# The Evolution of Counseling Psychology

**Donald H. Blocher, Ph.D.,** is a professor emertitus of counseling psychology at the State University of New York at Albany. Dr. Blocher received his Ph.D. in counseling psychology at the University of Minnesota. He is a Fellow of the American Psychological Association and a past president of the Division of Counseling Psychology. Dr. Blocher has served on the faculties of the University of Minnesota and the University of Western Ontario as well as at the University at Albany.

He was also a Fulbright Professor at the University of Keele in the United Kingdom. He has been a visiting lecturer at a number of universities in the United States and abroad. Dr. Blocher is the author of a number of books including *Developmental Counseling* now in its 4th edition, and has contributed numerous book chapters and journal articles to the counseling literature. Dr. Blocher has taught history in the public schools, served as a school counselor and school psychologist, and was an Intelligence Officer in the United States Air Force. He is currently engaged in writing and consulting.

# The Evolution of Counseling Psychology

**Donald H. Blocher,** PhD

 Springer Publishing Company

Springer Publishing Company, Inc.
536 Broadway
New York, NY 10012-3955

*Acquisitions Editor: Bill Tucker*
*Production Editor: J. Hurkin-Torres*
*Cover design by Susan Hauley*

00 01 02 03 04 / 5 4 3 2 1

---

**Library of Congress Cataloging-in-Publication Data**

Blocher, Donald H.
  The evolution of counseling psychology / Donald H. Blocher.
    p.  cm.
  Includes bibliographical references and index.
  ISBN 0-8261-1348-6
  1. Counseling—United States—History.  I. Title
  BF637.C6.B473 2000
  158'3—dc21

                                          00-020289
                                          CIP

---

Printed in the United States of America

**Photo Credits**
John Dewey, James McKeen Cattell, G. Stanley Hall, Leona Tyler, Lewis M. Terman, Jean Piaget, courtesy of the Archive of the History of American Psychology, University of Akron, Akron, Ohio. Donald Super, courtesy of Donald Blocher. Henry Borow, courtesy of Marian Borow. Alfred Binet, Sigmund Freud, Carl Jung, Alfred Adler, Carl Rogers, Ivan Pavlov, B. F. Skinner, courtesy of the University of Sonoma Web Site.

To Henry Borow,
a student of and maker of
the history of counseling psychology

# Contents

List of Figures                                                          ix

Preface                                                                  xi

Introduction                                                            xiii

## Part I   In the Beginning                                             1

Chapter 1    Guidance: A Product of the American            3
             Conscience

Chapter 2    The Rise of Applied Psychology                 33

Chapter 3    The Professionalization of Counseling          75
             Psychology

Chapter 4    The Search for a Professional Identity         97

Chapter 5    The Dawning of the Age of Psychotherapy       119

## Part II   Traditions, Traditions, Traditions           147

Chapter 6    The Individual Differences Tradition          149

Chapter 7    The Developmental Tradition                   177

Chapter 8    The Humanistic Tradition                      207

Chapter 9    The Behavioral Tradition                      233

## Part III   From Here to Uncertainty                     261

Chapter 10   From Theoretical Divisiveness to              263
             Eclectic-Integrative Therapies

Chapter 11    Coming of Age As a Profession                          291

Epilogue                                                            313

Appendix A    The Expansion of Counseling Psychology                317

Appendix B    Markers and Milestones in the Evolution              319
              of Counseling Psychology

*Name Index*                                                       *323*

*Subject Index*                                                    *333*

# List of Figures

| 1.1 | John Dewey | 21 |
|-----|------------|-----|
| 2.1 | James McKeen Cattell | 41 |
| 2.2 | Alfred Binet | 44 |
| 2.3 | Donald G. Paterson | 67 |
| 3.1 | G. Stanley Hall | 78 |
| 4.1 | E. G. Williamson | 98 |
| 4.2 | John Darley | 100 |
| 4.3 | C. Gilbert Wrenn | 104 |
| 4.4 | Leona Tyler | 107 |
| 5.1 | Sigmund Freud | 121 |
| 5.2 | Carl Gustav Jung | 125 |
| 5.3 | Alfred Adler | 127 |
| 6.1 | Lewis M. Terman | 167 |
| 6.2 | Donald Super | 173 |
| 7.1 | Jean Piaget | 180 |
| 7.2 | Henry Borow | 198 |
| 8.1 | Carl Rogers | 209 |
| 9.1 | Ivan Petrovich Pavlov | 235 |
| 9.2 | B. F. Skinner | 249 |

# Preface

Some years ago in one of those all too rare moments of reflection it occurred to me that I was only three lifetimes away from the very beginnings of modern psychology. It is generally agreed, as we will see, that what we call "scientific psychology" began with Wundt's laboratory at Leipzig around 1879. Similarly, applied psychology is seen to have begun with the work of Francis Galton in England at about the same time.

A short time later James McKeen Cattell, one of Wundt's first American students received his Ph.D. at Leipzig and went on to work briefly with Galton. Cattell coined the term "mental tests" and went on to a distinguished career in both academic and applied psychology. In 1911, E. K. Strong completed his Ph.D. with Cattell at Columbia, and in turn embarked on a distinguished career at Stanford. One of his students was C. Gilbert Wrenn, a pioneering leader of counseling psychology and my mentor and later colleague at the University of Minnesota. At this writing Gil Wrenn is alive and well and living in Arizona.

I have been moved since that realization to try to understand and make sense out of all of the ideas, ideals and events in those three generations that have produced what we presently call counseling psychology.

A dear friend and colleague who encouraged and stimulated me in the early phases of this project was the late Henry Borow. Unfortunately, his failing health and eventual death prevented our collaboration from really taking shape. This book is dedicated to him.

*Donald H. Blocher*
*Minneapolis, MN*

# Introduction

The history of counseling psychology is part of the history of the twentieth century. It was born out of the compassion, idealism and social concern that ushered in a century that seemed full of hope and promise for a better world and a richer and more fulfilling life for all. It has survived two world wars, the Great Depression, and the past 40 years of turbulence and turmoil.

The long trek from social reform to professional psychology is the story of many dedicated men and women whose ideas and ideals have paved the path to our present. There have been relatively few attempts to chronicle the lives and accomplishments of these pioneers. Much of our history seems to be buried in the musty pages of committee reports or proceedings of conferences and conventions.

What has seemed to be missing from this rather sketchy and scattered body of literature is some feeling for the people, the flesh-and-blood men and women, who in three brief generations have articulated the ideas, advocated for the ideals, and engaged in the conflicts, competition, and cooperation out of which has come what we presently call counseling psychology.

Noticeably absent also from most of our chronicles of events has been any real appreciation or understanding of the monumental social, economic and political forces that have shaped our lives and our century. The role of social reform, the contributions of applied psychology to two great wars, the boom and bust of applied psychology during the Roaring Twenties and the counseling of the despairing jobless in the Great Depression are all integral aspects of our history. The return of the veterans after World War II, our nation's descent into the Cold War, and the race for space have all molded our profession. The struggle for human rights, the Women's Movement, ethnic diversity, and multiculturalism are all vital parts of our past as well as our present.

This book is an effort to create a set of fresh perspectives within which we can better understand ourselves, our profession, and our century.

# PART I

# In the Beginning

# 1

# Guidance: A Product of the American Conscience

> Sometimes people call me an idealist. Well, that is the way I know I am an American. . . . America is the only idealistic nation in the world.
>
> —Woodrow Wilson
> Speech at Pueblo, CO
> November 8, 1919

History, like time itself, has no logical beginning and no discernible end. Every event, no matter how cataclysmic, is always preceded by others that have helped to shape and cement it into the endless mosaic that is human history.

It is historians, themselves, who choose the departure points and climactic events that best provide coherence and continuity to their own visions of a distant reality. The history of counseling psychology is no exception in this regard. It is possible to detect the roots of counseling in the education of squires in the Court of Charlemagne (Miller, 1961), or even to trace the origins of its literature to the earliest outputs of the Gutenberg Press (Zytowski, 1972). It is equally possible to choose the date of publication of a pioneering book, or the convening of a national conference (Aubrey, 1977) as points of departure from whence to unfold the story of counseling psychology's emergence as a profession. Such milestones may be important, but in themselves they seldom shed much light on the *zeitgeist* out of which a new profession actually came into being.

The history of counseling psychology is, after all, much more than a mere chronology of meetings and publications, organizations and

**3**

committee reports. It is rather a history of ideas, and the story of the men and women who generated, articulated, and applied those ideas on behalf of the values, causes, and ideals to which they were personally committed.

New ideas and new ideals are generally born out of active engagements with the overriding issues, problems, and conflicts that characterize the lives and times of the individuals who expound and advocate them. So it was with those whose pioneering vision and achievements helped to launch the counseling profession. Rather than to begin their story at any single, arbitrary point in time, it seems more reasonable to commence with a brief account of the events that were shaping the nature of American society around the beginning of the 20th century. These were the forces and events that energized the "spirit of the times" from whence came the ideas and ideals of the pioneers of what eventually became counseling psychology.

The years around 1900 in the United States were, to borrow Dickens' classic phrase, "the best of times and the worst of times." The years following the end of the American Civil War were witness to a veritable economic and social explosion. The full impact of the Industrial Revolution, combined with Westward expansion and a flood of immigration, created a new and vastly different America than that which had existed on the continent only a few years earlier.

Mark Twain called the period following the Civil War the "Gilded Age." It was a time of the amassing of great fortunes, of breathtaking technological advances, and of dramatic conquests and ruthless exploitation of natural and human resources.

Historian Sidney Lens (1969) described the transformation in this way:

> Statistics of growth were breathtaking. Population tripled from 23 million in 1850 to 76 million at the turn of the century. From 1859 to 1919 the value of manufactured goods increased by thirty-three times. Giant corporations and trusts dotted the country. Heavy industry, such as steel, replaced in importance light industry such as shoes, cotton goods, flour. The industrial revolution was finally in full swing, remaking the country in its own image. (p. 127)

The transformation of the country was geographical and psychological as well as economic. In the years following the Civil War, a parade of new states joined the Union. Most of these were carved out of the great heartland of the continent that only 20 years before mapmakers had labeled the "Great American Desert." The new states and the old were bound together in a frenzy of railroad-building. By 1890, the United States had more than 160,000 miles of railroads, or about one third of the world's total (Garraty, 1968).

The bonds that bound the American nation and people together were stronger than rails, however. As one social historian put it:

> So great numbers of Americans came to believe that a new United States, stretched from ocean to ocean, has miraculously appeared . . . publicists were savoring the word "nation" in this sense of a continent conquered and tamed. It was a term that most of all connoted growth and development and enterprise. . . . An age never lent itself more readily to sweeping, uniform description: nationalization, industrialization, mechanization and urbanization. (Wiebe, 1967, pp. 11–12)

One of the many ways in which this dramatic transformation affected the daily lives of ordinary people was in the ways in which they earned their living. The American ideal of making a living had, from the time of Thomas Jefferson, been that of the independent, self-employed farmer, artisan, or storekeeper. The expansion of slavery in the South had tarnished and threatened this ideal and the work ethic that grew out of it. In a very real sense, the Civil War was a struggle between two vastly differing economic systems and the consequences that flowed from each, as much as a conflict over the moral issue of slavery itself (Rodgers, 1978).

Abraham Lincoln, whose own career seemed to mirror the success theme—log cabin to White House—had constantly pointed up the differences between a "master-servant" economy in the South and the free labor economy of the North. In the late 1850s, Lincoln repeatedly told Northern audiences that "There is no permanent class of hired laborers among us" (Rodgers, 1978).

Even as the Civil War began, that claim was in the process of becoming an illusion. By 1870, a scant 5 years after the end of the war, when the first complete occupational census was taken, between 60 and 70% of the Northern labor force worked for wages. In the most highly industrialized states such as Massachusetts, the proportion was between 75 and 85%.

The changes in the nature of work in the newly industrialized society triggered new concepts of the work ethic and particularly vastly differing notions about the just rewards of labor. These ideas and the interplay of moral, intellectual, and economic issues that they triggered occupied the thinking of labor leaders, industrialists, and philosophers for the next half century.

It was the conflict between these sharply differing views of what constituted a just and healthy society that set the stage for the social reform efforts out of which the Guidance Movement, the forerunner of today's counseling psychology, first emerged.

The moral basis for widespread social reform movements quickly became apparent as the processes of industrialization and urbanization proceeded. Mark Twain's "Gilded Age" had a gold facade that was very thin indeed. The tremendous expansion of wealth, territory, and population that characterized the "Gilded Age" had not produced a new utopia on the American continent. The rapid increase of industrial production was accompanied by some improvements in material living standards. Real wages, that is, money wages equated for purchasing power, rose sharply in the 1870s and '80s as technological advances made labor more productive while the abundance of manufactured goods brought down prices (Garraty, 1968).

By far the most dramatic result of the new industrial era, however, was the astounding concentration of wealth and consequent political and economic power in the hands of giant corporations and the relative handful of people who controlled them. The economic, political, and social upheavals that were set in motion by this unprecedented concentration of wealth and power made the years around 1900 a turbulent and even violent period. A considerable portion of the burgeoning population had failed to benefit noticeably from the vast increase in total wealth. Even those who had profited temporarily often saw those gains vanish in the throes of financial panics and depressions, and the business failures and unemployment that inevitably followed.

Recent immigrants, Southern sharecroppers, prairie farmers, and unskilled factory workers all languished at the bottom of the newly established social and industrial ladder. The great safety valve in American society, the frontier, with its seemingly endless supply of cheap land and inexhaustible natural wealth, had disappeared. With it went the lure of adventure and the promise of a fresh start. By 1890, the West provided no escape from the harsh realities of urban slums and rural poverty (Norton et al., 1986).

These realities were indeed harsh for countless numbers of people. The economic and social conditions under which millions of people lived were almost incomprehensible to most Americans today.

The average annual earnings of American workers were between $400 and $500 per year. A standard wage for an unskilled laborer was a dollar and a half a day—when he could get work. According to the census of 1900, nearly 6 1/2 million workers were unemployed for some time during the year. Nearly 2 million were idle for 4 to 6 months of the year. The average working day was 10 hours, 6 days per week. Many workers had far longer hours. For example, in 1900, the hours in the New York garment industry were 70 hours per week (Allen, 1952).

Child labor was an accepted part of the economic scene. Some 26% of boys between the ages of 10 and 15 were considered "gainfully employed." More than a quarter of a million of such children worked in mills and factories.

Virtually no safety standards existed to protect workers, including children. In 1904, a careful assessment of poverty in the United States indicated that more than 10 million people were "underfed, underclothed and underhoused" (Allen, 1952, p. 56). This out of a total population of 76 million.

The results of these conditions were often social turmoil, bloody strikes, riots, increased crime, and political corruption. The journalists who kept these unsavory conditions before the American public were christened "muckrakers" by Theodore Roosevelt when their revelations hit too close to home.

## THE AWAKENING OF SOCIAL CONSCIENCE

The reaction of a great number of Americans from all walks of life to this widespread poverty, corruption, and abuse of power was a concerted demand for reform. This demand has been called "the awakening of the American conscience." It was within this awakening that the ideas and ideals that energized the Guidance Movement took root. The demand for reform had begun to gain momentum in the 1880s. As one historian put it:

> Dozens of groups and individuals came forward to demand civil service reform, the eight hour day, scientific agriculture, women suffrage, en-

forcement of vice laws, factory inspection, non-partisan local elections, trust-busting, wildlife conservation, tax reform, abolition of child labor, businesslike local government, regulation of railroad rates, less patronizing local charity, and hundreds of other causes . . . (Thelen, 1973, p. 200)

The onset of a devastating economic depression in 1893, together with the growing frustrations of reformers, led these disparate movements to coalesce into what became known as the Progressive Movement. This rising tide of reform and demand for greater social, economic, and political democracy was so powerful and pervasive that the period from 1900 to 1920 has been called "The Progressive Era" (Smith, 1985). The Progressive Era reshaped American Society into what we recognize today and brought with it the antecedents of the counseling profession.

The particular focus for reform that helped to energize the Guidance Movement concerned the nature of work in the new industrial world and the kind of preparation that was required for young people, if they were to be more than victims caught up in a system which they were unable to understand, and with which they were helpless to cope.

The arenas within which the Guidance Movement began were twofold. Reform of the educational system was a paramount objective, but the newly developed profession of social work was often more relevant for immediate action, simply because so few young people were actually in school, even at the tender age at which they were forced to begin employment.

In 1900 the average number of years of formal education was a little less than 7 years in the North and about 3 years in the South. In the South, the average public expenditure for education was $9.72 per pupil per year (Link & Catton, 1967).

Between 1900 and 1915, about 14.5 million new immigrants arrived in the United States. In the peak year of 1907 alone, more than 1.25 million new arrivals passed through open portals into the land of hope and opportunity.

The vast majority of these new Americans faced the challenge of learning a new language, adapting to a new culture, and at the same time earning a living for themselves and their children (Daniels, 1990).

Not surprisingly, the whole Progressive Movement focused upon the needs of youth. Historian Robert Wiebe (1967) put it this way:

If humanitarian progressivism had a central theme it was the child. . . . The child was the carrier of tomorrow's hope whose innocence and freedom made him singularly receptive to education in rational, humane behavior. (p. 169)

The reformers' central focus on children and youth was seen in their efforts to ban child labor, enforce compulsory education laws, improve urban environments with playgrounds and parks, and most of all, create schools attuned to the needs of all of the children of all the people.

The problems of preparing young people for stable and rewarding work in the industrial world was a key concern. In 1887 Edward Bellamy's utopian novel, *Looking Backward*, had described his vision of the society of the future. Bellamy, whose novel sold a million copies, had described the workings of an educational system that provided what would later be called vocational guidance.

The vocational education movement was the first effort to provide systematic preparation for entry into work. Most secondary schools of the time were essentially academies that were designed to prepare intellectually talented students for entry into colleges and universities.

## VOCATIONAL EDUCATION: PARENT TO VOCATIONAL GUIDANCE

The vocational education movement advocated radical changes in curriculum to include courses relevant to entry directly into the industrial world. A number of vocational high schools were opened. According to John Brewer (1942), the actual practice of vocational guidance probably began with a teacher named George Arthur Merrill, who began to include exploratory work experiences as part of the curriculum in a "manual training high school" in San Francisco around 1888.

In 1894 Merrill organized a new school, The California School of Mechanic Arts, that devoted its final 2 years to specialized preparation in a trade. This curriculum required that students choose a trade, which in turn required some assistance in the decision-making process. There was apparently no designated counselor, but the faculty and administrators furnished systematic assistance in the choice process.

The vocational education movement gained momentum rapidly during the 1890s and into the new century. Not all of its adherents were social reformers. Quite apart from the Progressive Movement, a rising chorus of criticism was directed toward public education.

The gigantic industrial system required skilled workers at an ever-increasing pace. The generally low level of educational attainment of workers entering the labor market was as much a source of concern to the "Captains of Industry" as it was to the social reformers.

Studies of school-leaving and educational achievement, such as "efficiency expert" Leonard Ayers' *Laggards in Our Schools*, published in 1909, spurred the demand for real changes in the public schools. The slogan for this demand was "social efficiency."

The vocational education movement was divided over the question of whether special vocational high schools should be created to train students, or whether the existing school curriculum should be broadened to meet the needs of non-college bound students. Germany, the great industrial rival of the United States at the turn of the century, had developed an elaborate system of special industrial schools to supply skilled workers to its industries.

In 1906, the National Society for the Promotion of Industrial Education (NSPIE) was formed. The NSPIE brought together a diverse and often conflicting set of interests and ideologies. It included bankers, industrialists, labor leaders, and philanthropists, as well as reformers and educators. From the first, the NSPIE was torn with dissension. Fortunately, the need for some kind of system of vocational guidance was generally recognized and accepted by all.

The foremost issue that provoked disagreement arose over the question of curricular reform of the existing public school, versus the desirability of creating a new system of industrial or vocational school education that was separate from and independent of the public school. Interestingly, the debate focused primarily around changes in what we would now call the junior high school years, because few people really believed that 12 years of schooling of any sort was a realistic option for the average student!

This issue served to crystallize the ideological differences within the vocational education movement. At the first national conference of the NSPIE, held in Chicago in 1908, the issue was hotly debated by two of the most charismatic and influential personalities of the time.

The opening address of the Conference was delivered by Charles Eliot, the President of Harvard University. Eliot had written for some years about the threat of industrialization to the work ethic, and to the need of human beings to experience satisfaction and fulfillment through work. He was opposed to labor unions and had been a member of the Committee of Seven of the National Education Association that in 1895 had affirmed the continuation of the academic, college-preparatory concept of high school (Rodgers, 1978).

Eliot proposed that NSPIE actively promote the development of a separate system of industrial schools for children from 14 to 17 years of age. He went on to urge that elementary school teachers should sort out their pupils in terms of their "evident or probable destinies" (Eliot, 1908, pp. 12–13). Eliot argued that nature had determined inequality among human beings and that a democratic society need only to provide those conditions that enable each individual to put forth his utmost effort (Stephens, 1970). Essentially, Eliot proposed a dual system of education, with students being assigned to academic or vocational tracks and schools at the end of elementary school, at about age 14.

Eliot was opposed on this issue by Jane Addams, one of the most visible and articulate humanitarian reformers of the times. Jane Addams was one of the founders of Hull House, a settlement house in Chicago. She was largely responsible for initiating the settlement house movement in America. Settlement houses were essentially community centers that provided a variety of services to workers, and especially to immigrants, living in the newly industrialized urban centers. Addams argued persuasively in favor of a single system of comprehensive high schools able to provide a wide range of educational opportunities for all children (Smith, 1985).

## THE CLASH OF MORAL PHILOSOPHIES

The differences between Eliot and Addams were far deeper than the question of the future setting for vocational education. Indeed, these differences stemmed from vastly differing social and moral philosophies.

Jane Addams was an exponent of the philosophical and religious movement called the "social gospel." The years from 1890 to 1920 saw a major change in the influence of organized religion, particularly in the large Protestant churches of the major urban centers. These changes involved the elevation of ancient Christian beliefs to new prominence in American religious thought. Essentially, these revived religious convictions emphasized the duty of Christians to create a society on earth, in the present time, that was in harmony with the will of God and which reflected the brotherhood of human beings. Together, these beliefs constituted a frame of reference and a divine mandate for the proponents of this new "social gospel" (Link & Catton, 1967).

These basic beliefs quickly put the preachers and followers of the social gospel movement into sharp opposition to a second stream of influence in social and philosophical thought that shaped the thinking of many intellectual leaders at the turn of the 20th century. This approach was termed "social Darwinism."

This movement sought to apply the principles that were seen to govern biological evolution, and the survival or extinction of animal species, to the conduct of human affairs. The chief proponent of Social Darwinism was the English philosopher Herbert Spencer. It was Spencer who coined the term "survival of the fittest."

For some social Darwinists, the concentration of wealth and the exploitation of both human and natural resources that characterized the Gilded Age seemed to reflect perfectly the struggle for dominance and survival that was seen as an inevitable part of the working of the natural world.

Clearly, social Darwinism and the social gospel movement represented antithetical views about a host of social, economic, and moral questions that confronted America at the beginning of the 20th century.

Interestingly, both social Darwinists and humanitarian progressives agreed upon the need for far-reaching and systematic reforms of educational institutions, although for quite different reasons. Their differences centered around the question of whether such reforms should be instituted in the name of "social efficiency" or of "social reconstruction."

Perhaps because of the dramatically differing social values represented in the vocational education movement and its complex political and economic agenda, a new group of caring and concerned people began to identify themselves as distinctly separate. These people were the pioneers of the vocational guidance movement. They were concerned not only with long-term social and educational reform, but also with the problem of providing immediate, practical assistance to the many thousands of young people who were leaving school to enter the labor market ill-prepared to cope with a highly complex and ruthlessly competitive world of work.

The question of the relationship between vocational education and vocational guidance has remained controversial. Brewer (1942) denied the existence of any substantial relationship between the two groups, while Stephens (1970) painstakingly pointed out that a great deal of overlap in leadership, interests, and directions obviously existed. These differences in interpretation are probably due to differing concepts of what vocational guidance involved and of its relationship to the larger progressive education movement. We will deal with that topic in subsequent pages.

## THE PARSONS LEGEND

At this point in the narrative enters the man who has been accorded the distinction of being the founder of vocational guidance. Frank Parsons' actual influence and contribution make this title much more a myth than a reality. A truly cynical student of history might decide that in order to become a "founding figure" in any area one needs to have three things—a charismatic personality, a great sense of timing, and an energetic publicist. Frank Parsons' had all three.

Actually, remarkably little is known about Frank Parsons, particularly of his personal life. A brief biographical sketch by Mann (1954) analyzed his political beliefs. Brewer (1942) sketched Parsons' career. The Brewer chapter drew on documents from the Vocation Bureau and conversations with several of Parsons' associates. While Brewer's account is more than slightly tinged with hero worship, it is probably the most comprehensive picture of Frank Parsons' life available.

Frank Parsons was born in New Jersey in 1854. At age 16, he entered Cornell University and graduated in engineering. His first position as a civil engineer for a railroad company was abruptly ended before it had really begun when the company went bankrupt in the financial panic of 1873. Parsons worked for a year as a manual laborer in a steel mill, experiencing first-hand the life of an industrial worker. He then obtained a teaching position in a public school. He began to study law with local attorneys and passed a bar examination.

About this time, Parsons suffered some kind of general breakdown, probably brought on by overwork. He spent 3 years in New Mexico "living in the open," and returned to New England in better health. Parsons practiced law and wrote or revised several legal treatises. He was a part-time lecturer at Boston University Law School from 1891 to 1902. During this period, he also served as a professor at two Midwestern colleges. He was forced out of one of these positions because of his radical political beliefs. During these years, Parsons published a dozen books on social and political issues.

He developed a social philosophy that he called "mutualism" which called for a gradual evolution into socialism. In 1895, Parson entered politics to become a candidate for mayor of Boston. He finished third in a narrowly decided election. Parsons was very active in progressive causes and organizations. He published a number of articles in a liberal periodical called *The Arena* that expounded both his political views and his growing interest in the problems of youth and education.

In 1905 Parsons helped to organize what was called the Breadwinner's Institute, an evening adult education program that operated under the auspices of Civic Service House, a settlement house in Boston's North End. This was apparently Parsons' first venture into youth work. He co-taught evening courses in "Industrial History," "Economics and Life Principles," and "Practical Psychology and Methods."

In 1907 Parsons was able to persuade philanthropist Pauline Agassiz Shaw, who was the principal financial supporter of the Civic Service House, to fund something called the Vocation Bureau of Boston, a social agency devoted to vocational guidance and counseling.

The Vocation Bureau opened its doors on January 13, 1908. Parsons' title was Director and Vocational Counselor. He prepared one report of its activities on May 1. Frank Parsons died on September 26, 1908. *Choosing A Vocation*, the book that finally brought him attention and adulation, was published by his friends and colleagues a year later.

It is difficult to assess the life and contributions of Frank Parsons. He was certainly not the founder of vocational guidance, nor was he really even an early pioneer in its practice. So far as we know, his professional counseling experience was a little over 6 months in duration.

*Choosing A Vocation* (1909) is a slender, almost pocket-size volume of 159 pages. Its simple framework for vocational counseling—self analysis by the client, knowledge of occupations and true reasoning about the two—is based upon common sense and an obviously very limited experience with the complexities brought to counseling by clients. The case descriptions cited show very little psychological insight or sophistication. Parsons apparently based judgments and subsequent advice heavily on initial impressions of the client's manner and physical appearance. Interestingly, the title page cites the author as Frank Parsons, Ph.D. According to Brewer (1942), no record exists of that degree.

Frank Parsons commanded the admiration and devotion of those who knew him. His friends and associates, particularly Meyer Bloomfield, the Director of Civic Service House, and Ralph Albertson, a friend and colleague, made sure that his work was remembered, often for far more than it was really worth.

The picture that emerges of Frank Parsons is that of a very intelligent and committed man whose own life was a search for meaning, satisfaction, and accomplishment. Frank Parsons never married. Brewer (1942) speculated that Parsons' volunteer evening work at Civic Service House was an effort to overcome his own loneliness. Perhaps young Frank Parsons had himself needed vocational counseling when none was available. He was engineer, steelworker, schoolmaster, lawyer, politician, peripatetic professor, and finally vocational counselor. A passage from the introduction to *Choosing A Vocation* may well have applied to Parsons' own life. He wrote:

> If a young man chooses his vocation so that his best abilities and enthusiasms will be united with his daily work, he has laid the foundations of success and happiness. But if his best abilities and enthusiasms are separated from his daily work, or do not find in it fair scope and opportunity for exercise and development; if his occupation is merely a means of making a living, and the work he loves to do is side-tracked into the evening hours, or pushed out of his life altogether, he will be only a fraction of the man he ought to be. (p. 3)

Whether Frank Parsons saw the lines quoted above to apply to his own life we will never know. His words have certainly represented a creed that has been accepted and acted upon by the generations of counselors who followed.

## BREAKING AWAY: THE BIRTH OF THE NATIONAL VOCATIONAL GUIDANCE ASSOCIATION

Clearly, vocational guidance and counseling did not originate with any single person, or in any one place. Instead, vocational counseling programs seem to have blossomed independently and almost simultaneously in a number of locations across the entire country. Guidance and counseling genuinely represent the original and spontaneous responses of a host of caring and concerned people to the human needs that they recognized to exist around them.

Anna Reed (1944) described more than a dozen guidance programs in operation before 1916 that were well enough organized and recognized for documentary evidence about them to be available. These projects included both school programs and those sponsored by social agencies. Cities represented included Boston, New York City, Chicago, Philadelphia, Cincinnati, Minneapolis, Hartford, Seattle, and Omaha. Programs were not confined to major cities. Grand Rapids, Michigan and DeKalb, Illinois, for example, both had early organized programs of vocational guidance. It seems likely that many other less well-known programs existed in schools and communities throughout the country.

It was natural that people engaged in these pioneering efforts should seek to communicate with and support each other. One of the first large-scale meetings of guidance people was held in Boston in 1910. This meeting was held two days prior to the 1910 annual conference of the NSPIE held in Boston. The timing of the meeting underscored the close ties that existed between vocational education and vocational guidance at this point, but also pointed to their imminent separation and independence.

The guiding organizer of this pioneering meeting of leaders in vocational guidance was Meyer Bloomfield, who had, after a brief interim, succeeded Frank Parsons as director of the Vocation Bureau. It was probably at this meeting that the Parsons legend was launched.

Armed with the newly published *Choosing A Vocation*, a book that seemed to provide both a coherent philosophical framework and a workable formula for professional practice, Bloomfield was able to confer upon Frank Parsons the mantle of founder of vocational guidance. Bloomfield by the way was listed as the copyright owner of *Choosing A Vocation*.

The roster of speakers and participants who attended the meeting gives a much clearer picture of the breadth and scope of the vocational guidance movement at this early date. Reed (1944) reported that delegates from 45 cities attended.

The participants included school superintendents, commissioners of education, philanthropists, businessmen, civic leaders, heads of social agencies, politicians, and, of course, counselors and social workers. The Honorary Conference Committee consisted of Senator Henry Cabot Lodge, Jane Addams, and G. Stanley Hall, President of Clark University and pioneering professor of adolescent psychology. Speeches were made by the Presidents of Massachusetts Institute of Technology, the University of Oklahoma, and, of course, Charles Eliot, the Harvard University President (Stephens, 1970).

Meyer Bloomfield was a master organizer and publicist who was able to turn out an impressive array of luminaries and leaders from many areas of society. Along with the luminaries were a number of people who had actually pioneered in professional practice. Ralph Albertson, Parsons' friend and colleague, Eli Weaver, who had established a guidance program at Boys High School in Brooklyn, and Jessie B. Davis, a high school teacher from Grand Rapids, Michigan who had begun counseling students several years before, all attended the Conference.

The Conference adjourned with two achievements. It clearly put vocational guidance on the path to visibility and recognition as a burgeoning force in educational and social reform. It also planted the seeds for an eventual separate association of vocational guidance professionals, although no specific plans were made.

A second national conference was held in October 1912 in New York City. The scant 2 years that elapsed between the Boston and New York conferences were eventful. A rising tide of interest in vocational guidance coincided with a powerful reform movement in public education. The settings in which guidance was to be practiced had begun to shift from social agencies concerned with out-of-school youth to the public schools themselves. The mounting criticism of public education, particularly in regard to school dropouts, had finally forced a literally soul-searching re-examination of the purpose and practices of American public education.

In 1912, the National Education Association appointed a Committee on Vocational Education and Vocational Guidance, as well as a commission on the Reorganization of Secondary Education (Stephens, 1970). Major changes in the nature of American public schools were underway, and the pioneering reformers of both vocational education and vocational guidance were in the forefront.

The New York Conference on Vocational Guidance in 1912 was held independently of the NSPIE meeting. The problems of the masses of school children literally dumped out of the school system to struggle in the work world was a central theme of the Conference. The approach to the problem that gained wide support was a "reconstructed educational system to fit youth for the world of work" (Stephens, 1970, p. 78).

Perhaps the most far-reaching accomplishment of the New York Conference was the appointment of a committee to consider the possibility of developing a national organization to promote the cause of vocational guidance. This Committee was chaired by Arthur Dean, Director of Industrial Education for the State of New York, and included Meyer Bloomfield of the Vocation Bureau of Boston and two high school teachers, Benjamin Gruenberg, of New York City, and Jessie B. Davis, of Grand Rapids, Michigan.

Considerable wrangling occurred in this committee over definitions of vocational guidance, and over control of the new organization. Apparently the founders of the profession were no less argumentative than their contemporary counterparts. The original Committee adjourned without agreeing on anything. It was replaced by a new group chaired by Jessie B. Davis, the English teacher from Grand Rapids, who was one of the true pioneers of school counseling and guidance. Plans were begun for the formation of the first national professional organization of guidance workers, The National Vocational Guidance Association.

These plans were continued at the meeting of the NSPIE in Philadelphia in December of 1912. The goals of the new organization, as reported by its planning committee, were both noble and lofty. The committee concluded that "Vocational education and guidance are generally recognized as two phases of the great economic and social movement to improve the condition of those who form the base of the human pyramid that we call civilization" (Stephens, 1970, p. 31).

## GUIDANCE RIDES THE CREST OF THE PROGRESSIVE MOVEMENT

The tie-in of these guidance pioneers to the reforms supported by the Progressive Movement was unmistakable. The election of Woodrow Wilson to the United States Presidency in 1912 was in many ways the high water mark of the Progressive Movement in American national politics. In 1908, William Howard Taft, Vice President under Theodore Roosevelt, had been elected promising to carry out the reform policies of his predecessor. He had, in Roosevelt's view, carried them out on a stretcher (Smith, 1985).

The mercurial Teddy Roosevelt had bolted from the Republican Party, taking with him its Progressive wing. Roosevelt formed a third party, the Progressive Party, or as it was called after him, the Bull Moose Party. The result was the election of Woodrow Wilson, the reform-minded Democratic governor of New Jersey and erstwhile president of Princeton University.

Although Woodrow Wilson's "New Freedom" policies proved less liberal than many progressives had hoped, much of the Progressive agenda was put into law during the next 8 years. Of particular importance to the adherents of vocational education and guidance was the passage of the Smith-Hughes Act and subsequent legislation to support and coordinate vocational education. At long last, support and recognition of vocational education and guidance had become part of American public policy. Also of importance was the passage of the Keating-Owens Act in 1916 which marked the beginning of a long constitutional struggle to abolish child labor in the United States.

Even before the arrival of the Wilson administration, a number of states had proceeded to support vocational education and guidance projects. Michigan was one of these states, the program in Grand Rapids pioneered by Jessie B. Davis was perhaps the most visibly successful in the country.

The NSPIE, together with the fledgling organization of vocational guidance people, decided upon a joint conference to be held in Grand Rapids in 1913. It was here that the new National Vocational Guidance Association came into full being (Norris, 1954).

The Grand Rapids Conference was at once a celebration of the successes of the Progressive Movement and a birthday party for vocational guidance. The list of dignitaries who addressed the joint convention of the NSPIE and the newly organized National Vocational Guidance Association was almost a *Who's Who* of national leaders of progressive causes.

Among them was Ida Tarbell, the queen of the "Muckrakers." She spoke on the vocational needs of women and gave impetus for the inclusion of home economics in the school curriculum. Owen Lovejoy, Secretary of the National Child Labor Committee, told the assemblage that not only must child labor be abolished and children provided vocational education and guidance, but that industry, itself, must be reformed to better meet the needs of people.

George H. Mead, the University of Chicago sociologist who had helped install vocational guidance programs in Chicago schools, told the audience that a democratic education required no separation between vocational training and academic preparation. Mead asserted that vocational education and vocational guidance constituted two avenues through which the community and its schools could work together (Stephens, 1970).

## GUIDANCE AND PROGRESSIVE EDUCATION

Perhaps the most influential and indeed prophetic voice heard in those jubilant days at Grand Rapids came from a young colleague of George Mead at the University of Chicago. Like Mead, he had worked with Jane Addams in the settlement house movement and had installed a vocationally oriented curriculum at the University of Chicago Experimental School. John Dewey urged a fully unified and integrated approach to vocational and academic education that would constitute a genuine revolution in secondary education.

John Dewey was to become the voice, the intellect and the missionary spirit that propelled the Progressive Education movement for the next three decades. Ironically, Progressive Education and vocational guidance became the sole surviving remnants of the Progressive Movement (Ryan, 1995).

It was the ideas and values of Progressive Education that broadened the concept of vocational guidance, from a program of one-shot services for school-leavers to a way of organizing and delivering a new curriculum aimed at preparing students to function as workers

**Figure 1.1    John Dewey**

and citizens in everyday life. In the process of this transformation, Progressive Education almost swallowed the Vocational Guidance Movement. Indeed, within a few years in many quarters vocational guidance was simply called guidance, and came to connote broadly constituted programs of pupil personnel services and a progressive philosophy of education.

We noted earlier that John Brewer (1942), writing a history of vocational guidance, vehemently denied that the vocational education movement had contributed significantly to the development of vocational guidance. This assertion in the face of a mountain of evidence to the contrary is probably due to the fact that for Brewer, and a host of others, guidance, vocational and otherwise, was perceived as rooted in a new and revolutionary concept of education based upon a radical philosophy that went far beyond the reforms advocated by the proponents of vocational education with their close ties to business and industry.

The man who sowed the seeds for this new approach to education was, of course, John Dewey. Social historians have assessed Dewey's impact on American education and culture in this way:

> Dewey set out to fulfill the American dream of a public school system that was the chief training ground for democracy. Repudiating the classical tradition that emphasized formal and polite learning, he advocated a curriculum that had meaning for an urban age and prepared the child to live in a democratic society. He taught, moreover, that curriculum and subject matter should be centered around the child's own experiences; and that "learning by doing" should supplant memorization of data that had no meaning to the child. . . . Dewey left such a deep imprint on American educational theory and practice that he can be said to have accomplished, almost single-handed one of the significant cultural revolutions of his time. (Link & Catton, 1967, p. 34)

Certainly John Dewey had a significant impact on the direction of a more broadly defined Guidance Movement. Ironically, the fortunes of the larger Progressive Movement as a force in national politics began to decline with the beginning of the First World War, or the Great War, as it was then called. The fragile coalition of progressive reformers split over support of American entry into the war, as well as other issues. By 1920, the Progressive Era was over and a war-weary, disillusioned nation was ready to return to what its new President, Warren Harding, called "Normalcy."

## GUIDANCE MOVES FROM IDEALISM TO PROFESSIONALISM

The Grand Rapids Conference and the birth of the National Vocational Guidance Association (NVGA) marked the beginning of another and equally profound set of changes. Guidance and counseling moved from being the domain of a group of dedicated and socially concerned amateur-do-gooders, if you will, to becoming a profession. The guidance pioneers, as we have seen, came from many walks of life. They included social workers, teachers, philanthropists, industrialists, professors, and public administrators.

Virtually all were social reformers motivated by deep-seated personal or religious beliefs. Jane Addams was a Christian socialist whose life was dedicated to actualizing the social gospel. Jessie B. Davis taught his students the moral value of hard work, ambition, honesty and good character. Eli Weaver and Anna Reed saw vocational guidance in terms of "social efficiency" and as a practical matter of fitting young people into the highly competitive industrial society. Frank Parsons, as we have seen, evolved a comprehensive philosophy of social reform and social reconstruction. All believed that both society and individual human beings could be improved and the human condition could so be made better (Rockwell & Rothney, 1961).

Anna Reed, herself a guidance pioneer, perhaps best articulated the dual commitments that energized the guidance movement in its early years. She wrote:

> During the closing years of the nineteenth century, the civilized world replied affirmatively to the age-old question, Am I my brother's keeper? Society had accepted the theory of the brotherhood of man and was ready to begin translation of the theory into practice. During the same years psychologists were busily engaged in translating into practice the theory of individual differences. Thus it happened that on the eve of the new century two theories—the one sociological and the one psychological and both fundamental to . . . guidance had crystallized . . . (Reed, 1944, p. 2)

The legacy that the guidance pioneers left to modern-day counseling psychologists was simple but profound: *We are all different, and we are all brothers and sisters.*

During the years that followed the birth of the NVGA, guidance workers and guidance programs both prospered and proliferated. The National Vocational Guidance Association began with about 100 members who grappled with the arduous task of converting a social movement into a respected profession. The NVGA began to develop ethical principles, standards for training, professional periodicals, and all of the tools and trappings necessary for a profession. The first professional journal for counselors was the *Vocational Guidance Bulletin,* first issued in 1915, which eventually became the *Vocational Guidance Quarterly.* The Association briefly disbanded in 1919, but was revived in 1920 with a total of 128 members (Norris, 1954).

From the first, the NVGA was beset with internal dissension between those who wished to maintain the vocational emphasis of the organization's founders and those who saw the term guidance as a broadly generic rubric to cover a broad and constantly developing constellation of professional services and settings (Norris, 1954). These tensions were not fully resolved until 1951 when NVGA joined with other personnel associations to form the American Personnel and Guidance Association. The APGA had a divisional structure to accommodate the diverse needs and interests of professional workers. That organization presently exists as the American Counseling Association.

## THE SEARCH FOR IDEALS AND IDENTITY

Vocational guidance, or simply guidance, depending upon one's perceptions and predilections, had come into the world amply endowed by its humanitarian parentage with all of the homely virtues such as faith, hope, and charity. Unfortunately, it was also born with a severe case of intellectual malnutrition. The lofty goals espoused by the founders of the movement seem from our vantage point in the closing years of the century to be noble, but naive, if not downright pretentious. Perhaps it is *our* problem in being unable to understand an age in which hope and optimism were still in fashion.

Other than the slender wisdom imparted by Frank Parson's little volume, based upon a lifetime of common sense and 6 months or so of professional experience, little was available to guide the guidance workers. Anna Reed, as noted in the quote rendered earlier, had generously attributed to psychology at least partial credit for the emergence of guidance.

In point of fact, when the counselor of 1913 sought enlightenment or assistance from the science of psychology, he or she found the cupboard very nearly bare. The field of industrial psychology in the United States had really just begun with the work of Hugo Munsterberg at Harvard, at about the same time that Parsons was beginning his brief career as vocational counselor. Munsterberg's classic book on industrial psychology was published in the United States in 1913, but had certainly not yet made a noticeable impact on counseling at that time. We will deal with that story further in Chapter 2.

The early years of guidance were in a sense a search for a practically useful and intellectually respectable set of principles and procedures and with them a professional role for the guidance specialist. As early as 1915, there were calls for the presence of a counselor in every school to help students sort through the complexity of course work in the newly diversified, comprehensive high schools (Miller, 1973).

As educational reform proceeded, the education profession itself examined the role of vocational guidance and decided that its implementation should reside primarily in the classroom. In 1918 a Committee on Vocational Guidance of the National Education Association's Commission on the Reorganization of Secondary Education came up with this definition:

> Vocational guidance, properly conceived, organizes school work so that the student may be helped to discover his own capacities, aptitudes and interests, may learn about the character and conditions of occupational life, and may himself arrive at an intelligent vocational decision. (NEA, 1918, p. 9)

This view was clearly consonant with our present view of vocational development and was certainly one that progressive educators were happy to espouse. The document went on to denounce the notion that anyone can foresee the future or determine what any child can or should become. This idea would have gladdened the hearts of the "non-directive" counselors who came along three decades later. Essentially, its view emphasized that good vocational development, like other aspects of psychological growth, should be natural and expected outcomes of a good general education. This point of view was elaborated by John Brewer (1932) in a volume called *Education as Guidance.* In a chapter entitled "Learning to Live, as the Only Genuine Curriculum" Brewer listed a set of criteria for good guidance practice that made it virtually synonymous with Progressive Education. His criteria were:

1. The person being guided is solving a problem, performing a task, or moving toward some objective.
2. The person being guided usually takes the initiative and asks for guidance.
3. The guide shows sympathy, friendliness and understanding.
4. The guide is guide because of superior experience, knowledge and wisdom.

5. The method of guidance is by way of offering opportunities for new experiences and enlightenment.
6. The person guided progressively consents to receive guidance, reserves the right to refuse the guidance offered and makes his own decisions.
7. The guidance offered makes him better able to guide himself. (Brewer, 1932, p. 22)

We can see rather clearly that the criteria offered by John Brewer in 1932 at a purely philosophical level comes remarkably close to our contemporary view of counseling psychology.

If we were to substitute words like "warmth," "empathy," "positive regard," or "expertness," "trustworthiness," and "attractiveness" at appropriate places, Brewer's formula would seem very modern indeed.

From 1920 to the mid-1930s, guidance in the secondary schools was largely seen as an activity performed by the classroom teacher as a part of the regular school curriculum. "Group guidance," "occupational exploration" units, and "life adjustment" courses flourished. Counseling was discussed, but was usually seen as the responsibility of classroom teachers, and was often provided in the form of well-intentioned but less than expert advice (Miller, 1973).

Not surprisingly, the number of full-time, professional guidance specialists did not grow rapidly. Large school districts often had Directors of Guidance or Pupil Personnel Services who helped to coordinate programs and adopt curriculum materials. In terms of school organization, guidance became one of several emerging special services, including school social work, school psychology, and school nursing.

Specialized student services were fairly new in American schools. They had begun in the late 1800s with attendance officers whose role was to enforce the compulsory education laws (Shear, 1965). As vocational guidance entered the schools, its coordination became an additional special service. The first guidance specialist in the Minneapolis schools, for example, had the title of Director of Attendance and Vocational Guidance (Reed, 1944).

Some of the impetus for the integration of guidance activities into the general curriculum was, of course, the compatibility of guidance philosophy with the goals and values of progressive education. This fit is hardly remarkable, since the movements stemmed from the same era of social reform. An equally powerful set of reasons had to do with the lack of availability and acceptance of means to accomplish what Parsons had termed the task of client self-analysis. It is surprising that school guidance programs were so slow to utilize the new technologies offered by the emerging fields of vocational and industrial psychology. The First World War had seen the development of large-scale aptitude testing for military selection and classification purposes.

## GUIDANCE AND THE NEW TECHNOLOGY OF TESTING

Immediately after World War I, a whole new industry grew up around the construction of a wide array of tests and inventories. With these instruments came numbers of applied psychologists to employ them, primarily in business and industry. Munsterberg's vision of a new vocational psychology rapidly became a reality. We will deal more thoroughly with this story in Chapter 2.

The first applications of the new technology of psychological testing for vocational guidance purposes came not in public schools, but in colleges and universities. With it came the new profession of vocational *counselor*, as opposed to guidance generalist, teacher, or administrator. With this development also came the marriage of vocational guidance and applied psychology.

Paul Hanus, an education professor at Harvard and one of the group of guidance pioneers in Boston, is said to have remarked that the original vocational guidance movement had "nothing to do with phrenology or psychology" (Stephens, 1970). Apparently, Hanus viewed that condition as one of bliss, rather than ignorance.

The impetus for the use of psychological tests came first from leaders in higher education (Williamson, 1965). Even before 1900, a number of college presidents had urged that individualized diagnoses of student aptitudes, temperament, strengths, and weakness be made prior to admission. Much of the concern came from the fact that colleges and universities were changing rapidly. The newly broadened college curriculum for the first time offered students a wide range of elective courses and majors. The students entering colleges and universities were also increasingly diverse in terms of backgrounds and aspirations.

In 1899 William Rainey Harper, the first president of the University of Chicago, had called for the scientific study of the college student. Harper had predicted that colleges would soon employ specialists who would analyze students' personalities in the same way physicians study patients' health (Williamson, 1965).

Very soon after the end of World War One Harper's prophecy was well on the way to becoming a reality. Several of the young psychologists who had helped to develop the Army's classification program with the Alpha and Beta tests returned to civilian life to inaugurate programs of research and counseling in universities.

Research programs were begun both in an effort to predict scholastic success, and to help students choose particular majors or professional schools. At Columbia University, Ben D. Wood began such a program that eventually led to the development of the comprehensive series of achievement tests published by the Cooperative Test Service (Paterson, 1938). In 1920 the University of Minnesota established the Testing Bureau under the leadership of Donald G. Paterson, another of the returning military psychologists. In 1916, the Minnesota legislature, in the flush of progressive reform had decreed that the University must admit any graduate of a Minnesota high school. As in many other states, this meant an increasingly variable college population. Donald Paterson began a program of research and test development that almost defined the armamentarium of vocational counselors over the subsequent three decades.

As early as 1919, the functions of the new college "personnel bureaus" that were the forerunners of today's college counseling centers were defined in terms of the utilization of psychological tests. One of them was described in these terms:

> The principal functions of the bureau are to obtain accurate data on each student, to codify the requirements of different professions, to supervise the use of tests, and to provide means whereby each student may be acquainted with his abilities and the requirements of the occupation in which he is interested. (Yoakum, 1919, p. 559)

Over the next 20 years, programs of research, test development, and counseling mushroomed in colleges and universities across the country. Schools such as the University of Iowa, Ohio State, Stanford, and California, as well as Minnesota, gave their names to whole new series and batteries of psychological tests and inventories. The mental testing movement was supported by the American Council on Education and the National Research Council. Creating and publishing tests became a growth industry in the private sector as well.

It seemed that the client analysis segment of the Parsonian model was finally brought to fruition. More important for counseling, perhaps, was the fact that the tools and techniques of psychological testing had at last provided a distinct and specialized professional role for counselors. This new role demanded specialized preparation and forever separated psychological counselors from the classroom teachers, public administrators, social workers, and other assorted reformers who had founded the Guidance Movement. Professional counseling was on its way.

The mental testing movement, with its cadre of enthusiastic young psychologists, brought a new direction and a new philosophical orientation to the fledgling profession. The new orientation arose from a deep-seated conviction in the power of science and scientific method to enlighten and reshape the world.

Where a Frank Parsons had placed his faith in the essential goodness of human beings, and a Jane Addams had believed in the eventual triumph of Christian virtues, the new breed of counselor psychologists believed just as firmly in a Newtonian view of the world. They perceived an orderly, lawful, and linear world of understandable and predictable people. They were sure that by diligent application of scientific methods, such understanding could be achieved, and the personal and collective destinies of human beings could be improved in the process.

Not even the most "Dewey-eyed" champions of progressive education were as imbued with a missionary spirit as were many of the mental testers. For better or for worse, the age of applied psychology had arrived.

# REFERENCES

Allen, F. L. (1952). *The big change: America transforms itself 1900–1950.* New York: Harper and Row.

Aubrey, R. F. (1977). Historical development of guidance and counseling and implications for the future. *Personnel and Guidance Journal, 56,* 288–296.

Brewer, J. M. (1942). *History of vocational guidance.* New York: Harper and Brothers.

Brewer, J. M. (1932). *Education as guidance.* New York: MacMillan.

Daniels, R. (1990). *Coming to America.* New York: Harper.

Eliot, C. W. (1908). Industrial education as an essential factor in our national prosperity. In *National Association for the Promotion of Industrial Education: Proceedings, 1908.*

Garraty, J. A. (1968). *The new commonwealth 1877–1890.* New York: Harper and Row.

Lens, S. (1969). *Radicalism in America.* New York: Thomas G. Crowell.

Link, A. S., & Catton, W. B. (1967). *A history of the United States since the 1890's* (3rd ed.). New York: Alfred A. Knopf.

Mann, A. (1954). *Yankee reformers in an urban age.* Cambridge, MA: Harvard University Press.

Miller, C. H. (1961). *Foundations of guidance.* New York: Harper and Row.

Miller, C. H. (1973). Historical and recent perspectives on work and vocational guidance. In H. Borow (Ed.), *Career guidance for a new age* (pp. 3–39). Boston: Houghton Mifflin.

National Educational Association, Department of the Interior, Bureau of Education. (1918). *Vocational guidance in secondary education.* (Bulletin No. 19). Washington, DC: Government Printing Office.

Norris, W. (1954). Highlights in the history of the National Vocational Guidance Association. *Personnel and Guidance Journal, 33,* 205–208.

Norton, M. B., Katzman, D. M., Escott, P. D., Chudcoff, H. P., Peterson, T. G., & Tuttle, W. M. (1986). *A people and a nation* (2nd ed.). Boston: Houghton Mifflin.

Parsons, F. (1909). *Choosing a vocation.* Boston: Houghton-Mifflin.

Paterson, D. G. (1938). The genesis of modern guidance. *Educational Record, 19,* 36–46.

Reed, A. Y. (1944). *Guidance and personnel services in education.* Ithaca, NY: Cornell University Press.

Rockwell, P., & Rothney, J. (1961). Some social ideas of pioneers in the guidance movement. *Personnel and Guidance Journal, 40,* 349–354.

Rodgers, D. T. (1978). *The work ethic in industrial America 1850–1920.* Chicago: The University of Chicago Press.

Ryan, A. (1995). *John Dewey and the high tide of American liberalism.* New York: Norton.

Shear, B. E. (1965). Pupil personnel services: History and growth. *Theory Into Practice, 4,* 133–139.

Smith, P. (1985). *America enters the world: A people's history of the progressive era and World War I.* New York: Penguin.

Stephens, W. R. (1970). *Social reform and the origins of vocational guidance.* Washington, DC: Monograph of the National Vocational Guidance Association.

Thelen, D. B. (1973). Social tensions and the origin of progressivism In J M Bannor, E. Hackney, & B. J. Berstein (Eds.), *Understanding the American experience* (pp. 187–208). New York: Harcourt Brace.

Wiebe, R. H. (1967). *The search for order 1977–1920*. New York: Hill and Wang.

Williamson, E. G. (1965). *Vocational counseling.* New York: McGraw-Hill.

Yoakum, C. S. (1919). College personnel research. *School and Society, 9,* 559.

Zytowski, D. G. (1972). Four hundred years before Parsons. *Personnel and Guidance Journal, 50,* 443–450.

# 2

# The Rise of Applied Psychology

> Psychology has a long past, but a short history.
>
> —Ebbinghaus

As the first faint stirrings of the vocational guidance movement were beginning to be felt, that is, during the years immediately following the Civil War, little in the way of organized psychology existed in America. There were no professors of psychology, no academic departments of psychology, and no psychological laboratories in American universities (Klein, 1970). Psychological clinics and child guidance centers were still decades away.

No psychological journals were published in English, and no Ph.D.s had yet been given. No one had yet taken a standardized intelligence test, nor a personality inventory. No one spoke of learning curves, referred to an IQ, diagnosed an inferiority complex, cited a correlation coefficient, or identified a Freudian slip. White rats were blissfully ignorant of the ins and outs of maze-running, and pigeons perched on statues in the park, rather than pecking for pellets in a Skinner Box.

Basically, what we now know as modern, scientific psychology was undreamed of in America. This doesn't mean, of course, that people did not have psychological problems, or that they were any less concerned about understanding themselves and their fellow human beings. Help with what we would call mental health problems was still the province of physicians, or of the clergy, as it had been for centuries. One of the many abuses that troubled the consciences of Americans during the Progressive Era was the plight of those confined in brutish, prison-like "insane asylums."

Historians tend to date the beginnings of scientific psychology to the advent of Wilhelm Wundt's laboratory at the University of Leipzig in Germany in 1879 (Boring, 1950). This event is usually taken to mark the emancipation of "scientific psychology" from the ancient domain of philosophy, and so to date its establishment as an empirical science. The selection of this time and place, like most of the "beginnings" established by historians, is probably somewhat arbitrary.

Since this chapter is concerned primarily with tracing the way in which applied psychology began in America, and particularly with the merging of the practice of counseling into the mainstream of professional psychology, that approximate time is as good a point at which to begin as any.

The birth of what we perhaps euphemistically call "scientific psychology" was, to say the least, a difficult delivery. Momentous and virtually insoluble issues that had defied resolution by philosophers for many centuries were part of the baggage that the fledgling discipline of psychology brought with it into the skeptical family of science.

Age-old controversies such as the nature-nurture debate, mind-body dualism, and the free will-determinism dilemma all helped to assure psychology a troubled childhood. Debates over the validity of experimental paradigms and differences in criteria for scientific evidence abounded. Unfortunately, many of these same controversies rage on as psychology moves through the second century of its adolescence (Hergenhahn, 1992).

Perhaps because of experimental psychology's preoccupation with weighty and insoluble issues, and its struggle to attain respectability in academia, the histories of experimental and applied psychology remained largely separate for the first half century of their existence. In one sense, they remain what Cronbach (1957) termed the "two disciplines of scientific psychology."

# THE BEGINNING OF APPLIED PSYCHOLOGY

If we accept that experimental psychology began in the 500-year-old halls of Leipzig University, we can trace the beginning of differential psychology, the foundation of early applied psychology, to a somewhat less prestigious institution. At about the same time that Wundt was undertaking his first attempts at psychological experimentation, some equally portentous events were occurring in London's fashionable West End.

The visitor to the Kensington district of London in the late 1880s might have strolled pleasant streets, admiring stately old Georgian architecture, or watched the mix of hansom cabs and aristocratic carriages that rumbled past. Our visitor might have sought out a sunny park bench to read the latest adventure of Sherlock Holmes in the popular *Strand* magazine. If one of London's frequent showers forced him indoors, our visitor might well have sought refuge in a place called the South Kensington Museum.

The South Kensington Museum was a far cry from the great British Museum, with its magnificent collections of Greek marbles and Egyptian sarcophagi. It did, however, have one distinction that eluded the British Museum itself. Quite arguably, the South Kensington Museum was the birthplace of applied psychology.

Along one of the Science Galleries was a long, narrow room containing a row of tables upon which were arrayed an assortment of odd paraphernalia that would have delighted the amateur inventor and gadgeteer. Picking up a handbill from the stack displayed near the doorway, our visitor would have been enlightened as to the purposes of this strange new facility as follows:

1. For the use of those who desire to be accurately measured in many ways, whether to obtain timely warning of remediable faults in development, or to learn their powers.
2. For keeping a methodological register of the principal measurements of each person, of which he may at any future time obtain a copy under reasonable restrictions. His initials and date of birth will be entered in the register, but not his name. The names are indexed in a separate book.
3. For supplying information on the methods, practice and uses of human measurement.
4. For anthropometric experiment and research, and for obtaining data for statistical discussion.

(From Pearson, 1924, p. 358)

For the paltry sum of "thruppence" (only two pence for repeat visitors), the "client" could undergo a variety of measurements supervised by the laboratory assistants. Physical measurements included head length, head breadth, standing height, height to the top of the knee, arm span, and a variety of other physical attributes. Functional measurements included strength of grip, breathing capacity, visual and auditory acuity, reaction time, and speed of striking a blow.

Many of the devices and instruments used were ingenious inventions devised by the founder of the facility. A number of these later became standard equipment in other laboratories. The facility at the South Kensington Museum was the brainchild of one of the most remarkable intellects of the 19th century (Forrest, 1974).

## FRANCIS GALTON: GENIUS AND GURU

Francis Galton was born near Birmingham, England, in 1822. He was a cousin of Charles Darwin. Their grandfather, Erasmus Darwin, was a physician, philosopher, and poet. Francis Galton's father was a wealthy banker.

Galton was a genuine child prodigy. He was able to read at age 2 1/2, and was reading the classics for pleasure by the age of 7. His early education was at home with private tutors. Later, when he entered boarding school, he had a thoroughly miserable experience.

Galton left boarding school at age 16 to study medicine at Birmingham General Hospital. He transferred to King's College in London and then moved to Cambridge, where he obtained a degree in 1843. He never completed a medical degree or practiced medicine, however.

Galton was independently wealthy after his father's death. He traveled the world, socialized with his wealthy friends, and served as a mapmaker with a scientific expedition to Southwest Africa. At age 32, he was awarded a medal from the Royal Geographic Society. He became President of that Society shortly after publishing two books on his experiences as an African explorer.

Francis Galton developed two great enthusiasms in his career as an independent but highly respected natural scientist. One was a passion to measure anything and everything that he could observe. The second was a determination to show that his cousin Charles Darwin's theories about natural selection applied to the human species, and particularly to establish the genetic basis of human intelligence. It was this quest that brought him to psychology.

Galton's passion for measurement led him to invent the weather map. He was the first person to use the terms "highs," "lows," and "fronts." He was the first person to suggest that fingerprints be used for personal identification. He tried to determine which country had the most beautiful women, the degree of boredom at scientific lectures, and the effectiveness of prayer. Francis Galton had insatiable curiosity and an genuinely original intellect.

Galton's truly consuming interest was in the genetic basis of individual differences. He studied the offspring of gifted parents to compare the frequency of eminence among their children as compared with the general population. In 1869, Galton published *Hereditary Genius: An Inquiry into Its Hows and Consequences.* He demonstrated that the offspring of illustrious parents were far more likely to achieve distinction than were the children of "ordinary" parents.

Galton coined the term "eugenics" and advocated social policies to promote marriage of gifted couples. Galton was the first person to use questionnaires to do survey research in psychology. He also was the first to use word association inventories, and he speculated about the existence and nature of unconscious mental processes well before Freud.

In 1884 Galton set up his first "anthropometric laboratory" at London's International Health Exposition and collected normative data on more than 9,000 individuals. It was this laboratory that was reopened at the South Kensington Museum. Altogether, more than 17,000 individuals were measured in these laboratories during the 1880s and 1890s (Johnson et al., 1985).

Although Francis Galton was primarily interested in the study of human intelligence, he had little in the way of direct measures of complex intellectual functioning, that is, what we would call "mental tests." These kinds of instruments would not come into wide use until after the turn of the century, toward the end of Galton's life. He and his associates used relatively primitive measures, such as reaction time and sensory discrimination and acuity.

Since Galton had few direct measures of intellectual functioning he was forced to make a set of sweeping and fateful assumptions in order to make his "anthropometric" measurements relevant to his search for a genetic basis for human intelligence. He reasoned that intelligence must be closely related to sensory acuity, since human beings could only learn about the world through observations made possible by the senses (Forrest, 1974).

This assumption was to have profound implications for the future of differential psychology and psychological measurement. It is clear that Galton was utterly convinced by his early genealogical studies that intelligence was a simple and straightforward function of genetic endowment, such as eye color or stature. His genealogical studies had been criticized early on for ignoring environmental factors (Hergenhahn, 1992). In responding to such criticism, Galton coined the phrase "nature vs. nurture" to characterize the heredity environment debate. He conducted pioneering studies of twins to support his views.

Even after sophisticated measures of intellectual functioning were in wide use, long after Galton's death, the basic notion that human intelligence was a unitary, innate, and genetically endowed function was to dominate differential psychology for decades. Interestingly, the search for biological foundations of intelligence still goes on, more than a century after Galton's early work (Vernon, 1993).

After Galton and his associates had collected their vast array of data from thousands of individuals, they were confronted by a host of methodological problems never before encountered by researchers. Their solutions to these problems created the second "culture" of psychology, an approach that was very different than the experimental methods that were evolving in German psychological laboratories. In the process of doing so, Galton and his colleagues essentially invented the field of statistics as we know it today.

Galton began by drawing on the work of the Belgian mathematician Adolph Quetelet, who had been one of the first to apply mathematical models to frequency distributions of human characteristics. Quetelet had found that many anthropometric measurements, such as height and girth, were distributed in frequency approximately in accordance with the "normal law." Interestingly, Quetelet saw these differences as "nature's error" in aiming at an ideal or "normal" condition. Today we call this tendency the bell-shaped probability curve (Boring, 1950).

Galton had formulated the basic notions of regression and correlation in connection with his studies of inherited characteristics. He first used the term "regression toward the mean" to describe the tendency of offspring to show less of a given characteristic than an extreme amount evident in a parent. At first, the concept of correlation was termed "Galton's function," before being christened the coefficient of correlation some years later.

Galton and his associates noted that their anthropometric data tended to fit the "normal curve," and so were able to begin to estimate the probability of occurrence of given deviations from the norm or average. This was, of course, the basis for inferential statistics. Galton invented the concepts of the median and of percentiles to describe central tendency and variability.

In 1904, Galton endowed a Professorship in Eugenics at the University of London. The first appointee to the position was Karl Pearson, who had worked with Galton for years, and who had helped to develop many of the statistical concepts used in their research. Together they had founded the journal *Biometrika*.

Karl Pearson was the inventor of that icon of elementary statistics courses, the Pearson Product Moment Correlation Coefficient. After Galton's death in 1911, the "Galton Professorship" led to the creation of a department of applied statistics that became the pre-eminent such program in the world.

Another Galton-inspired researcher and statistician was Charles Spearman. Spearman expanded upon early methods of correlation to produce a mathematical concept of intelligence. In 1904, Spearman published a paper in which he concluded that positive correlations among various types of measures of intellectual functioning must be due to the presence of a general factor which he called $g$. Eventually the $g$ factor came to be thought of as *intelligence*. Spearman also did much of the pioneering work on reliability of psychological measurement, and helped to lay the foundation for the development of factor analysis.

Perhaps the most remarkable thing about Francis Galton's career was that he quite literally laid down the theoretical and methodological structure for the study of individual differences and for the development of psychological measurement *before* any really sophisticated instruments were available with which to gather data. So compelling was Galton's genius that for the next half century psychologists were in the position of endeavoring to construct tests and obtain data in harmony with Galton's speculations about the nature of human intelligence. The notions that measured intelligence is fixed, unitary, genetically endowed and normally distributed all come from Francis Galton and his early associates. His views and methods were accepted more or less uncritically by an entire generation of applied and research psychologists who followed.

Galton was clearly the founder of applied psychology. He had entered the field to pursue his own set of purposes in extending

Darwin's ideas to the study of human heredity. As Boring (1950, p. 487) put it: "Wundt wanted to improve psychology; Galton, the human race."

Ironically, Galton's work was brought to America by one of Wundt's students. From the standpoint of modern psychology, Wundt's research went nowhere, but his students went everywhere, especially to America.

## APPLIED PSYCHOLOGY COMES TO AMERICA

James McKeen Cattell was one of the first Americans to complete a Ph.D. with Wilhelm Wundt at Leipzig. He completed his degree in 1886, having served as Wundt's research assistant. As a graduate student, Cattell published a half dozen scholarly papers, concerning reaction time or individual differences. Interestingly, some of his hypotheses about this research are still being investigated (Deary & Stough, 1996). After a brief sojourn in the United States, Cattell returned to Europe in 1887, to serve as a lecturer at Cambridge University. There he met Francis Galton and immediately shared his enthusiasm for the study of individual differences as well as many of his views about their nature. Cattell referred to Galton as the "greatest man whom I have known" (Watson, 1961).

James McKeen Cattell returned to the United States, where he accepted a position as professor of psychology at the University of Pennsylvania. There he established a psychological laboratory and continued research on measuring human abilities using Galton-style instruments. In 1890 Cattell published an article in the journal *Mind*, in which he was the first to use the term "mental tests." He went on to describe some 50 tests of the type used by Galton. In 1891, Cattell joined the faculty of Columbia University.

More than any other person, James McKeen Cattell set the direction for American psychology (Boring, 1950). He founded and/or edited six different journals in psychology and general science, including *Science, School and Society, The American Naturalist, Scientific Monthly*, and *Psychological Record*. He founded the biographical directory, *American Men of Science* (which included women).

In 1917, Cattell was dismissed from Columbia University because of his pacifist position in opposing American entry into World War

**Figure 2.1     James McKeen Cattell**

I. He was a man of strong principles and opinions, and was fearless in upholding his convictions. James Cattell went on to help found and direct the Psychological Corporation, the premier purveyor of psychological materials and instruments in the world. He died in 1944, the most senior and one of the most respected figures in American psychology.

One of Cattell's first research projects at Columbia University had been to test a large number of college students using Galton-type instruments, such as reaction time and visual and auditory discrimination. He and his associates found very low intercorrelations among these measures and virtually no relationship with external, real-world criteria, such as college grades.

The history of differential psychology in the United States, at least, might have been short and terminal if it were not for researchers interested in practical problems of education, particularly in the diagnosis and treatment of mental retardation.

## THE BIRTH OF THE CLINICAL METHOD

The person who replaced Cattell in the psychological laboratory at the University of Pennsylvania in 1892 was another of Wundt's American students, Lightner Witmer. Witmer had studied with Cattell at Pennsylvania and had traveled to Leipzig to finish his degree with Wundt at Cattell's suggestion. Witmer did not find in Wundt the kind of mentor that Cattell had seen. Witmer saw Wundt as autocratic and highly unscientific in attitude. Wundt required students to repeat experiments until they turned out as Wundt expected. He turned aside studies on variables such as reaction time because they were not "psychological," that is, not rooted in consciousness and based upon introspection. Witmer left Leipzig feeling that he owed nothing to Wilhelm Wundt (O'Donnell, 1985).

In 1896, Witmer started what he called the "psychological clinic." In the same year he presented a paper to the 4-year-old American Psychological Association in which he described the clinic as a new kind of social institution that combined service, research, and teaching of "psychological orthogenics" which included vocational, educational, correctional, hygienic, and industrial and social guidance (French, 1984).

Lightner Witmer was certainly one of the very first genuine applied psychologists in America. Today, he is often considered the founding figure of both school and clinical psychology (Benjamin, 1996). In 1907 Witmer founded a journal, *The Psychological Clinic*. This journal, as well as Witmer's own clinic, dealt primarily with problems of mental retardation and learning difficulties.

Perhaps the most significant legacy of the Witmer clinic was the name itself. From that time, the practice of psychology with individual clients and cases tended to be known as "clinical" psychology. At that point in time, the name referred almost solely to a method of applying psychological knowledge, rather than to a distinct professional group. Indeed, Witmer's clinic and his journal were more similar to today's psychoeducational or child study centers, and to the work of school psychologists, than to what we now call clinical psychology.

The next impetus for applied psychology came from neither England nor the United States. Rather, it was the work of two French physicians studying the same kinds of educational problems that had engaged Lightner Witmer. The two who accomplished that breakthrough in psychological measurement were, of course, Theodore Simon and Alfred Binet. It was Binet and Simon who first gave psychologists the basic tools with which to study complex mental functions directly.

## ALFRED BINET AND THE IQ

Alfred Binet (1857–1911) came from a family of physicians. He studied medicine, but turned away from medical practice to embark upon a career in psychology. He worked with Jean Charcot, the famous French psychiatrist, who had also been a mentor to young Sigmund Freud. Binet did a number of studies on hypnotism, a major tool in Charcot's treatment program.

While engaged in research at La Salpetriere Hospital Binet committed a blunder that haunted him for the rest of his life. He experimented with the use of magnets to change emotional responses. Binet passed magnets over various parts of a subject's body and claimed that he could convert fear of an object such as a snake into affection. Of course, other researchers were unable to replicate his results (Wolf, 1973).

Binet was finally forced to admit that his experimental methods were faulty. His spurious results were probably due to the subjects' expectations and responses to suggestion. Binet resigned his position in some disgrace, and spent the next few years studying the intellectual development of children (Hergenhahn, 1992).

His subjects this time were his own daughters. Binet invented several tests based upon simple intellectual tasks, not unlike those used by Jean Piaget some years later. He published several papers on child development.

In 1891, Binet, his reputation restored, joined the staff of a psychological laboratory at the Sorbonne. In 1899, Binet began a collaboration with a younger physician, Theodore Simon, who had worked in an institution for retarded children. Four years later, the two were commissioned to study the problems of educating such children. One

**Figure 2.2    Alfred Binet**

of their first tasks was to develop reliable ways of identifying mental retardation.

At the time, the kinds of tests used to identify retardation were essentially simple sensory measures of the type developed by Galton. Such instruments frequently misclassified children with visual or auditory handicaps as mentally retarded. As early as 1896, Binet had criticized such tests and had proposed that more complex, cognitively oriented instruments be developed to measure intellectual functioning directly. Binet suggested that tests be designed to measure functions such as memory, imagery, imagination, attention, and comprehension. He also included aesthetic appreciation, moral sentiment, and force of will in his comprehensive concept of human intelligence. Essentially, Binet proposed that intelligence be defined in terms of basic, cognitive functions, evidenced in everyday life, and that these be measured directly in terms of performance on relevant tasks (Wolf, 1973).

Between 1905 and Binet's untimely death in 1911, he and Simon constructed and revised a set of measures of intellectual performance that not only identified retardation, but also measured levels of intellectual development in children generally. The Binet-Simon Scale arranged a set of cognitive and motor tasks in an ascending order of difficulty. These tasks were administered to children ranging in age from 3 to 13. If three fourths of the children of a given age accomplished the task, that item was assigned to that age level in the scale.

The result was a comprehensive measure of a child's level of intellectual functioning in comparison to other children. In 1911, a German psychologist, William Stern introduced the term "mental age" to describe a child's score. He also suggested that the mental age be divided by the chronological age, and multiplied by 100, yielding the intelligence quotient, or IQ, that was to define human intelligence and focus the field of mental measurement from that time forward.

Ironically, Alfred Binet was vehemently opposed to both the concept of a "mental age" and to the use of the intelligence quotient to represent a fixed level of intellectual functioning (Wolf, 1973). Binet's approach to the definition, study, and measurement of human intelligence was almost diametrically opposed to that of Galton and his followers. Binet saw intelligence not as a single, unitary, and innate capacity, but as a composite of many abilities that emerged out of the processes of growth and development.

It is fascinating to speculate about how different would have been the history of psychology if Alfred Binet had lived to advance his vision of the nature of the human intellect, rather than to be remembered merely as the clever architect of the ubiquitous IQ test.

Ironically, a full century after Alfred Binet first proposed a multifaceted, developmental definition and approach to the study of human intelligence, the American Psychological Association commissioned a "blue ribbon" panel of distinguished psychologists to respond to the still-raging controversy over the nature, origins, and distribution of human intelligence (Neisser et al., 1996). In a report entitled "Intelligence: Knowns and Unknowns" the panel essentially concluded that we still do now know what intelligence is, how it develops, or why individuals and groups differ markedly on its measures. Predictably, the panel called for further research!

The Binet-Simon tests, however, represented an idea whose time had come. Within only a few years after the appearance of the revised scales in 1911, Binet-type tests were being translated and adapted for use throughout the world.

## MUNSTERBERG: PROPHET AND POPULARIZER OF THINGS TO COME

Some of the readiness to follow Binet's lead in developing measures of complex intellectual functions in the United States was probably due to the work of another of Wundt's students. Hugo Munsterberg was only 29 years of age when he accepted William James' invitation to join the Harvard faculty in psychology in 1892.

Young Hugo Munsterberg's experience with Wilhelm Wundt also was quite different from that of James Cattell, who, as Wundt's research assistant, had basked in the glow of his mentor's approval and encouragement. Munsterberg had proposed a line of research that was directly opposed to some of Wundt's most cherished theories. Wundt immediately shifted Munsterberg to a different area of research for his dissertation.

Upon graduation, however, Munsterberg took a position at the University of Freiberg and promptly published his rejected dissertation in expanded form. This triggered an animated controversy between Wundt and his former student, in which Munsterberg won academic respect and recognition but incurred the lasting enmity of his former professor (Roback, 1952).

Apparently, this feud limited Munsterberg's prospects for an academic career in Germany, and his acceptance of William James' invitation to join the Harvard faculty was at least partially an effort to secure a fresh start in a more hospitable environment.

As an experimental psychologist, Hugo Munsterberg was an original and creative thinker who challenged many of the prevailing ideas and approaches of his time. In this field, however, he was always in the shadow of his rival, Edward Bradford Titchener (1867–1927), another of Wundt's pilgrims to the New World. Titchener headed the psychological laboratory at Cornell University and, more by force of personality than by the lasting value of his research, became the dominating figure in American experimental psychology (Roback, 1952).

It was Hugo Munsterberg, more than any other of the early American psychologists, who promoted and extolled the practical benefits and possibilities of applied psychology. Munsterberg held both the Ph.D. and M.D. degrees. He wrote about the possibilities of psychotherapy and actually worked with some therapy cases.

Hugo Munsterberg wrote magazine articles, gave public lectures, and essentially founded the field of industrial psychology in America. As we noted in the previous chapter, Munsterberg foresaw the use of psychological tests in both vocational selection and guidance. His book on industrial psychology, published in the United States in 1913, attracted wide attention and set the stage for the rapid growth in applications of the new generation of psychological tests. Munsterberg was essentially the "popularizer" of American psychology (Roback, 1952). Munsterberg died in 1916, largely unappreciated for the contribution he had made to move applied psychology into the public eye (Hergenhahn, 1992).

## LEWIS TERMAN: ARCHITECT OF INTELLIGENCE

The work of Binet and Simon was brought to the United States very quickly. By 1910, translations of Binet items were available in English. Some difficulty was found, however, in fitting these items into an age scale with American subjects. It fell to a young Stanford professor to create the American version and to set the direction for mental measurement in the United States for the next half century.

Lewis Terman was born in 1877, the 12th of 14 children born to an Indiana farm family. He was a smallish, precocious child afflicted with tuberculosis. He was haunted by the fears of the disease and recurrences of its symptoms throughout his life. Much of Lewis Terman's early education came in one-room schools, including one taught by his elder brother.

The only college that Terman's family could afford was at a nearby "normal school," a kind of teacher's college. At the age of 17, Lewis Terman began his own teaching career in a one-room school much like the one he had attended a few years before. Terman returned to normal school several times, finally piecing together a Bachelor of Arts degree at the age of 22. In the interim he had taught in one-room schools and served as principal of a 40-student high school.

Terman's thirst for learning and education was unquenchable. He enrolled at Indiana University as an undergraduate to expand upon his normal school education. It was there that he developed his great commitment to psychology. Finally, in 1904, with financial aid from his family, Lewis Terman enrolled as a doctoral student in psychology at Clark University.

The president and grand guru of Clark University was G. Stanley Hall, the most famous and prestigious psychologist in America at that time. Hall had received the first Ph.D. in psychology granted in America under the tutelage of William James at Harvard. Hall then established the first psychological laboratory in the United States at John Hopkins in 1883.

In 1888, G. Stanley Hall became president of the newly established Clark University at Worcester, Massachusetts. In Terman's days at Clark, there were only about 50 full-time students, most graduate students in psychology, education, or philosophy (Shurkin, 1992).

Graduate education at Clark was stimulating and informal. There were no formal majors; no one took attendance; there were no grades. To register for a course, a student simply gave his or her name to the president's secretary. Upon finishing a prescribed set of courses, students took a 4-hour examination. If they passed they were given the Ph.D.

The moving spirit and intellectual force at Clark was clearly G. Stanley Hall. He taught, administered, guided, and inspired students. A highlight of the experience were evening seminars in Hall's home, the same home in which the American Psychological Association had been organized in 1892. Terman was tremendously influenced by Hall and encouraged by him to pursue the study of intelligence.

Terman had become interested in the study of intelligence while still a student at Indiana University. At Clark University, he conducted studies contrasting the abilities of high and low rated students as judged by school principals. Not surprisingly, he found the highly rated students superior on most criteria.

Terman's attitudes toward the mentally retarded, or "feeble-minded," as they were called even in scientific writing, were less than compassionate by today's standard. Like most American psychologists of the day, Terman saw mental retardation as a major social problem, and the retarded, themselves, as potentially anti-social beings who should be housed in mental institutions or "schools for the feeble minded" (Shurkin, 1992).

Terman passed his orals and was handed his diploma by none other than President Theodore Roosevelt at commencement ceremonies in 1905. (G. Stanley Hall knew how to turn out the rich and famous.)

Lewis Terman accepted a position as principal of a high school in San Bernadino, California. He was unhappy as a high school principal and accepted an offer to teach at the Los Angeles Normal School, which later became the University of California at Los Angeles. In 1909 he went back to Indiana University to teach. While there, he was recruited to the faculty of Stanford University as an assistant professor of education. This began one of the most remarkable and prolific careers in American psychology.

In 1910, the Binet items had been translated by Henry H. Goddard, another Clark University Ph.D., who became director of the Research Laboratory for the Study of the Feebleminded at the Vineland School in New Jersey. Goddard is remembered today for authoring a genealogical study of the pseudonymous Kallikak family that purported (in the manner of Francis Galton) to demonstrate the hereditary basis of mental retardation and the antisocial nature of the "feeble-minded." The work of Goddard and other American psychologists led to the passage of compulsory sterilization laws in some 20 states. (Galton would have been pleased!) Goddard also coined the term "moron," taken from the Greek term for foolish.

Goddard was apparently better at drawing genealogical charts than constructing psychological tests. Although Goddard administered his translated items to some 2,000 children and tried to draw conclusions from the results, his version of the Binet-Simon scales was severely flawed, if not foolish.

Lewis Terman began work with the Binet items in 1910 and quickly realized that adapting the methods devised by Binet and Simon for use with American children would require a major research effort. Over the next 2 years, Terman and his graduate students devised some new items, borrowed others from a variety of sources, and completely recalibrated the age scales on samples of American children. In the process, some 2,300 people were tested, including 1,700 "normal children," 200 children at both extremes, and 400 adults (Shurkin, 1992).

In 1912, with the help of graduate student H. G. Childs, Terman published his revision of the Binet scale and christened it the Stanford-

Binet, since all of the standardization work had been done there. Interestingly, there is no evidence that Terman ever corresponded with Alfred Binet, who died shortly before the Stanford-Binet was completed. Terman decided to use Stern's suggestion of expressing the results in terms of an IQ.

The impact of the Stanford-Binet on American applied psychology can hardly be exaggerated. For the next half century, the Stanford-Binet became the standard criterion against which almost all measures of intellectual functioning were compared and calibrated. Scores on the Stanford-Binet virtually came to define the concept of intelligence. In 1916, Terman published a monograph, *The Measurement of Intelligence*, that established his reputation as a premier scholar in American psychology. Even Lewis Terman was surprised at the immediate acceptance and uncritical acclaim that greeted his work. Clearly the Stanford-Binet Intelligence Scale represented an idea whose time had arrived.

At the same time that Lewis Terman and his associates were engaged in creating the Stanford-Binet, another psychologist, Frederick Kuhlman, was doing very similar work at the University of Minnesota. Kuhlman also published his test in 1912.

Terman's version was published by Houghton-Mifflin, who quickly sensed the commercial possibilities of the new instrument. They proceeded to advertise and promote the new test vigorously. Kuhlman's test was published by the University of Minnesota Press and languished in the relative obscurity produced by the anemic promotional efforts of an academic press.

It is ironic that the final operational definition of American intelligence was determined more by the entrepreneurial zeal of a profit-hungry publishing house than by any triumph of scientific discourse (French, 1984).

Terman, the diminutive Indiana schoolteacher, had suddenly become both a recognized scholar and a celebrity of sorts. He was promoted to full professor and given a special raise of $5,000 to keep him at Stanford. When one member of the Board of Trustees, future President Herbert Hoover, heard that Terman was being courted by the University of Iowa, Hoover pushed for another raise (Shurkin, 1992).

Terman immediately applied for a research grant to pursue his greatest interest, the psychology of the intellectually gifted. The grant and the grand design of Terman's epic longitudinal "genetic study of genius" was delayed by the impact of world events.

## PSYCHOLOGY AND THE GREAT WAR

In April, 1917, the United States entered the First World War. The declaration of war was followed by an outburst of patriotic sentiment. Psychologists were no less eager to participate in the war effort than were the rest of the population. The "War to End All Wars" had captured the popular imagination and mobilized the industrial, financial, and human resources of a nation that was indeed a "sleeping giant."

The president of the fledgling American Psychological Association in that fateful year of 1917 was one Robert Yerkes, a Ph.D. from Harvard, who had remained on the staff there as an instructor in comparative psychology. Yerkes was deeply interested in mental testing, and, ironically, had been one of the few vocal critics of Terman and the Stanford-Binet Scale. He had criticized the Terman-Binet approach as theoretically impure, and considered the item selection process as a concession to practical rather than theoretical criteria (Von Mayrhauser, 1992).

Only two weeks after the Declaration of War, Yerkes called a special meeting of the APA in Philadelphia to consider how psychologists could contribute to the war effort. Not surprisingly, it was decided that psychology's primary contribution should be in devising a testing program to help select and classify recruits entering the armed forces.

Shortly after this meeting, Henry Goddard hosted a conference of a select group of psychologists at the Vineland School to begin the process of developing a testing program for the entire army. Prominent among these psychologists were Lewis Terman and, of course, Yerkes.

This group received funds and space from the Philadelphia-based Committee on Provision for the Feebleminded and met for 2 weeks at the Vineland School to develop a plan. Yerkes led the effort to sell the idea of mass testing of recruits to the military, and succeeded so well that he was commissioned in the U.S. Army with the rank of major.

Drawing on group tests developed by one of Terman's students, Arthur Otis, this team proceeded to develop the famous Alpha and Beta tests. By the end of the war, one and three quarter million men had been tested.

Each army recruit was given the Alpha test. Those who were deemed illiterate (in English) were given the Beta test. The psychologists divided recruits into six classifications. The lowest group was discharged as unfit for military service, while the highest-scoring group was offered entrance into Officer's Training School. Only about 9,000 men were dismissed from service, while about 10,000 were assigned to labor battalions as a result of testing (Shurkin, 1992). At about the same time that Major Yerkes, and his legion of graduate students turned 2nd lieutenants, were busily testing a good share of the male population, another group of distinguished psychologists were also hard at work on behalf of the war effort.

These psychologists invented a comprehensive personnel classification system, the core of which was a military qualification card which recorded the results not only of group intelligence tests, but also trade tests, interview protocols, and rating scale results. Taken together, these instruments comprised a general personnel system that provided objective data for promotion and training decisions.

This system was the prototype for the systems of "scientific personnel management" that were used widely in business, industry, and education after the war. The qualification card was also the forerunner of the ubiquitous "cumulative record card" that was to be the centerpiece of school guidance activities for the ensuing half century.

Two of the key psychologists involved in this effort were Walter V. Bingham and Walter D. Scott. In the years immediately preceding America's entry into the Great War, a group of psychologists at Carnegie Institute of Technology had founded the first real academic department of applied psychology, and had proceeded to turn Hugo Munsterberg's vision of an industrial psychology into reality.

The Division of Applied Psychology at the Carnegie Institute pioneered the development of vocational aptitude tests, and began the process of measuring vocational interests. One of the members of this group was a Columbia Ph.D. who had earned his degree with James McKeen Cattell. E. K. Strong left the Carnegie group to move first to George Peabody and from there to Stanford University, where he developed the Strong Vocational Interest Blank which was derived in part from the work done at Carnegie (Super, 1983).

It is clear that the work of psychologists in World War I was not the beginning of applied psychology in America (Benjamin, 1996). Lightner Witmer had pioneered clinical work 20 years before the war. Actually, most of the substantive work that underlay the testing and classification program had been done by Terman and Otis at Stanford and by the Carnegie group led by Bingham and Scott well before the onset of war.

It is equally true, however, that the war experience had a very significant impact upon both the public's perception of the relevance of applied psychology, and the self-confidence and aspiration level of psychologists themselves (Sokal, 1984).

A number of the young psychologists involved in the Alpha and Beta projects returned to civilian life to launch careers at university counseling centers or in private consulting firms. The work of these psychologists produced a veritable deluge of new psychometric instruments that inevitably wrought major changes in business, industry, and education.

The new applied psychologists were inordinately proud of their achievements and contributions to the war effort. After the war, McKeen Cattell boasted that the value of the tests used by the Army was at least $1 billion (this at a time when a billion dollars was really worth something, even to the government). Apparently, the Army did not share the psychologists' appraisal of their own importance. General John J. Pershing, Commander of the American Expeditionary Force in Europe, thought that the importance of the personnel and testing program was overstated (Sokal, 1984). Significantly, the Army abandoned the program as soon as the war ended.

## PSYCHOLOGY IN THE ROARING TWENTIES

The decade of the 1920s was a period of excess and exuberance, of extremes and eccentricities as America rode an economic and emotional roller coaster from the end of the Great War to the beginning of the Great Depression. Women had finally gained the hard-won right to vote. Perceptions of "co-eds" and "flappers" replaced "suffragette" as a source of popular female stereotypes.

Henry Ford's Model T made personal transportation a part of everyday life. Motion pictures learned to talk, and gave birth to a peculiarly American phenomenon the "movie star," Jazz went from being a dirty word to becoming an icon of American culture.

Prohibition, the institution that Herbert Hoover called a "noble experiment," became the law of the land and ushered in an era of violence and lawlessness that made the Wild West seem tame by comparison. Terms like "bootlegger," "speakeasy," and "G-man" became part of the popular vocabulary. Al Capone ran Chicago and regulated competition in the beer business, with the tommy-gun in lieu of anti-trust laws.

The stock market rose faster than women's skirts, and Calvin Coolidge proclaimed that "What's good for business is good for the country." Certainly what was good for business was good for applied psychology.

In 1921 James McKeen Cattell organized a group of psychologists to found the Psychological Corporation. Psychological Corporation represented applied psychology by, with, and for psychologists, themselves. Cattell often referred to the Corporation as a "holding company" for psychologists (Sokal, 1984). The member psychologists were the stockholders, directors, and professional staff of the organization. The Corporation was to act as a public relations and advertising agent, a referral source, and a supplier of psychological materials and instruments. Customers were referred to member psychologists, and one half of the fees collected were to be devoted to psychological research.

This visionary scheme grew rather slowly at first, and eventually Cattell was forced out as managing director. When reorganized along more conventional business lines, however, Psychological Corporation became the nation's foremost supplier of psychological tests and materials.

At the same time that Cattell was marketing his vision of applied psychology, Walter Dill Scott was organizing the Scott Company. Scott, as we mentioned earlier, had been one of the pioneering industrial psychologists at the Carnegie Institute. He had written on the psychological principles involved in advertising, and had collaborated with Walter Van Dyke Bingham and others on the Army Classification System.

In 1919, Scott brought together a number of the psychologists who had worked on the wartime projects. The Scott Company was a full-fledged management consulting firm, probably the first in the world. The firm worked closely with more than 40 client companies around such areas as personnel selection and promotion problems, sales training, advertising, and labor relations. Besides its full-time staff, Scott Company utilized the services of distinguished consultants or "associates" including James Angell, Walter Bingham, E. L. Thorndike, John B. Watson, and Robert Yerkes. In 1923, the Scott Company disbanded, and its members went on to join other firms or establish ventures of their own. Ironically, Scott Company was not only one of the first psychological consulting firms in the country; it was one of the few that oversold neither the efficacy of its services, nor the power of its tests (Sokal, 1984).

By the mid-1920s, however, applied psychology was not only accepted by big business, it was on its way to becoming big business. The sweet smell of success was very much in the air in the 1920s, and its vapors were as intoxicating to applied psychologists as to their clients.

One history of psychology in the 1920s put it this way:

> Psychologists of the period showed a confidence possibly not seen at any other time in their science's history. . . . Specifically, this pattern saw the American psychologist of the 1920's approach one or another problem with extreme confidence. . . . This confidence led in some cases to important scientific, theoretical advances, and to results of genuine practical applicability. But more importantly, this confidence went farther, and thus the psychologists often vastly overstated their claims for the validity of their results and the usefulness of their work. These overstatements in turn led to exaggerated and unrealizable expectations of what psychology could do . . . (Sokal, 1984, pp. 275–276)

One frequently quoted example of the degree to which psychologists were intoxicated with the exuberance of their own verbosity was John B. Watson's masterpiece of overstatement in a 1925 book on behaviorism intended for the general public. Watson wrote:

> Give me a dozen healthy infants, well-formed, and my own specified world to bring them up in and I'll guarantee to take any one at random and train him to become any type of specialist I might select—doctor, lawyer, artist, merchant, chief and yes even beggar-man and thief, regardless of his talents, penchants, tendencies, abilities, vocations, and race of his ancestors. (Watson, 1925, p. 82)

John B. Watson was without doubt one of the most fascinating characters in the history of psychology. His meteoric rise to prominence as the self-appointed apostle of behaviorism, and his equally dramatic fall from grace in academia, are the stuff of plays and novels. His life could have furnished the plot for one of Sinclair Lewis's scathing denunciations of middle-class decadence and hypocrisy; or he could have been the protagonist in one of Eugene O'Neill's Freudian-flavored tragedies of family life gone wrong. We will chronicle more of his story in Chapter 9.

The supposed powers and virtues of the new science of psychology were trumpeted by many others, however. Popular books, newspapers and magazines all offered advice supposedly based upon psychological knowledge with little regard for either veracity or humility (Benjamin & Dixon, 1996).

Freudian psychology, with its emphasis on the destructive effects of repression and the intensity of libidinal impulses, seemed to fit perfectly the spirit of the times in 1920s America. Social revolutions in sexual mores, speech, fashions, and gender roles had transformed the society. Freud was interpreted, reinterpreted, and often misinterpreted to explain everything from flesh-colored silk stockings to the "Dance Craze."

Fortunately, not all of American psychology in the 1920s reflected the sensationalism, flamboyance, or hyperbole associated with figures like Watson or theories such as Freudian psychology.

Much very solid research was undertaken in the 1920s. Lewis Terman began his longitudinal study of intellectual giftedness, or what became known as "genetic studies in genius." Termans's epic study focused upon the lives and careers of more than 1,500 gifted children. Data on the "Termites," as they are sometimes called, are still relevant and still cited more than three quarters of a century later (Friedman et al., 1995).

Lewis Terman did not accomplish this tremendous study single-handed. Much of the field work of interviewing, testing, and selecting subjects was done by a team of four psychologists: Florence Fuller, Florence Goodenough, Helen Marshall, and Dorothy Yates. All four had previous experience in research with children and had been teachers. One, Florence Goodenough, went on to become a distinguished researcher in the area of child development and giftedness at the University of Minnesota. The study of intellectual functioning and the development of a multitude of psychological tests were a major preoccupation of psychology in the 1920s. At Stanford, besides Terman and his associates' work, E. K. Strong developed the Strong Vocational Interest Blank, and Truman Kelly (who was also assistant director of the Terman study) began to build on the work of Spearman to develop factor analysis as a psychometric tool.

Arnold Gesell, another of G. Stanley Hall's protégés, began pioneering studies in child development and founded the Yale Clinic of Child Development. W. F. Dearborn began the Harvard Growth Studies that followed a group of children from first grade to completion of high school.

Longitudinal studies in the manner of Terman were popular. Several major universities established institutes of child development and child welfare. These included the universities of Iowa, Minnesota, and California. The Fels Institute and the Merrill Palmer School also began impressive programmatic research efforts. The study of child and adolescent development became a major emphasis in American psychology during the 1920s (R. I. Watson, 1961).

## 1927: A PIVOTAL YEAR

The year 1927 was a time of triumphs and tragedies, of prophetic beginnings and monumental finishes. It was the end of the first full year of the "Great Bull Market," and confidence in the future was unbounded. George Herman "Babe" Ruth hit 60 home runs for the New York Yankees and was rewarded with the unheard of salary of $80,000 per year!

A 25-year-old ex-stunt pilot from Minnesota, Charles Augustus Lindbergh, soloed from New York to Paris and stirred the imagination and admiration of the world. The Lindy Hop rivaled the Charleston as America's favorite dance step. The state of Massachusetts executed Nicola Sacco and Bartolomeo Vanzetti, Italian immigrants and labor "agitators," for murder, in what historians consider a flagrant miscarriage of justice (Lens, 1969).

Henry Ford built the 15-millionth Model T and then stopped production of the "Tin Lizzie" that changed the face of a continent. (The new Model A was actually available in three colors.) After losing 36 pilots in 8 years, the Post Office terminated the Air Mail Service and consigned the mail to private contractors. The airline industry was born, and by the end of the year more than 5,000 paying passengers had flown the friendly skies of scheduled airline service.

Al Jolson starred in "The Jazz Singer," the first full-length "talking picture." There were 268 openings on Broadway as affluent America flocked to theatres and concert halls (Allen, 1952). The hit of the season was Jerome Kern and Oscar Hammerstein's "Show Boat." Sinclair Lewis published *Elmer Gantry*. Edward Kennedy "Duke" Ellington organized a new 10-piece band, began a epic engagement at Harlem's Cotton Club, and became a legend in American music.

CBS, the Columbia Broadcasting Company, joined its 3-year-old rival, NBC, to blanket America with everything from the Metropolitan Opera to the gridiron exploits of Harold "Red" Grange, the "galloping ghost" from Illinois. The mass culture in America was born.

Not all of 1927's endings and beginnings were outside of psychology, Edward Bradford Titchener died suddenly of a brain tumor. With him was buried the last vestiges of experimental psychology as the study of consciousness. Titchener—English by birth, German by education, and American by residence—had been the dominant figure in American experimental psychology since his arrival fresh from Wilhelm Wundt's Ph.D. factory in 1892.

Although differing from his mentor in some details, Titchener carried the Wundtian traditions and methods to the New World with greater fidelity and loyalty than any of Wundt's other American students. He passionately defended introspectionism as a method, and reiterated the view that psychology was the study of mind and consciousness. As attacks on the scientific legitimacy of German-style experimental psychology mounted, Titchener simply stiffened his resolution, and by sheer force of personality preserved his position, if not his influence, in American psychology.

Titchener resigned his membership in the American Psychological Association on several occasions only to be coaxed back into the fold. He was one of the few psychologists to boycott the war effort, believing that applied psychology was exchanging a science for a technology. In that, he was quite right.

By today's standards, Edward Titchener would have been seen as a faintly ridiculous figure who insisted on lecturing in academic robes and making solemn pronouncements firmly rooted in either mysticism or absurdity. Titchener's definition of mind, for example was "the sum total of human experience considered as dependent upon the experiencing person" (1917, p. 9). Ironically, many of the issues that underlay introspectionism are alive and well and living under the name mental representation (Gardner, 1985).

One of Titchener's favorite quotations was to the effect that when science comes to be useful, it ceases to be interesting. By that standard alone, Edward Bradford Titchener must have had one of the most interesting careers in the history of psychology.

The year of prophetic beginnings was evident in the publications produced in 1927. Ivan Pavlov, the Russian physiologist reluctantly turned psychologist, published *Conditioned Reflexes,* the book that reported the results of his famous "bell-food-salivation" studies that were to become a part of introductory psychology textbooks forever.

A young Wisconsin professor, Clark Hull, published a pioneering work called *Aptitude Testing.* Hull foresaw the use of normative test data arranged in expectancy tables and delivered by a "prediction machine," of which a prototype was actually built. Essentially, Hull anticipated the practice of computer-assisted counseling that was to come along a half century later.

Another profoundly prophetic publication in the year 1927 came from the pen of Leta Hollingsworth, a distinguished child and adolescent psychologist and a pioneering student of the psychology of women. In an article entitled "The New Women in the Making" for *Current History* she wrote:

> The essential fact about the New Women is that they differ among themselves, as men do, in work, in play, in virtues, in aspirations and in rewards achieved. They are women not woman. (Hollingsworth, 1927, p. 19)

It has taken the ensuing 70 years for Hollingsworth's "essential fact" to get through to both American society and the profession of psychology.

Perhaps the most profoundly prophetic publication of all in 1927 was a book entitled *The Logic of Modern Physic,* by P. W. Bridgeman. Bridgeman argued forcefully that definitions of scientific concepts and research procedures must be "operationalized" into directly observable procedures and communicated in terms of the actual processes that generated them. Without such specification, concepts and results were seen as devoid of scientific meaning. Bridgeman's book paved the way for what Herbert Feigl termed "logical positivism," an approach that was to dominate the philosophy of science in psychology for the next half century.

For many psychologists today, "operationism" or "logical positivism" is considered a straitjacket that constrained and curtailed the scope and direction of psychology as a science. Certainly, operationism helped to usher in what has been called the era of "physics envy" in American psychology. Experimental psychology turned away from the study of consciousness to concentrate on what has been facetiously called "rat morphology."

Perhaps, indeed, "operationism" has been a straitjacket. Given the grandiosity of applied psychology and the intellectual fuzziness of experimental psychology, it could well be that in 1927, at least, American psychology was badly in need of such a straitjacket.

Another bittersweet beginning and ending occurred in that fateful year of 1927. It was the "Dark Year," as he later called it, in the life of a struggling young writer. Armed with a note of encouragement from poet Robert Frost and straight out of college, he sought desperately to find his literary voice.

After a frustrating year of failure and rejection, the young man finally concluded that as a writer, he had nothing to say. In the course of seeking literary inspiration, he read the work of the celebrated giants, H. G. Wells and Bertrand Russell. The latter called J. B. Watson the greatest scientist of the century. H. G. Wells posed the question of what he would do if standing on a pier watching George Bernard Shaw drowning on one side and Ivan Pavlov struggling on the other. Wells went on to explain why he would save Pavlov and leave Shaw to the fish.

Turning to the works of Pavlov and Watson provided a totally different inspiration. In the fall of 1928, Burrhus Frederick Skinner began graduate work in psychology at Harvard. The rest, as they say, is history.

## PSYCHOLOGY'S WALK ON THE DARK SIDE

There was a dark side to all of the exuberance and excitement of the Roaring Twenties. Behind the frenetic facade of marathon dancing, movie star adulation, and highly publicized heroics was an ugly underlay of resurgent racism and blatant bigotry. The end of the Progressive Era, the horror of the World War, and the betrayal of Wilsonian idealism at Versailles left America in a mood of disillusionment, cynicism, and materialism.

The Bolshevik Revolution in Russia had shocked and threatened the country into fear and suspicion of all things foreign and "un-American." Home-grown racial antagonism and intolerance, never far beneath the surface of American society, was more distinct and destructive than ever.

In 1925, the revived Ku Klux Klan had a membership of about 5 million people (Link & Catton, 1967). The Klan with its platform of anti-Black, anti-Catholic, anti-Semitic, and anti-foreign sentiment wielded a degree of political power that is difficult for us to comprehend today. While the Klan's numerical strength was concentrated largely among lower middle-class, small-town Americans in the West, South, and Middle West, its message of hatred and intolerance pervaded the whole society.

Unfortunately, academia, the home base of most American psychologists, was hardly a sanctuary of enlightenment and tolerance. Many colleges and Universities had quota systems for both faculty composition and admission of students to limit numbers of Jews.

This "quota system" was so established that Lewis Terman advised one of his most promising doctoral students, one Harry Israel (who, as it happened, was not Jewish) to change his name. The young man accepted the suggestion and actually took his mother's maiden name. He went on to a distinguished career at the University of Wisconsin as Harry Harlow (Sokal, 1984).

Psychology and the rising tide of nativism and prejudice came together around the issue of immigration. As we noted in Chapter 1, the influx of immigrants to America in the late 19th and early 20th centuries was phenomenal. In the social and political climate of post-World War I America, the issue of immigration became powerful and polarized.

Restricting immigration had been a problem of prime concern to both political parties for a number of years. In 1921 an immigration bill had been passed that sharply reduced the total number of people admitted to the country. By 1924, however, the debate over immigration had taken a quite different turn.

The national debate over immigration focused not only on the question of how many immigrants were to be admitted, but also on the relative worth and desirability of various ethnic and religious groups who made up American society. The tone of this debate, and indeed the mood of the country, can be seen in a quote from the President of the National Institute of Immigration, one Broughton Brandenberg:

> It is not vain glory when we say that we have bred more than sixty million of the finest people the world has ever seen. Today there is to surpass us, none. Therefore any race that we admit to our body social is certain to be more or less inferior. (Quoted in Leahey, 1980, p. 260)

The role of psychologists in the formulation and passage of the Immigration Act of 1924 is a controversial and emotion-laden episode in the history of American psychology. To a considerable degree, the debate over immigration in 1924 was a debate over the virtues and worth of two groups of Americans. The "Old Immigrants," largely those who had arrived on these shores in the years prior to 1890, were predominantly Northern European Protestants—WASPS, if you will. The new immigrants, those arriving after 1890, were heavily drawn from Eastern and Southern Europe, and were frequently Catholic or Jewish in religion.

In the climate of Nativism and intolerance that permeated much of American society in the 1920s, the differences between the old and the new immigrants were seen as the differences between what was traditional, safe, and acceptable, and what was perceived as foreign, dangerous, and "un-American."

The entry of psychologists into this debate was largely an outgrowth of the testing movement. For a number of years, prominent psychologists, including people such as Goddard, Terman, and Yerkes, had trumpeted to the public the presumed danger presented by the "feebleminded." One of the major values of psychological tests was seen as their ability to identify these dangerous deviants and safely remove them from the mainstream of American life.

Immediately after the end of the First World War, psychologists began the task of analyzing the results of the military testing program. Test scores had been obtained, as we noted, on more than a million and a half men. Also available was the background data obtained on these individuals upon entry into military service.

When the test scores of recruits were analyzed by race and national origin, sharp differences among groups were found. Generally, a descending hierarchy was seen, with Northern Europeans at the top, those of Southern and Eastern European "stock" sharply lower, and Hispanic and African-American groups at the bottom.

As Shurkin (1992) described the pecking order:

> Immigrants were classified by nation of origin, with the smartest ones coming from Northern Europe and the dumbest from Southern Europe. The lighter the skin, the brighter the recruit. (p. 23)

The results of these analyses were reported in 1923 in a book entitled *A Study of American Intelligence* written by psychologist Carl C. Brigham of Princeton University. Brigham's book both documented the findings of the analyses of test scores and drew sweeping conclusions about the presumed intellectual differences among various ethnic groups and the public policy implications of those scores. The impact of Brigham's book was much like the storm of controversy stirred up by Herrnstein and Murray's *The Bell Curve* (1994) with the difference that in 1923, neither the general public nor the body politic were as well-informed about the nature and the limitations of psychological testing. The claim that tests directly measure a genetically endowed, innate, and fixed level of intelligence was probably considerably more credible then than today.

Some distinguished psychologists were quick to apply the military test data to the immigration debate. Actually, even before the War, Henry Goddard had taken his psychometrically flawed translation of the Binet items to Ellis Island, where he inflicted it upon a group of anxious and demoralized immigrants who stumbled off the steerage decks of ocean liners seeking admission to the "promised land." Despite the flaws in his homemade test, and the obvious limitations of the testing situation Goddard came up with a set of conclusions that were truly deserving of the term that he had coined, that is, "moronic." According to Goddard's results, 83% of the Jews, 80% of the Hungarians, 79% of the Italians, and 87% of the Russians were "feeble minded" (Kamin, 1995).

After the publication of the Brigham book, Robert Yerkes joined in the chorus of anti-immigration invective with a flight of unsupported and overblown rhetoric hardly befitting one who claimed to be a scientist. He wrote:

Whoever desires high taxes, full almshouses, a constantly increasing number of schools for defectives, of correctional institutions, penitentiaries, hospitals, and special classes in our public schools, should by all means work for unrestricted and non-selective immigration. (Yerkes, 1923, p. 365)

The Immigration Act of 1924 enacted into law most of the provisions urged by the mental testers. All immigration from Japan was prohibited, completing the exclusion of Orientals already in place. Quotas were established for immigration from Europe based upon the census data from 1890, clearly giving preference to Northern European immigrants. Since relatively few immigrants from those nations applied, overall immigration declined very sharply during the period prior to World War II. Many refugees from Nazi and Soviet persecution were turned away from American shores.

The role of the psychological community in the immigration debate is controversial, to say the least. Clearly, psychologists were far from unanimous in their interpretation of the military test data and its implications for the immigration debate. Indeed, when have psychologists ever been unanimous about anything? Clearly there would have been an Immigration Act with or without the intervention of psychologists, and it would have probably have discriminated against the "New Immigrants."

One of the inevitable temptations that confront both the writers and readers of history is the urge to make moral judgments based upon contemporary standards and values regarding the conduct of those who lived in another time, and whose life experiences led them to construe the world in vastly different ways.

It is possible to view the mental testers' infusion of psychology into the immigration debate as a shameful episode in our history, or simply to view it as the inevitable interplay between the social sciences and politics. Meara describes the encounter between psychology and social policy thus:

The pre-depression applied psychologists explicitly introduced politics into American psychology. They advocated for ideologies that they believed served the social order or the public interest. (Meara, 1989, p. 156)

The ideologies that many of the "mental testers" advocated were clearly based on Social Darwinism, although the term itself was out of vogue by the 1920s. Their view of the human condition was as a species whose members competed with each other for survival. It was, as Kamin (1995) put it, a "brutally pessimistic" doctrine. They were also deeply influenced by the eugenics movement founded by Francis Galton. While Galton had focused upon an effort to promote marriage between gifted people, the American eugenics movement centered around efforts to prevent the reproduction of retarded or handicapped individuals. Both of these ideologies are repugnant to a great many people at the close of the 20th century.

Rather than to attempt to pass judgment on the political correctness of those who acted on their values of eight decades ago, it is considerably more useful, and infinitely more fair, to examine the quality of the science that these pioneering psychologists preached and practiced.

No matter how pure or impure their motives may have been, their work was abysmally unscientific. The mental testers were, on the whole, oblivious to one of the most crucial distinctions in any empirical science. They were unable or unwilling to comprehend the distinction between observations and the inferences drawn from those observations. Psychological tests and inventories are simply ways of observing samples of behavior from which to infer other behavior. The inferences drawn are almost always based upon both the observations and some set of accompanying assumptions about the subject, the testing situation, and the domain of behaviors to be inferred.

There are myriad alternative explanations available for the patterns of test results obtained in the military testing programs, for example. Cultural biases in the tests themselves, unequal opportunities to learn, biases in the samples, stress-laden testing situations, and a host of other limiting factors were obvious and were pointed out by critics. They were studiously ignored or resisted by psychologists such as Goddard, Yerkes, Brigham, and their adherents.

An example of how simple-mindedly the mental testers saw their technology is clear in an introduction to a compendium of test descriptions intended as a handbook for teachers and counselors. The introduction, written by W. A. McCall in 1938, stated:

> Many years ago certain specialists sought to secure a monopoly of the privilege of using standard tests by trying to persuade educators to regard tests as possessing certain mystic properties. . . .
>
> Mental measurements are essentially similar to bodily measurements. If anyone proposed to abolish the making and use of the measurements

of pulse, temperature, blood pressure, et cetera we would call him crazy . . . (Paterson, Schneidler, & Williamson, 1938, p. xvii)

A half century after Galton began his program of "anthropometric" measurements at the South Kensington Museum, many psychologists still saw their instruments and the interpretations drawn from them as simple, straightforward, and essentially physiological measurements. The reasons for their mixture of ignorance and arrogance is unclear. The training programs from which they came certainly failed to equip these psychologists with the attitudes of skepticism, curiosity, and humility that are the essential attributes of science. Somewhere along the way, as Titchener and Boring predicted, these psychologists had indeed exchanged a science for a technology, and indeed a badly flawed technology that they did not fully comprehend.

Perhaps the most compelling explanation is the one tactfully suggested by Super (1983) when he described them as "intellectual" mediocrities. The ironic truth may well be that the IQ worshipers were themselves simply not bright enough to rise above the limitations of their training and the prejudices and biases of their times.

## WHERE HAVE ALL THE COUNSELORS GONE? GONE TO TESTING EVERYONE

By now it must be apparent to the reader that counseling and counselors, as such, played a very small part in the rise of applied psychology in America. By 1920, vocational guidance had largely moved out of social agencies into the schools and colleges. As we noted in Chapter 1, there were calls for the presence of counselors in every school as early as 1915 (Miller, 1961).

By 1920 the National Education Association had attempted to define vocational guidance in the schools. They recognized the need for counselors, but defined the function broadly, describing the counselor as something of a psychologist, but also a sociologist, an economist, and most of all, an educator (C. H. Miller, 1973). The concept of a counselor reflected much more the image of a program administrator than of a professional providing direct services to students.

In 1925, Donald G. Paterson described 14 functions of a college student personnel program (Williamson, 1965). Counseling was not one of them.

John Brewer (1932) described guidance almost entirely as an aspect of curriculum. He mentioned counselors almost in passing, warning them that they should expect no more pay than teachers. In discussing the counseling process, he described the counselor as needing to

> Learn how to receive students in the best manner: business-like without being formal, dignified but not pompous, friendly but not jovial, direct but not hurried, intimate when necessary but not inquisitive, helpful but not patronizing. (p. 157)

Brewer did not add that experience as a tightrope walker might be helpful!

One of the first books to deal directly with counseling process was Walter Bingham and Bruce Moore's *How To Interview* (1931). This

**Figure 2.3   Donald G. Paterson**

book dealt generally with interview situations, including areas such as selection and placement activities and opinion surveying, as well as counseling. The latter type of interview was considered as simply one type of generic interview situation. This book stayed in print in four editions for more than a quarter-century.

Basically, very little that we would recognize as counseling existed in either schools or universities during the 1920s and early 1930s. When one-to-one personal encounters occurred between students and guidance workers, the contact was much more in the form of direct advice-giving or test interpretation than anything we would term counseling today (C. Miller, 1961).

To some extent, this dearth of actual counseling services was due to the overwhelming impact of mental testing on American education. In 1922, Lewis Terman published a book titled *Intelligence Tests and School Reorganization*, in which he urged that students be tracked into groups labeled "gifted, bright, average, slow and special" based upon their IQs. A year later, in a speech to the National Education Association, Terman predicted that such IQ grouping would soon become standard practice in American schools. In his predictions, at least, Terman was quite right (Shurkin, 1992).

The spread of IQ testing in the schools and their use to group children into curriculum tracks was meteoric. The passage of child labor legislation, the enforcement of compulsory education laws, and the changing demographics caused by immigration and migration brought greater diversity into the schools than ever before. The dictum of progressive education that the public schools, including high schools, existed to teach all of the children of all of the people constituted a classic challenge to American education. Unfortunately, the rise of IQ testing and homogeneous grouping provided an equally classic cop-out.

Fass (1989) described the attraction of IQ testing to the schools in this way:

> For the schools, the IQ was a concept that seemed ideally suited to their new goals and problems. It seemed to establish a stable educational center by assuming an unvarying constant with in each child—his inborn capacity. . . .
>
> The IQ categorized children and made it possible for the schools to deal with them in group, class and hierarchical terms. That the IQ

ultimately also predefined children . . . and ironically the function of the school by establishing the primacy of innate ability over environmental stimulation was also a blessing. (p. 51)

As the IQ came to be considered the dominant characteristic of children, the functions of guidance programs were correspondingly simplified.

In an address to the National Education Association ironically titled "The Reorganization of the High School for the Service of Democracy," John Tildsley defined the task of the new comprehensive high schools as follows:

The high school must take every boy and girl from 13 to 18 years of age, *appraise* his ability, and discover his aptitudes by a series of *intelligence tests, group* him with other of approximately equal ability and then *assign* him subjects of study . . . (Quoted in Fass, 1989, p. 69) (italics added)

According to this formula, the functions of guidance were simple: *appraise, group,* and *assign*; not much need for counseling or counselors here. The role of guidance workers in the 1920s and 1930s were heavily shaped by this philosophy. These workers soon became the custodians of the massive testing programs and record-keeping systems that were the engine that drove the new test-centered schools.

In a strange and insidious way, guidance moved from its roots in progressivism and reform to a role as the guardian and gatekeeper of the status quo as defined by a fixed and unalterable entity, the IQ. All of this was done in the name of democratizing the schools and individualizing instruction.

The training of guidance workers quickly followed their new functions. Few textbooks in the 1930s dealt extensively with counseling as such (Super, 1954). Hamrin and Erickson (1939) in a book entitled *Guidance in the Secondary School* focused upon teachers as the heart of the guidance program. Paterson, Schneidler, and Williamson (1938), in a book entitled *Student Guidance Techniques*, described 97 different tests under more than 20 categories ranging from general aptitude tests to typewriting and stenography. Their brief mention of counseling procedures was largely to urge the counselor to give the appropriate tests before seeing the student directly. Perhaps the most forthright definition of guidance in this era of tests and records was given by Traxler (1945). He said simply:

> The central idea is to gather as much relevant information as possible about each pupil, organize it so that it shows both status at any given time, and growth over a period of years and use these data with understanding in the *distribution* and *adjustment* of individual pupils. (p. xiii) (italics added)

This era saw guidance moving from a philosophy of individual choice and self-direction to becoming a cog in the ponderous wheels of what can be called the "cult of adjustment."

In the end it was neither the cycles of educational reform nor the needs of school children that put the counseling component into counseling psychology, although the term "counseling" itself was still decades away. Rather, it was the desire to achieve professional status and recognition that supplied the impetus to define a specialized role of providing direct professional services to clients.

The need for some sort of separate professional identity was strong. The early model of psychologists as test-builders and teachers as test-users had been a notable failure. Individual counseling, while only a part of the generally recognized program of student personnel services, soon became an indispensable part.

The definition of a separate professional identity for psychologically trained student personnel workers required a broader and more sophisticated approach to counseling processes and procedures than those typically used by teacher-counselors, student advisors, program administrators, and others who were broadly termed student personnel workers.

One of the first contributions to a more sophisticated and thereby more professional approach to counseling was contributed by E. G. Williamson (1939a) in what was termed "the clinical method of guidance." Williamson set forth a six-step model of counseling procedures consisting of

1. Analysis or data collection;
2. Synthesis or collating of data;
3. Diagnosis or description of client characteristics and problems;
4. Prognosis or prediction of probable outcome;

5. Counseling treatment; and
6. Follow-up.

The clinical counseling approach obviously bore great similarity to a medical model. According to Williamson, it was derived from clinical approaches utilized in child guidance centers, as well as methods used in vocational counseling.

Williamson's clinical counseling model is historically important, not for its content, but for the way that it moved the practice of counseling to become a specialty in the professional practice of psychology. The emphasis upon data collection and analysis leading to diagnosis clearly defined clinical counseling as the province of psychologists. The opening paragraph of the 1939 article made this clear:

> Not all guidance workers are clinicians, and not all use clinical technics in assisting students. Psychometrists, registration advisors, teachers, dormitory directors and faculty advisers are all personnel workers but not necessarily clinical counselors. (p. 214)

The clinical counseling approach not only defined a systematic approach to counseling; it staked out a territory for psychologists as counselors and set in motion the series of events that would culminate in the inauguration of a new field called counseling psychology.

In the years from 1937 to 1945, E. G. Williamson and his colleagues at the University of Minnesota, including John G. Darley, Edward Bordin, Milton Hahn, and others explicated and expanded upon the clinical counseling approach to expound what has often been called the "Minnesota Point of View." They put counseling in a developmental framework that transcended the vocational guidance approach to include a wide range of personal and educational problems. Clinical counseling was firmly anchored in psychometrics and in the trait and factor approach to the study of personality. Most importantly, the counselor was defined as an expert, highly qualified, and specially prepared psychologist.

Only a few years after the clinical counseling approach was launched, it was rocked to its foundations by a new and radical challenge to its core assumptions. In 1942 Carl R. Rogers published *Counseling and Psychotherapy,* a "nondirective" approach almost diametrically opposed to the philosophical and theoretical underpinnings of the Minnesota Point of View.

The resulting controversy between directive and nondirective counseling both polarized and energized the field of counseling for the next quarter-century. It is important to understand, however, that these two often bitterly competing "camps" actually agreed upon several vital issues. Both saw counseling as a psychological specialty requiring high levels of graduate preparation. Both saw counseling as dealing with a wide range of human concerns and difficulties, and both helped set in motion the process that eventually led to the professionalization of counseling and so to the field of counseling psychology.

We will examine that story in Chapter 3.

## REFERENCES

Allen, F. L. (1953). *The big change.* New York: Harper and Row.

Benjamin, L. (1996). Lightner Witmer's legacy to American psychology. *American Psychologist, 51,* 235–236.

Benjamin, L., & Dixon, D. (1996). Dream analysis by mail. *American Psychologist, 51,* 461–468.

Bingham, W., & Moore, B. (1932). *How to interview.* New York: Harper and Row.

Boring, E. G. (1950). *A history of experimental psychology* (2nd ed.). New York: Appleton-Century-Croft.

Brewer, J. (1932). *Education as guidance.* New York: MacMillan.

Bridgeman, P. W. (1927). *The Logic of Modern Physic.*

Cronbach, L. J. (1957). The two disciplines of scientific psychology. *American Psychologist, 12,* 671–684.

Deary, I. J., & Stough, C. (1996). Intelligence and inspection time. *American Psychologist, 51,* 599–608.

Fass, P. (1989). *Outside in: Minorities and the transformation of American education.* New York: Oxford University Press.

Forrest, D. W. (1974). *Francis Galton: The life and work of a Victorian genius.* New York: Taplinge.

French, J. L. (1984). On the conception, birth, and early development of school psychology. *American Psychologist, 39,* 976–987.

Friedman, H., Tucker, J., Schwartz, J., Tomlinson-Keasy, C., Martin, L., Wingard, D., & Criqui, M. (1995). Psychosocial and behavioral predictors of longevity. *American Psychologist, 50,* 69–78.

Gardner, H. (1985). *The mind's new science: A history of the cognitive revolution.* New York: Basic Books.

Hamrin, S. A., & Erickson, C. E. (1939). *Guidance in the secondary school.* New York: Appleton-Century.

Hergenhahn, B. R. (1992). *Introduction to the history of psychology* (2nd ed.). Belmont, CA: Wadsworth.

Herrnstein, R. J., & Murray, C. (1994). *The bell curve: Intelligence and class structure in American life.* New York: Free Press.

Hollingsworth, L. S. (1927). The new woman in the making. *Current History, 27,* 15–20.

Johnson, R. C., McClearn, G. E., Yuen, S., Nagoshi, C. F., Ahern, F. M., & Cole, R. E. (1985). Galton's data a century later. *American Psychologist, 40,* 875–892.

Kamin, L. J. (1995). The pioneers of IQ testing. In R. Jacoby & N. Glauberman (Eds.), *The Bell Curve debate.* New York: Times Books.

Klein, D. B. (1970). *A history of scientific psychology.* New York: Basic Books.

Leahey, T. A. (1980). *A history of psychology.* Englewood Cliffs, NJ: Prentice-Hall.

Lens, S. L. (1969). *Radicalism in America.* New York: Crowell.

Link, A. S., & Catton, W. B. (1967). *American epoch* (Vol. II). New York: Knopf.

McCall, W. A. (1938). Two significant questions and two pertinent replies: Introduction. In D. G. Paterson, G. Schneidler, & E. G. Williamson (Eds.), *Student guidance techniques* (pp. xvii–xviii). New York: McGraw-Hill.

Meara, N. (1989). Presidential address. *The Counseling Psychologist, 18,* 145–167.

Miller, C. (1961). *Foundations of guidance.* New York: Harper and Row.

Miller, C. H. (1973). Historical and recent perspectives on work and vocational guidance. In H. Borow (Ed.), *Career guidance for a new age* (pp. 3–40). Boston: Houghton-Mifflin.

Neisser, A., Boodoo, G., Bouchard, T., Boykin, A., Brody, N., Ceci, S., Halpern, D., Loehlin, J., Perloff, R., Sternberg, R., & Urbina, S. (1996). Intelligence: Knowns and unknowns. *American Psychologist, 51,* 77–101.

O'Donnell, J. M. (1985). *The origins of behaviorism.* New York: New York University Press.

Paterson, D. G. (1937). The genesis of modern guidance: Introduction. In E. G. Williamson & J. G. Darley (Eds.), *Student personnel work* (pp. 3–10). New York: McGraw-Hill.

Paterson, D. G., Schneidler, G. G., & Williamson E. G. (1938). *Student guidance techniques.* New York: McGraw-Hill.

Pearson, K. (1924). *The life, letters and labours of Francis Galton.* London: Cambridge University Press.

Roback, A. A. (1952). *History of American psychology.* New York: Literary Publishers.

Shurkin, J. N. (1992). *Terman's kids.* Boston: Little, Brown.

Sokal, M. M. (1984). James McKean Cattell and American psychology in the 1920's. In J. Brozek (Ed.), *Explorations in the history of psychology in the United States* (pp. 273–327). Lewisbury, PA: Bucknell University Press.

Super, D. E. (1954). Comments on current books. *Journal of Counseling Psychology, 1,* 123–124.

Super, D. E. (1983). The history and development of vocational psychology: A personal perspective. In W. B. Walsh & S. Osipow (Eds.), *Handbook of vocational psychology* (Vol. I, pp. 5–38). Hillsdale, NJ: Erlbaum.

Terman, L. M. (1916). *The measurement of intelligence.* Boston: Houghton-Mifflin.

Titchener, E. B. (1917). *A text-book of psychology.* New York: The Macmillan Company.

Traxler, A. (1945). *Techniques of guidance.* New York: Harper.

von Mayrhauser, R. T. (1992). The mental testing community and validity. A prehistory. *American Psychologist, 47,* 224–253.

Watson, J. B. (1925). *Behaviorism.* New York: W. W. Norton.

Watson, R. I. (1961). A brief history of educational psychology. *Psychological Record, 11,* 209–242.

Williamson, E. G. (1939a). The clinical method of guidance. *Review of Educational Research, 9,* 214–217.

Williamson, E. G. (1939b). *How to counsel students.* New York: McGraw-Hill.

Williamson E. G. (1963). An historical perspective of the vocational guidance movement. *Personnel and Guidance Journal, 41,* 854–859.

Williamson, E. G. (1965). *Vocational counseling.* New York: McGraw-Hill.

Wolf, T. H. (1973). *Alfred Binet.* Chicago: University of Chicago Press.

Yerkes, R. (1923). Testing the human mind. *Atlantic Monthly, 121,* 358–370.

# 3

# The Professionalization of Counseling Psychology

> Psychology should be pure, but not too pure.
>
> —G. Stanley Hall

A ll through the summer of 1893, Chicago, "the town that Billy Sunday could not shut down," was dazzled by the sight and the sounds of a mighty World's Fair. America was celebrating the 400th anniversary of the supposed discovery of America by Christopher Columbus. The centerpiece of that celebration was the Columbian Exposition.

The tone of the Exposition, like the mood of the nation, was at once exuberant, festive, and patriotic. The Pledge of Allegiance, familiar to every schoolchild for the next century, was written especially for the opening ceremony.

All that was new and exotic was displayed at the Exposition for the amusement, amazement, and sometimes edification of fairgoers. The motion picture camera, an electric automobile, and the Liberty Bell were all prominent attractions.

A mile-long entertainment strip created a giant "Midway" that became a standard feature for fairs ever after. The sensation of the Midway was George Ferris's remarkable invention that could carry 40 passengers on a revolving journey some 250 feet above the glittering fairgrounds. Less lofty attractions were the abdominal undulations of a troupe of Egyptian belly dancers. One of the many side shows featured the legerdemain of a young magician named Harry Houdini.

One of the minor, if slightly more cerebral, attractions at the Fair was the psychology exhibit. The exhibit itself was neither very original nor, for that matter, very American. It was clearly patterned after Francis Galton's booth at the London Health Exhibition, that, as we noted, came to rest at the South Kensington Museum. Fairgoers who were scandalized by the belly dancers or too acrophobic to enjoy the Ferris Wheel could take a series of Galton-type tests and examine a collection of brass instruments, mostly drawn from European laboratories (Blumenthal, 1991).

The exhibit was the brainchild of Joseph Jastrow, a young professor at the University of Wisconsin, and a tireless publicist, promoter, and prophet of the powers and potentialities of scientific psychology. Jastrow exceeded in enthusiasm even Hugo Munsterberg, although he occupied a somewhat less lofty pulpit than the Harvard Laboratory.

The psychology exhibit was noteworthy in that it marked the first effort in America to interpret the new science to the public, and that it carried at least the tacit endorsement of a new scientific society. Jastrow had outlined his plans for the exhibit the previous December at the first annual meeting of the American Psychological Association (APA) held at the University of Pennsylvania. In one of those strange, convoluted quirks of history, the Exposition and Jastrow's exhibit were actually part of the impetus for the founding of the APA.

## THE FOUNDING OF THE APA

The American Psychological Association came about as a natural outgrowth of the development of modern research universities in America. During most of the nineteenth century, American colleges tended to be oriented toward character development and dominated by sectarian religious groups. Americans interested in higher learning in the sciences typically went to Europe, particularly to Germany; witness, for example, Wilhelm Wundt's stable of American scholars at Leipzig.

One of the consequences of the Gilded Age with its concentration of wealth and industrial power was that very large amounts of money became available for endowments to found new or transform old universities to pursue advanced study in the sciences, and in the process to generate the research needed to shape the great industrial enterprises. The University of Chicago, for example, was simply created by John D. Rockefeller and his Standard Oil mega-fortune. A number of state universities, particularly those in the West and Midwest, transformed themselves into research universities with public funds as well as private endowments.

The transformation of the universities created a new class of academic scientists, housed in universities, but immersed in the pursuit of knowledge (and eminence) on an international scale. Those new academic specialists had far more in common with their counterparts in other universities, whether in Europe or America, than with colleagues in other disciplines officed down the same hallway.

The result of all of this was the creation of scientific societies. One of the first of these, the American Association for the Advancement of Science, had actually been founded in 1848. It, however, was a general umbrella organization open to all. Even after establishing a number of divisions in 1882, the AAAS did not offer the kind of identity, prestige, and publication opportunities that the new class of academics sought.

By 1892 the time was ripe for the tiny group of scholars interested in the new and somewhat ambiguously defined discipline of psychology to organize. The guiding hand that shaped the organizational process was none other than Grenville Stanley Hall's.

## G. STANLEY HALL: FOUNDER, FATHER FIGURE, AND FLIM FLAM MAN

G. Stanley Hall has already been mentioned several times in this narrative. He was without doubt one of the most fascinating, controversial, and complex characters in the history of psychology, or any other science. Hall was the first Ph.D. in American psychology, and a student of theology with a lifelong interest in history and religion. He was a charismatic and caring teacher, and a highly respected scholar in several disciplines. (Bringmann, Bringmann, & Early, 1992) He was also an accomplished and inveterate liar, a shameless self-promoter, and, on occasion, a shady manipulator of men and money.

**Figure 3.1   G. Stanley Hall**

As Sokal (1992) put it, "Throughout his career Hall seemed to deal loosely with the truth" (p. 113).

G. Stanley Hall was a native New Englander born in 1844 on a farm in the Berkshire mountains of Western Massachusetts. He completed grammar school at 16, attended a private academy, and entered Williams College, where he graduated in 1867 (Ross, 1972).

Hall then entered Union Theological Seminary studying theology, philosophy, and the classics. He spent a brief time as a student pastor, then headed for Europe to study theology and philosophy in the Universities of Bonn and Berlin. When the money he had been given by a benefactor ran out, he returned to the United States in 1870 and completed a degree at Union Seminary, but was never ordained (Vande Kemp, 1992).

Hall taught philosophy at Antioch College and then became an instructor in English at Harvard. In 1878 he received the first psychology Ph.D. ever awarded there. His dissertation was directed by William James, and was the first in America on a psychological topic: "The Perception of Space."

Immediately after graduating, Hall returned to Europe to travel and to study physiology at Leipzig. Wilhelm Wundt was not his major professor, and though Hall made much of their very limited association later, Wundt was apparently neither impressed nor charmed by the brash and ambitious Yankee. When Hall later wrote a biography of Wundt, the latter dismissed it as pure invention (Benjamin, Durkin, Link, Vestal, & Acord, 1992).

G. Stanley Hall returned to the United States in 1880, one of the most brilliant and superbly educated figures in American academic life. He joined the faculty of Johns Hopkins, one of the most prestigious of the new research universities. In Hall's few years at Hopkins, he opened the first psychological laboratory in America, organized the first formal Ph.D. program in psychology, and graduated six Ph.D.s, among them Joseph Jastrow. Another of Hall's doctoral students at Johns Hopkins was John Dewey

While at Hopkins, Hall also founded *The American Journal of Psychology*. The financing of this journal was an example of his style. In the early years of scientific psychology, considerable public confusion existed between the terms "psychological research" and what was then called "psychic research," that is, the study of "spiritualism"—the effort to communicate with the dear departed.

Hall's mentor William James maintained a lifelong interest in spiritualism, much to the detriment of his reputation as a scientist. When Hall was seeking financial support for his new journal, he obtained money from several confirmed "spiritualists" who apparently believed that they were contributing to a journal devoted to the study of the supernatural. Hall did not bother to enlighten them on the differences between "psychic research" and scientific psychology (Coon, 1992).

Hall accomplished a great deal in his brief tenure at Johns Hopkins. His penchant for political intrigue and self-promotion, however, led him to seek broader horizons with greater status, autonomy, and power. In 1888, Hall became the founding President of Clark University at Worcester, Massachusetts. Jonas Clark, a wealthy Boston industrialist, put up the money to fund the new university, but succeeded in influencing little but its name.

For 4 years Hall continually deceived Jonas Clark about the institution's goals and policies. Hall assembled a world-class faculty, making extravagant promises that he could not possibly keep. Finally, in 1891, a disgusted Clark withdrew all financial support (Sokal, 1992).

By January of 1892, Clark University's all-star faculty had endured enough of Hall's arbitrary ways and doubledealing. Finally, in April of that year, William Rainey Harper, the President designate of the soon-to-open University of Chicago, came to Worcester armed with Rockefeller's bottomless bankroll and simply hired away the most distinguished of Clark University's faculty.

A lesser man than G. Stanley Hall would have been daunted by such a resounding reversal of fortune. As Hall contemplated this revolting set of developments, however, opportunity knocked loudly in the form of a letter from a former student. Joseph Jastrow announced that he was coming east to garner support for his proposed exhibit at the Columbian Exposition.

Hall seized upon Jastrow's trip as an opportunity to reassert his leadership and prestige. In July of 1892, Hall gathered a small group of psychologists in the study of his home in Worcester, and while Joseph Jastrow pleaded for support for his exhibit at the great fair, G. Stanley Hall quietly orchestrated the formation of the American Psychological Association with himself as its first president.

## THE FOUNDING MEMBERS

No complete and official roster of the original membership exists (Sokol, 1992). It is generally accepted that 26 men had accepted membership in the new organization, and had agreed to elect five others, including three Leipzig graduates, Hugo Munsterberg, Edward Pace, and E. B. Titchener, who were about to take up professorships in American Universities, but who had not yet arrived. Five of the group were colleagues of Hall at Clark, and four more were his former students.

The names of the founding members were as illustrious as their intellectual pedigrees and professional interests were varied. William James, John Dewey, Josiah Royce, James McKeen Cattell, and Hall, himself, were all academic stars of the first magnitude. The group included psychiatrists, philosophers, and pedagogists as well as experimentalists. All were, of course, White males. Sokol (1992) described the group:

In their diversity, however, these 31 men shared at least two other significant traits (besides their sex). First, they were all quite young. Aside from Cowles (aged 54), James and George T. Ladd of Yale (both 50) were the oldest, and Hall, himself was only 48. At least six were in their 20's and their average age was about 35. Like most of the university-based research-oriented fields of the nineteenth century, psychology was a young man's science. (p. 114)

The first few years of APA's existence did not run smoothly. The collisions of massive egos must have reverberated through the halls at that first meeting at the University of Pennsylvania and in subsequent meetings. There were wrangles over the control of journals. Most of the early psychological journals were privately owned, and were sources of power and patronage for their owner-editors.

By 1898, the philosophers had begun to walk out, after failing to obtain a separate section for philosophy. It was becoming clear that the future of the organization lay with science and not philosophy. The umbilical cord that had connected American psychology to its past was cut forever.

The tension that has tugged at the heart and soul of organized psychology throughout its existence was asserted very early.

## SCIENCE VS. PRACTICE: THE THORNY PATH TO PROFESSIONALIZATION

Few of the original members of the APA saw themselves as professionals offering psychological services directly to the public. They were primarily philosophers, educators, and experimentialsts. The common bond that brought them together was a commitment to purely academic psychology founded in research and teaching.

As early as 1896, however, as we noted earlier, Lightner Witmer had shared his vision of a new professional psychology that combined research with practice and that addressed a wide variety of human needs and problems. Witmer had challenged the fledgling organization to help "throw light on the problems that confront humanity" (Witmer, 1897, p. 1). It is fascinating to speculate about how different the future and fortunes of psychology might have been if Witmer's call to focus the field on real people and the real world, instead of the laboratory, had been heeded. As it turned out, Witmer's impact on the APA and on the future of psychology was negligible (Benjamin, 1996).

Witmer's failure to influence psychologists on behalf of his vision of a new scientific-practitioner oriented approach was probably due to four factors (Reisman, 1976). First, most of his colleagues saw themselves purely as scientists; secondly, few had any training or experience in delivering of services; thirdly, few were willing to take risks in attempting to apply their knowledge; and finally, Witmer had a talent for antagonizing his colleagues. Witmer had once so angered Hugo Munsterberg that he threatened to bar a APA meeting from the Harvard campus unless Witmer was expelled from the organization.

For twenty years the influence of professional concerns on the affairs of the APA was almost nonexistent. Several abortive attempts to establish some sort of standards for the growing array of psychological tests were made, with no real results (Resnick, 1997).

## PRACTITIONERS ORGANIZE

By 1916, the voices of practitioners were finally strong enough to be heard in the APA. Concerns about the use of psychological tests by unqualified people, as well as the low status of psychologists in state mental institutions, were raised at the annual meetings in 1915 and 1916 (Resnick, 1997).

Finally, in 1917, at the annual convention in Pittsburgh, an effort was made to organize a new association of practitioners. The new group, called the American Association of Clinical Psychologists, was formed to define, establish and promote standards in the field of clinical psychology. The term "clinical psychology," coined by Witmer in 1907, was adopted to distinguish the new profession. A total of eight men and women founded the new association (Sokal, 1992). They then recruited about 40 others. The immediate question confronting this group, of course, was its relationship, if any, with the APA.

The broader question was clearly the professionalization of applied psychology. The practitioners sought some kind of certification for what was broadly termed "consulting psychology" which included clinical, industrial, and educational psychologists. Such certification would set standards for training and practice, but, more importantly, set in motion a process leading to professional recognition and identity.

To some extent, the Great War and psychologists' role in the war effort overshadowed these first halting steps toward professionalization. The very existence of the new organization was threatening to some of the academic psychologists who saw in it the seeds of dissolution for the APA. Shortly after the end of the war, a joint business meeting between the AACP and APA was held which resulted in a reunification. In exchange for promises to pursue the issue of certification for consulting psychologists, the clinical group, led by Wallace Wallin and Leta Hollingworth, agreed to dissolve the autonomous organization and to form a section of Clinical Psychology within the APA.

The events surrounding the return of the clinical psychologists to the APA fold, and the ensuing years, are somewhat obscure. Wallin complained many years later that certain of the proceedings of the reunification meeting had been mysteriously lost and never published (Routh, 1994).

Some confusion also existed regarding the labels of clinical psychologist, consulting psychologist, and other varieties of applied psychologists. Generally, "consulting psychologist" was the broader term, and tended to refer to psychologists operating in private practice, and thus offering psychological services directly to the public. Many clinical psychologists worked in hospitals and other institutions. Incidentally, the first psychologist in the United States to have a full-time private practice was probably David Mitchell, a student of Lightner Witmer (Routh, 1994).

In 1921, an independent New York State Association of Consulting Psychologists was formed to promote high standards of professional qualifications. In the same year, this group became a division or state chapter of the Clinical Psychology section of APA (Hilgard, 1987). Resnick (1997) referred to the New York group as follows:

> By 1921, sufficient pressure by the applied psychologists had been exerted to form a *Division of Counseling Psychologists* within the A.P.A.'s SCP. (Resnick, 1997, p. 464) (italics added)

Resnick cites the 1987 Hilgard volume mentioned above. That reference clearly labels the New York group as the "Division of Consulting Psychologists" (p. 626) and notes that it was deleted from the APA constitution in 1932.

Some of the confusion about these events may stem from the fact that, according to Strickland (1988), the New York applied psychologists operated under several names and with several affiliations. Her version of events was:

> Attempts to develop a "pure science" of psychology left few opportunities for attention to clinical issues and social activism within the A.P.A. In the early 1930's the New York State Psychological Association, in an attempt to respond to issues of ethics, licensing and standardization of training, became the *Association of Counseling Psychologists* (italics added) (ACP). By 1937 ACP had become so strong that the Clinical Section within APA voted to disband and join the ACP. A new name, the American Association for Applied Psychology (AAAP) was adopted and this independent national group became home for many clinical practitioners. (p. 104)

The New York group of applied psychologists deserves a great deal of appreciation for their leadership in the struggle for professionalization of psychology over a 20-year period. Although they may have been the first group to use the name "counseling psychologist," it is clear that they are in no way the direct ancestors of the present day Division of Counseling Psychology (Division 17) of the APA.

The reasons for the disenchantment of professional psychologists with the APA throughout the twenties and thirties were clear. Despite the supposedly firm promises to pursue certification of consulting psychologists that were part of the reunification agreement, little actual progress was made.

A combination of foot-dragging and stonewalling by the governing powers of APA prevented any real progress toward professionalization. By 1926, an anemic certification procedure had been put in place that failed to prescribe any real standards of training or experience. By paying a fee of $35, a member could be certified. Only about 25 psychologists were ever certified, and the whole procedure was soon abandoned (Samelson, 1992).

So frustrated were the members of the Standing Committee on Certification that they blamed the whole debate on the personality traits of the academic psychologists, stating in a final report that "Scientific men are predominantly schizoid, and seldom exhibit the capacity for resolute common action . . . " (Quoted in Samelson, 1992, p. 125).

By 1927, the Clinical Section was hardly more than a paper-reading group that influenced little beyond the scheduling of symposia at the annual conventions. The APA as a whole was becoming progressively more research-oriented and less supportive of professional practice during the late twenties and thirties. In 1925, a provision was made for "associate" membership, bringing in a group who had the privilege of paying dues, but who could not vote or hold office.

In 1927, a bylaws amendment was passed requiring published research beyond the doctoral dissertation as a requirement for regular membership. A year later an additional amendment was passed requiring that associates in the Clinical Section must also be associates of the APA. Clearly the APA wanted to limit, if not totally exclude, practitioners. As late as 1941, an official APA resolution deplored the existence of organized blocs or caucuses in a scientific organization (Routh, 1994). Clearly the "schizoid" group had won. The acknowledged leader of the "pure science" group, incidentally, was Edwin Boring.

As described in the quote from Strickland, the struggle for professionalization of psychology was finally forced outside the APA.

## COUNSELING COMES OF AGE IN THE GREAT DEPRESSION

On the morning of October 24, 1929, the bubble on which the world economy had floated for nearly a decade burst. In the course of the next few weeks $30 billion in paper value had vanished into thin air in the United States alone. The myth of Wall Street's invulnerability was shattered, and the Great Depression was on its way.

The human consequences of the Depression are almost incomprehensible today. Hundreds of banks simply closed their doors, and hundreds of thousands of uninsured savings accounts dissolved. By 1933, 14 million workers were unemployed. There were no unemployment benefits for the jobless or Social Security insurance for the aged.

Thousands of unemployed men took to the roads in search of nonexistent jobs. The homeless and destitute huddled in cardboard and tarpaper shanty towns called "Hoovervilles" around the fringes of every major city.

One social historian described the psychological impact of the Depression thus:

> It marked millions of people inwardly-for the rest of their lives. . . . Most of them had been brought up to feel that if you worked hard and well and otherwise behaved yourself you would be rewarded by good fortune. Here were failure and defeat and want visiting the energetic along with the feckless, the able along with the unable, the virtuous along with the irresponsible. They found their fortunes interlocked with those of a great number of other people in a pattern complex beyond their understanding and apparently developing without reason or justice. (Wiebe, pp. 148–149)

The impact of the Depression on family life was catastrophic. The number of marriages actually declined by more than 25% from 1929 to 1932. The birth rate dropped by about 15%, while the divorce rate increased sharply (Link & Catton, 1967).

A whole generation of young people was unable to complete an education, get a job, or marry, have children, or begin normal adult lives. They were indeed as much a Lost Generation as their counterparts in the Great War.

The educational system was in shambles. Educational expenditures decreased by nearly 20% nationwide and the decreases in teachers salaries averaged nearly one-third (Link & Catton, 1967). Colleges and universities were even harder hit than public schools. Enrollments in higher education dropped by a little less than 10% from 1931 to 1934. The state colleges and universities were especially vulnerable, losing almost a third of their financial support.

On March 4, 1933, Franklin Delano Roosevelt was inaugurated as President of the United States. He delivered his famous "We have nothing to fear but fear, itself" inaugural address to a demoralized nation whose faith and hope in its own institutions had been sadly eroded.

Franklin Roosevelt's New Deal responded to the nation's crisis by launching a series of what were seen as radical social and economic experiments. Clearly, the social, political and economic philosophies that had characterized the Roaring Twenties were as dead as had been Herbert Hoover's chances of re-election. The nation was thoroughly disenchanted with rugged individualism, "the survival of the fittest," and all of the trappings of Social Darwinism and laissez-faire economics.

Many of the New Deal Programs were focused on the needs and problems of young people. Strangely enough, it was from these desperate and often hastily contrived efforts to stem the tide of social dissolution that counseling as we know it came into its own.

## Counseling the Unemployed

No one really knows how many youth were unemployed during the Depression era. Estimates range from 3 to 6 million workers under the age of 25 who were unemployed at the depth of the Depression between 1933 and 1935. Several massive federal programs were launched to help these young people.

In 1933 the Civilian Conservation Corps, or CCC, was established eventually providing training, jobs and sometimes counseling for a quarter of a million young men. In 1935 the National Youth Administration was created with the objectives of encouraging job training, counseling, and placement services for youth. In 1938 the U.S. Office of Education established an Occupational Information and Guidance Service to coordinate and support vocational counseling services nationwide.

In 1935 a federally supported American Youth Commission undertook an extensive series of investigations into the needs of young people. Using information gleaned from thousands of individual interviews, they documented the need for equalizing educational opportunities and providing vocational training and counseling.

Not all Depression-era counseling efforts were direct outgrowths of the New Deal. As early as 1931, the Minnesota Employment Stabilization Research Institute was established by the University of Minnesota under the leadership of Donald G. Paterson. Many thousands of job-seekers were tested and counseled at the Institute's Occupational Analysis Clinic and in public employment offices in Minneapolis, St. Paul, and Duluth, Minnesota. A substantial proportion of applicants were placed in jobs despite the depressed economic conditions.

The Minnesota program of research and service provided a model for other programs and developed a research base that documented the usefulness of aptitude testing in vocational counseling (Super, 1983). The program became essentially a prototype for the United States Employment Service's approach to testing some years later.

Other counseling and job placement programs were established by private agencies. In 1934, a young Donald Super worked as a vocational counselor with the YMCA in Cleveland, Ohio. In 1938, the B'nai B'rith Vocational Service Bureau opened in Washington, D.C. A year later, the Jewish Occupational Council was formed to coordinate all Jewish vocational services.

The Adjustment Service was established in New York City in 1933. It was made possible by the cooperation and sponsorship of many different people, agencies, and private businesses. During the existence of the Service, more than 16000 clients were counseled. One of the significant features of this program was that broad-based counseling services were provided. The individual client was seen as a whole human being and a constellation of specialized services were made available (Miller, 1961). Similar smaller and less well-publicized program operated throughout the country.

## Counseling in the Child Guidance Clinics

As we noted earlier, the area of scientific psychology that experienced the greatest financial support in the 1920s was the child study movement. The natural extension of that interest and support was in the provision of psychological services to children and adolescence.

The child guidance movement was partially, at least, an outgrowth of the larger mental hygiene movement spearheaded by Clarence Beers circa 1910. We will discuss this movement in more detail in Chapter 5. Stemming from the mental health movement, a number of child guidance centers or clinics were established prior to the First World War. Some, like Witmer's original clinic, were sponsored by universities or medical schools.

A remarkable proliferation of child guidance clinics occurred in the years following the First World War. By 1939, at least 116 centers had been designated as child guidance clinics (Louttit, 1939). Most of these were headed by psychiatrists, but also utilized staff psychologists. A survey of the activities of these psychologists showed that around 70% indicated that they were engaged in providing educational and vocational guidance. These were the most frequently reported activities after testing. Only about a third of the psychologists reported doing psychotherapy (Louttit, 1939). These reports make clear why the title of "Association of Counseling Psychologists" may have been a comfortable one for the New York applied psychologists in the 1930s. On the eve of the Depression, a young Ph.D. fresh from Columbia University began a 12-year career at a child guidance center in Rochester, New York. His name was Carl Rogers.

Definitions of clinical psychology in this period were broad, vague, and varied, emphasizing primarily the employment of a method for studying individuals (Louttit, 1939). In the 1930s, applied psychology differed little from setting to setting. Similar principles and techniques were utilized in clinics, industrial, and business settings and in colleges.

## Counseling in Colleges and Universities

The final arena within which counseling came to the fore in the 1930s was in what came to be called "College Personnel Work." Although American colleges, with their emphasis on character-building, had long utilized deans and professors in working with individual students, the modern approach was an outgrowth of the rise of applied psychology.

Shortly after the end of World War I, Walter Dill Scott, who as we saw, had pioneered industrial psychology at Carnegie Institute and founded the Scott Company, accepted the Presidency of Northwestern University. One of his first acts was to appoint an applied psychologist, L. B. Hopkins, to organize a comprehensive personnel program along the same lines that had been recommended by Scott Company consulting psychologists for their clients in business and industry (Williamson, 1965).

This program included research on selection and a comprehensive system of student records, as well as a program of vocational counseling and placement. The Northwestern program made the Personnel Office the central coordinating agency in promoting student development (Lloyd-Jones, 1929). Counseling was an important part, but only a part of this total program. In the foreword to Lloyd-Jones' history of the program, Walter Dill Scott gave a simple, succinct definition of personnel work as he saw it: "Personnel work is the systematic consideration of the individual, for the sake of the individual, and by specialists in the field" (Lloyd-Jones, 1929, p. v).

Scott's brief definition both provided a credo and staked out a territory for applied psychologists in higher education. A similar comprehensive student personnel program was also developed at the University of Minnesota by Donald G. Paterson and E. G. Williamson.

The Northwestern and Minnesota student personnel programs soon became models for other universities. The role of professional counselors in these programs gradually expanded, and the doctoral programs that were associated with them at places like the University of Missouri, Ohio State University, Columbia University and the University of California, as well as at Minnesota, trained a cadre of young psychologists who were instrumental in defining the field of counseling psychology only a few years later.

By the late 1930s material on counseling was appearing in the literature. In 1938 C. Gilbert Wrenn wrote one of the first major reviews of counseling in schools and colleges. He defined counseling as a one-to-one, highly personal helping relationship. Even then Wrenn felt compelled to justify the necessity for counseling services, as opposed to general guidance procedures, by citing surveys of the needs of youth.

Wrenn cited recent books by Strang (1937), Williamson and Darley (1937), and Elliot and Elliot (1936) as well as the classic Bingham and Moore (1931) volume. In 1939, E. G. Williamson published his *How to Counsel Students*, and in 1942 Carl Rogers published *Counseling and Psychotherapy*. Counseling had begun to establish its own literature and to create its own identity.

In a small way, the Great Depression did for counseling what the First World War had done for applied psychology generally. Counselors across a wide range of settings and at various levels of preparation had responded to a national crisis and to the needs of a very large number of citizens. The need for counseling and counselors had been recognized by government and by communities, colleges, and universities throughout the land.

Perhaps more importantly, counseling had begun to evolve from the rudimentary "test them and tell them" model of early vocational guidance to a process rooted in an appreciation and respect for the complexity, integrity, and uniqueness of each individual. In a word, counseling had moved from advising and admonishing to listening and learning.

By the beginning of a second great war, counseling had achieved a degree of public awareness and acceptance that put it at the threshold of professionalization.

## THE REORGANIZATION OF APA

The Great Depression was finally ended by the Japanese attack on Pearl Harbor and the frantic flurry of defense spending that immediately preceded it. On December 7, 1941, for the second time in less than a quarter century, the United States was at war.

Again, individual psychologists were heavily involved in the massive mobilization of human resources on behalf of the war effort. The Army General Classification Test replaced the old Alpha. On of the notable achievements of psychologists was the design and management of the Aviation Psychology Program which selected air crewmen for the Army Air Forces (Super, 1983). A number of distinguished psychologists were involved in this program and in similar kinds of personnel selection and training programs throughout the Armed Forces.

An unexpected outgrowth of the war effort was the beginning of a process of reunification of organized psychology.

The precise reasons and motivations behind the move toward reunification seem obscure. The AAAP was only 5 years old and thriving. It had acquired its own journal, *The Journal of Consulting Psychology*, and had formed a number of sections to represent the varied interests of its members. Its first president was Douglas Fryer, followed by luminaries such as Donald G. Paterson, Walter Van Dyke Bingham, and Carl Rogers.

A second dissident group had also formed in 1937. The APA had been conspicuously absent from the efforts to alleviate the effects of the Depression, and had been seemingly unconcerned about the turmoil and human suffering caused by both the Depression and the rise of Fascism in Europe. Even though these events had impacted the lives of countless psychologists they were apparently outside the purview of a "scientific society."

As one psychologist put it in 1940:

When the United States entered the big world depression, psychologists did nothing as a group, and have so far done nothing . . . one might conclude that psychologists were oblivious to the fact that our social institutions were rattling around our ears. (Grundlach, 1940, p. 613)

The upshot of APA's official indifference to both the Depression and world affairs was the formation of the Society for the Psychological Study of Social Issues. The APA had finally lost both its professionalism and its social conscience.

The self-perpetuating oligarchy that controlled the APA had been notably successful both in preserving its own power, and in protecting the dubious virtue of the organization as a scientific society. Time after time, they had rebuffed the entreaties of both the professional and socially concerned segments of the membership.

Financially, the organization was more than solvent. The creation of a group of second-class, nonvoting "associate" members had been a financial master stroke. Associates paid dues and supported journals. In another very shrewd move, APA had acquired virtually all of the major privately owned psychological journals.

In 1940, the APA enjoyed a $5,000 financial surplus (Bulatao, Fulcher, & Evans, 1992). Unfortunately, psychology as a science was running a knowledge deficit that approached intellectual bankruptcy. A one historian of the period put it:

> There was neither a shared paradigm, nor a consensus on evaluative criteria, nor even a common language. The center of the science was in disarray, and the insistence of the APA leadership on maintaining the high level of formal credentials may have been an inverted reflection of this condition. (Samelson, 1992, p. 32)

By 1940 the membership elite had grown by only 88 individuals, while the number of associates had increased by over 1300 (Samelson, 1992). Further, more than two thirds of the members had received their Ph.D.s prior to 1925. As its ruling elite approached dinosaur status, the APA was faced with the first real challenge to its supremacy. As Benjamin (1997) noted, "For the first time psychology seemed truly divided" (p. 728).

Ostensibly, the pressure to reunify organized psychology came out of the war effort through the intervention of the National Research Council. How the issue actually impacted upon the war effort seems very unclear.

The official version of events was elaborated by Wolfle (1946) in the newly founded *American Psychologist*, Volume 1, No. 1 (Reprinted in the *American Psychologist,* July, 1997):

> The series of events which culminated in the new constitution started in 1942 in the deliberations of the National Research Council's Emergency Committee in Psychology. The Emergency Committee met with the Council of Directors of the APA and the Board of Governors of the American Association for Applied Psychology (AAAP) in September, 1942 to discuss possible changes. Plans were initiated for an intersociety constitutional convention. This convention met on May 29–31, 1943 with representatives of all national psychological organizations present. Discussion was held on kinds or reorganization which might best serve the professional needs of psychology. The work of the convention was carried on by a continuation committee which was succeeded in September, 1943 by a joint APA-AAAP constitutional committee. (1997, p. 721)

Actually, it seems very probable that the motivations behind the reconciliation between APA and the dissident groups were more pragmatic than patriotic. The pretext of reorganizing to further the war effort seems to have been a face-saving illusion that permitted compromise to move forward despite personal animosities. In any event, more than 2 years of hard-nosed bargaining and negotiation occurred before the resolution of the final arguments. The war was nearly over when the final votes were taken in 1944, and the merger did not actually take effect until late 1945, a few months after the war's end.

The fine hand that guided the many months of behind-the-scene bargaining that finally brought reunification and a new APA constitution belonged to none other than Robert Yerkes. Yerkes was one of the few leading psychologists with an intimate knowledge of government, having continued to work with the National Research Council after the end of the First War. He also had close relationships with leaders in both APA and AAAP.

The task of reconciliation was not as formidable as it might have appeared on the surface. More than one fourth of the voting members of APA were also members of AAAP and a number of its leaders were "insiders" in APA. The second president of AAAP, for example, was Donald G. Paterson, who had served as Secretary of the APA (having succeeded Carl Brigham).

In any case, Yerkes proved to be an able diplomat. He assembled a hand-picked subcommittee under the aegis of the National Research Council. This group consisted of six men and one woman and included such diverse personalities as Edwin Boring and Carl Rogers. Other members were Edgar Doll, Alice Bryan, Calvin Stone, Earnest Hilgard, and Richard Elliott. All of the major constituencies were represented. Ironically, the group met at Vineland Training School, where the planning group of World War I psychologists had brought forth the Alpha and Beta testing programs. When this group was able to agree on a plan for constitutional reform, the die was cast and a new and reformed APA was on its way to reality.

The reform created the APA as we know it today. A divisional structure was created to represent specialties and special interests, and to elect the governing Council of Representatives. Both members and associates were given the right to speak, vote, and hold office. The ability of the Board of Directors to nominate their own successors, as in the bad old days, was curbed.

Perhaps most significantly, the new constitution defined the organization as both a scientific society and a professional association. The new constitution was a giant step toward professionalization for psychology. It also opened the door for counseling and counselors to define a new psychological specialty, and to find a place at the table of organized psychology.

The story of how that door was opened and how counseling psychology came in follows in Chapter 4.

## REFERENCES

Benjamin, L. (1996). Lightner Witmer's legacy to American psychology. *American Psychologist, 51,* 235–236.

Benjamin, L. (1997). The origin of psychological species: History of the beginnings of American Psychology Association Divisions. *American Psychologist, 52,* 725–732.

Benjamin, L., Durkin, M., Link, M., Vestal, M., & Acord, J. (1992). Wundt's American doctoral students. *American Psychologist, 47,* 123–131.

Bingham, W. V. D., & Moore, B. C. (1931). *How to interview.* New York: Harper and Row.

Blumenthal, A. L. (1991). The intrepid Joseph Jastrow. In G. A. Kimble, M. Wertheimer, & C. L. White (Eds.), *Portraits of pioneers in psychology* (pp. 75–88). Washington, DC: American Psychological Association.

Bringmann, W. G., Bringmann, M. W., & Early, C. E. (1992). G. Stanley Hall and the history of psychology. *American Psychologist, 47,* 281–299.

Bulatao, E. Q., Fulcher, R., & Evans, R. B. (1992). Appendix: Statistical data on the American Psychological Association. In R. B. Evans, V. S. Sexton, & T. C. Cadwallader (Eds.), *100 years: The American Psychological Association in historical perspective* (pp. 391–394). Washington, DC: American Psychological Association.

Coon, D. J. (1992). Testing the limits of sense and science: American experimental psychologists combat spiritualism, 1880–1920. *American Psychologist, 47,* 143–151.

Elliott, H. S., & Elliot, G. L. (1936). *Solving personal problems.* New York: Henry Holt.

Evans, R. B. (1992). Growing pains: The American Psychological Association: from 1903–1920. In R. B. Evans, V. S. Sexton, & T. C. Cadwallader (Eds.), *100 years The American Psychological Association: A historical perspective* (pp. 73–90). Washington: American Psychological Association.

Evans, R. B., Sexton, V. S., & Cadwallader, T. C. (Eds.). (1992). *100 years: The American Psychological Association: A historical perspective.* Washington: American Psychological Association.

Grundlach, R. H. (1940). Psychologists understanding of social issues. *Psychological Bulletin, 37,* 613–620.

Hilgard, E. R. (1987). *Psychology in America: A historical survey.* New York: Harcourt Brace Jovanovich.

Link, A. S., & Catton, W. B. (1967). *American epoch* (Vol. 2) (3rd ed.). New York: Alfred A. Knop.

Lloyd-Jones, E. (1929). *Student personnel work at Northwestern University.* New York: Harper.

Louttit, C. M. (1939). The nature of clinical psychology. *Psychological Bulletin, 36,* 361–389.

Miller, C. A. (1961). *Foundations of guidance.* New York: Harper and Row

Reisman, J. M. (1976). *A history of clinical psychology.* New York: Irvington.

Resnick, R. J. (1997). A brief history of practice-expanded. *American Psychologist, 52,* 463–468.

Rogers, C. R. (1942). *Counseling and psychotherapy.* Boston: Houghton-Mifflin.

Ross, D. (1972). *G. Stanley Hall: The psychologist as a prophet.* Chicago: University of Chicago Press.

Routh, D. K. (1994). *Clinical psychology since 1917: Science practice and organization.* New York: Plenum Press.

Samelson, F. (1992). The APA between the World Wars: 1918 to 1941. In R. B. Evans, V. S. Sexton, & T. C. Cadwallader (Eds.), *100 years:*

*The American Psychological Association: A historical perspective* (pp. 119–147). Washington: American Psychological Association.

Scott, W. D. (1929). Foreword. In E. Lloyd-Jones, *Student personnel work at Northwestern University.* New York: Harper.

Sokal, M. M. (1992). Origins and early years of the American Psychological Association. In R. B. Evans, V. S. Sexton, & T. C. Cadwallader (Eds.), *100 years: The American Psychological Association: A historical perspective* (pp. 43–72). Washington: The American Psychological Association.

Strang, R. (1937). *Counseling technics in college and secondary school.* New York: Harper.

Strickland, B. R. (1988). Clinical psychology comes of age. *American Psychologist, 43,* 104–107.

Super, D. E. (1983). The history and development of vocational psychology. In W. B. Walsh & S. H. Osipow (Eds.), *Handbook of vocational psychology* (Vol. I, pp. 5–38). Hillsdale, NJ: Erlbaum.

Vande Kemp, H. V. (1992). G. Stanley Hall and the Clark School of Religious Psychology. *American Psychologist, 47,* 290–298.

Wiebe, F. L. (1952). *The big change: America transforms itself 1900–1950.* New York: Harper.

Williamson, E. G. (1939). *How to counsel students.* New York: McGraw-Hill.

Williamson, E. G. (1965). *Vocational counseling.* New York: McGraw-Hill.

Williamson, E. G., & Darley, J. G. (1937). *Student personnel work: An outline of clinical procedures.* New York: McGraw-Hill.

Witmer, L. (1897). The organization of practical work in psychology. *Psychological Review, 4,* 116–117. (From a 1896 speech at the American Psychological Association meeting in Boston).

Wolfle, D. (1946). The reorganized American Psychology Association. *American Psychologist, 1,* 3–6. Reprinted in *American Psychologist, 52,* 721–724.

Wrenn, C. G. (1938). Counseling with students. In *Guidance in educational institutions: 37th yearbook of the National Society for the Study of Education* (pp. 110–143). Washington, DC.

# 4

# The Search for a Professional Identity

If you don't know what business you are in, conceptualize what business it would be useful to think you are in.

—John Naisbitt

The winter of 1945–46 was one of relief and rejoicing for the American people. The four long years of war and bloodshed had ended and millions of young men and women were returning home from far flung corners of the world. The threat of further wars, and the frightful consequences of the nuclear age, were as yet blissfully unrealized.

For American psychologists, it was also the beginning of a new age. Professional psychology was at last recognized and valued both by the public and within its own ranks.

In September 1944, the APA had approved a new constitution and a set of by-laws that provided for as many as 19 new divisions. Early in 1944, a ballot had been mailed to about 6,000 people identified by a federal manpower agency as psychologists. That ballot was sent regardless of organizational affiliations or the lack thereof. The psychologists were asked to express their preferences for divisional membership. Nineteen proposed specialties were listed, and opportunity was provided for write-in votes.

The list included personnel psychology, as well as both business and industrial psychology. Of the 3,680 responses, a total of 417 respondents picked personnel psychology as either a sole or multiple

**97**

choice. The only specialty to exceed personnel psychology was clinical, with 768 votes (Benjamin, 1997). There were also apparently a number of write-in votes mentioning guidance in schools or colleges.

It is not clear exactly how the results of this balloting were translated into the final list of divisions presented in the bylaws and approved at the 1944 convention. Apparently, a political process influencing the final choices was at work. For example, school psychology, which was not even on the ballot, and which received a total of five write-in votes, became Division 16 (Benjamin, 1997). (Perhaps the ghost of Lightner Witmer intervened.) Division 17 was assigned to what was originally termed the Division of "Personnel and Guidance Psychologists."

The process by which this decision was implemented, and the way in which the actual founding of the Division was accomplished, is, strangely enough, still shrouded in a degree of mystery. What is clear is that the central figures in the process were two psychologists from the University of Minnesota: E. G. Williamson and John G. Darley.

**Figure 4.1   E. G. Williamson**

As we noted in Chapter 2, Williamson and Darley were instrumental in the effort to define, refine, and otherwise legitimize "clinical counseling" as a psychological specialty at the doctoral level. Both Williamson and Darley had been students of Donald G. Paterson. Both were relatively young, and while rising stars, were certainly not members of the "inner circles" of APA or AAAP.

Several senior Minnesota psychologists were, however, key players in the long process of negotiation that culminated in reorganization. Richard Elliott, the longtime chair of the psychology department, was, as we saw, an original member of Yerkes' "Emergency subcommittee." John E. Anderson, Director of the Institute of Child Welfare at Minnesota, was President of APA in 1943 and had presided over many of the deliberations. Donald Paterson, with a foot planted firmly in each of the rival camps, was a pivotal behind-the-scenes player in the whole process. Certainly their influence would have been sufficient to catapult Williamson and Darley into prominence in the divisional organizing process.

Provisional chairpeople were appointed by the APA to guide the organization of the new divisions. The provisional chair for Division 17 was Edmund Williamson. Little of what transpired between the awarding of divisional status in September, 1944, and the first business meeting is known.

Conspicuously absent from any known involvement in the new division was Carl Rogers. At this point in his career, Rogers was essentially a counseling psychologist (Hilgard, 1987). In 1945, after 4 years on the Ohio State faculty, Rogers had established the Counseling Center at the University of Chicago. Rogers held a Ph.D. degree from Teachers College, Columbia University. His 1942 book, *Counseling and Psychotherapy* had, as we noted, presented an approach to counseling almost diametrically opposed to the Minnesota point of view. Rogers had actually first presented his ideas on "nondirective" counseling in 1940 at a symposium held at the University of Minnesota, where he had experienced a somewhat hostile reception (Rogers, 1961).

Rogers had been actively involved in training counselors to work with returning veterans in the last years of the war. He had published widely in the counseling literature, including writing the chapter on counseling for the 1945 *Review of Educational Research*. With J. L. Wallen, Rogers published *Counseling with Returned Servicemen* (1946).

**Figure 4.2   John Darley**

It is interesting to speculate about why Carl Rogers was not involved in the organization of the new division, and to wonder how different the history of counseling psychology would have been if he had been one of its principal founders.

The best account of the founding of Division 17 is in the very sketchy report authored by C. Winfield Scott (1980) as Division Historian in 1963, nearly 20 years after the fact. According to Scott, there were some informal and virtually impromptu meetings held among psychologists at various locations. It must be remembered that the war was still on for much of this time, and most of the younger psychologists were still in the military or in other government service.

It is clear that John Darley represented the new Division at an APA business meeting in December, 1944, and volunteered to write a set of bylaws which were then approved by Williamson. Scott (1980) described the actual beginning of the new organization:

> Insofar as official records go the division sprang full bloom at the
> first annual business meeting of the Division, September 5, 1946 in
> Philadelphia, Pennsylvania. One might be more metaphoric and say
> that it emerged in maturity from the brows of Edmund G. Williamson
> and John G. Darley who in minutes of this meeting were listed as being
> respectively, president and secretary-treasurer. (p. 25)

The names and roles of others who may have helped in the founding
are largely unknown. Besides Williamson and Darley, Scott mentioned
only Hugh Bell, Carrol L. Shartle, Mitchell Dreese, and G. Frederic
Kuder. In the original assignment of provisional officers, Catherine
Miles had been named as provisional secretary. The first representatives of the Division to the APA Council were Alvin C. Eurich, Harold
A. Edgerton, and Carrol Shartle (Scott, 1980).

For the decade after that momentous morning in Philadelphia, the
Division of Counseling and Guidance, as it soon chose to call itself,
wrestled mightily with questions of definition and of inclusion and
exclusion as it struggled essentially to invent itself and grow some sort
of professional identity.

The founders and early leaders of the Division were largely university
professors and administrators engaged in preparing guidance workers
of all sorts for the schools and colleges (Pepinsky, 1984). Except for
Williamson and Darley's rudimentary vision of the "clinical counselor,"
as a prototype, counseling psychologists as we know them today
simply did not exist prior to 1945.

In the decade after 1945, a veritable blizzard of conference reports,
position papers, and other declarations of faith and opinion sought
to clarify the basic questions of who are we?, what are we doing?,
and how do we differ from others? In the end, these questions of
definition and identity were shaped far more by events in the real
world than by all of the rhetoric emanating from committee rooms
and conference tables.

## Veterans Come Home: Counselors Go to Work

Almost as soon as the mushroom clouds dissipated over Hiroshima
and Nagasaki, and the ink dried on the surrender papers signed on
the battleship *Missouri*, the stream of homeward-bound GIs began
to pour back into the country. Eleven million men and women were

separated from the military and returned to the bosom of a grateful nation.

Even before the end of the War, a series of legislative acts had inaugurated the process of helping returning veterans to move back into civilian life. The first of these was Public Law 16, the Disabled Veterans Rehabilitation Act. This legislation provided a variety of rehabilitation services, including vocational counseling and training for those veterans with service-connected disabilities. A year later, in 1944, Public Law 346, popularly known as the G.I. Bill extended limited education and training benefits, including counseling, to all World War II veterans. Eventually, similar benefits were extended to veterans of the Korean War which began in 1950. Altogether, in the decade following World War II, more than 10 million veterans received benefits of some kind through the Veterans Administration.

Obviously, not all of these veterans had returned unscathed. In 1946 some 74,000 veterans were being cared for in Veterans Administration hospitals. Of these, 44,000 were classified as neuropsychiatric patients (Hilgard, 1987).

Altogether, the end of war and the return of the veterans created a totally unprecedented demand for psychological services, and thrust professional psychology into a key role in the return of American society to peacetime status.

As the Veterans Administration was assigned the task of both caring for disabled veterans and administering the benefit programs, it was quickly forced to seek additional professional help. The V.A.'s Division of Vocational Rehabilitation supplemented its own counseling resources by contracting with colleges and universities to provide for educational-vocational counseling services to help veterans utilize the broad-based educational benefits available to them under the G.I. Bill. Numerous new counseling centers in both community and college-based settings were created and/or expanded with the help of V.A. contracts or subsidies (Pepinsky, 1984).

Similarly, the Veterans Administration's Division of Medicine and Neurology expanded its services, both within hospitals and in outpatient facilities, to treat patients with neuropsychiatric disabilities. Perhaps the most significant step in the development of professional psychology came out of this dramatic need for additional professional personnel. In a series of sweeping actions, the Veterans Administration defined the position of clinical psychologist as a doctoral-level specialty, complete with internship requirements; endowed the position with status and salary equivalent to that of MD's; and opened the door for psychologists to provide direct treatment to patients, including psychotherapy (Hilgard, 1987).

These sweeping changes were accomplished in close collaboration with the APA, and especially with the leadership of the new Division of Clinical Psychology. It was suddenly incumbent upon APA to define and monitor standards of training, designate and accredit doctoral programs, and essentially to manage a suddenly transformed and expanding profession. The transformation in status and importance was almost miraculous. Less than four years after being reluctantly admitted to the church, professional psychology was now leading the choir.

APA dealt with the increased demand for clinical psychologists and proliferation of training programs by holding a national conference on training in August of 1949 in Boulder, Colorado. Even before the reorganization of APA, joint committees of APA and AAAP had agreed that Ph.D. programs should be four years in length, including a year of internship (Hilgard, 1987).

The Boulder Conference reviewed previous recommendations regarding training and produced a lengthy set of recommendations for the training of clinical psychologists that became known as the "Boulder Model," or sometimes the "scientist-practitioner" model of training. This model was to dominate the preparation of professional psychologists for the next 25 years. It essentially grafted clinical training, including practicums and internship, onto traditional, academically oriented Ph.D. preparation in psychology with its strong emphasis on research methodology.

The Boulder model had the advantage of providing a rationale for preparing professional psychologists within traditional academic psychology departments. The sudden expansion of clinical programs within such departments created considerable friction between the two groups of faculty. Much of that friction was lubricated by the massive infusion of federal money in the form of training grants and stipends.

The sudden demand for professionals quickly spread to counseling as well as clinical psychologists. By 1950 it was clear that the Veterans Administration was ready to designate another doctoral-level specialty for counseling personnel if the Division of Counseling and Guidance

(Division 17) were to explicate and upgrade its standards for training and practice in the same way that clinical psychology had done (Pepinsky, 1984).

## Counseling Psychology Gets Its Name

A process similar to that which led to the Boulder Conference was quickly undertaken in Division 17. In September, 1951, an invitational conference attended by some 60 leading psychologists interested in counseling and guidance was convened by the current president of Division 17, C. Gilbert Wrenn at Northwestern University.

Out of this conference, and the work of the committees that laid its ground work, came both a new set of standards for training and a new name for the Division: that of counseling psychology. As Donald Super (1955) put it:

**Figure 4.3   C. Gilbert Wrenn**

In 1951, rather suddenly, but not unexpectedly, a new psychological job title came into use in the United States, and a hitherto somewhat amorphous and debatable field of psychology emerged as clearly a field in its own right. The job was that of *counseling psychologist* and the field was that of *counseling psychology*. (p. 3)

Counseling psychologists and their parent organization have spent the second half of the 20th century trying to define exactly what this new field is all about. The impetus for both the name change and the upgrading and explication of training standards very clearly came from the Veterans Administration.

Within a few months after the adjournment of the Northwestern conference, the Veterans Administration announced the creation of two major positions, Counseling Psychologists (Vocational) and Counseling Psychologist (Vocational Rehabilitation and Education). Training requirements were on the same level as those for Clinical Psychologist. This action was quickly followed by a program of financial support for training counseling psychologists underwritten by the Veterans Administration.

## Coming of Age in the 1950's

The decade that followed the Northwestern Conference and the advent of the newly named Division 17 was outwardly one of progress and prosperity for counselors and counseling psychology. The Veterans Administration counseling efforts and the Ph.D. training programs and internships that grew up around them were a mainstay of jobs and of financial support for the new field. The Korean War provided a second generation of returning veterans with educational benefits as well as the scars of war.

The influx of veterans into the colleges and universities changed higher education in America forever. The new generation of college students was more diverse in age, abilities, and social and ethnic backgrounds than ever before. Many were married, and family life became an accepted part of the college campus environment for the first time.

College counseling centers were rapidly expanded on large campuses, and were proliferating rapidly throughout higher education. Counseling psychologists had arrived to practice in a variety of settings and were working with a wide range of clients and an ever-lengthening list of client concerns. In 1950, the APA accreditation process was extended to counseling psychology training programs (Evans et al., 1992). Counseling psychology was officially part of the family of professional psychology.

The field was also developing in a substantive and scholarly sense. Early in 1954, the *Journal of Counseling Psychology* was founded. Four distinguished counseling psychologists, C. Gilbert Wrenn, Donald Super, Milton Hahn, and Harold Seashore, started the new journal with their own funds. The new journal was an outlet for the host of new ideas and research findings that were generated in the rapidly expanding world of counseling psychology. Eventually, the journal was transferred to the APA and remains the flagship journal for the field.

The 1950s were a period of ferment as new theoretical formulations and empirical findings emerged. These ideas were articulated in a number of seminal books that helped to give substance and focus to the field.

Perhaps the most articulate and influential intellectual leader in the early years of counseling psychology was Leona Tyler. Leona Tyler was in her mid-thirties when she abandoned a career as a high school teacher to begin graduate work in psychology with Donald Paterson at the University of Minnesota. After completing a Ph.D. just prior to World War II, she began a distinguished career at the University of Oregon. Tyler's *The Work of the Counselor* (1953) was the most balanced and well-integrated articulation of the so-called Minnesota Point of View. Tyler helped to move the field from a static, almost mechanical preoccupation with testing and prediction to a broadly balanced view of counseling that focused on facilitating client development.

Throughout her career of more than 30 years, Leona Tyler personified the spirit of counseling psychology as a blend of scholarly inquiry and professional practice. She was recognized across the world of psychology and was the first counseling psychologist to become president of the APA.

In 1954 another seminal book appeared. Harold and Pauline Pepinsky produced *Counseling Theory and Practice*, a book that did more to provide a rationale for the scientist-practitioner model of training for professional psychologists than did the whole book-length report of the Boulder Conference. The Pepinskys pointed out that the basic

**Figure 4.4   Leona Tyler**

methods of science, observation and inferences about those observations, are precisely the tools inevitably utilized by counselors as they endeavor to understand and relate to their clients.

They proposed a careful and continuing process of hypothesis testing through which the counselor could build a tentative and testable understanding of the client. The Pepinsky's model of counselor cognition laid the groundwork for much future research on clinical judgment and decision-making over the next 40 years.

In 1955 Edward Bordin published *Psychological Counseling*, an essentially psychodynamic approach to counseling. Bordin's book broadened the concept of counseling to virtually define it as an effort to promote general personality development, rather than to alleviate specific client-presenting problems. Bordin also attempted to treat counseling as a process firmly rooted in psychological theory, rather than as a pragmatic "seat of the pants" approach. He defined the psychological counselor as *"a psychological practitioner who aids people with those problems of behavior in which the critical issues have to do with their emotions and motivations"* (Bordin, 1955, pp. 3–4).

Perhaps the most influential and certainly the most contentious book of the decade was Carl Roger's *Client-Centered Therapy* (1951). Rogers dropped the term "counseling" in the title and forever after referred to his approach as "therapy." He retained the term "client" rather than "patient," however, possibly because of a long history of conflict with psychiatrists (Hilgard, 1987). By whatever title, Rogers' book was enormously influential among counselors and counseling psychologists. Rogers tied his approach to perceptual theory and phenomenology. He gave primacy to the self-concept as the central construct in personality functioning.

The directive-nondirective controversy raged on for more than 20 years, dividing counseling psychology into competing camps. However, it also focused research on counseling process and the counseling relationship.

By the end of the 1950s counseling was firmly defined as a psychologically oriented process requiring a high level of training and expertise, and directed to both a wide range of client concerns and to basic issues and processes of personality development. As the decade began, counseling was virtually bereft of theoretical foundations. By the end of the 1950s it was blessed or cursed, depending upon one's view, with an embarrassment of competing theoretical riches.

## THE DEVELOPMENT OF ETHICAL PRINCIPLES

Perhaps the most significant achievement of professional psychology in the years immediately following the reorganization of APA was in the development and dissemination of a set of ethical principles for the practice of professional psychology. For many years prior to reorganization, applied psychologists had looked in vain for support in developing ethical standards. In 1938, the old APA had appointed a Committee on Scientific and Professional Ethics. It had agonized for a number of years over the question of whether a formal ethical code or set of principles was really needed. Finally, in 1947, after the reorganization was fully implemented, the decision was finally taken to develop such a statement.

This decision was not taken without opposition. Some members argued that ethical codes could never be explicit enough to cover all ethical transgressions, and that loopholes or ambiguities would prove to be a refuge for scoundrels.

Despite opposition, a Committee on Ethical Standards was appointed, chaired by Edward Tolman. This committee decided that an effective and comprehensive set of ethical principles could only be established after some empirical investigation was done. A second committee was then appointed chaired by Nicholas Hobbs, a prominent clinical psychologist. Counseling psychologists Donald Super and Harold Edgerton were also on the Committee. The Committee decided to adapt a critical incident technique developed by counseling psychologist, John Flanagan

In 1948, all 7,500 members of the APA were surveyed by mail and asked to share experiences involving ethical problems, and particularly to describe specific circumstances and processes involved in making ethical decisions (Pope & Vasquez, 1991). The committee received over 1,000 reports of such critical incidents. These were then classified and analyzed to define and describe the range of ethical dilemmas confronted by psychologists.

The information obtained was used to define six basic areas of ethical standards and principles. These included (1) public responsibility, (2) professional relationships, (3) client relationships, (4) research, (5) writing and publishing, and (6) teaching.

A draft set of standards was published and discussed among the membership. Revisions were made and in 1953 the *Ethical Standards for Psychologists* was formally adopted.

Beginning in 1954, a standing committee on ethics began the task of establishing enforcement and adjudication procedures. For more than 40 years APA has worked to earn the public trust by defining, enforcing, and revising statements of ethical conduct.

## COUNSELING AND COUNSELING PSYCHOLOGY: A ROSE IS A ROSE; OR IS IT?

Even as the Northwestern conference replaced the title of "counseling and guidance" with the term "counseling psychology," the new field diverged from its historical antecedents in an even more profound way. In that same year of 1951, a group of professional associations in the field united to form the American Personnel and Guidance Association (APGA). The new association included the National Vocational Guidance Association, which, as we saw, had pioneered the professionalization of the entire field. The new association also represented in its divisions college personnel workers, counselor educators and, very shortly, school counselors and rehabilitation counselors.

The new APGA, as it was originally called, represented most of the fields and settings from which counseling psychology had just emerged. Many of the leaders of the Division of Counseling Psychology were also college counselors or counselor educators.

Throughout the 1950s and beyond, the Division of Counseling Psychology and the APGA (now the American Counseling Association) maintained a sort of parallel, if occasionally uneasy, pattern of coexistence. A considerable overlap of leadership was evident with a number of leading counseling psychologists holding offices in both organizations.

The differences between counselors and counseling psychologists were far from clear. The field of guidance had always been multidisciplinary (Wrenn, 1962). The field had been influenced by progressive education, sociology, and economics, as well as by psychology. Many counselors with the doctorate did not see themselves as psychologists, and many counselor education programs were not in departments of either psychology or educational psychology.

Problems of multiple identities were especially real for faculty and graduates of counseling psychology programs housed in schools of education. Many of these had large master's-level counselor education programs, as well as APA-accredited counseling psychology programs.

These identity problems became more acute with the passage of the National Defense Education Act. Early in 1957, in the midst of the Cold War, the then Soviet Union put *Sputnik 1*, a basketball-sized piece of hardware, into orbit around the earth. A month later, *Sputnik 2* was launched, with a dog named Laika aboard. In the United States the reaction was one of shock, shame, and self-recrimination.

In point of fact, the problem was largely that the Soviets' hired ex-Nazi rocket scientists had outperformed the American purchased crew of expatriate German rocketeers. By some sort of convoluted set of mental processes, apparent only to politicians, the Congress decided that the fiasco was due to the fact that American school children did not take enough science and mathematics courses.

The result, predictably, was a new law called the National Defense Education Act (NDEA). It provided for, among other things, a massive infusion of guidance counselors into the schools to ensure that junior and senior high school students were exposed to the appropriate amount of science and mathematics.

For many years, guidance in the schools had received scant attention. Standards of certification of guidance counselors varied widely from state to state, and were often both antiquated and minimal. The role of counselors in many school systems was that of a minor administrative functionary who presided over testing programs and cumulative records cards, rather relating directly to students.

The NDEA legislation provided for the inauguration of special Counseling and Guidance Institutes funded directly by the Office of Education, including stipends for students. Essentially, a new federally mandated and financed program of counselor education was put into place to recruit, prepare, and upgrade school counselors. Within five years after the passage of the NDEA legislation, nearly 14,000 counselors and counselor trainees had participated in the institutes (Borow, 1964).

It was soon apparent that counseling psychology saw a vital role for itself in this virtual revolution in counseling and counselor education. In 1961, the APA Division of Counseling Psychology issued a report attempting to specify the psychological content of graduate preparation programs for school counselors (APA, Division of Counseling Psychology, 1961). Clearly, however, the influence of counseling psychology on the roles and training of guidance counselors had passed to the APGA. A similar process occurred a short time later with rehabilitation counselors, as federally supported programs were instituted.

As an organization, the Division of Counseling Psychology virtually abdicated its influence over the very fields that had nurtured it historically (Pepinsky, 1984). College personnel work, school guidance and counseling, and rehabilitation counseling had all found homes for themselves outside of the umbrella of counseling psychology. Many individual counseling psychologists continued working in these fields and accepted the reality of multiple identities and allegiances.

While counseling psychology seemed to prosper in terms of growth both in number and settings served, at another level the picture was one of turmoil, conflict, and even discouragement. The crucial formative years for the field were in the period from the Northwestern Conference in 1951 to another major reassessment at the Greyston Conference in 1964.

In 1963, C. Winfield Scott, the Division Historian, in the same report cited earlier, surveyed the 17 past presidents regarding their views on both past achievements and current issues for counseling psychology. Strangely, the tone of many of these comments seemed both negative and pessimistic.

The past presidents mentioned the cleavages within the division between education and psychology and between vocational and personal counseling orientations, as well as between counseling and clinical psychology. Throughout most of the comments ran the theme that counseling psychology had not yet developed a professional identity.

A quote from John Darley, one of the two principal founders of the field nearly 20 years before, sounded a typical note:

> I have some conviction that the division has not lived up to its potentials, and this seems to me to be the result of two historical forces: the major surge in the broad field of clinical psychology, and the inability of the divisional membership in 17 to define the roles and functions of a counselor. (John G. Darley, 9/12/62, quoted in Scott, 1980)

E. J. Shoben put his discontent with the state of the field even more bluntly:

> There were signs that . . . counseling psychology as a professional group seemed more inclined to claim full professional status rather than to achieve it through imaginative and sustained work. (E. J. Shoben Jr., 8/9/62, quoted in Scott, 1980)

The feeling of confusion and ambiguity about professional role and identity had persisted, despite numerous reports and articles attempting to define the field. Super's article (1955) on the transition between counseling psychology and vocational guidance had been widely quoted. The Division, itself, issued reports on counseling psychology as a specialty (1956) and on standards for training of counseling psychologists (1952). Both reports were published in the *American Psychologist*.

## The Crisis of Confidence

Much of the atmosphere of self-doubt that seemed to pervade at least the leadership of the Division in the early 1960s may well have stemmed from an incident in 1959, in which the Education and Training Board of the APA apparently gave serious consideration to eliminating counseling psychology as a recognized and approved specialty. This would have eliminated the accreditation process, and would probably have sounded a death knell for the counseling psychology training programs. The rationale behind these efforts is not altogether clear. Pepinsky (1984) attributed the difficulty to jurisdictional disputes over entitlements to government funding between clinical and counseling psychology. Although both specialties were equally new insofar as APA sponsorship was concerned, clinical psychology was clearly far more powerfully entrenched within the APA's political structure. If an attempt was to be made to reduce competition for funding, clearly, counseling psychology would be the one to face extinction (Pepinsky, 1984).

The Education and Training Board appointed a three-person panel consisting of Irwin Berg, Harold Pepinsky, and E. J. Shoben to write a report on "The Status of Counseling Psychology: 1960." Pepinsky and Shoben were past presidents of the Division; Berg was a future president of the Division. All were highly qualified psychologists who had published widely and held a variety of leadership positions.

The report that these three leaders of the Division prepared for dissemination to the APA Board that virtually held the power of life or death over the Division of Counseling Psychology was scathing. They approached the task with a kind of prosecutorial zeal. The opening paragraph of this supposedly objective report began

> There is clear evidence that counseling psychology is declining. Because there is a large number of psychologists who currently bear the counseling label, the indications of a vanishing specialty are not at once apparent. (Berg, Pepinsky, & Shoben, 1980, p. 105) (Original, 1959)

The report went on to catalog the sins and shortcomings of counseling psychology. The main thrust of the report was a very unfavorable comparison between clinical and counseling psychology. Many of the unfavorable comparisons were probably true, while others were doubtful. None was really documented in a way that might be expected in a report of this magnitude, carrying as it did a very serious set of possible consequences.

The report ended by proposing three possible courses of action. The first alternative proposed was a "fusion" of clinical and counseling training—essentially, a merger with clinical psychology. The other alternatives involved total shifts in focus and emphasis that verged on the ridiculous; for example, focusing on the problem of global population control as a central mission.

The report apparently went to both the Education and Training Board and to the Division 17 governing board. It must have been received by the latter as a kind of bombshell. Three of its most distinguished leaders had essentially proposed the dismantling of the field 15 years after its inception. Interestingly, Irwin Berg, the first author of the report, went on to run for and be elected to the presidency of the Division in 1963–64. It seems a little like the captain of the Titanic, after striking the iceberg, volunteering to take the ship out on her next voyage.

The actual consequences of the report were apparently negligible. The E. and T. Board had by that time gone on to other, hopefully less partisan problems. The Berg et al. (1980) report was never published, or made available to the membership. It was in effect suppressed until John Whiteley (1980) resurrected it, along with the Win Scott Report, for inclusion in his book of historical readings nearly 20 years later. This too seems strange from an organization supposedly committed to the free exchange of ideas.

The Divisional response was apparently to commission its own study on the status of counseling psychology conducted by Leona Tyler, David Tiedeman, and C. Gilbert Wrenn (1964). This report, which was written in 1961 and published in 1964, painted a much more positive picture of the status of counseling psychology, and it received the full endorsement of the Division's Executive Committee. The Tyler et al. report made a case for the continuation of the field of counseling psychology as a matter of social responsibility.

This whole episode leads to the inescapable conclusion that many of the troubles besetting counseling psychology in the early 1960s were the result of dissension and distrust among its own leaders. Clearly, the field also suffered from a severe case of sibling rivalry with Division 12, the Division of Clinical Psychology.

One of the major differences between clinical psychology and counseling psychology as professional organizations was in the quality of experienced political leadership available. Clinical psychologists had been working for more than 40 years to attain some degree of status and autonomy from psychiatrists, and some modicum of support and recognition from experimental psychology.

Clinical psychologists had founded the New York Association of Consulting Psychologists and had ultimately formed the American Association of Applied Psychologists. They had, in hard-fought negotiations with the old APA, finally won recognition and a voice in the affairs of American psychology.

Clinical psychology was no more clearly defined than was counseling psychology in the years prior to the War (Louttit, 1939). It had, however, worked very closely with government agencies to secure the breakthrough in recognition and status given by the Veterans Administration and the National Institute of Mental Health. Organized clinical psychology entered the new APA as a cohesive group, led by people who were politically astute and entrepreneurial in spirit.

The Division of Counseling Psychology, on the other hand, had come into the world of organized psychology in a very different way. It was organized essentially by E.G. Williamson and John Darley to, as the latter put it, "protect the integrity of the field of counseling as a legitimate applied specialty within the new APA organization" (quoted in Scott, 1980, p. 29).

Counseling psychology had no history of political struggle and did not really have a grassroots organization. Most of the many thousands of practicing counselors did not consider themselves psychologists, and would have not been accepted as psychologists by the APA. The Division of Counseling Psychology in its early years was not really even an organization of counselors. In 1957, only 22% of the members indicated that counseling was their principal job function (Tyler et al., 1964).

Neither the early membership nor the leadership of Division 17 set out to advance a political cause. They came from many different backgrounds and had a variety of professional roles. Many were members of other Divisions of the APA; a great many were also active in the APGA, and were highly involved in preparing counselors under the NDEA programs.

Many of the early leaders, people like Leona Tyler, Donald Super, and Gilbert Wrenn, among others, saw participation in Division 17 as part of a career-long commitment to develop and shape a new area of psychological knowledge and, with that knowledge, evolving a new professional specialty.

For some others, however, membership and leadership in the Division seems to have been largely an exercise in personal and professional status-seeking. To some extent, counseling psychology was seen as an elitist group within the constellation of counseling and guidance professions. In 1959, Granger published the results of a doctoral dissertation indicating that counseling psychology, as ranked by other psychologists, was at that time the least prestigious of the some 20 psychological occupations. This finding was not terribly surprising, given the recency of the field. The title itself had only been in existence for some 7 years. The Granger study was obviously the source of great consternation, and was cited in almost all of the papers and reports that dealt with counseling psychology's identity and future or lack thereof.

Perhaps much of the urge to meld with clinical psychology was based on the realization that continued identification as a counseling psychologist was not likely to enhance one's prestige and status within the psychological pecking order.

## LEGITIMACY RESTORED: THE GREYSTON CONFERENCE

The period of prolonged and agonized navelgazing and soul-searching reached a climax with the Greyston Conference in January of 1964. The conference was planned and orchestrated by Donald Super and Albert Thompson of Columbia University. It was held at Columbia's Conference Center at the beautiful old Dodge family mansion, Greyston House, overlooking the Hudson River. Some 60 counseling psychologists were invited. The conference was a festive celebration of the status quo, and the theme was frankly self-congratulatory.

One after another, the luminaries of counseling psychology came forward to detail the genuinely impressive list of accomplishments achieved in the 13 years since the Northwestern meeting. Joseph Samler described the expanding work settings of counseling psychologists. Leona Tyler pointed out that counselors no longer appraised clients, but rather assisted them in self-appraisal. John Darley observed that pecking orders are an inevitable part of life, and that counselors can live with being looked down upon by clinical psychologists, secure in the knowledge that clinical psychologists in turn are looked down upon by psychiatrists.

The conference produced a detailed report (Thompson & Super, 1964) on the preparation of counseling psychologists, the ostensible purpose of the meetings. Drs. Shoben, Pepinsky, and Berg were not among the invitees, even though Berg was the current president of Division 17.

The conference disposed of the identity issue neatly and pointedly. They simply stated that "Counseling psychologists are no longer a group of people in search of professional identity, but rather a group, some members of which have an identity problem" (Super & Thompson, 1964, p. 27).

The congenial gathering of counseling psychologists adjourned on an upbeat note. The warm glow from inside Greyston House had a distinctly rose-colored hue, while the view of the Hudson and the Palisades across the river was inspiring, and as the author can attest, the food was excellent.

## REFERENCES

American Psychological Association, Division of Counseling Psychology. (1961). *The scope and standards of preparation in psychology for school counselors.* (Multi-lithes report.)

American Psychological Association, Division of Counseling Psychology, Committee on Definition. (1956). Counseling psychology as a specialty. *American Psychologist, 11,* 282–285.

American Psychological Association. (1953). *Ethical standards for psychologists.* Washington, DC: Author.

American Psychological Association, Division of Counseling and Guidance, Committee on Counselor Training. (1952). Recommended standards for training counselors at the doctoral level. *American Psychologist, 7,* 175–181.

Benjamin, L. (1997). The origin of psychological species: History of the beginnings of American Psychological Association Divisions. *American Psychologist, 52,* 725–732.

Berg, I., Pepinsky, H., & Shoben, E. J. (1980). The status of counseling psychology: 1960. In J. Whiteley (Ed.), *The history of counseling psychology* (pp. 105–113). Monterey, CA: Brooks-Cole. (Original, 1959)

Bordin, E. (1955). *Psychological counseling.* New York: Appleton-Century-Crofts.

Borow, H. (1964). Milestones: A chronology of notable events in the history of vocational guidance. In H. Borow (Ed.), *Man in a world at work* (pp. 45–66). Boston: Houghton-Mifflin.

Evans, R. B., Sexton, V. S., & Cadwallader, T. C. (Eds.). (1992). *100 Years: The American Psychological Association: A historical perspective.* Washington: American Psychological Association.

Granger, S. G. (1959). Psychologists' prestige rankings of 20 psychological occupations. *Journal of Counseling Psychology, 6,* 183–188.

Hilgard. E. R. (1987). *Psychology in America: A historical survey.* New York: Harcourt Brace Jovanovich.

Louttit, C. M. (1939). The nature of clinical psychology. *Psychological Bulletin, 36,* 361–389.

Pepinsky, H., & Pepinsky, P. (1954). *Counseling theory and practice.* New York: Ronald Press.

Pepinsky, H. B. (1984). A history of counseling psychology. Unpublished manuscript.

Pope, K. S., & Vasquez, J. F. (1991). *Ethics in psychotherapy and counseling.* San Francisco: Jossey-Bass.

Rogers, C. R. (1951). *Client centered therapy.* Boston: Houghton-Mifflin.

Rogers, C. R. (1961). *On becoming a person.* Boston: Houghton-Mifflin.

Scott, C. W. (1980). History of the Division of Counseling Psychology: 1945–1963. In J. M. Whiteley (Ed.), *The history of counseling psychology* (pp. 25–40). Monterey, CA: Brooks-Cole (A report originally submitted in the Executive Committee of Division 17 in 1963).

Super, D. E. (1955). The transition from vocational guidance to counseling psychology. *Journal of Counseling Psychology, 2,* 3–9.

Thompson, A., & Super, D. E. (Eds.) (1964). *The professional preparation of counseling psychologists.* New York: Columbia Teachers College.

Tyler, L. (1953). *The work of the counselor.* New York: Appleton Century.

Tyler, L., Tiedeman, D., & Wrenn, C. G. (1964). The current status of counseling psychology: 1961. In D. E. Super & A. Thompson (Eds.), *The professional preparation of counseling psychologists* (pp. 151–162). New York: Columbia Teachers College.

Wrenn, C. W. (1962). *The counselor in a changing world.* Boston: Houghton-Mifflin.

# 5

# The Dawning of the Age
# of Psychotherapy

Psychotherapy is an undefined technique applied to unspecified problems, with unpredictable outcome. For this technique we recommend rigorous training.

—Victor Raimy

## FREUD COMES TO AMERICA

It was a sultry Sunday afternoon in late summer, in the house where the APA had been born some 17 years earlier. An excited, if slightly weary, traveler recently arrived on the liner *George Washington*, 8 days out of Bremen, chatted with his host. The talk of the world that week was of the return of Robert Peary, the Arctic explorer. The date was September 5, 1909. Peary had reached the North Pole, and Sigmund Freud had arrived in America.

The occasion that brought Freud to the United States was a promotion worthy of G. Stanley Hall's entrepreneurial genius. Hall had decided to celebrate the 20th anniversary of Clark University, and of his own presidency, with a scientific extravaganza of heroic dimensions. He had held a similar program a decade before to celebrate his 10th anniversary, but the *Clark University Vicennial Conference on Psychology and Pedagogy* outshone all of Hall's previous triumphs. The Psychology Conference was simply one part of a distinguished series of convocations that included programs on

119

mathematics, physics, chemistry, and biology, as well as on international relations and child welfare (Evans & Koelsch, 1985).

It was the foremost in the series, however, that marked a new chapter in the history of American psychology. Hall had originally wanted to have appearances by both Wilhelm Wundt, his former professor, and Sigmund Freud. The former tartly refused the invitation on grounds that he was engaged in preparing for the 500th anniversary of the University of Leipzig.

The Clark faculty had voted to invite Herman Ebbinghaus, who apparently accepted, but who died a few months before the conference. Alfred Binet was also invited, but declined. William Stern, the soon-to-be inventor of the IQ, accepted an invitation to appear. Carl Jung, then Freud's closest disciple, also accepted an invitation to speak and to receive an honorary degree. A third close associate of Freud, the Italian psychoanalyst Sandor Ferenczi, attended the conference, but did not present a paper. American psychoanalysts, Ernest Jones, later Freud's biographer, and A. A. Brill, his American translator, also were in the audience.

Although a number of distinguished American psychologists, including E. B. Titchener and Franz Boas, as well as psychiatrist Adolf Meyer, were on the program, the Conference was clearly a showcase for Sigmund Freud and psychoanalysis.

G. Stanley Hall was probably the only psychologist in America, perhaps the only one in the world, who would have extended such an invitation to Sigmund Freud. At this point in his career Freud was not well known in Europe, and many who were aware of his work considered his ideas as somewhere between the speculations of a hopeless eccentric and the obscene fantasies of a dirty old man. William Stern, for example, had criticized Freud's work as utterly unscientific and had incurred Freud's lasting hostility. They were, ironically, shipmates on the transatlantic crossing (Rosenzweig, 1994).

Hall, however, had followed Freud's work for more than 10 years, and like Freud was interested in the nearly taboo topic of sexuality in children and adolescents. Hall lectured about sex drives and masturbation in his courses in adolescent psychology. Women were, of course, excluded from the lecture hall when such indelicate subjects were discussed (Evans & Koelsch, 1985).

Freud made five formal presentations in German to an assemblage that included most of the eminent American professors in psychology

**Figure 5.1    Sigmund Freud**

of the day. William James, Joseph Jastrow, and James Cattell were among the distinguished members of the audience.

For Freud, the lectures were a major milestone on the way to worldwide recognition. He later recounted his reaction:

> As I stepped out to the platform at Worcester to deliver my Five Lectures on Psychoanalysis it seemed like the realization of some incredible day-dream: psychoanalysis was no longer a product of delusion, it had become a valuable product of reality. (Freud, 1925/1952, p. 99. Quoted in Evans & Koelsch, 1985, p. 945)

Freud's five lectures covered the basics of psychoanalysis from Oedipal complexes to slips of the tongue. They were later published in book form, and still constitute the most succinct statement of his views. He was modest and sincere, and apparently well-received by most of his listeners. William James supposedly greeted him with the accolade that the future belongs to you. Titchener, however, was unimpressed. The great defender of introspectionism thought psychoanalysis was utterly unscientific!

Regardless of the reaction of the eminent professors congregated in the immediate audience, Freud was a great public relations success. With his usual flair for publicity, G. Stanley Hall had arranged for widespread press coverage of the Freud lectures and later had even planted a laudatory "anonymous" article in *The Nation*, an influential national magazine (Evans & Koelsch, 1985).

Somehow psychoanalysis captured the imagination of the American people. in a totally unprecedented way. Within a few year after the Clark Conference, psychoanalysis has eclipsed all other forms of psychotherapy in terms of media attention and public awareness. Freudian ideas, in all their manifestations, in art and literature as well as psychotherapy, had become part of American culture (Cushman, 1992).

Sigmund Freud had clearly not invented psychotherapy, nor was he the first to bring it to America. Freud had learned to use hypnosis in treatment while working with the French psychiatrist, Jean Martin Charcot, and had later worked with Josef Breuer, who had invented what he called the "talking cure." Together Freud and Breuer published a book on the treatment of hysteria. Freud evolved the cathartic approach invented by Breuer into the use of free association and dream analysis, and so into the grand design and theory of psychoanalysis.

Psychotherapy was practiced in the United States well prior to Freud's journey across the Atlantic. Perhaps the most central figure in the development of psychotherapy and the study of psychopathology in America was Morton Prince. Prince received a medical degree from Harvard in 1879. He traveled widely in Europe and published extensively, particularly in the areas of dissociation and multiple personality disorders.

Prince was the leader of a small group of psychologists and psychiatrists, including Hugo Munsterberg, who practiced and studied psychotherapy. Many of Prince's ideas, such as automatism, complexes, conflicts, repression and symbolism, had become familiar in the work of leading students of psychopathology. Most of these concepts were originated well before they became part of psychoanalysis (Hilgard, 1987).

Unfortunately for Prince and his fellow American pioneers in psychotherapy, it was Sigmund Freud who captured the popular imagination, and so was often credited with not only inventing psychoanalysis, but also with being the originator of psychotherapy.

As Morton Prince, himself, put it:

> Freudian psychology had flooded the field like a full rising tide, and the rest of us were left submerged like clams buried in the sands at low water. (Murray, 1956, p. 293)

The ascendancy of Sigmund Freud and psychoanalysis to a position of undisputed leadership of the field of psychotherapy was not good news for psychologists interested in the practice of psychotherapy. Although Freud, himself, considered psychoanalysis a part of the science of psychology rather than of medicine, the lines of demarcation were drawn very differently in the United States than in Europe (Cohen, 1992).

In the United States, the medical profession quickly established monopolistic control of psychoanalysis and effectively excluded non-medical personnel from either psychoanalytic training or practice. In the 1920s, the New York state legislature actually passed a law making it illegal for anyone to practice "lay analysis," that is, nonmedical analysis. Since practitioners of psychoanalysis began training by taking their own "training analysis," psychologists were effectively excluded from the field (Cohen, 1992).

Strangely enough, the United States became the haven of orthodoxy for psychoanalysis. Toward the end of his life, Freud is said to have remarked only half-jokingly that there were many things that he had written about psychoanalysis that he would have liked to change, but hesitated because of the reaction of the New York Psychoanalytic Society.

In Europe, on the other hand, the psychoanalytic movement quickly began to spin off dissident theories and therapies. The grand design of psychoanalysis had actually taken shape around the weekly meetings of a small group of practitioners working in Vienna as they met weekly to discuss cures and cases. Sigmund Freud was of course the undisputed and highly authoritarian leader of this group in its early days.

Out of their collegial interaction, early psychoanalysis evolved from an informal, almost tentative approach to treatment to become a formal and highly systematic psychotherapy (Cushman, 1992). Even Freud's early patients were aware of the ways in which their own symptoms and discomforts were woven into the grand mosaic of psychoanalysis. Freud was apparently seen by them as a caring and committed therapists, however (Kaplan, 1967).

Freud's little circle of like-minded colleagues was soon torn with dissension. One by one Wilhelm Stekel, Alfred Adler, Carl Jung, Wilhelm Reich, and Otto Rank withdrew or were expelled from the group as a result of disagreements with the "Master." Each went on to establish his own variant form of theory and therapy while Freud continued to elaborate his own views and to promulgate them as the true gospel of orthodox psychoanalysis.

Freud was deeply hurt and disappointed by these defections, but apparently never associated them with his own autocratic leadership behavior. An associate, Franz Alexander, recounted an experience at a dinner party in Freud's home when he bitterly complained of his disciple's desertions. An aged aunt spoke up saying "Sigi, the trouble with you is that you just don't understand people" (Hilgard, 1987, p. 641).

Ironically, it was Carl Jung, the once trusted friend and confidante who accompanied Freud on the visit to America, who perpetrated the ultimate betrayal. It was Jung, as a Nazi collaborator and leader of a Nazi sponsored psychoanalytic establishment, who denounced Freudian ideas as "the Jewish science" and pronounced it as unfit to minister to the Aryan soul (Cushman, 1992).

## Psychoanalysis and Psychotherapy Between the Wars

Even as psychodynamic theories proliferated and the ex-disciples of Sigmund Freud came into prominence, Freudian and neo-Freudian thinking came virtually to define the study and practice of psychotherapy in America.

In terms of professional development, American psychoanalysis was organized around "psychoanalytic societies" that served as professional organizations, training institutes, and accrediting bodies. This

**Figure 5.2    Carl Gustav Jung**

model followed the pattern established by Freud and his associates in Vienna. They had created the Vienna Psychoanalytic Society, which in 1912 had established an informal "watchdog committee" of six individuals to maintain and oversee the psychoanalytic movement (VandenBos, Cummings, & Delcon, 1992).

In the United States, similar societies were founded in major cities during the 1930s. These societies tended to spawn sectarian groups based upon a kind of professional genealogy. Since the key aspects of psychoanalytic preparation were centered around the "training analysis," each practitioner could eventually trace his or her lineage back through several generations of training analysts and ultimately to Freud and the Vienna group or one of the competing gurus. Gradually, each of these groups tended to develop unique emphases and approaches that distinguished it from others.

Of Freud's dissident disciples, only Alfred Adler and Otto Rank, the last to defect, settled in America. Rank's "will therapy," based on the supposed anxiety of birth trauma separation, was influential in the field of social work. The Rankian approach was made prominent by Jesse Taft and Frederick Allen at the Philadelphia School of Social Work. Carl Rogers was introduced to Rank's ideas by social workers early in his career. Rank's belief in the existence of constructive forces, or the "will to health," within the individual and his emphasis on the importance of relationships influenced Rogers and supported views he had developed in his own clinical work (Rice & Greenberg, 1992).

Adlerian theory, called Individual Psychology, attracted a notable following in the United States, although it never achieved the popularity and visibility of orthodox psychoanalysis. Adler became best known for his concept of the inferiority complex, and the individual's attempts to compensate or overcompensate for it. Adler was also interested in the dynamics of family constellations, and Adlerian theory has strongly influenced family therapy in America.

Over time, a number of significant new leaders and innovators in more orthodox psychoanalytic thinking emerged in America. These included Erich Fromm, Frieda Fromm-Reichmann, Harry Stack Sullivan, and Karen Horney. Since they departed markedly from traditional psychoanalytic teachings, they are sometimes termed neo-Freudians. They had in common a rejection of oedipal conflict as the sole source of pathology. They looked to social learning and cultural demands as sources of difficulty.

In addition to the psychoanalytic societies, a number of prominent centers of psychoanalytic practice were established during the 1920s and 1930s. These provided long-term residential care for patients undergoing lengthy psychoanalytic treatment. The more posh of these were often something of a cross between the old-fashion health spas of the nineteenth century and fashionable resort hotels that offered psychoanalysis along with room service.

Several became very well-known, such as the Austen Riggs Center in the Berkshire mountains at Stockbridge, Massachusetts; the Menninger Clinic at Topeka, Kansas; and the Chestnut Lodge Sanitarium outside of Washington, D.C. The most prestigious of these "centers"

**Figure 5.3    Alfred Adler**

attracted very distinguished analysts to their staffs, and consequently produced a stream of scholarly books and papers.

The type of lengthy treatment and residential services provided, often lasting for years, was obviously very expensive. Even non-residential psychoanalysis was far beyond the financial reach of all but the wealthiest Americans. To a considerable extent psychoanalysis during the period between the wars specialized in treating the neuroses and peccadilloes of the rich and famous (Vandebos et al., 1992). Visiting one's analyst was often considered a fashionable and prestigious form of conspicuous consumption, not unlike driving a new Duesenberg or Rolls Royce.

The practice of psychoanalysis was effectively walled off from the mainstream of both American psychiatry and psychology during the period by a number of factors. Training in psychoanalysis was outside of the framework of university medical schools and was limited in access, as well as lengthy and expensive. In terms of practice, psychoanalysis had little direct impact on the treatment of the mentally ill in the United States.

Psychoanalytic theory, on the other hand was enormously influential in shaping theories of personality development, approaches to psychopathology, and eventually approaches to other forms of psychotherapy. As psychoanalytic theory evolved during the period, it underwent changes that made it more amenable to applications other than classical psychoanalytic treatment.

Freud's original formulation of personality dynamics conceptualized the ego, that is the rational, problem-solving functions of personality, as perpetually caught between the irrational demands and impulses of the id, and the equally irrational burden of guilt and anxiety imposed by the super-ego.

One of the most important revisions of classical psychoanalysis, termed ego psychology, postulated the "autonomy of the ego" (Hartmann, 1939). This approach was far more optimistic about the potential of the individual to function in rational, goal-directed ways than was the original Freudian formulation. Similarly, neo-Freudians like Sullivan, Erikson and Horney saw the crux of many personality problems as rooted in interpersonal difficulties rather than always residing in deeply repressed intra-psychic conflicts.

These revisions and reformations of theory pointed to the possibility of shorter, more directly focused approaches to treatment. The gradual evolution of revised psychodynamic approaches to personality development and psychopathology in turn laid down a foundation for new approaches to psychotherapy.

Psychodynamically oriented therapies of various persuasions tended to dominate the field well into the 1950s. These therapies varied in many details, especially in terms of the basic nature of human needs and motivations postulated, depending on the particular school or revision from which they were derived. They shared in common, however, several basic tenets. All were "insight therapies." They tended to see "insight" about one's past experiences as crucial to the behavior change process. They also tended to be "uncover and cure therapies" that focused upon the patient's past, particularly childhood experiences, as a major source of present symptoms and difficulties. Finally, they saw the role of the therapist as interpreting to the patient the real meaning of denied, repressed, or disguised material.

These basic psychoanalytic concepts were the foundation of much of psychotherapy and were a much more significant part of the growth of the field than was classical psychoanalysis itself. By the 1950s, these ideas virtually defined traditional psychotherapy.

# PSYCHOTHERAPY AND MENTAL HEALTH

At about the same time that Sigmund Freud was elaborating his theories to the assembled psychologists in Worcester, another very different kind of message had recently been enunciated. In 1908, Clarence Beers, a former mental patient, had published *The Mind That Found Itself*, based upon his own experience with mental illness. William James had contributed an introduction to the book, and its publication marked the beginning of a national movement to promote public understanding and concern for mental illness and programs of prevention and treatment for its victims and potential victims.

Beers had gone to Adolf Meyer, the Swiss-born dean of American psychiatry, who advised him to call his cause the "mental hygiene movement." Meyer was notable among American psychiatrists of his day in that he saw an important role for psychiatry outside of mental hospitals. Meyer had a broad view of the causes of psychological disturbances. His wife, Mary, visited the families of patients to learn more about their backgrounds. As early as 1904 she became the first American psychiatric social worker (Hilgard, 1987).

Meyer's innovative ideas about mental health, essentially a forerunner of today's community psychology, merged with Clarence Beers' zeal to improve the lot of the psychologically disturbed and led to the eventual establishment of the National Association for Mental Health. This group advocated not only for the improvement of mental hospitals, but even more importantly for the development of programs of prevention at the level of families, schools, and community.

Many of the ideas and commitments about prevention, early intervention, and family and community outreach that are integral to the modern practice of counseling psychology were pioneered more than 80 years ago by Beers, Meyer and their followers in the mental hygiene movement. They laid the groundwork for the eventual establishment of the National Institute of Mental Health after World War II, and finally for the community mental health legislation of the 1960s.

The battle to improve mental hospitals and the treatment of acutely disturbed patients was an agonizingly slow and often tragic one. The treatment, or rather mistreatment, of the mentally ill was one of the areas in which the awakening of the American conscience, represented in the Progressive Movement, was deeply concerned. Indeed, the Mental Hygiene movement was a part of the wave of reform initiated by Progressivism.

Acutely disturbed people were typically incarcerated in warehouses of human misery euphemistically called mental hospitals. Most Americans believed that mental illness was hereditary, violence-prone, and incurable. People who were afflicted with mental illness were stigmatized and often ostracized from society and rejected even by family. Medical treatment for the acute mental illnesses was primitive, ineffectual, and verged upon the barbaric.

By Beers' time, psychiatry as a medical specialty had been in existence for more than a century with relatively little progress in either the efficacy or humanitarian aspects of treatment. The founding figure in American psychiatry is generally considered to be one Benjamin Rush of Philadelphia. Rush was a signer of the Declaration of Independence, and wrote the first American textbook on psychiatry. He was a Quaker reformer who advocated temperance, abolition of slavery, and improved education for women.

As a physician, Rush established the first free medical dispensary in the United States. In terms of care of the mentally ill he advocated for clean cells, kind treatment, qualified attendants, and what we might call occupational therapy. Rush was undoubtedly a sincere, committed, and well-intentioned man. His views on mental illness, however, is described by Grinker below:

> Rush's psychiatric therapies included a tranquilizing chair into which patients were strapped until they were quiet, other mechanical constraints, whippings when necessary, "shock treatment" by immersion in cold water, and gyration to produce rushing of blood to the head. He insisted that there was one disease and one treatment for its etiology of convulsive action in the cerebral capillaries. The treatment was severe purging and excessive bloodletting, which Rush also advocated as a sure cure for yellow fever. (Grinker, 1970, p. 25)

In the middle of the nineteenth century a truly remarkable woman, Dorothea Dix, crusaded tirelessly for reform of living conditions in prisons and mental hospitals (there was little difference between the two). Dix was a schoolteacher who retired from teaching because of her health. Ironically, she spent the rest of her life campaigning for humanitarian cases and reforms.

Dorothea Dix worked at reform some 40 years before the progressive movement, and her pleas very often fell on deaf ears and uncaring politicians and bureaucrats. In many "asylums" the only improvements were to switch from restraining patients with chains to using leather straitjackets and manacles.

In Europe, humane treatment of the mentally ill had progressed rapidly due to the efforts of physicians such as Philippe Pinel and William Tuke. New approaches to caring for the mentally ill focused on kind and caring treatment, or what was known as "moral treatment," an approach that would be called milieu therapy today (Grob, 1966).

Much of the impetus for the adoption of the "moral treatment" approach came from educated laymen, such as Horace Mann and Dorothea Dix, rather than physicians. The humanitarian interests of such people were related to their religious views. Around the turn of the nineteenth century, a major religious movement called the Great Awakening had focused attention on humanitarian causes in much the same way as the "Social Gospel" did a century later.

Moral therapy emphasized kind, individual care and utilized occupational therapy and religious exercises, as well as amusements and games, or what we would call recreational therapy. Above all, it emphasized kind treatment, without threats of physical violence and used a minimum of physical restraints. Essentially, this new therapy implied the creation of a healthy psychological environment for individual patients and for the hospital, itself. In some settings, follow-up results showed that moral treatment obtained very positive results (Grob, 1966).

Unfortunately, the influence of the moral treatment approach began to wane after the middle of the nineteenth century. As urbanization and immigration increased, the patient population became larger and more diverse in ethnic and religious backgrounds. Mental hospitals became larger and more bureaucratic. The "therapeutic hospital" gave way to the "custodial hospital" (Grob, 1991). Individual care of patients deteriorated and the use of physical restraints resumed. The mental hospital changed from a healing institution to an agent of social control (Sharma, 1970). The medical profession moved into what Grob (1991) termed "administrative psychiatry."

By the 1930s electric shock, insulin shock, and cranial lobotomies were in fashion, and mental hospitals were increasingly crowded warehouses of human misery. The custodial hospital was in full bloom.

The Mental Hygiene Society continued to advocate for more effective and humane care for mental patients. It was supported by journalistic exposés, books, and even motion pictures documenting and detailing the horrors of so-called mental hospitals. Ultimately, the treatment of mental patients was reformed by a combination of chemicals and court orders, rather than by appeals to conscience.

The advent of the tranquilizing drugs in the 1940s and 50s was the catalyst for new approaches to treatment, including psychotherapy. The courts essentially prohibited the warehousing of the mentally ill in "hospitals" that simply incarcerated patients under the pretext of providing treatment.

The Mental Hygiene Movement was notably more successful in its efforts to support preventive programs and early intervention, particularly for youth. The Child Guidance Movement, which we referred to in Chapter Three, as well as major programs of research on child development, were a result of the increased awareness of mental health problems stimulated by Clarence Beers, Adolf Meyer, and their successors.

## Psychologists and Psychotherapy

In the period between the two world wars, psychologists were only rarely engaged in the practice of psychotherapy. As we noted above, they were effectively excluded from the practice of psychoanalysis, and even as newer and more flexible approaches to psychotherapy emerged, psychologists were seldom in a position to practice anything that was called psychotherapy. Psychotherapy was still defined as medical treatment administered solely in medical settings by physicians, or under their direct supervision, and was accepted as such by organized psychology (Humphreys, 1996).

Two settings in which psychologists were directly engaged in working with clients or patients other than in a purely assessment role were the child guidance clinics and the university counseling centers. As we noted in Chapter 3, these settings were precisely the ones from which professional psychological counseling emerged. These two settings are also cited as the primary places in which psychologists began to practice psychotherapy (VandenBos et al., 1992). Child guidance clinics were almost always run by psychiatrists. Clinical psychologists in those settings simply called their approaches to treatment counseling, re-education, or child guidance, and so escaped the wrath of the medical profession and the threat of being accused of practicing medicine. In the college counseling centers, coming as they did out of the historical framework of progressive education and the Guidance Movement, fewer such difficulties were encountered.

It seems clear that in the 1930s and 1940s what Williamson and Darley called clinical counseling, what Rogers called nondirective counseling, and that which Bordin a little later referred to under the umbrella term of "psychological counseling" differed from what was called psychotherapy in many medical settings in name only. It was primarily a matter of psychologists using terminology that was safe and acceptable in the organizations in which they operated, while psychiatry continued to dominate not only medical settings, but the medical jargon as well.

As Garfield (1981) put it:

> In the late 1930s, clinical psychology was a rather small and undistinguished specialty and psychotherapy was not a major activity of clinical psychologists . . . I can assure from my own recollections that the future of clinical psychology did not look particularly bright at that time and that psychology's involvement with psychotherapy was unpredictable. (p. 174)

The first real opportunities for psychologists to practice psychotherapy came during World War II when the need for therapists simply overwhelmed the supply of psychiatrists available. Psychologists, social workers, and nurses were pressed into service to provide therapy for the very large numbers of neuropsychiatric casualties of the war (Resnick, 1997). The same shortages existed in the early postwar years and led to the upgrading of psychologists' role and status in the Veterans Administration that was described earlier.

Even in these emergency conditions, however, psychotherapy was practiced only under the supervision and control of psychiatrists. Psychologists were clearly not accepted as autonomous professionals in the practice of psychotherapy.

The real dilemma in the postwar years was for the trickle of psychologists who aspired to careers in independent practice. Rollo May, who was awarded the first Ph.D. in clinical psychology from Columbia University in 1948, was a pioneering psychologist and psychotherapist in New York City in the early 1950s. He described the dilemma of private practice psychologists in those years:

My memory goes back to the years of 1955 and 1956, when there were only a handful of us in the whole state of New York practicing psychotherapy.

We thought of those as "the Dangerous Years." We few psychologists were continually under the threat of being declared outlaws. . . . I recall those days when the legislators of the state of New York had before them a bill . . . that would make all psychotherapy a branch of medicine. If this passed we would be explicitly outlawed and possibly arrested for practicing medicine. (May, 1992, p. xxxiii)

Gradually, license and certification laws for psychologists began to provide a measure of legal protection and legitimacy for the private practice of psychology. Clinical psychologists were, however, "Johnny-come-latelys" to the practice of psychotherapy. The "scientist-practitioner" model of training for clinical psychologists that had opened the doors to employment in the Veterans Administration after World War II had provided little in the way of formal preparation for the practice of psychotherapy. The designers of these new training programs apparently hoped that psychologists would not go into private practice, but instead would do psychotherapy only in the context of treatment teams that included psychiatrists (Humphreys, 1996). The coaches captains and quarterbacks of such "teams" were, of course, to be psychiatrists.

The emphasis in preparation of clinical psychologists was, not surprisingly, weighted heavily toward assessment and psychometrics, including the administration and interpretation of intelligence tests, personality inventories, and other diagnostic measures. In the internship phase of preparation, psychotherapy was not undertaken until late in training, and then only with the permission and supervision of psychiatrists. This approach was characteristic of internship training both within the Veterans Administration and in other hospital settings (Humphreys, 1996). Until well into the 1950s, the professional practice of clinical psychologists was essentially testing (Resnick, 1997). As Garfield (1981) noted:

[T]he majority of practicing clinical psychologists were employed in medical installations where they were under the nominal or actual supervision of psychiatrists. Staff and case conferences were presided over by senior staff psychiatrists, and the psychologists' role most frequently was to present the results of psychological test evaluations. (p. 176)

This situation stood in sharp contrast to the training of counseling psychologists during the same period. At the Northwestern Conference in 1951, which laid down guidelines for the training of counseling psychologists, considerable attention was given to practicum training in counseling (Bordin & Wrenn, 1954). Supervised experience in counseling was a primary requirement in counseling psychology programs (Committee on Counselor Training, 1952).

## Counseling and Psychotherapy

One of the issues that has haunted the field of counseling psychology for nearly a half century has been the differences, if any, between counseling and psychotherapy. It is clear that the issue was not given paramount importance in the early years of the Division of Counseling Psychology, that is, in the early 1950s.

Gilbert (1952), writing a review of the counseling literature for the *Annual Review of Psychology*, simply concluded that distinctions between counseling and psychotherapy are unnecessary and artificial. Wrenn (1954), in writing the "Counseling Methods" chapter of the *Annual Review of Psychology* 2 years later, made no attempt to distinguish between counseling and psychotherapy, but simply included studies under either rubric that were done in a nonmedical setting.

From today's vantage point, the agonizing debate over presumed differences between counseling and psychotherapy that began in the 1960s seems unproductive and superficial. In 1951, Carl Rogers published his classic *Client Centered Therapy* and ever after referred to his approach as psychotherapy. The Rogerian approach, however, actually had far more adherents among those who identified themselves as counselors than among any other group.

The 1960s saw the effort to distinguish counseling from psychotherapy waged primarily by counseling psychologists themselves in an effort to achieve an identity separate from clinical psychology or the other mental health professions. The historical antecedents of counseling were, as we saw, rooted in education and vocational guidance, rather than in clinics or hospitals. Counseling had no history of struggles for recognition or autonomy from psychiatry or organized medicine.

For counseling types the problem was, as we saw in Chapter 4, a fragile sense of identity as psychologists, coupled with a keen sense of competition from clinical psychologists who during the 1960s began flocking to the practice of psychotherapy. For many counseling psychologists in the 1960s, perceptions of what constituted psychotherapy were rooted almost solely in images of traditional psychoanalysis or psychoanalytically oriented therapies.

The traditional psychodynamic therapies were of long duration and focused on uncovering and interpreting repressed material, breaking down defenses, and ostensibly bringing about major personality change. Such approaches were obviously both foreign from and antithetical to what many counseling psychologists saw as the historical, philosophical, and theoretical foundations of their field. As counseling psychologists tended to put it: Psychotherapy is about discovering why you are feeling anxious, counseling involves doing something about it.

One of the factors that complicated both the identity problems of counseling psychologists and the distinction between counseling and psychotherapy was the rapid changes that were occurring in the area of vocational counseling. The "test them and tell them" approach to vocational counseling, which was really a perversion of Parsons' process of "true reasoning," had finally fallen into total disrepute. It was replaced by a realization that vocational life and vocational decisions were inevitably intertwined with the emotional and motivational facets of an individual personality (Pritchard, 1962; Samler, 1961; Thompson, 1960). This trend is further discussed in Chapter 6.

For many years, some of the less cognitively complex counselors and counselor educators had endeavored to keep life simple by categorizing client concerns into neat little compartments labeled "vocational-educational problems" and "emotional problems." The latter category could then be ruled out of the counselor's domain and cast into the murky waters of psychopathology.

As vocational counseling began to deal with feelings, anxieties, and motivations, meaningful distinctions between counseling and psychotherapy were even more difficult to maintain.

Numerous attempts were made at definitions of counseling that would provide a separate and unique identity for counseling and counselors, while recognizing the full psychological complexity and integrity of clients. Tyler (1960) wrote of counseling as "minimum change

therapy." Brammer and Shostrum (1960) saw counseling and psychotherapy on a continuum with counseling characterized by such terms
as "educative," "supportive," and "emphasis on normality." Psychotherapy, on the other hand, was described as "analytic" and "recon-
structive" with "a focus on unconscious processes."

Almost all of these definitions recognized the very close similarity
between counseling and therapy. Hahn (1953) pointed out that the
two processes cannot be clearly distinguished. He noted that counselors sometimes practiced what therapists would call psychotherapy
and therapists did what counselors would see as counseling, yet, he
maintained, the two are different.

Stefflre (1965) reviewed more than a dozen definitions that attempted to distinguish the two processes. He concluded that such
distinctions were necessary only to justify the inclusion of non-psycho-
logically trained "counselors" who clearly were not competent to do
psychotherapy. He wrote wryly that "just as first aid may shade into
the practice of medicine, so counseling may shade into psychotherapy,
but no one thinks it is impossible to distinguish between the application
of a band-aid and brain surgery" (pp. 16–17).

Many of the definitions listed were lengthy and tedious enumera-
tions of tendencies and shadings that, in the aggregate, were suppose
to discriminate between counseling and psychotherapy. Almost all of
these distinctions obviously perceived psychotherapy as purely psychodynamic, delving into the unconscious, lasting for months or years,
and aimed at some kind of total transformation of the client's personality. Such a view was totally out of touch with the newer therapies that
were already emerging in the 1960s.

Most of the definitions perceived counseling clients as "normal."
When this almost meaningless term was elaborated, it typically meant
relatively high-functioning, not institutionalized, and employed and
self-supporting. These are of course precisely the same kinds of people
who typically sought out, persisted in, and profited from psychotherapy as well as counseling. Indeed, in the pre-health insurance years
of the 1950s and 1960s, given the out-of-pocket cost of therapy, a
client certainly needed to be employed and self-supporting.

It seems clear, as Stefflre (1965) noted, that much of the energy
expended in these definitional calisthenics was devoted to providing
umbrella definitions that would cover the varied activities of the wide
assortment of personnel workers who had the words "counselor" or

"counseling" embedded in their titles or job descriptions. Most of these workers were prepared in counselor education programs housed in the same academic departments that operated counseling psychology programs. The senior faculty of such departments were very frequently the leaders of the Division of Counseling Psychology and the writers of the Procrustean definitions cited above.

During the 1960s, particularly, a host of new personnel workers were prepared in counselor education departments, usually with the assistance of generous government subsidies. School guidance counselors, rehabilitation specialists, employment service placement people, and a variety of college personnel workers were all prepared in such settings.

According to Stefflre (1965), the average length of graduate preparation for most of these people at that time was less than one academic year, with fewer than one half of their credits in psychology. The principal duties of these workers were tremendously varied. College personnel workers ran admissions programs, managed residence halls, and regulated fraternities, for example. School guidance people kept cumulative record files, administered testing programs, maintained libraries of college catalogs and occupational information, constructed class schedules, and registered students. They were often responsible for providing services to four or five hundred students or more. Actual counseling interviews, when they occurred, were brief and irregular. Guidance counselors frequently struggled to establish a professional role, obtain time actually to see students, and avoid being relegated to the role of minor administrative functionaries. Similar, non-psychological functions were often the rule in employment service and rehabilitation settings.

All of these people performed important and worthwhile functions within the organizations that they served. Very few, however, were engaged in or aspired to do psychological counseling.

With the benefit of hindsight, it seems clear that rather than stretching definitions of counseling to ridiculous lengths in order to include a heterogeneous group of people who, after all, had their own professional organization (APGA), the leaders of counseling psychology would have better served the field by specifying its role within the family of professional psychology. A simple statement to the effect that psychological counseling is a form of psychotherapy practiced by psychologists that includes, but is not limited to, assistance with personal problem-solving, decision-making, and life planning would have sufficed to clarify the nature of counseling psychology.

Perhaps the conflicting allegiances and interpretations of the historical traditions of the field made even this kind of consensus impossible. The attempt to paper over the divisions among counseling psychologists accomplished at the Greyston Conference in 1964 certainly did little to resolve issues or advance the field.

The failure to achieve consensus on credible definitions of counseling and its relationship to psychotherapy early in the history of the field has produced a series of negative consequences. Considerable confusion still exists about the differences between the two processes, and counseling is typically denigrated as a result. In a recent book edited by Corsini and Wedding (1995) that, ironically, has actually sometimes been used to prepare counselors, the editors' introduction defines counseling and psychotherapy as follows:

> Essentially, counseling stresses the giving of information, advice, and *orders* [italics added] by someone considered to be an expert in a particular area of human behavior, while psychotherapy is a process of helping people discover why they think, feel and act in unsatisfactory ways. A counselor is primarily a teacher, while a psychotherapist is essentially a detective. (p. 3)

The failure of counseling psychology to clarify and disseminate definitions of psychological counseling that justify its status as a specialty in professional psychology has hampered the growth and acceptance of the field. Although one may suspect that Corsini and Wedding's version of the psychotherapist as detective may resemble Inspector Clouseau more than it does Sherlock Holmes, the spectre of the counselor defined in 1995 as merely the giver of "information, advice and orders" is a discouraging one.

In a bitterly worded complaint about the failure of the field to develop and communicate a clear and positive identity, Weigel (1978) put his finger squarely on the problem with an aptly worded title: "We Have Seen The Enemy And They Is Us . . . " In the same edited volume, titled *The Present and Future of Counseling Psychology* (1978), Parker and Hurst lamented the choice of the name of the field in a paper called "Counseling Psychology; Tyranny of a Title." Clearly, the identity problems that beset the field in the 1960s were not laid to rest either at Greyston House or since.

## The Decline of Psychoanalysis

By the middle of the 1950s, the psychodynamic therapies from which the early counseling psychologists were so eager to divorce themselves were already in sharp decline. The story of psychoanalysis and psychoanalytic therapies to that time had been one of grandiose claims of success supported by relatively little solid research evidence (Garfield, 1981). As more and more psychologists with research training began to do psychotherapy and to evaluate it, those claims were greeted with steadily increasing skepticism.

Perhaps the most highly publicized and certainly one of the most scathing criticisms of traditional psychotherapy came from Hans Eysenck in a widely read article in the *Journal of Consulting Psychology* in 1952. Eysenck essentially challenged the total efficacy of traditional psychotherapy by comparing results of outcome studies with rates of spontaneous remission of symptoms in untreated cases.

The 1952 Eysenck article, and a series of further studies published by him and others, touched off a veritable storm of controversy. For the next 30 years a long series of critiques and rebuttals of critiques enlivened the psychotherapy literature.

The Eysenck critique did not discredit psychotherapy in the long term. It certainly did not discourage psychologists from practicing therapy, or patients from accessing it. Numerous flaws in Eysenck's sweeping conclusions were found and new studies were undertaken. The Eysenck critiques did usher in a new wave of interest in psychotherapy research that both advanced knowledge and opened the door to radically new approaches to therapy.

By the end of the 1950s psychoanalytic theories and the therapies derived from them had already lost their pre-eminent position in the mental health field. The increasing skepticism about the efficacy of psychodynamic treatments alluded to above was obviously one reason for this fall from grace.

Within psychiatry itself, however, a dramatic change had occurred in the perception of mental illness and its etiology. "Biological" psychiatry had begun to replace "psychodynamic" psychiatry (Bowen, 1987). The tremendous success of the tranquilizing and antidepressant drugs had virtually revolutionized the treatment of acute mental illnesses. The old-fashioned "mental hospitals" were almost emptied in the course of a few short years. Somatic causes and somatic "cures" became the focus of American psychiatry.

As the aura of infallibility that had surrounded psychoanalysis, at least in the public eye, faded, strident criticisms of psychoanalysis as scientific theory began to be heard and heeded. The resurgence of behaviorism pointed up the contrast between a psychology based upon observables and the slippery and apparently untestable propositions that were the foundation of psychoanalysis.

As psychotherapy research burgeoned, the demand for testability and accountability in psychotherapy grew among both researchers and practitioners. The decline of psychodynamic approaches opened the door to a whole host of new therapies, often based upon assumptions and propositions virtually antithetical to those of Freud and his followers (Hilgard, 1987).

## The Rise of the New Therapies

The first of the new therapies was Carl Roger's Client-Centered Therapy. Rogerian counseling and therapy was received by counseling and clinical psychology as a virtual revolution in treatment compared with either psychodynamic therapies or the "directive" trait and factor approaches. It had little impact, however, on psychiatry or psychiatrically directed treatment (Garfield, 1981). Because Client-Centered Therapy and the era of "humanistic psychology" that it ushered in were so important to the development of counseling psychology, they will be dealt with separately in Chapter 8.

By the 1960s a new set of therapies had also emerged, based generally upon behavior theory and specifically on the learning approaches advanced by B. F. Skinner. They too will be discussed separately in Chapter 9.

In addition to the humanistic and behavioral approaches, a whole series of new therapies burst upon the scene in the 1960s. Fritz Perls' (1969) Gestalt Therapy, William Glasser's (1965) Reality Therapy, Albert Ellis's (1962) Rational Emotive Therapy, and the Counter-Conditioning Therapy of Joseph Wolpe (1958) were all articulated, studied, and won large and vocal groups of adherents including counseling psychologists.

We will not attempt to describe all of these and the host of other individual and group therapies that emerged in the 1960s here. Taken together, they did indeed revolutionize the practice and popularity of psychotherapy in America. They were especially important to counseling psychologists. For the first time, there were psychotherapeutic approaches that were reasonably brief and based upon theories and assumptions that were neither alien nor repugnant to the historical and philosophical foundations of counseling. The new therapies were, on the whole, amenable to research and had begun to produce a growing body of process and outcome studies. In short, they seemed appropriate and applicable to the practice of counseling psychology. Perhaps the most important legacy of psychoanalytic thinking to influence counseling psychology was its emphasis on personality development. This is discussed further in Chapter 7.

The New Therapies and the changes that came with them were momentous. First, they led to the demystification of psychotherapy. As early as 1938, Francis Robinson at Ohio State University had begun to record counseling sessions (Schmidt & Chock, 1990). In 1940, when Carl Rogers came to Ohio State, facilities were expanded and the recording of interviews was an established part of both training and research in counseling and psychotherapy.

By the 1960s psychologists could observe the therapeutic styles of "gurus" like Roger, Perls, and Ellis on film or audio- or videotape. Most trainees, had themselves been taped or observed in interview situations.

Even more importantly, the 50-year-old monopoly of medicine over training and practice had been finally and forever broken. Psychotherapy was practiced legally and effectively by clinical, counseling and school psychologists, social workers, nurses, and a variety of counselors, as well as by psychiatrists. A therapist no longer needed a goatee and a Viennese accent to be recognized. Therapy was practiced in schools, colleges, hospitals. community agencies, clinics, and private practices with or without the supervision of psychiatrists.

## RESEARCH ON PSYCHOTHERAPY

By the 1980s the great debate begun by Eysenck on whether psychotherapy actually works had given way to more pertinent and searching questions of when, where, how, why, and for whom psychotherapy helps. A number of large-scale, well-funded studies of psychotherapy

outcomes were accomplished beginning in the 1960s. The proliferation of such studies and the wide range of methods, samples, and
criteria used made any clear-cut conclusions difficult.

Questions of why psychotherapy works, or what kinds of treatment
work best for which patients, remain and are the focus of much current
research. Perhaps most disturbing to psychologists is the fact that
little convincing evidence exists to show that level or type of training in
psychology is related to success as a psychotherapist (Peterson, 1995).

## THE AGE OF PSYCHOTHERAPY ARRIVES

Perhaps of the greatest importance to the practice of psychotherapy
was the fact that, for the first time, the cost and availability of psychotherapy made it a realistic option for a large segment of the population.
The resulting growth in numbers of both patients and practitioners
was phenomenal. In 1960 about 14% of the population was estimated
to have received any kind of mental health service from any source.
By 1990, that percentage had more than doubled, and 65 million
Americans were estimated to have received mental health services at
some point in their lives. By the mid-1980s more than 150 thousand
psychotherapists were estimated to be practicing in the United States
(VandenBos et al., 1992).

The change that occurred as psychotherapy became part of American culture was clear. Once, the only people who saw therapists were
the very rich, the very famous, or the very neurotic. By the 1980s,
all sorts of people from all walks of life, for all sorts of reasons, were
seeking out or thinking of seeking out psychotherapy. The age of
psychotherapy had indeed arrived.

As an organized profession, counseling psychology was ill-prepared
to relate to or profit from the astounding success of psychotherapy
as an American institution. In the 1960s, confronted with competition
and challenges from clinical psychology, counseling psychology had
taken refuge in expounding upon the presumed differences between
counseling and psychotherapy even as these differences were disap-
pearing before their eyes.

The myopia induced by navel-gazing on the part of organized counseling psychology has had a pronounced negative effect on the growth

and acceptance of the field. From a position at the cutting edge of developments in psychotherapy in the university counseling centers and child guidance clinics during the 1940s and 1950s, counseling psychology has had to struggle to avoid being left in the dust created by the "psychotherapy explosion."

# REFERENCES

A.P.A. Division of Counseling Psychology, Committee on Counselor Training. (1952). *The practicum training of counseling psychologists.* Washington, DC: American Psychological Association.

Brammer, L., & Shostrum, E. (1960). *Therapeutic psychology.* Englewood Cliffs, NJ: Prentice Hall.

Bordin, E., & Wrenn, C. G. (1954). The counseling function. *Review of Educational Research, 24,* 134–146.

Bowen, M. (1987). Psychotherapy past, present and future. In J. K. Zeig (Ed.), *The evolution of psychotherapy* (pp. 32–40). New York: Brunner/Mazel.

Cohen, L. D. (1992). The academic department. In D. K. Freedheim (Ed.), *History of psychotherapy* (pp. 731–764). Washington, DC: American Psychological Association.

Corsini, R. (1995). Introduction. In R. Corsini & D. Wedding (Eds.), *Current psychotherapies* (pp. 1–14). Itasca, IL: Peacock.

Cushman, P. (1992). Psychotherapy to 1992: A historically situated interpretation. In D. K. Freedheim (Ed.), *History of psychotherapy* (pp. 21–64). Washington, DC: American Psychological Association.

Ellis, A. (1962). *Reason and emotion in psychotherapy.* New York: Lyle Stewart.

Evans, R. B., & Koelsch, W. A. (1985). Psychoanalysis arrives in America. *American Psychologist, 40,* 942–948.

Eysenck, H. (1952). The effects of psychotherapy: An evaluation. *Journal of Consulting Psychology, 16,* 319–324.

Garfield, S. (1981). Psychotherapy: A 40-year appraisal. *American Psychologist, 36,* 174–183.

Gilbert, W. (1952). Counseling: Therapy and diagnosis. In *Annual Review of Psychology* (pp. 357–380). Palo Alto, CA: Annual Reviews, Vol. 3.

Glasser, W. (1965). *Reality therapy.* New York: Harper and Row.

Grinker, R. R. (1970). The continuing search for meaning. *The American Journal of Psychiatry, 127,* 25–31.

Grob, G. N. (1991). *From asylum to community.* Princeton, NJ: Princeton University Press.

Grob, G. N. (1966). The state mental hospital in mid-nineteenth century America: A social analysis. *American Psychologist, 21,* 510–523.

Hahn, M. (1953). Conceptual trends in counseling. *Personnel and Guidance Journal, 31,* 231–235.

Hartmann, H. (1939). *Ego psychology and the problem of adaptation.* New York: International Universities Press.

Hilgard, E. R. (1987). *Psychology in America: A historical review.* New York: Harcourt Brace Jovanovich.

Humphreys, K. (1996). Clinical psychologists as psychotherapists. *American Psychologist, 51,* 190–197.

Kaplan, D. M. (1967, December). Freud and his own patients. *Harper's,* pp. 99–107.

May, R. (1992). Foreword. In D. K. Freedheim (Ed.), *History of psychotherapy* (pp. xx–xxviii). Washington, DC: American Psychological Association.

Murray, H. A. (1956). Morton Prince. *Journal of Abnormal Psychology, 52,* 291–295.

Parker, C., & Hurst, J. (1978). Counseling psychology: Tyranny of a title. In J. Whiteley & B. Fretz (Eds.), *The present and future of counseling psychology* (pp. 21–28). Monterey, CA: Brooks/Cole.

Perls, F. (1969). *Gestalt therapy verbatim.* Moab, UT: Real People Press.

Peterson, D. R. (1995). The reflective educator. *American Psychologist, 50,* 975–983.

Pritchard, D. H. (1962). The occupational exploration process: Some operational implications. *Personnel and Guidance Journal, 40,* 674–680.

Resnick, R. J. (1997). A brief history of practice: Expanded. *American Psychologist, 52,* 463–468.

Rice, L. N., & Greenberg, L. S. (1992). Humanistic approaches to psychotherapy. In D. K. Freedheim (Ed.), *History of psychotherapy* (pp. 197–224). Washington, DC: American Psychological Association.

Rogers, C. R. (1951). *Client-centered therapy.* Boston: Houghton-Mifflin.

Rosenzweig, S. (1994). *The historic expedition to America* (1909). St. Louis, MO: Rana House.

Samler, J. (1961). Psycho-social aspects of work: A critique of occupational information. *Personnel and Guidance Journal, 39,* 458–465.

Schmidt, L., & Chock, S. (1990). Counseling psychology at Ohio State University: The first 50 years. *Journal of Counseling and Development, 68,* 276–281.

Sharma, S. (1970). A historical background of the development of nosology in psychiatry and psychology. *American Psychologist, 25,* 248–253.

Stefflre, B. (1965). Function and present status of counseling theory. In B. Stefflre (Ed.), *Theories of counseling* (pp. 1–29). New York: McGraw-Hill.

Thompson, A. S. (1960). Personality dynamics and vocational counseling. *Personnel and Guidance Journal, 38,* 350–357.

Tyler, L. (1960). Minimum change therapy. *Personnel and Guidance Journal, 38,* 475–479.

VandenBos, G. R., Cummings, N., & DeLeon, P. H. (1972). A century of psychotherapy: Economic and environmental influences. In D. K. Freedheim (Ed.), *History of psychotherapy* (pp. 65–102). Washington, DC: American Psychological Association.

Weigel, R. G. (1978). I have seen the enemy and they is us—and everyone else. In J. Whiteley & B. Fretz (Eds.), *The present and future of counseling psychology* (pp. 56–61). Monterey, CA: Brook/Cole.

Wolpe, J. (1958). *Psychotherapy by reciprocal inhibition.* Stanford, CA: Stanford University Press.

Wrenn, C. G. (1954). Counseling methods. In *Annual Review of Psychology.* Palo Alto, CA: *Annual Reviews, 5,* 337–357.

# PART II

# Traditions, Traditions, Traditions

## INTRODUCTION

In Part 1, we traced in roughly chronological fashion the origin and evolution of historical events, and the responses to them, that have helped to shape modern counseling psychology: from its inception as part of a social movement created largely by reformers, philanthropists, visionaries and assorted "do-gooders," to its present position as a specialty in the practice of professional psychology. We have attended only in passing to the intellectual substance in terms of theory, research, and values that has nourished and informed the field.

At least four major streams of thought and theory can be identified as shapers of our current professional identity. These are really no longer separate streams of influence. Rather, they have slowly become loosely woven threads that together form the fabric of contemporary counseling psychology. These threads that now serve to unite and integrate the intellectual infrastructure of the field can be termed the Individual Differences Tradition, the Developmental Tradition, the Humanistic Tradition, and the Behavioral Tradition.

Each has contributed mightily to the evolution of counseling psychology. Once, they were conflicting, and competing ideologies vying for the loyalty and commitment of warring factions. Today, few counseling

**147**

psychologists would deny the impact that each has had and continues to have on theory and practice.

Yet, each of these traditions represents a different view of human nature and of the human condition. Each represents a different set of lenses through which to construe ourselves and our clients. Each also has a separate, fascinating and unique history, complete with its cast of heroes and even occasional villains. To understand either where we have come from, or where we are going, we must first understand these traditions and the people who created them. Together, they are both our legacy from the past and our passport into an uncertain future.

# 6

# The Individual Differences Tradition

If it moves measure it. If two things move together correlate them.

—A graduate student's definition of Dust Bowl empiricism

When James McKeen Cattell completed his Ph.D. with Wilhelm Wundt in 1886, he returned to the United States full of enthusiasm and eager to spread the gospel of German-style scientific psychology. Unfortunately, he found few interested listeners in academia. Few American universities were interested in hiring psychologists, if indeed they even knew what psychologists did.

Young McKeen Cattell's father, the elder James Cattell, was understandably upset by this turn of events. By this time, he had a considerable financial investment in his son's psychological education. After the younger Cattell had received a number of polite expressions of disinterest in his academic credentials from major universities, his father went so far as to travel all the way to Leipzig to demand a personal letter of recommendation for his son from Wundt. We do not know how the august Wilhelm Wundt reacted to the irate father of his former research assistant demanding such a letter, but the elder Cattell at length returned to America with the recommendation and a handful of research papers that McKeen had done enroute to his dissertation (O'Donnell, 1985).

James Cattell, Senior, proceeded to lobby energetically on behalf of his son's gainful employment. The University of Pennsylvania had, some time before, received an endowment from the estate of a wealthy spiritualist who wished the university to create a professorship in

**149**

philosophy for someone to examine the validity of modern spiritualism.

Meanwhile, the unemployed McKeen Cattell had returned to Europe to establish an unofficial laboratory at Cambridge and there to meet and come under the influence of the eminent Francis Galton. Cattell worked briefly with Galton and his colleagues at the South Kensington Laboratory. Cattell had always been interested in the psychology of individual differences. He returned to America in 1887 to the position his father had promoted at the University of Pennsylvania with the princely salary of $300 per year (about what a schoolmaster teaching in a one-room school on the prairie would have received in those days).

James McKeen Cattell, however, this time had brought with him from Europe something that America was far more willing to buy into than Wundt's brand of slightly soiled and suspect experimentalism. He brought with him trait and factor psychology.

Within 4 years, Cattell had moved to Columbia University to a more lucrative position where he no longer had to pretend an interest in "psychic research." In the process, he coined the term "mental test" and set in motion the phenomenal movement that dominated applied psychology in America for the next half-century.

By 1893 Cattell was busily inflicting his "mental tests" on the undergraduate population at Columbia, and, as we saw, Joseph Jastrow, with the blessing of the fledgling APA, had opened his little psychological sideshow in the shadow of the Ferris wheel on those dusty fairgrounds of Chicago.

Exactly 50 years later, in 1943, Broadway saw another opening of another show. As the curtain rose, the audience saw ten air cadets in stiffly starched khakis and white sidewall haircuts standing at attention before an ominous array of laboratory apparatus while a white-coated examiner droned out a set of instructions.

The cadets seated themselves before the apparatus, grasped a metal rod, and were directed to hold it so steadily that it did not touch the electrically charged aperture surrounding it. Each time a cadet made an error, a light flashed. Each cadet was told to keep an accurate account of his "mistakes."

The examiner explained that the purpose of the test went far beyond measuring mere muscular control. The examiner explained the purpose in these terms:

The test you are to take now will measure your ability to remain steady under pressure. The pressure will consist of your anxiety to succeed in air-crew training. It will consist of your own fear that you will be eliminated. It will consist of your own weaknesses and secret doubts. It will consist of jumping nerves that you cannot control.

The test will pit you against yourself. Every man has fear. Every man has tenseness. Every man has weakness and jumping nerves and secret doubts. But not every man can control these things. (Quoted in Napoli, 1981, pp. 134–135)

As the scene continued the trials went on and the almost sadistic "examiner" forcefully reminded his "subjects" of the possible consequences of their mistakes. After four more trials exactly like the first, the test was over.

The stage lights faded and the curtain fell. The scene was from Moss Hart's *Winged Victory*, a semi-documentary drama and later motion picture about the role of the Army Air Corps in World War II.

One drama critic declared that the scene depicting the cadets undergoing the "steadiness under pressure test" was experienced as an ordeal by every member of the audience. A year later, people all over the country got a chance to witness this diabolical challenge to the cadet's sense of competence and self-esteem. In actuality, the scene was not entirely accurate. Even before the play opened, a revised version of the steadiness-under-pressure test had been abandoned after Air Force psychologists had shown it to be totally ineffective in selecting aviation cadets (Napoli, 1981).

What was both real and disturbing, after 50 years of applied psychology, was the public perception of psychologists and of the tests and inventories that virtually defined their professional practice. For many people, psychologists were seen as unfeeling and uncaring instruments of a technological society who were willing to sacrifice the best interests of the individual to the purposes of their employers.

Psychological tests were often seen as the means for revealing the weaknesses, frailties, and inadequacies of people, rather than providing information to enhance their well-being and self-esteem. In the 50 years prior to the end of World War II, the history of trait-and-factor psychology, as it came to be called, was one of great technological and practical progress with a record of positive contributions to countless individuals. The programs of vocational guidance and counseling undertaken during the Great Depression that were described earlier were notable examples. From a public relations stand-point, however, those 50 years were disastrous.

## INDIVIDUAL DIFFERENCES AND DARWINIAN BIOLOGY

Trait-and-factor psychology was born out of the study of individual differences that was an essential part of Darwinian biology. The evolution of species as described by Darwin was based upon the "natural selection" of individual organisms possessing superior characteristics or traits that ensured their ability to survive and reproduce and thus pass on their genes in the competitive environments found in nature. Indeed, it was Charles Darwin, himself, who coined the term "individual differences" to identify the scientific study of these kinds of phenomena.

As we saw earlier, Charles Darwin's half-cousin, Francis Galton, soon began to apply the notion of such an evolutionary process to the human species, while Herbert Spencer and others used evolutionary principles to concoct a political and philosophical movement called Social Darwinism.

The study of the individual differences existing among members of a specific species was thus at the center of nineteenth-century evolutionary biology. The study of psychological individual differences in human beings was seen by early researchers as an obvious and straightforward extension of such an evolutionary biology.

In biology, a trait was simply viewed as a tendency of an individual organism to react or function in a particular way. Two crucial aspects of this functioning were of interest to the biologist. The first aspect to be understood was the way in which the specific trait or tendency contributed to an increased probability in the organism to survive and reproduce successfully. The second problem was to establish that the characteristic was actually acquired and transmitted genetically to offspring. In Darwinian terms, then, a trait was simply a genetically transmitted stable characteristic proved to be adaptive in a given environment.

In terms of the psychology of individual differences, the problems are clearly not the same. Knowledge of human psychological characteristics that are stable, that is, that persist over time, and that are manifested across situations may be of great scientific interest and practical utility, whether or not they are directly genetically transmitted. Thus the usefulness of an applied psychology based upon the study of individual differences may have relatively little to do with evolutionary biology.

It was the failure of early researchers and applied psychologists to recognize and appreciate this distinction that haunted trait-and-factor psychology for its first 50 years and in fact is still the source of controversy, today.

## COUNSELING AND THE TRAIT-AND-FACTOR MODEL

The application of individual differences research to practical human problems is almost universally seen as the genesis of applied psychology (Dawis, 1992). As we saw in Chapter 1, such research was relatively insignificant in the early years of the Guidance Movement. Not until after World War I did psychometrics and what came to be called trait-and-factor psychology make a notable impact on counseling and guidance. The story of the heyday of trait-and-factor psychology is essentially one of its influence in the 1920s and 1930s. Aubrey (1977) maintained that the decline of the trait-and-factor approach in counseling began around 1940 and was virtually complete by the mid-fifties. Meara (1990) asserted that the individual differences model was not really central to the science of psychology after the end of World War II. The history of this decline is one of both scientific changes and sociopolitical factors.

For some 20 years, however, trait-and-factor psychology and the empirical base from which it was drawn—the study of individual differences—virtually dominated American applied psychology. It was in fact expertise in the use of psychological tests that first identified the counselor and later of course, the counseling psychologist, as a key player in the processes of educational and vocational guidance. It is not too much to say that without psychological tests to administer and interpret, there would have been no counseling psychologists.

Trait-and-factor psychology was quite a different entity from the other basic approaches to psychology spawned in the formative years of the field. It was not a separate or unique theory of human development or dysfunction, such as psychoanalysis and all of its myriad derivatives. It was not even a clearly defined "school" or approach to the science like "structuralism," "functionalism," or "behaviorism."

## The Basis of Trait-and-Factor Counseling

In point of fact, trait-and-factor psychology is not easy to define. Even E. G. Williamson, considered an arch-proponent of the trait-and-factor approach and what was loosely termed the Minnesota Point of View, was hard-pressed to provide a clear or concise definition (Williamson, 1965). Stripped of excess verbiage, the view essentially assumes that individual human beings contain within themselves behavior potentials or predispositions that when carefully measured allow accurate and useful predictions to be made about the individual's future success and satisfaction in a wide variety of situations, most notably in educational and vocational activities.

From this basic assumption, the implication is that information about these predispositions or traits will be helpful to individuals in devising plans and making decisions about their vocational and educational futures. As the fields of interest measurement and later personality measurement developed, this point of view was extended beyond aptitudes to include other traits and tendencies, and, indeed, to include predictions about success, satisfaction, and survival in a variety of situations beyond the educational and vocational realms.

A key element in the whole definition is the nature of psychological traits. As applied psychology developed, the scope of "Traits" went far beyond the Darwinian definition. In 1931, Gordon Allport set forth a list of criteria with which to determine if a specific sample of behavior constituted a "trait." According to Allport (1931, p. 368) a trait:

1. has more than a normative existence, that is a name;
2. is more generalized than a habit;
3. serves to *determine* behavior;
4. may be identified and measured empirically;
5. is relatively independent of other traits;
6. is not solely a product of moral or social judgment;

7. may be seen either within an individual or in how it is distributed in a population.

Clearly, a trait is seen to exist inside an individual and to determine behavior consistent with its predisposition across a variety of situations, and to persist over time.

The concepts of trait psychology are in contradiction to either the "empty organism" view of radical behaviorism, that searched for the causes of behavior in external reinforcement, or the less extreme social learning view, that sets the causes of behavior in patterns of socialization, habits, or customs.

Some 35 years later, Allport (1966) reiterated his view of the reality of traits in what he called heuristic realism. This position:

> holds that the person who confronts us possesses inside his skin general-ized action tendencies (or traits) and that it is our job to discover what they are. (p. 3)

As psychological measurement revealed that traits were often complex, consisting of more than single tendencies, or measured by clusters of items, the concept of factors was added. For more than a century, the questions of the existence, nature, and significance of trait concepts has been debated. Since traits are seen to exist inside the individual, they can never be directly observed. They must always be inferred from samples of behavior. Psychological tests and inventories are devices for making observations that allow trait inferences to be made and presumably checked against other behavior. The concepts of reliability and validity are measures of the consistency and accuracy with which this is accomplished.

In terms of counseling, we can extend Allport's definition of "heuristic realism" to say that clients have within them action tendencies that are partially, at least, determinants of their future success and satisfaction, and that it is our job as counselors to discover those tendencies in order to help the client better to understand self, develop full potentials, and achieve a degree of personal satisfaction and happiness.

In terms of this definition, probably almost all counseling psychologists are to some extent trait-and-factor psychologists. The importance given to this kind of activity of course varies widely across counselors.

The emphasis of trait-and-factor psychology has always been practical, specific, and empirical, and was usually bereft of high-flown speculations about the human condition. The earliest practitioners were heavily influenced by Darwin and evolutionary biology, as we have seen. In actuality, however, the utilization of tests and test results in counseling has little to do with philosophical orientation.

One of the oddities about the history of differential psychology is that its first and most sophisticated contributions were essentially methodological ones rather than theoretical and substantive. Galton and his colleagues, such as Karl Pearson and Charles Spearman, developed the mathematical and statistical foundations for studying large-scale arrays of data. The principles of correlational and factor analysis were laid down long before any accompanying theoretical framework other than Darwinian biology had provided coherent sets of questions to which they could be addressed.

Perhaps the most enduring legacy of the trait-and-factor approach has been the sophisticated quantitative and statistical methodology that it has bequeathed to modern counseling psychology (Dawis, 1992). The present methodological sophistication of research in counseling psychology is very largely a legacy from the trait-and-factor approach. That methodology was based on a linear, orderly, and almost Newtonian view of the world and of human behavior which has sometimes limited the scope and creativity of research in the field. At times, unfortunately, these methods have seemed to provide a set of powerful and complex methodological approaches for which there were few equally sophisticated questions.

## THE SEARCH FOR INTELLIGENCE

The first great quest of trait-and-factor psychology involved the effort to understand the nature of human cognitive functioning. We traced much of this history in Chapter 2. The upshot of this first phase of research was of course the enthronement of the IQ and what Spearman termed $g$, as the *sine qua non* of human intelligence. In America, the Stanford-Binet can be seen as the basic measure of that quantity. By the early 1930s there were already challenges to the notion of a unitary definition of intelligence (Thurstone, 1931). L. L. Thurstone extended Spearman's concept of a two-factor approach to cognitive functioning to evolve the concept of a set of separate but equal "primary mental abilities" (Thurstone, 1938). The Thurstone measures were derived from factor analysis, and The Primary Mental Abilities Test was the first factor-analytic multiple-ability test battery (Dawis, 1992). It was also the first instrument published by a new psychological publisher, Science Research Associates.

During the Great Depression, research and applications of multiple-ability approaches to differential individual assessment were done at the University of Minnesota under the direction of Donald G. Paterson. After the end of World War II the United States Employment Service built upon this work to develop the General Aptitude Test Battery with accompanying norms for specific occupations (Dvorak, 1956). This probably constituted the high water mark of the trait-and-factor approach in applied psychology.

## MEASURING INTERESTS AND PERSONALITY

At about the same time that trait-and-factor psychology was busy trying to define and quantify concepts of intelligence and special aptitudes, other psychologists were extending that approach to the measurement of vocational interests and general personality characteristics.

E. K. Strong published the Strong Vocational Interest Blank in 1927, adding a form for women in 1933. His classic work the *Vocational Interests of Men and Women* was published in 1943. Strong concluded that entry and persistence in specific occupations could be predicted from scores on interest inventories at a rate better than chance. He also concluded that vocational interests or preferences were quite stable over time. Strong established the study and measurement of vocational interests as a major aspect of vocational counseling and of counseling psychology. Strong's work and that of his successors have pointed up the stability of interest patterns across the lifespan. His method of comparing the responses of subjects to criterion groups was a major contribution.

A second line of research on interest measurement was begun by Frederick Kuder using a different methodology. Kuder published the

Kuder Preference Record in its full form in 1943. His approach was to compare subjects' scores or responses across interest areas, rather than in terms of specific occupations. Kuder's instrument has also become a standard tool in vocational counseling.

The measurement of personality characteristics began very early in the trait-and-factor era. Robert Woodworth prepared one of the first personality inventories for use during World War I. Robert Bernreuter published a personality inventory in 1931. The personality inventory that was destined to become the most famous and durable of all, the Minnesota Multiphasic Personality Inventory (MMPI), was developed in 1940 by psychologist Starke Hathaway and psychiatrist J. C. Mc-Kinley. It was published and widely used by 1943. Since that time, additional scales have been added, and the MMPI has been a standard clinical tool in all of the helping professions. The MMPI utilizes a comparison method somewhat similar to Strong's method in comparing subjects' scores with those of criterion groups with specific clinical diagnoses.

The growth of personality measurement after World War II was truly phenomenal. Factor-analytic methods were used to develop instruments such as The 16 Personality Factor Questionnaire developed by R. B. Cattell in 1950. A wide variety of personality measures exist and are extensively used in both psychological research and professional practice.

## THE TRAIT-AND-FACTOR LEGACY

The history of the trait-and-factor approach is strange indeed. For 20 years the psychometric approach both revolutionized and dominated applied psychology. Its legacy in terms of psychometric principles and test design and construction virtually permeates the science and practice of psychology today. Each year hundreds of new psychometric instruments are designed for research purposes. Dawis (1992) estimated that more than 70 such instruments appear each year in research reports in the *Journal of Counseling Psychology* alone.

Without the technology of psychological measurement, we would simply not have the field of psychology in anything that resembles its present form. As a technology, measurement has made steady and often dramatic progress over the 100-year history of scientific psychology.

Despite this record of positive contributions and continuous progress, the trait-and-factor approach seems to have fallen from grace, at least in the field of counseling psychology. Today, the term "assessment" has all but replaced "diagnosis" or "appraisal" as a term to denote the effort to understand clients. A 1991 survey of counseling psychology training programs (May & Scott, 1991) indicated that while training in the use of psychometric instruments is required in virtually all programs, the most widely used assessment procedure in internship settings is the clinical interview. The current emphasis in counseling psychology seems to be on "qualitative assessment" (Goldman, 1990). People like Munsterberg, Terman, and Paterson must be spinning in their graves!

## THE NATURE-NURTURE CONTROVERSY

As we noted in Chapter 2, the controversy about the origin of intellectual characteristics has been present in the field of psychology from the very beginning. Indeed, as we saw, it was Francis Galton, himself, who coined the phrase "nature vs. nurture" to describe the debate.

In the United States, most of the pioneer mental testers were, like Galton, firmly convinced that what they were measuring was an innate, fixed, and unitary trait in the Darwinian sense, and that it was genetically transmitted. As Terman's work in building the Stanford-Binet test was widely acclaimed and used, the nature-nurture controversy quickly became more heated.

The first collision between the hereditarian position regarding IQ testing and the environmental or developmental view was in the form of a more or less public debate between Lewis Terman and journalist Walter Lippmann. Lippmann had been a protégé of the old muckraker Lincoln Steffens, who had, in fact, studied psychology with Wundt in Leipzig.

Lippmann was deeply concerned and incensed about what seemed to be the social and political implications of IQ testing. After the public furor over Brigham's interpretation of the Alpha and Beta test results, and Yerkes' intrusion into the immigration debate that we noted earlier, Lippmann proceeded to denounce IQ testing in general and Terman's claims about the Stanford-Binet test in particular.

In the early 1920s Lippmann published articles in the *New Republic* and *Century* magazines pointing to discrepancies in results obtained with the Army intelligence tests and those produced with the Stanford-Binet. Essentially, he suggested that results obtained from intelligence tests were more a function of the particular test than of the characteristics of the people being tested. He sharply challenged the notion that Terman or the other mental testers were actually measuring anything that could accurately be termed "intelligence." As we noted earlier, this was not greatly different from the position taken much earlier by Alfred Binet.

Lippmann attacked the claims of Terman and others that their tests measured any innate or genetically endowed characteristics. He pointed to the dangers of categorizing people, and was particularly concerned about the effects of labeling schoolchildren within IQ categories.

Lewis Terman quickly reacted to these criticisms (Block & Dworkin, 1976). He immediately suggested that Lippmann as a journalist should not have the effrontery to criticize the work of scientists. Terman attempted to heap scorn on the writer, and only defended his scientific claims in very general terms (Shurkin, 1992). Terman did admit that tests could not measure "pure intelligence," but rather, assessed intellectual ability and other factors. Terman's defense of testing was published in the *New Republic* and he was widely supported by others of the "mental testers." A notable exception was John Dewey, who echoed Lippmann's concerns about the dangers of categorizing and labeling schoolchildren.

Dewey dismissed the claims of the mental testers in very strong terms. The idea of abstract, universal superiority and inferiority was for him an absurdity that masqueraded under the title of science. He deplored any effort to use IQ tests to classify students or assign people to vocations as undemocratic as well as unscientific.

Terman quickly got the worst of this exchange in the journalistic arena, and attributed his defeat to the ignorance of the general population regarding scientific matters. Actually, a journalistic debate of this kind between future Pulitzer Prize-winning columnist Lippmann and Lewis Terman was tantamount to a battle of literary wits with an unarmed man.

Terman soon became engaged in another debate over the meaning of IQ scores, this time within the field of psychology. The next antagonist was George G. Stoddard, the Director of the Child Welfare Research Station at the University of Iowa, one of the pioneering and most highly respected centers for research in child psychology.

The battleground this time was in a scientific publication, the 1928 yearbook of the National Society for the Study of Education (NSSE). In 1928 Terman had chaired the *NSSE Yearbook* Committee and had focused upon the nature-nurture debate. The opposing points of view were aired in a set of scholarly articles that allowed each side to claim victory, and, as is usual in this kind of exercise, changed no minds.

The controversy simmered on for the next decade with the gradual formation of two opposing camps, each headquartered in different universities, and each producing a steady stream of totally contradictory research findings and conclusions.

The controversy flared up again when George Stoddard chaired the same *NSSE Yearbook* Committee in 1938. Stoddard invited Terman to reopen the formal debate. This time Stoddard had data that he believed directly discredited Terman's hereditarian position of an innate, fixed, and unitary intelligence. A longitudinal study by Beth Wellman had found not only that the early IQ scores of children were not fixed, but that they may actually increase with education, a finding that has since been replicated many times and is today generally accepted. The Iowa results suggested that the IQ scores of children could be changed markedly by the nature and quality of the environment in which they lived and went to school.

Terman took the publication of the Iowa study and the conclusions drawn from it as a direct attack on his career and reputation (Shurkin, 1992). He sent forth a contingent of students, former students, and colleagues to do battle with the Iowa environmentalists. Florence Goodenough, once a member of the original Stanford Testing team and a respected psychologist at Minnesota, went to meetings about the proposed yearbook. Quinn McNemar, another former Terman student, was commissioned to reanalyze the Iowa data and did in fact uncover a number of errors and inconsistencies.

Finally, Terman and Stoddard engaged in an open debate at a meeting held at Stanford University in July 1939. Terman apparently arranged the meeting so that he had a full hour to speak while Stoddard had only 10 minutes to respond. Terman's speech was loaded with sarcasm and vindictiveness, to the extent, according to Stoddard, of making faces when he mentioned any of the Iowa psychologists (Shurkin, 1992).

The debate, or more accurately the public brawl, went on for the next several years in a whole series of public meetings, conferences, and publications. Terman clearly waged the battle in an acrimonious and vindictive way. He misrepresented the opposing views shamelessly (Shurkin, 1992). Indeed, the position taken by Wellman had been simply that intelligence was a product of genetic and environmental interaction, a view that is almost universally accepted today.

As one views the emotional intensity with which the whole nature-nurture debate was played out in the 1920s and 30s, it is difficult to reject the proposition that the whole controversy was not scientific at all. It seems probable instead that it was the collision of two totally incompatible worldviews, each with conflicting social and political philosophies. The effects of this kind of controversy on public perceptions of psychology in general, and on psychological testing in particular, were obviously negative.

## PSYCHOLOGY AND SOCIAL DARWINISM

In Chapter 1, we pointed out that Social Darwinism represented one of the views of the human condition that energized the debate over social justice in the United States at the turn of the twentieth century. The Progressive Movement was very largely organized in opposition to Social Darwinism and its view of the survival of the fittest—or, in reality, the most ruthlessly competitive.

It is difficult today to imagine the intellectual upheaval produced by Darwin's ideas during the latter years of the nineteenth century. In the 30 years that followed the publication of *The Origin of Species* in 1859, the influence of Darwin reached into almost every branch of the life sciences. The conflict between Darwin's ideas and the teachings of organized religion and conventional philosophies produced an epidemic of crises of conscience for thinkers everywhere.

Nowhere were Darwin's ideas more cataclysmic than in the newborn field of psychology as it struggled to burst out of the cocoon of traditional philosophy. For many of the new "scientific psychologists," Darwinism seemed to herald the revolution which would at last bring to bear the insights of science on human affairs. It is perhaps not surprising that Darwinism seemed attractive to many of the pioneers of American psychology. What is surprising was the uncritical and untempered reception that they gave to its supposed political and social implications.

As we saw, G. Stanley Hall was probably the most prestigious and influential American psychologist at the turn of the twentieth century. Hall was such a devotee of Darwinian ideas that he liked to call himself the "Darwin of the Mind." Hall's social and political views were profoundly pessimistic in terms of his lack of confidence in the intellectual capabilities of the average human being. Hall distrusted not only the ability of people, but also individualism and democracy themselves.

Grinder and Strickland (1963) summed up Hall's social views in this way:

> [T]he most serious evil of democracy as he saw it was its encouragement of concern for individuals. Hall argued that "pity" must not be extended to the downtrodden "because by aiding them to survive it interferes with the process of wholesome natural selection by which all that is best has hitherto been developed." (p. 392)

It was predominantly G. Stanley Hall's students, people like Goddard, Terman, and Kuhlman, who spread the technology and gospel of mental testing across the land. Ironically, however it was also John Dewey, who had been a student of Hall's at John Hopkins, who provided the most eloquent opposition within psychology to the extravagant claims of the mental testers.

The social and political ideas that pervaded the mental testing movement during the 1920s and 1930s were not the product of any single thinker or group of thinkers inside or outside of psychology. These ideas were firmly linked with the events and ideas that energized American society after World War I. Progressivism as a social and political force in American life was a casualty along with the 112,000 young Americans who died in the "War to End All Wars." As we noted earlier, cynicism, materialism, and hedonism were the order of the decade as America returned to "normalcy." Harding's successor, the dour New Englander Calvin Coolidge, periodically awoke from his afternoon naps in the White House to proclaim that "the business of America is business."

Applied psychology, with its technology of testing and its comforting reaffirmation of the presumed superiority of white, middle-class, Protestant males, was the darling of "Big Business" and a perfect reflection of the times. Whether in selling corn flakes or selecting college students, applied psychology with its technology of testing was a symbol of American confidence and competence. Mental testers and efficiency experts seemed to epitomize the triumph of American know-how. How could one fail to have confidence in the future (and stock) of enterprises operated on principles of scientific management and psychometric selection? The downside of the Roaring Twenties seemed to receive little attention in a country with an urge to dance and a thirst for bathtub gin.

The United States at the end of the 1920s was a study in contrasts and contradictions. It was a nation of tremendous cultural, economic, and social diversity that saw itself as one nation, united and indivisible through the magic of the "melting pot." It contained the richest cities in the world and millions of disease-ridden and malnourished subsistence farmers. It proclaimed itself a land of freedom, tolerance, and opportunity—and fostered a fiercely defended system of racial segregation and officially sanctioned bigotry (Barone, 1990).

As America stood poised on the brink of the Great Depression, the overriding and pervasive theme of its history was what it had been from the very beginning. The burning and insoluble question was and still is who is really an American? Disagreement over what it means to be an American had sparked countless Indian Wars, a great Civil War, and had pitted North against South, Black against White, immigrant against pioneer, Protestant against Catholic against Jew, and Anglo against Hispanic. The technology of mental testing was a tiny part of the whole patchwork of privilege and prejudice that riddled the society.

Beginning in 1933, Roosevelt's New Deal ushered in not only a change in economic policies, but a major shift in the values and priorities in American society. Over the next 8 years, America limped slowly and unsteadily out of the Depression until World War again convulsed the nation. As America coped with the Great Depression and entered World War II, profound changes in social values and perceptions of social problems were accelerated. The ultimate horror of the Holocaust revealed the terrible consequences of bigotry and the insanity behind the concept of a "Master Race."

The changing social climate of the postwar years brought desegregation in education and the Women's Movement, as well as the Civil Rights struggle, and brought back in the 1960s an era and spirit of reform reminiscent of the heady days of the Progressive Era. Trait-and-factor psychology and the technology of mental testing that it had brought to dominance in applied psychology were gradually pushed into the background in favor of ideas and approaches that were more compatible with the spirit of the times.

## THE DECLINE AND FALL OF THE MENTAL TESTING MOVEMENT

By the mid-1950s the "tyranny of testing," as its critics liked to call the mental testing movement, had clearly fallen into disrepute and was passing into relative obscurity as a dominant force in applied psychology and education. Throughout the 1960s and 1970s, a long series of court decisions had sharply circumscribed the use of psychological tests for both educational placement and selection of employees (Bersoff, 1981). While the courts moved in to protect the public from psychological tests and testers, it was in fact more the misuse of tests by school systems and other organizations than the nature of the tests themselves that created problems (Reschly, 1981). Also for the first time the effects of cultural differences on test scores began to be recognized and taken seriously (Miller-Jones, 1989). Test bias became a phenomenon to be studied.

Some of the decline of psychological testing was due, as we saw, to changes in the attitudes and values of the society. Some of the decline was also due to progress in the science of psychology itself.

New concepts of validity, together with a greater insistence on methodological sophistication in the construction and standardization of psychometric instruments, brought closer scrutiny to the characteristics of tests themselves (American Psychological Association, 1954). Many of the extravagant claims made by authors and publishers of tests were discredited.

By the beginning of the 1980s, nearly a century after James McKeen Cattell coined the term "mental tests," it was clear that so-called intelligence tests predicted very little relevant behavior outside of the school and college environment (Bersoff, 1973). As David McClelland (1973) put it, "The games people are required to play on aptitude tests are similar to the games teachers require in classrooms" (p. 1). A careful review of some 35 major research studies done after 1950 (Samson, Graue, Weinstein, & Walberg, 1984) found that the mean correlation between even the combination of grades *and* test scores predicted only about 2.5% of the variance on criteria of occupational success. These criteria were defined by variables such as income, career satisfaction, and performance ratings of effectiveness. When test scores on the ACE college aptitude test alone were used, the mean correlation was statistically non-significant at .02. As McClelland (1973) pointed out, the vast majority of validity studies for so-called intelligence tests had focused on predicting grades from test scores, when neither had much relationship to success in the world outside of schools. These findings were consistent with those studies done as early as 1902.

After all of the claims, counterclaims, invective, and denunciations that had surrounded a century of efforts to define and quantify human intelligence, it had become clear that the whole controversy was much ado about very little. The old-style IQ-worshipping mental testers departed center stage, not with a bang, but with a whimper.

## A BORN AGAIN DIFFERENTIAL PSYCHOLOGY

What was left of the mental testing establishment has clearly been on the defensive over the past 40 years. Lewis Terman (1954), himself, shortly before his death in 1956, had written what was virtually an epitaph for himself and for the early years of trait-and-factor psychology. He ignored the years of controversy over the nature-nurture issue and wrote of the quest to identify and understand exceptional talent. His longitudinal study of the gifted was clearly the crowning achievement of trait-and-factor psychology.

Nearly 15 years after Terman's death, Lee Cronbach (1970), who was himself one of Terman's "gifted kids," defended the testing move-

**Figure 6.1    Lewis M. Terman**

ment as an important force in the creation of opportunity in American Society. Clearly, the *zeitgeist* had changed and a new "born-again" generation of differential psychologists had begun to emerge.

The 1970s and '80s saw a veritable procession of articles contributed by one after another of the leaders and luminaries of the "new psychology of individual differences." Many of these prefaced their new ideas with faint apologies for the sins of the past, but most focused upon new definitions and concepts of aptitudes and tests themselves. Together, these provided the substance for a new psychology of individual differences.

Along with the revised concepts came a new "social context" for testing that has attempted to put testing into the service of equal opportunity and greater social justice (Gordon & Terrell, 1981; Holtzman, 1970). The most important aspects of this new approach were the redefinition of crucial concepts of traits, particularly aptitudes and specifically of intelligence.

## The New Aptitudes

The new definitions of intelligence were much broader and more flexible than the old concepts of Spearman's *g* or Stanford-Binet IQ. Wesman (1968) declared that intelligence is an attribute, not an entity lurking within the individual. He defined that attribute broadly, if vaguely, as the sum total of the learning experiences of the individual. David Wechsler (1975), author of the other standard measure of intelligence, denied that intelligence is a quality of mind, and instead defined it as an aspect of behavior. Intelligence, according to Wechsler, is not a singular trait or ability and must be seen as an overall or global capacity, and is not even entirely a function of cognition. It may in fact involve emotion and motivation as well as cognition: "Intelligence is the capacity for an individual to understand the world about him and his resourcefulness to cope with its challenges" (p. 139). Clearly, Wechsler's definition goes far beyond cognition to encompass general human effectiveness. Clearly, also, it goes far beyond what is measured in any single intelligence test.

These much broader and more flexible views of intelligence and how it develops were echoed by numerous others as the new psychology of individual differences emerged (Carroll & Horn, 1981; Frederiksen, 1986; Glaser, 1981). Ironically, the new concepts of intelligence had come full circle to embrace the ideas first formulated by Alfred Binet at the beginning of the century.

As we noted earlier, the concept of a multifaceted intellect had been pioneered by L. L. and Thelma Thurstone as early as 1938. Their work on basic factors in intellectual performance was carried on by J. P. Guilford (1968). Guilford, through factor analysis, identified as many as 120 relatively independent or unique abilities that define what he termed the "structure of intellect." Guilford proposed classifying these in terms of the kinds of information processing involved, the kinds of content involved and the products arrived at.

More importantly, Guilford and the other factor analysts lent empirical support to the new broader, more flexible concepts of intelligence. According to Guilford (1968)

> It would be best to regard each intellectual ability of a person as a somewhat generalized *skill* that has *developed* through the circumstances of experience, *within a certain culture* and that can be devel-

oped by means of the right kind of exercise. There may be limits to abilities set by heredity, but it is probably safe to say that very rarely does an individual really test those limits. (p. 610) (italics added)

Clearly, these definitions represent a final repudiation of the original trait-and-factor approach. The broadening of our concepts of intelligence has continued unabated over the past 30 years. Howard Gardner (1983) promulgated a "theory of multiple intelligences" that posits the existence of at least six distinct types of intelligence-linguistic, musical, logical-mathematical, spatial, bodily-kinesthetic, and personal. Clearly, the nature of what we are willing to call intelligence resides primarily in the eye of the beholder. Even more recently, Goleman (1995) has proposed the concept of "emotional intelligence." The new breed of differential psychologists have even had the common sense to suggest that we start testing for common sense (Sternberg, Wagner, Williams, & Horvath, 1995). Even Alfred Binet might well be overwhelmed by the ways in which his speculations about the nature of intelligence have been expanded.

As one looks back over the history of the trait-and-factor approach, with its technology of mental testing, it seems clear that the sources of controversy and perhaps the seeds of its eventual decline were simple. They were planted by the uncritical acceptance of Galton's notion of a fixed, unitary, and genetically based intelligence, eventually designated as the IQ, and by the emotionally charged and generally unscientific collision of intransigent social attitudes and worldviews that were touched off by the nature-nurture debate.

If we accept, for example, Guilford's definition given above, there seems to be little scientific or practical basis for much of the conflict and controversy that has fulminated for nearly a century. The nature-nurture controversy has been like a smoldering volcano that erupts every few years to spew the ashes of confusion and contradiction across the landscape. The latest eruption occasioned by Herrnstein and Murray's *The Bell Curve* (1994) was simply déjà vu all over again.

Despite all of the controversy surrounding aptitude tests, a survey of psychologists and educators considered specialists in psychometrics (Snyderman & Rothman, 1987) showed that such psychologists overwhelmingly believe that tests can tap most of the important aspects of intelligence; that such tests are, however, racially and socio-economically biased; that they are limited by the confounding effects of nonintellectual factors on performance; and that they are frequently misused and misinterpreted. Despite these limitations, they consider such tests useful in many situations.

What has kept the testing controversy so heated for so long has not so much been disagreement about the sources and extent of individual differences in intellectual functioning, but rather sharp disagreements about the supposed implications of such differences in terms of social, economic, and political issues.

Interestingly, other areas of differential psychology dealing with nonintellectual aspects of personality have proceeded largely unimpeded by controversy to define differences; for example, in basic personality patterns and in mood and emotional responsiveness. Such research has suggested the existence of a basic personality trait structure that applies to all people, across all cultures (McCrae & Costa, 1997). Other research has pointed to strong genetic effects on feelings of well-being or personal happiness (Lykken & Tellegen, 1996). Apparently, human beings are much less threatened by the thought that their basic personality patterns are circumscribed, or that their chances for happiness are genetically determined, than by attempts to sort out the sources, nature, and distribution of what we call intelligence.

## COUNSELING PSYCHOLOGY AND THE DECLINE OF THE TRAIT-AND-FACTOR MODEL

It was the trait-and-factor model that had provided the final piece in the Parsonian pattern of vocational counseling. Knowledge about occupations, coupled with knowledge about self, that is, knowledge about measured traits, provided the essential ingredients. True reasoning about the two was left in the hands of the counselor, with varying degrees of participation and responsibility assigned to the client.

The Parsonian model seemed to have worked well for some 50 years. Most of the Depression-era counseling of the unemployed, and the Veterans Administration's counseling programs that greeted the returning GIs, were clearly based on a slightly updated version of the 1909 Parsonian blueprint. The counselor, slowly emerging from the cocoon of vocational guidance to become a counseling psychologist, was armed with the *Dictionary of Occupational Titles* in one hand and Buros' *Mental Measurement Yearbook* in the other.

New tests were developed, published, and used in bewildering profusion. The Bennett Mechanical, The O'Connor Finger and Tweezer Dexterity, the Purdue Pegboard, The Minnesota Clerical and the Minnesota Paper Form Board, along with a dozen more, were standard equipment in the vocational counselor's arsenal. Patients in a VA hospital referred for vocational counseling often faced a 4- or 5-hour barrage of psychological tests before they had a chance really to talk with a counselor. For many, the Battle of the Bulge must have seemed like a cakewalk in comparison. The arrival of the General Aptitude Test Battery with its accompanying catalogue of Worker Trait Requirements was hailed as a marvelous accomplishment that put all the tests in one yawn-inducing basket.

Ironically, it was not the slowly dawning realization that most of the test scores predicted little more than continuing profits for the test publishers that sparked the decline of aptitude testing in counseling. The question to test or not to test had become a central issue in the burgeoning directive vs. nondirective counseling debate. Aptitude testing came to be seen as part and parcel of the directive approach and unbecoming to a truly client-centered counselor. Various expedients, such as having the clients choose the tests to be taken, or involving the client fully in test interpretation, were urged, to little avail. Counseling was in the process of an almost religious conversion from the worship of the IQ to the adoration of the self-concept.

Fortunately, interest inventories and even personality measures managed to survive the new orthodoxy. Since inventories supposedly have no right or wrong answers, they were apparently seen as less potentially abrasive to tender self-concepts than were tests.

The demise of "test them and tell them" counseling was in itself no great loss. The problem that its departure left, however, was nothing less than a void in the whole rationale for vocational counseling. The Parsonian model was based upon the tacit assumption that people made clear, conscious, and one-time choices that permanently defined their occupational futures. The notion was probably not really defensible even in the slower-moving economy that marked Frank Parson's abbreviated counseling career. By the 1950s, the idea was patently absurd. The post-World War II years saw kaleidoscopic changes in the world of work. Whole new industries in fields like electronics, chemistry, and air-space technologies were creating hundreds of occupations and opportunities that were literally undreamed of a few years before. Life planning was clearly by necessity becoming lifelong planning.

The expansion of opportunity for millions of women and minority members that accompanied the social changes of the 1960s similarly redefined the whole concept of both vocation and planning.

The decline of the trait-and-factor model of vocational counseling triggered a kind of feeding frenzy of criticism and condemnation of traditional vocational-educational counseling. A deluge of articles with titles like "Do We Have a Theory of Vocational Choice?" (Carkhuff, Alexik, & Anderson, 1967); "Vocational Theories: Direction to Nowhere" (Warnath, 1975), and even "Vocational Planning: The Great Swindle" (Baumgardner, 1977) seemed to sound a death knell to any and all approaches to vocational counseling. This period of disillusionment probably marked the beginning of the decline of interest and emphasis on vocational counseling that has marked the last 20 years of the evolution of counseling psychology.

## From Vocational Choice to Career Development

Not all counselors and counseling psychologists were ready to give up on vocational counseling. More moderate and constructive criticisms of the older approaches attempted to set new directions for a revised and broader view of vocational psychology. Much of this revision of thinking sought to broaden the field by considering the impact of general personality dynamics on vocational life and satisfaction.

Writers such as Thompson (1960), Samler (1961), Pritchard (1962) and Calia (1966) all sought to integrate concepts of personality development and vocational satisfaction and effectiveness.

The most influential leadership in redefining vocational counseling came from Donald Super. In 1957, Super published his *Psychology of Careers*, a landmark publication that moved from a preoccupation with vocational choice to a view of "career" as a lifelong, psychologically integrated pattern of aspiration, compromise, and synthesis that represented an important aspect of total lifespan development. Borow (1959) proposed that the scientific infrastructure for vocational counseling lay not in a trait-and-factor model of differential psychology, but instead was rooted in developmental psychology, with its newfound emphasis on lifespan personality development.

**Figure 6.2    Donald Super**

The new approach to differential psychology and vocational behavior has set in motion several lines of research that have helped to move forward career counseling. The work of John Holland that began in the 1950s as a new theory of vocational choice (Holland, 1959) set in motion a 40-year line of inquiry that is probably the most impressive empirical product to come out of counseling psychology. Holland's matching model of personality characteristics with vocational environments has demonstrated that the individual differences tradition is still alive and well in counseling psychology. Super's Career Patterns studies and Lofquist and Dawis's line of research on work adjustment are similar examples of research that has bridged the gap between trait-and-factor psychology and career development.

In Chapter 7 we will examine the legacy of the "Developmental Tradition" and in the process examine the ascendancy of concepts of career development.

## REFERENCES

Allport, G. (1931). What is a trait of personality? *Journal of Abnormal Psychology, 25,* 368–373.

Allport, G. (1966). Traits revisited. *American Psychologist, 21,* 1–10.

American Psychological Association. (1954). *Technical recommendations for psychological tests and diagnostic techniques.* Washington, DC: Author.

Aubrey, R. F. (1977). Historical development of guidance and counseling and implications for the future. *Personnel and Guidance Journal, 56,* 288–296.

Barone, M. (1990). *Our country: The shaping of America from Roosevelt to Reagan.* New York: The Free Press.

Baumgardner, S. R. (1977). Vocational planning: The great swindle. *Personnel and Guidance Journal, 55,* 17–24.

Bersoff, D. M. (1973). Silk purses into sow's ears: The decline of psychological testing and a suggestion for its redemption. *American Psychologist, 28,* 892–899.

Bersoff, D. M. (1981). Testing and the law. *American Psychologist, 36,* 1047–1056.

Block, N. J., & Dworkin, G. (1976). Heritability and inequality. In N. J. Block & G. Dworkin (Eds.), *The IQ controversy* (pp. 410–540). New York: Pantheon Books.

Borow, H. (1959). Modern perspectives in personnel research. *N.S.S.E. Yearbook, 58,* 210–230.

Calia, V. F. (1966). Vocational guidance: After the fall. *Personnel and Guidance Journal, 45,* 320–327.

Carkhuff, R., Alexik, M., & Anderson, S. (1967). Do we have a theory of vocational choice? *Personnel and Guidance Journal, 46,* 335–345.

Carroll, J. B., & Horn, J. L. (1981). On the scientific basis of ability testing. *American Psychologist, 36,* 1012–1020.

Cronbach, L. J. (1970). Mental tests and the creation of opportunity. *Proceedings of the American Philosophical Society, 114,* 480–487.

Dawis, R. (1992). The individual differences tradition in counseling psychology. *Journal of Counseling Psychology, 39,* 7–19.

Dvorak, B. (1956). The General Aptitude Test Battery. *Personnel and Guidance Journal, 35,* 145–152.

Frederiksen, N. (1986). Toward a broader conception of human intelligence. *American Psychologist, 41,* 445–452.

Gardner, H. (1983). *Frames of mind.* New York: Basic Books.

Glaser, R. (1981). The future of testing. *American Psychologist, 36,* 923–936.

Goldman, L. (1990). Qualitative assessment. *The Counseling Psychologist, 18,* 205–213.

Goleman, D. (1995). *Emotional intelligence.* New York: Bantam.

Gordon, E. W., & Terrell, M. D. (1981). The changed social context of testing. *American Psychologist, 36,* 1167–1171.

Grinder, R. E., & Strickland, C. E. (1963). G. Stanley Hall and the social significance of adolescence. *Teachers College Record, 64,* 390–399.

Guilford, J. P. (1968). Intelligence has three facets. *Science, 160,* 615–620.

Herrnstein, R. J., & Murray, C. (1994). *The bell curve: Intelligence and class structure in America.* New York: Free Press.

Holland, J (1959). A theory of vocational choice. *Journal of Counseling Psychology, 6,* 35–43.

Holtzman, W. H. (1970). The changing world of mental measurement and its social significance. *American Psychologist, 85,* 546–553.

Lykken, D., & Tellegen, A. (1996). Happiness is a stochastic phenomenon. *Psychological Science, 7,* 186–189.

May, T. M., & Scott, K. J. (1991). Assessment in counseling psychology: Do we practice what we teach? *The Counseling Psychologist, 19,* 396–413.

McClelland, D. C. (1973). Testing for competence rather than for intelligence. *American Psychologist, 28,* 1–14.

McCrae, R. R., & Costa, P. T., Jr. (1997). Personality trait structure as a human universal. *American Psychologist, 52,* 509–516.

Meara, N. (1990). Presidential address. *The Counseling Psychologist, 17,* 144–167.

Miller-Jones, D. (1989). Culture and testing. *American Psychologist, 44,* 360–366.

Napoli, D. S. (1981). *Architects of adjustment: The history of the psychological profession in the United States.* Port Washington, NY: Kennikat Press.

O'Donnell, J. M. (1985). *The origins of behaviorism.* New York: New York University Press.

Pritchard, D. H. (1962). The occupational exploration process. *Personnel and Guidance Journal, 40,* 674–680.

Reschly, D. J. (1981). Psychological testing in educational classification and placement. *American Psychologist, 36,* 1094–1102.

Samler, J. (1961). Psycho-social aspects of work: A critique of occupational information. *Personnel and Guidance Journal, 39,* 458–465.

Samson, G. E., Graue, M. E., Weinstein, T., & Walberg, H. J. (1984). Academic and occupational performance: A quantitative analysis. *American Educational Research Journal, 21,* 311–321.

Shurkin, J. N. (1992). *Terman's kids.* Boston: Little, Brown.

Snyderman, M., & Rothman, S. (1987). Survey of expert opinion on intelligence and aptitude testing. *American Psychologist, 42,* 137–144.

Sternberg, R. J., Wagner, R. K., Williams, W. M., & Horvath, J. A. (1995). Testing common sense. *American Psychologist, 50,* 912–927.

Strong, E. K. (1943). *The vocational interests of men and women.* Stanford, CA: Stanford University Press.

Super, D. (1957). *The psychology of careers.* New York: Harper.

Terman, L. M. (1954). The discovery and encouragement of exceptional talent. *American Psychologist, 9,* 221–230.

Thompson, A. S. (1960). Personality dynamics and vocational counseling. *Personnel and Guidance Journal, 38,* 350–357.

Thurstone, L. L. (1931). Multiple factor analysis. *Psychological Review, 38,* 406–427.

Thurstone, L. L. (1938). Primary mental abilities. *Psychometric Monographs, 1,* 1–121.

Warnath, C. F. (1975). Vocational theories: Directions to nowhere. *Personnel and Guidance Journal, 53,* 422–428.

Wechsler, D. (1975). Intelligence defined and undefined: A relativistic appraisal. *American Psychologist, 30,* 135–139.

Wesman, A. G. (1968). Intelligent testing. *American Psychologist, 23,* 267–274.

Williamson, E. G. (1965). *Vocational counseling.* New York: McGraw-Hill.

# 7

# The Developmental Tradition

> The professional goal of the counseling psychologist is to foster the
> psychological development of the individual.
>
> —APA, Division 17 (1952)

The 18th of October, 1911, was a sad day for the students and
faculty at the little elementary school in Rue Grange-aux-belles
in the then outskirts of Paris. The day was especially bitter for
Principal Vaney, for he had lost a dear friend and colleague. Together,
some 6 years before, they had founded in the school the Laboratory
of Experimental Pedagogy. Grange aux-belles was the first laboratory
school in Europe and one of the first in the world. Arguably, it can
be seen as the birthplace of experimental school psychology.

The laboratory was closely affiliated with the "Free Society for the
Psychological Study of Children," an association of teachers, school
administrators and psychologists devoted to the study of education
and child development. *La Societé*, as it was called, had lost its guiding
light and driving force. A plain, black framed announcement appeared
in the *Bulletin* of the *Societé* saying simply that its president had
died of cerebral apoplexy at the age of 54. The following year the
Society honored its fallen leader by changing its name to the *Societé
Alfred Binet*.

Alfred Binet was clearly France's greatest psychologist, yet he died
frustrated and bitter at the lack of recognition that he had received
in his own country. He was passed over three times for appointment
to a chair at the Sorbonne. Binet was a proud, prickly and perfectionistic man who savagely criticized those with whom he disagreed. He

**177**

was a failure at political gamesmanship and academic intrigue. Ironically, he has been remembered and honored abroad as the architect of the intelligence test and of the IQ. Binet, as we saw earlier, never accepted the concept of "mental age" or the IQ as useful indices of intelligence (Wolf, 1973).

## DISCOVERING THE DEVELOPING MIND

Binet's view of intellectual functioning was broader, deeper, and more complex than those of the psychologists who came before him. As his colleague Theodore Simon remarked, Binet had sought to penetrate the human mind, to analyze its very wellsprings, and to understand it as a complete entity. Perhaps he followed an impossible dream. Certainly the gargantuan task that Binet had set for himself was barely begun when his life came to an end. Alfred Binet had succeeded, however, in pointing the way to a view of human intelligence that focused on higher-level functions and those that developed out of interaction with the environment.

Binet approached a "constructivist" position in psychology, but stopped just short of seeing the mind as creating its own reality. He defined intelligence in these terms:

> intelligence is before all a process of knowing that is directed toward the external world, that works to reconstruct it in its entirety, by means of the little fragments that are given to us. (Quoted in Wolf, 1973, p. 205)

For Binet, intelligence was expressed in four essential functions: comprehension; inventiveness, or creativity; direction, or focus; and criticism. Binet's true work and pioneering vision was carried on not by Lewis Terman and the other test-makers, who perpetuated his name, but by another very different line of research and theory that ironically also flowed out of the little school in Rue Grange-aux-belles.

Less than 3 years after Alfred Binet's untimely death, Europe descended into the maelstrom of madness called World War I. The tragedy of the Great War pushed Binet's dream of understanding the human intellect far into the background. Millions of men died in the blood-soaked mud of Flanders, the horrors of mustard gas, phosphorus shells, and thousand-gun artillery barrages took precedence over the pursuits of academia. A new term, "shell shock," entered the lexicon of psychological disabilities and Sigmund Freud coined the term "thanatos" to darken his already somber view of the human condition.

A few months after the end of the war, Theodore Simon returned to Rue Grange-aux-belles to launch a project aimed at translating and restandardizing a set of new intelligence tests developed by Cyril Burt in Great Britain. The supply of young French psychologist to survive the war was thin, indeed. Simon settled upon a 25-year-old Swiss botanist, zoologist, amateur philosopher, and want-to-be psychologist to revitalize Binet's pedagogical laboratory at Rue Granges-aux-belles. The young man who accepted his first position in Binet's old laboratory was named Jean Piaget.

Piaget was born in 1896 in Neuchatel, Switzerland. He was the son of an academic who wrote prolifically about medieval literature and history. His mother was apparently emotionally disturbed; family life was often tumultuous and upsetting. As a child, Piaget identified with his father and tended to retreat into study and writing. Later in his life, when asked about his tremendous productivity as a scholar, Piaget remarked that he was essentially a worrier for whom only work could provide relief (Fancher, 1990).

Piaget's first scientific fascination was with birds. In childhood he produced a small handwritten book entitled *Our Birds* and at age 10 had his first scientific article published, an essay describing a partly albino sparrow. His report appeared in a local journal of natural history.

Shortly after this, Piaget became a sort of volunteer assistant to the curator of Neuchatel's museum of natural history. Between the ages of 15 and 19 he published 21 reports and papers in assorted international journals. The readers of these journals were unaware of his age, and one offered him a job as curator of a museum in Geneva. Young Piaget had to refuse because he had 2 years of high school remaining.

Piaget was apparently an unhappy, if highly productive, adolescent. He dabbled in philosophy, was plagued by religious doubts, and had rather fragile health. At age 20 he was forced to spend a year resting and recuperating in the mountains. During this time he wrote a philosophical novel that was published, but received little acclaim.

After recovering Piaget entered a doctoral program at the University of Neuchatel and at 22 received his Ph.D. in natural history. At this tender age, already an internationally known zoologist, a published

**Figure 7.1    Jean Piaget**

novelist, and an amateur philosopher, Jean Piaget decided to study psychology.

Piaget first went to Zurich, where he studied briefly with Freud's ex-disciple, Carl Jung. There he learned a little about abnormal psychology, and a lot about the quasiscientific approaches of psychoanalysis. Seeking an approach that was somewhat more rigorous than psychoanalytic interpretations of dreams and delusions, Piaget journeyed to Paris and the Sorbonne. There, quite by chance, he encountered Theodore Simon and so began his career as a psychologist in the very laboratory left empty by the death of Alfred Binet nearly a decade before.

Piaget accepted the assignment of translating and restandardizing Burt's tests of "reasoning," although he was far from convinced that the psychometric approach was the way to understand intellectual functioning. He quickly found, however, that carefully and sensitively administering the tests to children could lead to some surprising discoveries. As Piaget administered the individualized tests, he found that he was considerably more interested in the wrong answers that his child subjects gave than in the right ones.

Piaget began to engage his subjects in conversations patterned after psychiatric interviews to find out how they arrived at their responses to test items. Out of this simple process came Piaget's revolutionary approach to the study of intellectual functioning. Once again, the schoolchildren of Rue Granges-aux-belles had helped to open a doorway to greater understanding of the human mind.

Piaget refined his technique of interrogation of children into what is called the "genetic approach" (genetic meaning developmental, not genetically determined) and launched a 60-year career that transformed developmental psychology. Most of those who had interpreted and often misinterpreted Alfred Binet's work had conceptualized the intellectual development of children as a sort of incremental process in which new knowledge and skills gradually increased in an almost additive sense. The concept of mental age, rejected by Binet, but essential to the concept of IQ seemed to capture this sort of neat linear progression nicely.

What Piaget discovered in his patient and painstaking study of children was quite different. Piaget found a pattern of development characterized by discrete stages, each of which was qualitatively different from both that which preceded and that which followed.

Piaget spent only about a year with the children of Rue Granges-aux-belles. He soon returned to Switzerland to become director of research at the J. J. Rousseau Institute in Geneva. He remained affiliated with the Institute until his death in 1980. It is somehow fitting that Piaget spent his life tirelessly studying the development of children at an institution named for Jean-Jacques Rousseau, the philosopher, reformer, and prophetic voice of developmental psychology. More that a century before Piaget's birth, Rousseau had written a treatise for teachers. In the introduction to *Emile* in 1762, Rousseau wrote these words:

> We do not know childhood. Acting on the false ideas we have of it the farther we go the farther we wander from the right path. Those who are wisest are attached to what it is important to know without considering what children are able to apprehend. *They are always looking for the man in the child, without thinking of what he was before he became a man.* J. J. Rousseau (p. 1) (italics added)

A century and a half after Rousseau wrote this complaint, Jean Piaget, more than any other psychologist, devoted his life to understanding what the child was and how he or she thought and reasoned along the thorny path to adulthood.

Besides demonstrating the existence of qualitatively different stages of thinking and reasoning in children, Piaget also expounded a very different view of how intellectual functioning developed. He believed that new ways of thinking and reasoning, that is, intelligence itself, grows out of action or active engagement with the environment. Perhaps drawing on his experience as philosopher, he was opposed to concepts of passive learning, or the belief that human beings merely copy reality. Rather, Piaget was a true "constructivist" who went beyond Binet's thinking to view knowledge as a set of transformations of reality. For Piaget, people literally choose and create knowledge out of experience. What we call knowledge is one possible way of construing the world. Knowledge, then, was seen as a system of transformations that become more and more adequate, that is, useful (Piaget, 1970). The need or drive to understand the world and to create knowledge out of experience was seen as a biological given, virtually wired into the developing organism.

Piaget's 60 years of tireless observation and voluminous publications attracted myriad students and adherents of his "genetic epistemology." He quite literally reshaped the ways in which psychologists think about childhood and intelligence.

## DEVELOPMENTAL PSYCHOLOGY IN AMERICA

The great leaps forward for developmental psychology during the early years of the twentieth century were not confined to Europe. Indeed, some of Piaget's ideas about intellectual development were actually anticipated by James Mark Baldwin. It was Baldwin, not Piaget, who first attempted a synthesis of philosophy and the life sciences by describing a stage-by-stage process of intellectual development (Broughton, 1981).

Despite his achievements, Baldwin made little permanent impact on psychology, while Piaget, who quite consciously drew upon Baldwin's work, was clearly the one who visibly and definitively changed the field of developmental psychology (Cahan, 1984). The story behind James Mark Baldwin's failure to make a lasting contribution to the field, and of his descent into disgrace and obscurity, is as strange and ironic as any that could be depicted in a tragic novel.

# The Rise and Fall of James Mark Baldwin

In the portentous summer of 1892, when the little group of visionary psychologists met in G. Stanley Hall's house in Worcester to form the APA, James Mark Baldwin was already one of the most prestigious and visible American psychologists. Along with James McKeen Cattell and Hall himself, James Mark Baldwin was one of the dominant voices in American psychology.

In 1895, 3 years after the formation of the APA, Baldwin published *Mental Development in the Child and in the Race*, a volume that helped to establish him as the prime mover in American developmental and child psychology. Baldwin was educated at Princeton, and, like many of the psychologists of his time, was trained in philosophy and theology. He had made the obligatory pilgrimage to Germany and the psychological laboratories of Berlin and Leipzig. Baldwin, like Lightner Witmer, was utterly unimpressed with Wilhelm Wundt. Unlike Witmer, however, Baldwin returned to Princeton to complete his Ph.D. Throughout his career, Baldwin steadfastly opposed the German brand of "structuralism" in experimental psychology and is considered one of the pioneers of "functionalism" in American psychology. For Baldwin, the introspective analysis of the individual mind and it supposed contents was narrow, mechanical, and both uninteresting and unconvincing. The structural approach, as he saw it, simply ignored the basic tendency of human beings to respond actively and creatively to the natural and social forces that surround them.

Baldwin began his academic career as professor of philosophy at a Presbyterian college called Lake Forest University in Illinois. He described the place as a small institution exploiting a large name (O'Donnell, 1985). Like many of the sectarian colleges of the day, it was devoted primarily to the education of candidates for the ministry and specialized in sending missionaries to China. Neither purpose appealed to either Baldwin's interests or his talents.

In 1889 Baldwin obtained the chair in metaphysics and logic at the University of Toronto. He established a psychological laboratory there and published his *Handbook of Psychology*, a volume that firmly established his reputation. By 1892, Baldwin was established in an endowed chair at Princeton and was recognized as one of the premier psychologists in America. In 1894 Baldwin cofounded the

*Psychological Review* and soon made it the most influential journal in the field. In 1897, he was elected president of the APA.

In 1903 Baldwin moved to Johns Hopkins University and revived the original laboratory founded by G. Stanley Hall and literally dismantled by Hall upon his move to the presidency of Clark University.

For the next 5 years, Baldwin occupied the very pinnacle of prestige and influence in American psychology. In 1909 Baldwin succeeded in securing funds to establish an animal laboratory. He brought in a relatively unknown professor from the University of Chicago to direct its research. The new arrival was none other than John B. Watson, the soon to become prophet and promoter of behaviorism in American psychology.

In December 1909, a few short weeks after Watson arrived at Johns Hopkins, the unthinkable happened. Baldwin abruptly entered Watson's office to announce his resignation from the University and his imminent departure from the United States. In one inexplicable moment, John B. Watson inherited both the chairmanship of the psychology department at Hopkins and the editorship of the *Psychological Review*. At the same time, the most powerful and prestigious American psychologist departed under a cloud of scandal into a self-imposed exile in Mexico and eventually Europe. Baldwin was 48 years old.

The incident that precipitated the fall from grace of James Mark Baldwin is almost impossible to comprehend in today's world. Sometime before his resignation, Baldwin had been arrested in a police raid on a Baltimore brothel. He had given a false name at his arrest and had managed to keep the entire incident quiet. A little later, Baldwin was invited to run for the Baltimore School Board. Upon his acceptance, a local newspaper reported the entire affair. On the basis of this incident, which Baldwin always claimed was misinterpreted, he was forced to resign from Johns Hopkins (Hergenhahn, 1992). Baldwin spent 5 years consulting at the National University of Mexico. He then moved to France and taught in a French university. He died in Paris in 1934, largely ignored as a significant figure in American psychology.

## G. Stanley Hall: "The Darwin of the Mind"

The individual who did succeed in placing developmental studies at the cutting edge of American psychology was G. Stanley Hall. It was

Hall who stamped the concept of adolescence with the connotation of "storm and strife" firmly into the American consciousness (Muuss, 1968). His two-volume work *Adolescence* elevated the study of the teen years from simple acceptance as a natural part of the developmental process to a period seen as both especially crucial and as particularly problematic in the attainment of full adulthood.

Hall's actual contribution to the understanding of adolescence, as opposed to his success in raising the public's consciousness of its importance, was, in fact, minimal. Like most American psychologists of his time, G. Stanley Hall, as we saw, was fascinated with and fully immersed in Darwinian biology. Hall sought to unify the precepts of evolutionary theory with the growing body of knowledge about human development. Never one afflicted with false modesty, Hall, as we noted earlier, liked to refer to himself as "The Darwin of the Mind."

Hall promulgated a rather underbaked theory in which he proclaimed that the psychological development of the individual parallels the evolutionary history of the species. He drew on some research and theory in biology that noted similarities in embryo development across species that seemed to suggest a progression through evolutionary stages. Biologist Ernst Haeckel (1896) had speculated that some kind of law or principle could be derived from this phenomenon. Haeckel coined the phrase "Ontogeny recapitulates philogeny," that is, embryological development in an individual organism passes in condensed form through stages of evolutionary development in the history of the species. Hall tried to build a theory of psychological development around this rather flimsy foundation. His "recapitulation theory" divided the life span into five developmental stages: infancy, childhood, preadolescence, adolescence, and adulthood. He described the years prior to adolescence as an extension of embryological development. More importantly, Hall identified the period of adolescence as the crucial phase in development that allowed or prevented the blossoming of the individual into a healthy full adulthood.

Hall's recapitulation theory was not long taken seriously by psychologists. Edward L. Thorndike, the pioneering educational psychologist, among others, pointed to the many flaws in Hall's theory and concluded that the influence of the theory was not due to evidence, but to the attractiveness of its rhetoric (Thorndike, 1913). None of the critical reactions by his colleagues really diminished the popular impact of Hall's emphasis on the significance of adolescence, however.

G. Stanley Hall was 60 years old in 1904 when his massive two-volume treatise appeared. Clearly, he saw this as his magnum opus, the great life's work that capped his career. The sheer sweep and scope of its subject matter was both amazing and, like Hall himself, unabashedly pretentious. The full title of the work was *Adolescence: Its Psychology and Its Relations to Physiology, Anthropology, Sociology, Sex, Crime, Religion and Education*. In 1,373 pages, G. Stanley Hall made his pronouncements and prescriptions regarding almost every conceivable aspect of childhood and adolescence. In 1907, he mercifully abridged the work into a single-volume edition to make it more accessible to parents, teachers, normal schools, and college classes. This revised edition clearly put the emphasis on child-rearing and teaching (Hilgard, 1987).

Stripped of its rhetorical and pseudoscientific trappings, Hall's message about adolescent development was a slightly updated and toned-down version of the Rousseauian approach: to let nature take its course, unfettered by strenuous or repressive efforts at socialization. It was an appropriate and timely message in an era in which childrearing and teaching was heavily colored by a "spare-the-rod" mentality.

While Hall's scholarly contribution to the understanding of psychological development was a modest one, his role as an ardent and effective advocate for child-centered causes and organizations was paramount. In Chapter 1 we noted that Hall was a speaker and organizer for early guidance conferences. Similarly, he was a driving force in forming the National Association for the Study of Childhood in 1893. Throughout his checkered career, G. Stanley Hall was a constant and effective voice in promoting both scientific study and public policy decisions relating to the welfare of children and adolescents.

## The Social Impetus for Developmental Psychology

G. Stanley Hall's writing and organizational efforts helped to make the issue of child and adolescent development a major part of the Progressive agenda. Along with Hall, John Dewey's role in the Progressive Education movement kept issues relating to child and adolescent development in the public eye. Dewey was forcefully enunciating the view that the goal of education was optimal development.

In this classic book *Democracy and Education* (1916) Dewey had spelled out the basic philosophical substance that underlaid progressive education. He put forth his views in these words:

> [E]ducation means the enterprise of supplying the conditions which insure growth. . . . The criterion for the value of school education is the extent to which it creates a desire for continued growth and supplies the means for making the desire effective in fact. (pp. 51, 53)

The result of the chorus of voices such as Hall's and Dewey's, among many others, was to focus public attention and public policy on the needs of children and adolescents. As we noted earlier, during the years between the world wars, developmental psychology was one of the most visible, productive, and well-funded areas of psychology. Many Universities established well-endowed child welfare research and service programs.

One of the first and most noteworthy of these new centers was the Iowa Child Welfare Research Station at the University of Iowa. Ironically, it was loosely patterned after another research facility, the Agricultural Research Station operating at Iowa State University. As one of its advocates put it, the Child Welfare Research Station was established in the hope that someday we might know as much about rearing children as we do about raising pigs. The Iowa station was funded by the Legislature in 1917 and soon became a model for similar facilities throughout the country.

The mental hygiene movement, mentioned previously, also helped to focus attention on the psychological problems of children and youth. Among the beneficiaries of this public awareness of and financial commitment to developmental studies and service programs were the three institutions that together provided the cradles for what became counseling psychology. Funding and support for child and adolescent programs meant funding and support for child guidance clinics, college student personnel programs, and school guidance.

As we saw earlier, medical domination of American psychoanalytic organizations effectively excluded psychologists from the direct practice of psychotherapy or treatment of mental illness. The settings in which psychological counselors could practice were precisely those devoted to the needs of developing children and adolescents.

The emphasis on development as the central thrust of school guidance remained strong even after the first flush of progressive education had passed on. Hamrin and Erickson (1939) in a text for preparing guidance counselors put it this way:

> There must be someone in the school with the responsibility, the interest, the time and capacity to "know" each child as an individual and to integrate the many influences affecting the child into a positive program of growth and development. (p. 37)

Clearly, the person to whom they referred was the school counselor.

Even after the field was divided over the directive-nondirective controversy that raged on through the 1950s and '60s, a common commitment to the goals of psychological development remained one of the few concepts in the field of counseling in which a firm consensus could be found.

E. G. Williamson (1958), writing from a background in student personnel work and a strong commitment to the directive school of thought, defined counseling in this way.

> Counseling is a peculiar type of relatively short-term human relationship between a "mentor" with some considerable experience in problems of human development and in ways of facilitating that development, on the one hand, and a learner . . . who faces . . . difficulties in his efforts to achieve . . . forward moving development. (p. 521)

Carl Rogers (1962) who spent much of his early career working in a child guidance clinic gave his endorsement to the developmental view in these terms:

> The purpose of most of the helping professions, including guidance and counseling is to enhance the personal development, the psychological growth . . . of its clients.
>
> The effectiveness of any member of the profession is most adequately measured in terms of the degree to which, in his work with his clients he achieves this goal. (p. 64)

Leona Tyler (1958) in describing the central focus of counseling psychology identified its developmental thrust in this way:

> For me the basic principle out of which . . . a synthesis grows is that of *development*. (p. 3)

Similar pronouncements were made by the founders of the Divisions of Counseling Psychology as they attempted to give definition and substance to the field (Whitely, 1984).

Ironically, many of the ideas that provided enough scope and substance to concepts of development to allow them to become the central focus of counseling psychology's emerging professional identity came out of psychoanalytic theory and the many revisions and additions that were spun off from it. Developmental psychology, as it was conceptualized in the child welfare research centers, child guidance clinics, and other facilities through the 1920s and '30s was focused almost solely upon children and adolescents. Development was seen to cease and to culminate with the arrival of adulthood. By the 1940s, a new approach to development was underway.

## LIFESPAN DEVELOPMENT

Psychoanalytic theory was, in essence, a theory of human development. Sigmund Freud posited the existence of a series of psychosexual stages of development. The basic energy that drives development was seen as sexual in nature and was derived from libido. According to Freud, the whole body was a source of sexual pleasure, but this pleasure was centered or concentrated in different parts of the anatomy at different stages of development. At any given stage, the area of the body in which sexual arousal and stimulation was focused was called the erogenous zone. The erogenous zones gave the stages of development their respective names. They were termed the oral stage, the anal stage, the phallic stage, the latency stage, and finally the genital stage.

According to this theory, the first three stages were all experienced in the first 5 years of life; the latency stage was seen to last from about age 6 to puberty; and the genital stage encompassed the rest of the lifespan (Alexander, 1948).

The most important aspect of Freud's developmental stage theory was his notion that either under- or overgratification of sexual impulses led to fixation, or an interruption of emotional development at that stage. Such fixations were seen to determine the formation of given personality types that persisted for many years into adulthood. Thus, according to Freud, adults could be classified as "oral," "anal," and "phallic" types, and so on, thus determining the basis of personality traits that originated in early development.

Much of the public criticism of psychoanalysis was based upon Freud's notions of infant and childhood sexuality that offended and scandalized Victorian views of childhood innocence and purity. Freud's views of the crucial nature of childhood and adolescence for healthy adult development were very much in tune with those of G. Stanley Hall, who, as we saw, had been instrumental in bringing Freud to America.

Since various aspects of adult psychopathology were seen to develop out of childhood fixations or traumas, the chief function of the therapist was to search for the origin and cure of problems in psychosexual development going back into early childhood. So was born the "uncover and cure" approach to psychotherapy that, as we saw, was a traditional part of most therapies well into the 1950s.

Interestingly, however, one of the earliest aspects of orthodox Freudian theory to be questioned by the many revisions and variations that were spun off from psychoanalytic theory was its emphasis on the crucial role of the psychosexual stages in the formation of adult pathology.

Several major changes in emphasis marked the advent of the neoanalytic theories. These changes set the stage for the creation of a new set of psychosocial theories of lifespan development. As we noted earlier, a group of psychoanalytically-oriented personality theorists sometimes called "ego-psychologists" began to put much greater emphasis upon the rational, reality-oriented, problem-solving functions inherent in human personality. These "ego" functions were seen by these revisionist theorists as much more significant than they had been conceptualized in Freud's original and markedly pessimistic view of the human condition. Freud's gloomy vision of a humankind at the mercy of thwarted infantile, libidinous impulses was replaced by an increased appreciation of the positive, resilient, and adaptive capacities of human beings (Fromm, 1941; Hartmann, 1939).

At the same time, these neoanalytic theorists began to envision the seeds of psychopathology as sown much more broadly and pervasively across the lifespan, rather than simply arising out of the curbing or indulging of childish sexual impulses. The new theories encompassed the whole lifespan. They saw the whole developmental history of the individual as involved in the formation of complex patterns of interpersonal relationships that virtually defined the individual personality (Sullivan, 1947).

Finally, analytic theorists such as Freud's former disciple, Carl Jung, began to see developmental issues not simply as latent reactions to childhood traumas and turmoil, but as full-blown and immediate crises born out of the realities of contemporary experiences that could occur across the entire lifespan. Jung labeled the tumultuous upheavals that sometimes occurred in middle age the "midlife crises" (Jung, 1933).

The psychoanalytic theorist who did the most to put together the pieces of the lifespan developmental puzzle was Erik Erikson. His classic formulation of the "Eight Stages of Man" (Erikson, 1950) put the neoanalytic theoretical concepts together to produce an integrated developmental model that specified eight chronological stages reaching across the entire lifespan. Each stage was characterized by a central, overriding developmental task or challenge that must be accomplished or resolved if future development was to proceed optimally. The theoretical model pointed not only to possible sources of psychopathology, but also envisioned a path of healthy and effective personality development when crises and critical tasks were mastered stage by stage.

Erikson's model deviated from an orthodox Freudian view in that it was psychosocial rather than psychosexual. Rather than seeing development as driven almost solely by inner, instinctual forces, of which the individual is an almost passive and unconscious victim, Erikson saw development as a process of continuing, lifelong interaction between maturational and aging processes unfolding within the individual, and the social institutions and influences constantly at work in the environment.

Robert White (1960) elaborated on this kind of perspective when he characterized the seeds of personality development not as growing out of psychosexual stages, but rather as rooted in an innate striving or drive virtually wired into the developing human being. White described this drive in what he called the "concept of competence," that is, the developing capacity of the organism both to survive and to grow. By his definition, the competence of an organism meant its fitness or ability to carry on those transactions with the environment which result in its not only maintaining itself, but actually growing and flourishing. From this view, development was seen to proceed out of the lifelong striving of human beings to master and control their environment. Out of this striving comes the actualization of the individual's highest talents, potentials, and abilities.

At about the same time that these revisions of psychoanalytic theories were being articulated Robert Havighurst (1953) coined the term "developmental tasks" to describe the host of challenges and hurdles confronting individuals as they move along developmental pathways. Havighurst defined a developmental task as a task which arises at or about a certain period in the life of an individual; successful accomplishment of the task leads to happiness and to success with later tasks, while failure leads to unhappiness, disapproval by society, and difficulty with subsequent tasks. Havighurst pointed up the relationship between developmental processes and education and articulated a step-by-step interaction between the two.

These new views of development, and the opportunities for intervention that they implied, were profound. They were particularly revolutionary for the practice of counseling and psychotherapy.

Personality traits or tendencies were no longer seen as etched in stone in infancy or early childhood. Human beings were no longer seen to carry within themselves a set of ticking time bombs fashioned out of traumas and fixations buried deep in their developmental histories. People were no longer seen as passive and largely helpless victims of an unconscious tug of war between irresistible sexual impulses and the stern, irrational, and unforgiving mandates of society as reflected in the super-ego.

The new perspectives opened the door to new and different kinds of psychotherapeutic interventions. People were seen as potentially able to change both feelings and behavior through rational discourse. Since development was a lifelong process, interventions could be targeted at crucial points across the lifespan where particularly troublesome crises or transitions were likely to occur. Counselors positioned in schools, colleges, or community agencies were potentially able to identify and even reach out to prevent or minimize growth-arresting transitions early. It was possible to conceptualize clients as developmentally "stuck," rather than sick.

Most profoundly, the laborious and painful process of "uncover and cure" represented by classical psychoanalysis was no longer the only game in town.

## Lifespan Developmental Research

The new approaches to personally theory triggered a burst of interest in the process of adult development. A whole series of long-term longitudinal studies of the adult years was undertaken in the decades that followed the changes in personality theories. Vaillant (1977), Levinson, Darrow, Klein, Levinson, and McKee (1978), Neugarten (1979), Lowenthal, Thurnher, and Chiriboga (1975), and Gould (1978) were among the best known of these researchers on the problems and processes of adult development and the transitions and discontinuities that form its fabric.

The results of these pioneering studies were surprisingly similar in terms of their broad conclusions. Generally, they saw developmental patterns as related to chronological stages, and supported a psychosocial or interactionist view of the relationship between maturational and environmental forces. Some differences emerged across studies in terms of the timing of life stages and patterns of response to them. However, several rather clear generalizations emerged across the studies and had important consequences.

These generalizations included:

1. It is not the isolated traumas of childhood that shape the course of human lives. but rather the quality of sustained relationships with other people.
2. Developmental change is continuous across the life span.
3. Developmental change is pervasive, touching psychological, social, and physiological domains.
4. Lifespan development is influenced by many factors. No single characteristic such as intelligence, education, or family origin is all-important and controlling.
5. The full context of past development and present situation must be considered if we are to understand an individual life.

The changes wrought by these revisions in theory and the research findings that supported them produced a whole new vision of human development and psychological interventions. This new vision saw capacity for change and progress that stretched across the lifespan. Development could be facilitated not merely in adolescence or early adulthood, but the "window of opportunity" for constructive change was opened wide.

The idea that the experiences of the early years inevitably constrained the characteristics of later life gave way to the proposition that personality is continually being transformed by interactions with the environment, making the course of human development more open than had been believed earlier (Brim & Kagan, 1980).

## Concepts of Optimal Development

One of the offshoots of the new approaches to personality theory was an increasing interest in the nature of optimal development. For many years, the focus of both psychology and psychiatry had been on all that was abnormal or maladaptive in human behavior.

As more optimistic views of human personality prevailed, attempts were made to specify the elements of optimal development. One of the first of these was formulated by Marie Jahoda (1958). She described the healthy or "normal" person simply as one who actively masters the environment, behaves with a degree of consistency, and perceives oneself and the world realistically. She also saw the healthy person as one who is able to function effectively without making undue demands upon others.

Shoben (1957) provided a slightly expanded definition of the normal personality. Obviously, the term "normal," with regard to human behavior, is a very slippery one that can be used to describe what is most frequent in a statistical sense; what is expected or demanded within a given culture; or what is approved or desired within a particular ethical or moral framework.

Shoben attempted to specify four sets of characteristics of a "normal" person that he maintained could be arrived at independently of social norms of statistical averages. His model of the normal personality included:

1. The willingness to accept the consequences of one's own behavior.
2. The capacity to function within interpersonal relationships.
3. Acceptance of and discharge of obligations to society.
4. Commitment to some set of ideals and standards for behavior.

The simple and straightforward definitions of writers like Shoben and Jahoda were soon followed by much more elaborate and often idealistic recitations of desirable personality traits and characteristics. Humanistic psychologists such as Abraham Maslow (1954), Gordon Allport (1963) and Carl Rogers (1964) all proposed elaborate definitions of higher-level human functioning. Most of these were either pure "armchair" descriptions or were based upon rather limited research or clinical observations. In the aggregate, these descriptions sounded a little like grown-up versions of the Boy Scout Oath and Law.

This "bag of virtues" approach to the study of human effectiveness, as it was sometimes called, produced an almost superhuman list of "shoulds" and "should nots," creating something that more resembled a set of lofty aspirations for human conduct than practical criteria by which to gauge adequate functioning.

When one reads Maslow's list of the 15 characteristics of the "self-actualized" person, one suspects that such individuals would also be faster than a speeding bullet, more powerful than a locomotive, and able to leap tall buildings at a single bound. They probably would also never need an underarm deodorant.

The interest and attention to optimal development and positive functioning, however, produced useful concepts regarding patterns of development that seemed to provide greater resistance to the onset of psychopathology. White's original concept of competence as a kind of psychological "immunization" was followed by concepts of "hardiness" (Kobasa, 1979) and "resilience" (Garmezy, 1974). Despite their tone, most views about optimal development and human effectiveness have provided useful concepts for counselors and therapists engaged in working with clients struggling to meet the crises, challenges, and vicissitudes of everyday life (Gelso & Fassinger, 1992).

From the standpoint of the development of counseling psychology, these ideas were much more than simply a set of convenient conceptual tools. They were, for counseling psychology, a veritable reason for being. When Donald Super (1955), in a now-classic article, attempted to explain the transition from vocational guidance to counseling psychology—and, in the process, to distinguish between counseling and clinical psychology—he observed that the focus of clinical psychology was clearly on psychopathology, while the practice of counseling psychology was oriented around what he called "hygiology," or the nurture of psychological health and well-being. In point of fact, the body of psychological research and theory that was to provide the conceptual infrastructure for such a specialty had only began to emerge in the 1950s. Without the interest in and attention to lifespan development and human effectiveness, counseling psychology as a separate and distinct psychological specialty would have had a very undistinguished and perilous existence.

## THE RISE OF VOCATIONAL DEVELOPMENT

As we noted earlier, the end of World War II saw traditional occupational psychology and the model of vocational counseling that it had spawned move perilously close to extinction. As we saw in Chapter 6, the old Parsonian matching model augmented by trait-and-factor psychometrics was under attack on practical, scientific, and sociopolitical grounds. Many counselors were ready to renounce the view that the single act of vocational choice-making was the supreme event in occupational life, and that the actuarial method was the sole vehicle with which even that event could be best accomplished (Borow, 1959).

The counseling of millions of returning veterans, diverse in age, education, ethnicity, and social class, had pointed up the inadequacy of the old approaches in dealing with the complexities that these clients brought to the counselor. The old model had assumed the problems originated solely out of information deficits.

As counselors, vocational and otherwise, became more aware of and concerned with the complexities and nuances that shaped and shaded the lives of their clients, the psychometric approach seemed less and less adequate. As Borow put it, the dominance of the trait-and-factor model represented "a period in which the regression equation was tacitly assumed to hold all the answers to student adjustment" (1959, p. 212). Counselors were clearly looking for more convincing approaches.

As interest in lifespan development research and theory began to blossom, alternative conceptions of both vocational life and vocational counseling began to emerge. One of these new concepts was that of "career" as a broad psychological construct that transcended and subsumed the notion of isolated choices and static levels of adjustment. The notion of *career* envisioned vocational behavior as a lifelong, psychologically integrated pattern of behavior that shaped a major social role that potentially provided structure and meaning to a human life. As much as any other social role, career was seen as mediating the individual's lifestyle and furnishing the conditions for fulfillment or failure in meeting needs and aspirations.

The new vocational theorists quickly began to draw upon the insights emerging from lifespan developmental psychology to provide substance to their concept of career development. Miller and Form (1951) and Super (1957) both drew upon Charlotte Buhler's (1933) concept of development as an orderly and predictable sequence of life stages to describe career development. Super (1957) postulated six distinct stages of career development:

(a) explorations: developing a self-concept;
(b) reality testing: the transition from school to work;
(c) floundering or trial processes: attempting to implement a self-concept;
(d) establishment;
(e) maintenance; and
(f) decline.

Two pioneering programs of research organized around the new developmental frameworks were launched in the 1950s. The Harvard Studies in Career Development (Tiedeman, O'Hara, & Baruch, 1963), and the Career Pattern Studies directed by Super at Columbia (1957). A theoretical model of vocational development that helped to broaden conceptions of career behavior was Ann Roe's (1956) psychoanalytically flavored model of vocational behavior as an aspect of basic personality development.

By 1964, the transition from the old actuarial or Parsonian model of vocational guidance to the newer and broader concept of career development was virtually accomplished. The National Vocational Guidance Association celebrated the 50th anniversary of its humble beginnings in Grand Rapids in 1913 with the publication of *Man in a World of Work* (Borow, 1964), a masterful and truly comprehensive anthology of distinguished contributions to the literature of career development. Clearly it was an idea whose time had come.

Henry Borow, the editor, described the transformation in these words:

What is youth as worker-to-be? What is he subsequently as adult worker? He is an organism in development through a series of life stages,

**Figure 7.2    Henry Borow**

confronting at each stage a set of interrelated problem-solving conditions (development tasks). The conditions are both imposed by society
as prerequisites of psychological and social growth, and self-imposed
out of an enlarging capacity for understanding reality . . . (p. 364)

## DEVELOPMENTAL EDUCATION

The pioneering work of Jean Piaget almost single-handedly redirected
and rejuvenated developmental psychology and the study of cognitive
development. Ironically, this work was largely ignored by applied
psychologists in America for almost 40 years. This was perhaps due
to the fact that American psychologists, fixated upon the paramount
importance of the IQ, saw cognitive growth as largely a function of
maturation that proceed almost automatically to the limits imposed
by the individual's genetic endowment. Cognitive growth, as measured
by IQ tests, as we saw earlier, seemed to culminate at about age 15.

As interest in lifespan development grew, some applied psychologists began to look at the Piagetan model and to perceive new opportunities to nurture and to enhance aspects of cognitive functioning beyond childhood.

Several aspects of Piaget's "genetic epistemology" were seen to fit nicely with the conceptual foundations of lifespan developmental approaches.

As we noted, Piaget emphasized that thoughts, ideas, and strategies grow out of actions. His was an interactionist view of behavior and development rather than either a hereditarian or purely environmentalist perspective. Piaget saw life itself as a continuous creation of increasingly complex ways of thinking, and a progressive balancing or testing of these cognitive processes with challenges and realities posed by the environment. Although most of Piaget's own research had been done with children, there was no reason to suppose that these same basic processes did not continue across the lifespan. Cognitive development, that is, changes in the way we construe, interpret, and literally transform our world, evolves out of our continuing struggle to make sense out of a complex and often confusing world.

Piaget also posited a built-in, innate motivational system to drive the cognitive developmental processes that he observed. His concept of the need to understand was not unlike White's concept of competence or the need to explore, manipulate, and finally to master the environment.

For Piaget, the basic need to understand and make some degree of sense out of our encounters with the environment meant that a kind of dissonance or disequilibrium is established when we confront situations or phenomena that our present ways of thinking cannot explain or comprehend. This kind of dynamic mismatch between our habitual ways of construing events and unfamiliar or perplexing problems furnishes the basic elements conducive to cognitive development. Such situations are very much the kind frequently experienced by clients in counseling and psychotherapy.

Piaget had also noted, along with the lifespan developmentalists, that transitions between stages of development are often accompanied by anxiety and turmoil.

By the 1960s a number of developmentally oriented personality theorists had begun to look to the Piagetan model and to integrate it with views of lifespan development. Harvey, Hunt, and Schroder

(1961), Kohlberg (1969), Perry (1970), and Loevinger (1976) all articulated theoretical models to account for processes of intellectual, social, and moral growth and their roles in general personality development. At about the same time, George Kelly (1955) had produced a theoretical model of personality which, while not a developmental stage model like those mentioned above, put cognitive changes at the heart both of the therapeutic enterprise and of personality functioning.

Cognitive developmental changes were seen, in these newer theories, to be different from other kinds of human learning in that they are seen to be irreversible and to follow an invariant sequence. Individuals cannot slide back down the developmental ladder to lower-level stages once they are established on a given rung.

While there is no guarantee that any given individual will ever develop to reach a higher stage, the sequence of stage changes is considered to be similar across individuals and even across cultures. In other words, no one can skip a stage on the way to the top of the developmental pyramid.

The cognitive developmental view was noticeable different than other theories in that it does not make the assumption that higher levels of cognitive functioning are inevitable. Rather, it is seen that without specific kinds of learning experiences, large percentages of the general population may spend their lives languishing at or near the bottom of the developmental totem pole. The challenge was clearly there for applied psychologists to design educational or therapeutic interventions to move individuals to higher levels of cognitive functioning.

Two of the most influential of the cognitive developmental approaches were Lawrence Kohlberg's (1969) model of moral development and Jane Loevinger's (1976) approach to ego development. The latter was intended to subsume other, more limited domains.

Counseling psychologists Ralph Mosher and Norman Sprinthall (1970) proposed programs of what they called "deliberate psychological education" to promote cognitive development. In many ways, the developmental education movement as it grew over the 1970s and 1980s was an updating and reaffirmation of John Dewey's emphasis on development as the core of the educational enterprise and to the role of guidance as an integral part of progressive education.

The cognitive developmental approach has influenced counseling psychology over the past 30 years to a far greater degree than it has been able to reform the educational establishment. Various cognitive developmental models have been proposed as a framework for counseling (Kegan, 1980; Swenson, 1980), and a number of special developmental programs have been utilized in social skills training, gender awareness, cross-cultural education, and counselor education programs. The cognitive developmental approach has also become a central feature of the study of career development (Neimeyer, 1988).

## THE IMPACT OF THE DEVELOPMENTAL TRADITION

While the trait-and-factor tradition clearly dominated the formative years of counseling as a profession, it is difficult to escape the conclusion that the field of counseling psychology could not have flourished or even survived without the ideas, energy, and professional niche furnished to it from the emphasis on understanding and facilitating human development across the lifespan. Beginning with the very earliest pronouncements that christened the new field at or shortly after the Northwestern Conference in 1951, the new division of counseling psychology established its identity and staked its claim to uniqueness around developmental concepts and approaches (Whiteley, 1984). Writers like Tyler (1958), Super (1980), Blocher (1966), Okun (1984), Schlossberg (1984), and Danish, D'Angelli, and Ginsberg (1984) have all articulated and underscored the central role of development to the science and practice of counseling psychology.

In 1966 Blocher's book *Developmental Counseling*, articulated a comprehensive approach to counseling organized around Erik Erikson's life stage concepts. This approach envisioned the successful bridging of problematic life transitions as a central aspect of counseling. The goals of counseling were seen to focus around the social roles, developmental tasks and coping behaviors at each life stage (Blocher, 2000, 4th ed.).

As Gelso and Fassinger (1992) pointed out, the relationship between counseling and development has waxed and waned and has been often marked by ambivalence. The siren call of white-coat psychology, together with the notion that the sicker the patient the higher the status of the healer, has often tended to deflect counseling psychologists from their roots.

Clearly, however, the developmental approach is very much alive and well and living at the core of counseling psychology research and practice. Fassinger and Schlossberg (1992), writing in the *Handbook of Counseling Psychology*, articulated what could be viewed as a basic creed for developmental counseling and therapy

> Inherent in our philosophy is a non-pathological focus on normalcy and day-to-day problems of living with an emphasis on strengths and adaptive strategies in our clients. . . . We see ourselves as educators, we emphasize the empowerment of individuals, we value preventive as well as ameliorative intervention efforts and we work for enhanced functioning in all people . . .
>
> Our scope includes environmental as well as individual intervention . . . the effective use of community resources and social political advocacy where appropriate. . . . We emphasize developmental approaches to working with people including attention to their sociocultural context and the influence of gender, race, age, ethnicity, sexual orientation, (dis) ability and socio-history. These characteristics give us the unique opportunity to be in the forefront . . . of . . . effective service delivery. (p. 244)

The statement above very eloquently summarizes the legacy given us in the developmental tradition as it is being applied in contemporary counseling psychology.

## REFERENCES

Alexander, F. (1948). *Fundamentals of psychoanalysis.* New York: Norton.

Allport, G. (1963). *Pattern and growth in personality.* New York: Holt, Rinehart.

Blocher, D. H. (2000). *Counseling: A developmental approach* (4th ed.). New York: Wiley.

Blocher, D. H. (1966). *Developmental counseling.* New York: Ronald Press.

Borow, H. (1959). Modern perspectives in personnel research. *N.S.S.E. Yearbook, 58,* 210–230.

Borow, H. (Ed.) (1964). *Man in a world at work.* Boston: Houghton-Mifflin.

Brim, O., & Kagan, J. (Eds.) (1980). *Constancy and change in human development.* Cambridge, MA: Harvard University Press.

Broughton, J. M. (1981). The genetic psychology of James Mark Baldwin. *American Psychologist, 36,* 396–407.

Buhler, C. (1933). *Der menschliche lebenslauf als psychologishes problem* [The course of human life as a psychological problem]. Leipzig: Hirzel.

Cahan, E. D. (1984). The genetic psychologies of James Mark Baldwin and Jean Piaget. *American Psychologist, 20,* 128–135.

Danish, S. J., D'Augelli, A. R., & Ginsberg, M. R. (1984). Life development interventions: Promotion of mental health through the development of competence. In S. Brown & R. Lent (Eds.), *Handbook of counseling psychology* (pp. 520–544). New York: Wiley.

Dewey, J. (1916). *Democracy and education*. New York: The Free Press, MacMillan.

Erikson, E. (1950). *Childhood and society*. New York: Norton. (2nd ed. published 1963).

Fancher, R. E. (1990). *Pioneers of psychology* (2nd ed.). New York: Norton.

Fassinger, R., & Schlossberg, N. (1992). Understanding the adult years. In S. Brown & R. Lent (Eds.), *Handbook of counseling psychology* (2nd ed., pp. 217–250). New York: Wiley.

Fromm, E. (1941). *Escape from freedom*. New York: Rinehart.

Garmezy, N. (1974). Children at risk: The search for the antecedents of schizophrenia. *Clinical Psychologist, 19,* 55–125.

Gelso, C. J., & Fassinger, R. E. (1992). Personality development and counseling psychology: Depth, ambivalence and actualization. *Journal of Counseling Psychology, 39,* 275–298.

Gould, R. (1978). *Transformations: Growth and change in adult life*. New York: Simon and Schuster.

Haeckel, E. H. (1896). *The evolution of man*. New York: Appleton. (Originally published 1874).

Hall, G. S. (1904). *Adolescence: Its psychology and its relation to physiology, anthropology, sociology, sex, crime, religion and education*. New York: Appleton.

Hamrin, S., & Erickson, C. (1939). *Guidance in the secondary school*. New York: Appleton-Century.

Hartmann, H. (1939). *Ego psychology and the problem of adaptation*. New York: International Universities.

Harvey, O. J., Hunt, D. E., & Schroder, H. M. (1961). *Conceptual systems and personality organization*. New York: Wiley.

Havighurst, R. (1953). *Human development and education*. London: Longmans Green.

Hergenhahn, B. R. (1992). *An introduction to the history of American Psychology* (2nd ed.). Belmont, CA: Wadsworth Publishing.

Hilgard, E. R. (1987). *Psychology in America: A historical survey*. New York: Harcourt Brace Jovanovich.

Jahoda, M. (1958). *Current concepts of positive mental health*. New York: Basic Books.

Jung, C. (1933). *Modern man in search of a soul*. New York: Harcourt Brace.

Kegan, R. (1980). Making meaning: The constructive developmental approach to persons and practice. *Personnel and Guidance Journal, 58,* 373–380.

Kelly, G. (1955). *A theory of personality: The psychology of personal constructs*. New York: Norton.

Kobasa, S. C. (1979). Stressful life events, personality and health: An inquiry into hardiness. *Journal of Personality and Social Psychology, 37,* 1–11.

Kohlberg, L. (1969). *Stages in the development of moral thought and action*. New York: Holt, Rinehart, Winston.

Levinson, D., Darrow, C., Klein, E., Levinson, M., & McKee, B. (1978). *The seasons of a man's life*. New York: Ballantine.

Loevinger, J. (1976). *Ego development*. San Francisco: Jossey-Bass.

Lowenthal, M., Thurnher, M., & Chiriboga, D. (1975). *Four stages of life: A comparative study of men and women facing transitions*. San Francisco: Jossey-Bass.

Maslow, A. (1954). *Motivation and personality*. New York: Harper.

Miller, D. C., & Form, W. H. (1951). *Industrial sociology*. New York: Harper and Brothers.

Mosher, R. L., & Sprinthall, N. A. (1970). Psychological education in secondary schools: A program to promote human development. *American Psychologist, 25,* 911–924.

Muuss, R. E. (1968). *Theories of adolescence* (2nd ed.). New York: Random House.

Neimeyer, G. J. (1988). Cognitive integration and differentiation in vocational behavior. *The Counseling Psychologist, 16,* 440–475.

Neugarten, B. (1979). Time, age and the life cycle. *American Journal of Psychiatry, 36,* 887–898.

O'Donnell, J. M. (1985). *The origins of behaviorism*. New York: New York University Press.

Okun, B. (1984). *Working with adults: Individual, family and career development*. Monterey, CA: Brooks/Cole.

Perry, W. (1970). *Intellectual and ethical development in the college years*. New York: Holt, Rinehart, Winston.

Piaget, J. (1970). *Genetic epistemology*. New York: Norton.

Roe, A. (1956). *The psychology of occupations*. New York: John Wiley and Sons.

Rogers, C. R. (1962). The interpersonal relationship: The core of guidance. In R. Mosher, R. F. Carle, & C. D. Kehas (Eds.), *Guidance: An examination*. New York: Harcourt Brace and World.

Rogers, C. R. (1964). Toward a modern approach to valuing in the mature person. *Abnormal and Social Psychology, 68,* 160–167.

Rousseau, J. J. (1762). *Emile* (translated and abridged by W. H. Payne). New York: Appleton, 1926.

Schlossberg, N. K. (1984). *Counseling adults in transition*. New York: Springer.

Shoben, E. J. (1957). Toward a concept of the normal personality. *American Psychologist, 12,* 183–190.

Sullivan, H. S. (1947). *Conceptions of modern psychiatry*. Washington, DC: William Alonson White Foundation.

Super, D. (1955). The transition from vocational guidance to counseling psychology. *Journal of Counseling Psychology, 2,* 3–9.

Super, D. (1957). *The psychology of careers*. New York: Harper.

Super, D., and Associates (1957). Vocational development: A framework for research. (Career Pattern Study, Monograph No. 1.) New York: Teachers College.

Super, D. E. (1980). A life span, life space approach to career development. *Journal of Vocational Behavior, 16,* 282–298.

Thorndike, E. L. (1913). *Educational psychology*. New York: Teachers College.

Tiedeman, D. V., O'Hara, R. P., & Baruch, R. W. (1963). *Career development: Choice and adjustment*. Princeton, NJ: College Entrance Examination Board.

Tyler, L. (1958). Theoretical principles underlying the counseling process. *Journal of Counseling Psychology, 5,* 3–10.

Vaillant, G. (1977). *Adaptation to life*. Boston, MA: Little, Brown.

White, R. (1960). *Competence and the psychosexual stages of development* (Nebraska Symposium on Motivation). Lincoln, NE: University of Nebraska Press.

Whitely, J. M. (1984). A historical perspective on the development of counseling psychology as a profession. In S. D. Brown & R. W. Lent (Eds.), *Handbook of counseling psychology* (pp. 3–55). New York: Wiley.

Williamson, E. G. (1958). Value orientation in counseling. *Personnel and Guidance Journal, 36,* 520–528.

Wolf, T. H. (1973). *Alfred Binet*. Chicago: University of Chicago Press.

# 8

# The Humanistic Tradition

> How do we know? When we first encounter this question we are apt
> to think of some of the impressive machinery of science. . . . In the
> last analysis, knowledge rests on the subjective. I experience; in this
> experiencing, I exist; in this existing, I in some sense *know*. All knowl-
> edge including all scientific knowledge, is a vast inverted pyramid
> resting on this tiny, personal base.
>
> —Carl Rogers (1965)

In the autumn of 1956, the Minnesota Counseling Association
held its annual conference. In this pre-NDEA year, the Association
represented a relative handful of high school counselors, a small
group of university or college counselors, and counselor educators,
along with a scattering of members from community agencies. That
the Association existed at all was due largely to the leadership of
Willis E. Dugan, long-time counselor educator and advocate of school
counseling, from the University of Minnesota's Department of Educational Psychology.

The meeting was held in the auditorium of one of the new suburban
high schools that ringed the Twin Cities as the Baby Boomers began
to reach adolescence. In view of the limited membership and visibility
of school counseling in that era, it was surprising to find the auditorium
virtually overflowing with eager listeners.

The occasion was the collision of the two opposing views of counseling and psychotherapy that had polarized, yet energized, the field for
more than 15 years. For the first time, E. G. Williamson and Carl R.
Rogers would share the same platform to engage in what the audience,
at least, saw as the crucial debate that would finally define the issues and

determine the future of the great directive-nondirective controversy. It might also bring to the surface what many believed was a personal feud between these two pioneers of professional counseling.

At the appointed hour, the two speakers took the stage, shook hands briefly, and sat stiffly at opposite ends of a table as the moderator made the usual laudatory remarks of introduction.

Dean of Students Williamson presented a polished and tightly organized review of his version of what was being called the "Minnesota Point of View." His tone was formal, even crisp, and only a trifle warmer than he might have used with a group of overimbibing fraternity brothers in his Office of Disciplinary Counseling. For Williamson the counselor was clearly an expert, a mentor, and a representative of all that was rational, proper, and virtuous in a civilized society.

As Carl Rogers approached the podium, his thoughts must have turned to the day 16 years earlier in December of 1940 when he delivered a paper at a University of Minnesota symposium. It was one of those rare occasions in a Minnesota winter when the atmosphere inside was even chillier than outside.

On that December day, Rogers was just entering his academic career as Professor of Psychology at the Ohio State University. He later described the Minnesota presentation as "my first experience of the fact that a new idea of mine, which to me can seem all shiny and glowing with potentiality, can be to another person a great threat" (Rogers, 1961, p. 13).

Rogers' presentation to the counselors of Minnesota on that autumn morning in 1956 was totally different in style, tone, and content from that of Williamson's. Rogers spoke in eloquent generalities of his own experiences and resulting understandings as a therapist. He was a year away from his classic pronouncement about the "necessary and sufficient" conditions for therapeutic change, but the direction of his thinking was unmistakable. For Rogers, the essence of counseling was relationship. All of the trappings of psychological sophistication and technical expertise were peripheral, if not antithetical, to the almost magical properties of an "I-thou" encounter.

Neither speaker mentioned the other's ideas or even acknowledged their differences. After a few polite questions from the audience, the great debate that was not a debate was over. To the author and the other graduate students sitting in the back of the hall, the reaction was like that of children invited to a 4th of July fireworks celebration

**Figure 8.1    Carl Rogers**

that had somehow fizzled in a unexpected rainstorm. As one of the audience remarked in filing out, the two speakers were like ships that passed in the night without so much as the toot of a whistle.

What the more experienced and perceptive members of the audience probably saw was that the differences that separated Carl Rogers and Ed Williamson were indeed so basic and so profound that they really precluded any meaningful dialogue, and certainly prevented any kind of compromise or melding of points of view. Rogers rather clearly won the contest of charisma, but the ship of ideas on which he was embarked was headed for a very different port than Williamson could or would have chosen to reach.

Carl Rogers was born in 1902 in Wisconsin. He grew up in what he described as a loving, yet deeply and sternly religious family. Carl's father was a successful business man who moved his family to a Wisconsin farm to escape the temptations of suburban life. As Carl described his family, they were different from others in terms of a puritanical lifestyle with no alcoholic beverages, no dancing, no cards or theater, very little social life, and much *work*.

He was apparently a rather lonely adolescent who turned to books. He became something of an authority on moths, and showed an early interest in scientific agriculture.

Carl Rogers entered the University of Wisconsin intending to major in agriculture. During this time, he attended several emotionally charged religious conferences and abruptly decided to become a minister. He shifted his college major from agriculture to history to better prepare for a religious career. One of the formative experiences of this period of Carl Rogers' life was a trip to China to attend a World Student Christian Federation Conference. He described this as a situation in which he was forced to accept the fact that sincere and deeply committed people could differ widely in terms of religious beliefs and could also see the world in very different ways.

Carl Rogers entered Union Theological Seminary in 1924 to prepare for a career in the ministry. He spent 2 years there, but left apparently because his own developing beliefs were incompatible even with this very liberal institution.

Rogers went literally across the street to enroll at Columbia Teachers College in its psychology program.

In 1926, there were few clearly defined doctoral programs in any areas of applied or professional psychology. Rogers took courses in what we would now call educational psychology at Teachers College. There he found a strong trait-and-factor orientation. He began doing clinical work with children under the supervision of Leta Hollingsworth, whom he described as a sensitive and practical person. Certainly, as we saw earlier, Leta Hollingsworth was committed to the future of professional psychology. At this point, Rogers formally shifted into the area of child guidance which, as we saw, was one of the new fields that contributed to the development of both clinical and counseling psychology.

After completing an internship in a Freudian-oriented child guidance center in New York City, Rogers accepted a position as a psychologist in a Child Guidance Center in Rochester, New York at a salary of $2,900 a year. Rogers was to stay in this position for the next 12 years, completing his doctorate while there.

It was in Rochester that Carl Rogers developed his views of counseling and therapy. He was influenced by social work and the Rankean version of psychoanalytic thinking. At one time, Rogers virtually thought of himself more as a social worker than as a psychologist. The 1930s were, as we saw, dark days for professional psychologists. Rogers joined the New York State Association of Consulting Psychologists and played a part in the organization of the American Association of Applied Psychology. He was President of that group during the crucial negotiations for the reorganization of APA and was elected to the Presidency of APA soon after its reorganization.

In 1940, Rogers accepted his first academic position as a full professor of psychology at the Ohio State University. Five years later he accepted a position as Director of the Counseling Center at the University of Chicago. In 1957, Rogers returned to his *alma mater* as Professor of Psychology and Psychiatry at the University of Wisconsin. Six years later, at the height of international prestige and influence, Rogers' academic career ended there under strange and somewhat mysterious circumstances.

As one views Carl Rogers' career and the characteristics and influences that guided his development, it seems clear that dominant forces were the strength of his penchant for independent thinking coupled with a powerful work ethic. Rogers was a true maverick who considered and then moved beyond the tenets of organized religion, trait-and-factor psychology, Freudian and Rankian psychoanalysis, and a variety of philosophical orientations to build a powerful and ultimately highly persuasive view of counseling and psychotherapy. In the process, he also helped to redefine the nature of virtually all positive human relationships.

Summing up Carl Rogers' achievements and contributions to psychology is difficult, indeed. He pioneered a new approach to psychotherapy known successively as "nondirective," "client-centered," and "person-centered." He was the first therapist to record and publish complete cases of psychotherapy. He was one of the first to do filmed or live demonstrations of actual therapy interviews. He carried out or encouraged more research on therapeutic process and outcome than had ever been undertaken before. Yet today little of that research is remembered or even viewed as relevant. He profoundly influenced all of the helping professions, from guidance counseling to clinical psychology and psychiatry, yet as theory, his formulations are now given little credence. Rogers virtually founded the encounter group movement—an approach that has also faded into obscurity. He was one of the leaders of "humanistic psychology." Yet, in spite of, or because of all this, his influence is still profoundly felt in counseling psychology. Ironically, controversy followed Carl Rogers even to the grave. His obituary (Gendlin, 1988) credits Rogers as a founder of counseling psychology. Gendlin's tribute was later followed by a comment written by Don Super (1989) disputing that claim. This must represent the only rebuttal to an obituary in the history of psychology.

## FROM NONDIRECTIVE COUNSELING TO HUMANISTIC PSYCHOLOGY

As powerful as Carl Rogers' personal influence was on the field of counseling and psychotherapy, it was undoubtedly the way in which his ideas meshed with both those of other thinkers and with the spirit of the times that produced such profound effects. When Carl Rogers' ideas were first showered upon the field in the 1940s, they fell upon very fertile soil.

As we noted in Chapter 6, the decline of trait-and-factor psychology was well underway as it fell increasingly out of tune both with both popular values and scientific realities. In education, and in counseling and psychotherapy, generally, the postwar era was a period of profound discontent with both the techniques and the value systems that underlay much of what went on in schools and colleges, as well as in counseling offices.

As we saw in Chapter 2, the 1930s were the heyday of what its critics called the "cult of adjustment." In educational parlance, "adjustment" was little more than a code word for conformity. Too often, conformity itself was conceptualized as psychological passivity and a careful avoidance of any kind of "boat-rocking" activity.

Personal adjustment as a major goal of education, and, indeed, of much of counseling and psychotherapy, was devoted to "helping" individuals to "fit in" and "get along" in terms of existing social norms and prevailing organizational practices. Surviving and eking out a living in the terrible Depression years with rampant unemployment, constricted opportunities, and active suppression of dissent or dissatisfaction with the status quo seemed to place a premium on adjustment as an optimal state of being.

It was a time in which guidance people talked of "counseling students out" of unrealistic aspirations or expectations. By the 1950s, it was not unusual to meet successful college graduates, including those with advanced degrees, who had been actively discouraged from even considering college by guidance counselors.

The adjustment emphasis was just as strong in the field of psychotherapy as in education, or guidance. One therapist (Halleck, 1971, p. 3) termed psychotherapy the "handmaiden of the status quo." Women, for example, who expressed career aspirations beyond those of housewife or mother were very often labeled as maladjusted, and the psychotherapeutic wheels turned to grind them back into their "proper role" in society.

Lest we think that the "cult of adjustment" has been finally eradicated from the field of counseling and psychotherapy, a simple reading of a metropolitan newspaper will demonstrate its hardiness. Today's criminal justice system has made counseling and psychotherapy the number one alternative to incarceration. Upon conviction, or even before, culprits are routinely condemned to "terms of psychotherapy" for a wide range of offenses ranging from drunken driving and domestic abuse to window-peeping and indecent exposure. Therapy or jail is still a common choice facing violators in our criminal justice system The "cult of adjustment" is still very much alive and well and living in every courtroom in America.

The end of World War II and the tremendous expansion of aspirations and opportunities brought about by the GI Bill, the Women's Movement, and the Civil Rights struggle made personal choice and personal autonomy highly cherished values. The harmony of these new values with "nondirective" and "client-centered" approaches to counseling and therapy seems unmistakable.

By the end of the war, millions of American women were fully aware of the tremendous contributions they had made to the war effort, both in defense plants and in maintaining the home front. Eleven million men returned from literally conquering the world, and in the process rescuing it from totalitarian tyranny, bigotry, and genocide. Millions of these men and women had themselves grown up in poverty, discrimination, and oppression in their own land. A passive adjustment to the status quo was no longer what they were looking for. Change was in the air.

Nowhere were the changes coming more rapidly than in higher education. As the veterans began to exercise their educational benefits, enrolling in great numbers in colleges and universities, time-honored traditions, mores and values were challenged. Many of these primarily undergraduate institutions were sponsored and controlled by religious groups and quite consciously focused their efforts on character-building. Well-intentioned efforts were often perceived by the new breed of college student as paternalistic, patronizing, and hypocritical.

In the 1940s and early 1950s, for example, it was still common for female college students to be treated much like books on reserve in the college library. Women were required to sign out or be signed out of residence halls after 6 p.m. and to be returned no later than 10 p.m. (11 p.m. on Saturday), presumably with virtue and virginity intact. This kind of virtual guardianship often came at the hands of institutions and administrations actively engaged in practicing and perpetuating blatant race and sex discrimination in their own operations. The double standard in terms of sexual behavior was an official part of student personnel policy in a great number of institutions of higher learning.

The winds of change began to blow on college campuses soon after the end of World War II and culminated in the 1960s with thousands of college students in virtual rebellion against their own institutions. For the first time in the history of American higher education, campuses were hotbeds of social and political activism. The anti-war movement, the Civil Rights struggle, and the Women's Movement coalesced to produce a storm of protest against the status quo. All too often, protest turned into violence, with tragic consequences for all concerned.

The philosophical basis for much of college student personnel work, and indeed for much of counseling in educational settings, had been built upon the concept of in *loco parentis*, the idea that educators represented and acted for and in the place of parents. In the 15 years that followed the end of the war, that concept became increasingly untenable.

It is little wonder that the challenges to what were perceived, at least, to be paternalistic and authoritarian approaches to counseling were enthusiastically received. Carl Rogers was not the only critic of directive counseling, but the most coherent and compelling theoretical formulations to move the field came from his fertile mind and facile pen.

In 1939, Rogers was in his 11th year as a staff psychologist in the Child Study Department of the Society for the Prevention of Cruelty to Children in Rochester. As Rogers put it later, it was a dead-end job, professionally. During this period, he actually published a personality inventory to be used with children, The Rogers Personality Adjustment Inventory.

In 1939 Carl Rogers published his first book, *The Clinical Treatment of the Problem Child*. It was, as he indicated in the preface, the product "of more than a decade of daily clinical experience with all of the varieties of maladjusted children which a modern American community can produce" (p. vii).

This volume is a thorough and relatively conventional review of the methods, approaches, and techniques then in use in child clinical psychology. It features chapters on diagnosis, particularly on the use of personality inventories, and describes treatment strategies as diverse as summer camps, foster home placement, play therapy, and what he rather awkwardly termed "interview therapy." The task of writing this book while working full time in the arduous and emotionally draining role of therapist must have been a true test of the work ethic with which he was imbued in childhood. Clearly, however, it was also Carl Rogers' ticket out of Rochester.

A sensitive reading of this book suggests a therapist struggling to find anything that works, and seeking desperately to find when something does work, why it works. As Rogers described approach after approach, the creeping shadows of doubt and ambivalence were all too apparent. In a discussion of the use of personal influence and advice in working with children, for example, he acknowledges its prevalence, cites several authorities, and—almost as an aside—remarks that "such methods place emphasis upon the notion of remaking the individual rather than of releasing his own strengths" (p. 300).

*The Clinical Treatment of the Problem Child* broke little new ground for Rogers as either therapist or theoretician, but it served admirably to get him out of Rochester. He attributed an invitation to join the faculty at Ohio State University as full professor to the publication of this book.

## Directive vs. Nondirective: A Real or Rhetorical Question?

It was 2 years after arriving at Ohio State that Rogers published the book that set him apart forever as a therapist and theoretician,

*Counseling and Psychotherapy* (1942). This book did not present a full-blown theory, but rather drew the battle lines, identifying his own approach as nondirective while labeling most of what was going on elsewhere in the field as directive. It seems very probable that what had transformed a loose collection of lingering doubts into a set of fiercely held convictions was Rogers' experience in studying the therapeutic process through the use of actual recordings and transcripts. One gem of information that came out of this kind of study was the observation that directive counselors use six times as many words per interview as do nondirective counselors. (It is not clear whether Rogers counted head nods or "Um huhs," however.)

The 1942 book carried the first complete verbatim transcribed psychotherapy case ever published (Kirschenbaum & Henderson, 1989). It was an 8-session case called "The case of Herbert Bryan" and it put a new and potent weapon in Carl Rogers' hands in his war on directive counseling, that is, a record of what actually goes on in counseling sessions.

*Counseling and Psychotherapy* was much more a personal manifesto than a theory of counseling. Rogers presented data from his counseling process studies and introduced his verbatim case study. Even in this first, introductory presentation of his views, however, Rogers set a combative tone that was to color and cloud the directive/ nondirective debate for the next 20 years. Not content with examining the differences in use of techniques between his directive and nondirective counselors, Rogers immediately imputed basic philosophical and even personal differences between the two. One wonders if the hostile reception given to him and his new ideas 2 years before had helped to harden the almost prosecutorial tone of his 1942 book.

Rogers described what he saw as the implicit purposes of directive and nondirective counselors:

> The first basic difference in purpose centers around the question of who is to choose the client's goals. The directive group assumes that the counselor selects the desirable and the socially approved goal which the client is to attain, and then directs his efforts toward helping the subject to attain it. An unstated implication is that the counselor is *superior* to the client since the latter is assumed to be *incapable* of accepting full responsibility for choosing his own goal. (Rogers, 1942, p. 127) (italics added)

The above indictment has to be one of the most sweeping and least supported statements ever to appear in what purported to be a scholarly work. It represented an accusation that many counselors had vehemently rejected since the days of Frank Parsons. It would have been complete anathema to people such as John Brewer or John Dewey whom we quoted earlier.

Rogers contrasted his own views to the straw man he had just set up in these terms:

> Non-directive counseling is based on the assumption that the client has a right to select his own goals, even though these may be at variance with the goals the counselor might choose for him. . . . The non-directive viewpoint places a high value on the right of every individual to be psychologically independent, and to maintain his psychological integrity. The directive viewpoint places a high value on social conformity and the right of the more able to *direct the less able*. (Rogers, 1942, pp. 127–128) (italics added)

These sweeping statements were not only masterpieces of oversimplification and overstatement, but constituted a virtual declaration of war. As we saw above, the developing spirit of the times, however, was with Carl Rogers.

For almost a decade after the publication of *Counseling and Psychotherapy*, the directive-nondirective debate was carried on very largely at the level of philosophical differences, and, unfortunately, very often, in terms of personal invective. In the 1942 book Rogers had specified rather clearly what he was against, and had given some descriptions of what he termed nondirective counseling. Very little in the way of a theoretical framework or rationale was provided. Nondirective counseling and therapy was at this point a small bundle of techniques largely involving reflections of feeling, restatement of content, or simple acceptance of a communication. Watching student counselors attempt to incorporate these techniques into a counseling style was a little like watching a mechanical puppet programmed to nod, smile, and say "Um huh" no matter what the client said or did.

Clearly, at this point, nondirective counseling was an effect desperately seeking a set of psychological causes. In his first effort at theory-building, Rogers turned to the social psychological construct of self as the key variable in therapeutic change.

The self was almost a taboo topic in early scientific psychology because it had been virtually equated with soul by spiritualists, who asserted that it was selfhood that would continue to exist after death. One psychologist who ignored this taboo was William James. James had continued a lifelong infatuation with Spiritualism and the study of "psychic phenomena," much to the embarrassment of his contemporaries in American psychology.

One of James's students, Mary Whiton Calkins, who was, by the way, the first woman to become president of the APA, had made self psychology a part of her view of mental functioning. The sociologist Charles H. Cooley saw the concept of self as a key aspect of human interaction that provides a social context for all roles and relationships. He wrote of the "looking glass" self as the product that emerges as we begin to see ourselves as others perceive us.

Another sociologist and social psychologist who advanced the construct of self was George Herbert Mead who, as we saw, was a colleague of John Dewey and an early advocate of both vocational counseling and progressive education. Mead made the concept of self contrasted with others the basis for social role theory, which became one of the cornerstones of modern sociology.

Perhaps the most significant source of Rogers' version of self theory was a book by Prescott Lecky called *Self-Consistency: A Theory of Personality* (1945). Lecky suggested that the course of personality development was largely a struggle to develop a consistent and satisfying view of the self, and that failure to achieve such a view, or "self-concept," was a source of anxiety and psychological dysfunction.

Rogers proceeded to develop a one-construct personality theory around the self-concept and the lifelong struggle to establish, protect, and enhance it. The aspect of self on which Rogers focused was really self-esteem or self acceptance. The self-concept was viewed as positive or negative, and psychological well-being was virtually equated with having a positive self-concept.

Although other researchers had seen the self as complex and varied, arising out of all of the individual's various roles and relationships, the Rogerian version focused only upon self-esteem or acceptance.

Rogers unveiled his self theory in his 1947 Presidential address to the American Psychological Association. He attributed the approach to his experience as a therapist (Hilgard, 1987). Rogers launched a line of process and outcome research at the University of Chicago

Counseling Center using as a criterion of therapeutic effectiveness changes in "self-acceptance," that is, the strength of the relationship between the self-description produced by client and the description of that client's ideal self. These were obtained using a Q sort methodology. Much of this research was published in an edited book titled *Psychotherapy and Personality Change* (Rogers & Dymond, 1954).

Almost a decade after the publication of *Counseling and Psychotherapy*, Carl Rogers and his associates produced the first comprehensive and coherent theoretical framework for what he by then termed Client-Centered Therapy.

## Client-Centered Therapy: The 1951 Model

*Client-Centered Therapy: Its Current Practice, Implications and Theory* (Rogers, 1951) was perhaps the most influential book on psychotherapy in America since Freud's *Five Lectures on Psychoanalysis*. Although Carl Rogers' name alone graces the title page, a long and somewhat strange preface credits by name some 21 people "who are most likely to find portions of their own thoughts included in this book" (p. ix).

The book traces the history of the client-centered approach, gives much attention to therapists' attitudes, rejects the necessity for differential diagnosis, and contains several separately authored chapters on specific applications. Most noticeably, the combative tone of the 1942 book is missing. Differences with other viewpoints are recognized without the sweeping condemnation invoked earlier.

Perhaps the most interesting and ultimately influential chapter is titled "A Theory of Personality and Behavior." It is clear that in the years between his presidential address in 1947 and the publication of *Client-Centered Therapy*, Rogers had greatly expanded his theoretical framework to include a phenomenological approach. Phenomenology is a view drawn from both philosophy and psychology that holds that each person has his or her own essentially private and unique world of reality, and behaves in terms of that reality. Rogers reiterated his view that all people possess an inner growth force which, when released, will direct them unerringly along the path to further development. Threats to the self-concept were seen to cause distortions in the client's perceptions and also to stifle the growth force.

The task of the therapist in Client-Centered Therapy then was defined as sharing the client's private reality insofar as possible, and reducing threat to the client's self-concept, thereby helping the client to perceive the world more accurately and to behave more effectively in the directions set by the inner growth force. Clearly, these rather formidable therapeutic tasks were to be accomplished as a result of a very special and powerful kind of therapist-client relationship that was largely a function of the therapist's basic attitudes. The precise nature of that relationship was still not fully spelled out.

## The Relationship Conditions Emerge

In *Client-Centered Therapy* (1951) Rogers suggested that progress in counseling or therapy would be likely to occur if the therapist were

(1) congruent or genuine in the relationship;
(2) if the therapist experiences unconditional positive regard for the client; and
(3) if the counselor demonstrates accurate empathic understanding of the client.

The emphasis in this formulation was clearly on the attitudes or inner state of the therapist, rather than upon what the therapist actually does. Even empathic understanding might be demonstrated in a wide variety of largely unspecified ways.

This was the era of what has been facetiously termed the "sunlamp school of psychotherapy." The therapist needed only to shine the rays of his or her inner genuineness and unconditional positive regard on the client for wonderful things to begin to happen. In some published cases, it was argued that such changes were actually occurring during long periods of complete silence. Long silences were not unusual in client-centered interviews.

A down side of this approach was that counselors who could not achieve such successes were often viewed as personally flawed, judgmental, incongruent and insensitive, all cardinal sins.

Six years after the publication of *Client-Centered Therapy*, Carl Rogers issued the most famous and most sweeping pronouncement of his controversial career (Rogers, 1957). He defined the basic conditions that he asserted were necessary and sufficient for therapeutic change. These conditions were described as:

1. The two persons are in psychological contact.
2. The first, whom we shall term the client, is in a state of incongruence, being vulnerable or anxious.
3. The second person, whom we shall call the therapist, is congruent or integrated in the relationship.
4. The therapist experiences unconditional positive regard for the client.
5. The therapist experiences an empathic understanding of the client's internal frame of reference and endeavors to communicate this experience to the client.
6. The communication of the therapist's empathic understanding and unconditional positive regard is to a minimal degree achieved.

No other conditions are necessary. If these six conditions exist, and continue over a period of time, this is sufficient. The process of constructive personality change will follow. (p. 96)

This pronouncement is probably one of the most sweeping knowledge claims ever advanced in American psychology. Not even J. B. Watson's claim of environmental supremacy, discussed earlier, could top Rogers' claims of the magic of relationship. There was modest rejoicing in the camps of those still smarting from Rogers' attacks of 15 years before. This time, they were sure that Carl Rogers had clearly stepped across the boundaries, if not of reason, then at least of reputable science.

It is much more probable that the "necessary and sufficient" conditions manifesto was more a product of Carl Rogers' growing disenchantment with the rigors and restrictions of traditional scientific epistemology and methodology than of a sudden attack of dementia.

In 1956 Rogers had participated in a symposium, or really, a debate, with B. F. Skinner around the issues of determinism versus free will. The papers from the symposium were published in *Science* (1956) and were widely read and discussed among behavioral scientists of all persuasions. Rogers' paper was entitled "Some Issues Concerning the Control of Human Behavior." It marked the beginning of his conversion to the tenets of humanistic psychology and a throwing off of the shackles that he and a number of other psychologists felt were imposed by a positivistic, highly experimental, and statistically bound psychology. For Carl Rogers, the rules of scientific evidence had changed. Not only were the lives of people not determined by external reinforcement, but the nature of scientific knowledge was not determined solely by tests of statistical significance. In an autobiographical book (Rogers, 1961) Rogers described a wrenching inner struggle as he abandoned many of the tenets of traditional science.

In 1958, in a speech to the American Personnel and Guidance Association, Rogers expanded on his definition of "The Characteristics of a Helping Relationship" (Rogers, 1958). Again, the emphasis was on the personality of the counselor, as Rogers set forth a set of soul-searching questions that the counselor must ask of self before entering a therapeutic relationship. At no point did Rogers really define relationship conditions in terms of what the therapist would actually do or say. The therapeutic vehicle for the healing power of the therapeutic relationships was clearly the therapist's personality.

## Client-Centered Therapy with Schizophrenics

Shortly after returning to the University of Wisconsin as Professor of Psychology and Psychiatry, Carl Rogers launched the largest and most ambitious study of his career. Using funding from the National Institute of Mental Health and a variety of other sources, Rogers organized a large-scale study of the effects of Client-Centered Therapy and, more specifically, of his specified "relationship conditions," in the treatment of hospitalized schizophrenics. The general consensus among clinical psychologists was, and still is, that this population is not amenable to treatment with any form of psychotherapy.

Clearly, this study was intended to constitute the acid test of the "necessary and sufficient" theorem, and was to be thrown directly into the teeth of Rogers' many skeptics and critics. The project apparently turned into an unmitigated disaster, both scientifically and in terms of relationships among the researchers themselves. The design problems were clearly horrendous, and the task of organizing and controlling variables must have been mind-boggling.

The study was reported in a 1967 volume initially published by the University of Wisconsin Press and appearing well after most of the principal researchers had departed the University of Wisconsin. The volume was edited by Rogers, with the collaboration of Eugene T.

Gendlin, Donald Kiesler, and Charles B. Truax (1967). It contains material authored by some 16 other contributing authors and "commentators."

This book has to be one of the strangest and most laborious reports of a research project ever compiled. Rogers claimed support of his theoretical approach, but the absence of clear-cut results of almost any kind was unmistakable. Much of the book is devoted to transcribed verbatim excerpts from cases and descriptions of client-therapists interactions. The study did mark the beginning of a 15-year effort to build rating scales for measuring relationship conditions.

In the introduction, Rogers mentioned the morale factors and conflicts that plagued the staff. Apparently warmth, empathy, and unconditional positive regard were in short supply among the researchers themselves. One of the principal researchers was Charles B. Truax, who was apparently in charge of the monumental task of rating samples of taped interviews from the hundreds of therapy sessions. At the point of final analysis of these crucial pieces of data upon which the whole study really depended, the Truax data abruptly disappeared. Rogers' described the situation in these terms:

> Dr. Charles B. Truax organized the initial data collection and analysis. The ratings on which his studies were based mysteriously disappeared and have not been recovered. This unfortunate fact made Dr. Truax' preliminary reports unusable in this book. (Rogers et al., 1967, p. xviii)

The original samples were apparently re-rated by other raters and the new data were entered in the final results.

Eugene Gendlin, who was a principal coordinator of the project, was, as we noted, the author of Carl Rogers' obituary in *The American Psychologist* (Gendlin, 1988). In describing Carl Rogers' administrative style, Gendlin asserts that

> [I]n Wisconsin (where Rogers was invited to do research with schizophrenics) his organizational model could not cope with even one deliberately unethical person, (who removed the data, tried to publish it, and then, destroyed it so that much work had to be done again). (p. 128)

This incident has been the source of considerable rumor and conjecture. Whatever the true circumstances, the "schizophrenic study" marked the end of Carl Rogers' academic career and his formal research activity. Perhaps Rogers' growing discontent with conventional research methods and his espousal of new and radical approaches to learning and professional education, as well as the debacle of the "schizophrenic study," contributed to his decision to join the Western Behavioral Sciences Institute in LaJolla, California and later The Center for Studies of the Person.

For 15 years after the Wisconsin study, efforts to measure relationship conditions constituted one of the most active lines of research in both clinical and counseling psychology. Much of this line of research was described in a book by Charles Truax and Robert Carkhuff (1967). This research effort endeavored to translate Rogers" concepts of the attitudes and inner states of the therapist into observable behaviors and specific therapeutic interactions. Unfortunately, the effort proved to be one of the many "blind alleys" traveled by psychological research. In 1978, one of the last major reviews of this research (Lambert, DeJulio, & Stein, 1978) examined the relationship between therapeutic outcomes and therapists' interpersonal skills such as empathy, regard, and genuineness. Conclusions "include the idea that Rogerian hypotheses have been only modestly supported," and "the efficacy of popular interpersonal skills training models has not been demonstrated" (p. 467). By 1994, a major review of "The Status of the Counseling Relationship" did not even cite this line of research (Sexton & Whiston, 1994).

## Existentialism: From Thought to Therapy

The term "existentialism" is not indexed in *Client-Centered Therapy*. In *On Becoming a Person* (Rogers, 1961) Rogers noted that on a trip to Mexico in the winter of 1952 he "immersed himself" in the writings of the nineteenth-century Danish existential philosopher Soren Kierkegaard. This apparently marked the beginning of a profound change in both Rogers' thinking and in his approach to therapy. In this, he joined a group of other distinguished American psychologists.

Existentialism is an approach to philosophy that stresses the primacy and overriding importance of each individual's direct and immediate experiencing in the search for understanding and meaning in living. The position of Kierkegaard, as well as of later existentialists, was that both objective reality and the individuals' uniquely human "subjective reality" must be recognized and respected in order to grasp the full meaning of either an individual's life or the general human condition. This position is, of course, related to the phenomenological view discussed earlier.

Existentialism was to some degree a reaction to the analytical and reductionistic approaches to both philosophy and science in the nineteenth and early twentieth centuries. In psychology, as we have seen, trait-and-factor, psychoanalytic, and behavioral approaches all sought to partition, classify and reduce human behavior to a neat and relatively simple set of forces or causes, operating either within the individual or within the environment. To some extent, the search for general principles or laws governing human behavior could be seen as a "mechanizing" and dehumanizing of total human experience.

Existentialism as a philosophy and as a basis for psychotherapy became prominent in Europe after the end of the Second World War. Europeans had experienced the horrors of total war, the Holocaust, and their aftermath in a much more personal and immediate way than had most Americans. The realities of a nuclear age were also much more vivid to a population that had lived through two world wars in one generation.

The new existential therapies that arose in Europe rejected the biological and deterministic views of psychoanalysis and its derivations and developed an approach that emphasized the human need and capacity for giving meaning to life or existence. Many of the aspects of modern urbanized and industrialized society were seen to alienate people from their own experiencing, and to deprive them of the opportunity to find genuine meaning in their existence. Traditional psychotherapies were viewed to be part of the problem rather than the solution.

Existentialists were suspicious of the artificiality of "grand designs," whether in terms of political ideologies, personality theories, or prescriptive therapies. Kierkegaard is said to have remarked that the builders of such grand systems are like a man who constructs a magnificent castle, and then goes to live in the adjoining barn.

It seems clear that the concepts of existentialism and existential therapies resonated with the ideas and values that were evolving in Carl Rogers' approach. Kierkegaard's ideas were introduced to American psychologists by Rollo May in a book titled *The Meaning of Anxiety*

(May, 1950). May focused upon Kierkegaard's concept of existential "dread" and interpreted it to support the notion that anxiety and loneliness are pervasive and inevitable aspects of the human condition.

By the early 1960s, the views of a variety of existential therapists and philosophers such as Binswanger, Boss, Frankl, Sartre, and Jaspers were widely read and discussed by American psychologists. Psychologists such as Abraham Maslow, Gordon Allport, and Hadley Cantril were drawing upon existential concepts to broaden and enrich basic concepts of the "Nature of Man." Therapists such as Rollo May, Irving Yalom, James Bugental, and Thomas Szasz, along with Rogers, were reevaluating their views of therapy. In counseling psychology, Cecil Patterson was applying the new ideas to a variety of counseling situations.

Existential notions not only resonated with the views of American psychologists; they were very much in tune with the total American experience of the 1960s. Distrust of and discontent with institutions and social, political, and religious ideologies were rampant. Philosophies and psychotherapies that centered upon individual experience and looked to individual perceptions as the final source of validity were welcomed.

A new "third force" in American psychology was recognized and christened Humanistic Psychology.

## HUMANISTIC PSYCHOLOGY: THE THIRD FORCE

The 1960s were an era of "idol-smashing" in counseling and therapy as well as in politics (Zax, 1980). Both psychoanalysis and behavior therapy came under attack on both philosophical and scientific grounds. New therapies burst upon the scene in dazzling profusion. Gestalt Therapy, introduced by Fritz and Laura Perls, was influenced both by the German Gestalt psychologists and by the existential writings of Martin Buber and Paul Tillich (Rice & Greenberg, 1992).

Various group approaches devoted not only to therapy, but to self-actualization, the development of human potential, sensitivity training, and a host of other outcomes proliferated as they stirred the imagination and opened the pocketbooks of the populace. They promised to fulfill a yearning for "something more" in their lives than two cars and a house in the suburbs. As with most popular enthusiasms, the encounter group movement had both a thoughtful and psychologically sound side and a lunatic fringe of sensationalism, superficiality, and cynical exploitation.

Openness and self-disclosure and confrontation were often equated with "growth" and "sensitivity." The "transparent self" (Jourard, 1964) was seen as the epitome of optimal development. Out on the lunatic fringe, the "marathon nude T-Group" and other caricatures of psychological helping were the subject of journalistic derision and/or indignation (Gross, 1978).

After leaving Wisconsin, Carl Rogers became deeply involved in the encounter group movement and tried to build a new, psychologically sound, and existentially oriented concept of positive human relationships on all levels and in all aspects of personal interaction. He had clearly moved beyond even "person-centered therapy."

It is not entirely clear how Client-Centered Therapy, Gestalt Therapy, the European Existential therapies and various approaches to conceptualizing the "Nature of Man" came together under the rubric of Humanistic Psychology. To many psychologists not part of the new movement, the term was both annoying and confusing. By 1977, an Association for Humanistic Psychology was represented in the exhibitor's section of the APA Convention Program. This group defined itself in these terms: "We are a worldwide network organized to develop the human sciences in ways that recognize our distinctively human qualities" (quoted in Wertheimer, 1978, p. 740). Clearly, the purpose of humanistic psychology has been from the beginning to reform, revolutionize, or subvert traditional psychology, depending upon one's point of view.

Royce (1967) credited humanistic psychology with not only being a "third force" in psychology, but with being founded on a "third way of knowing" that goes beyond empiricism and rationalism, the generally accepted bases for science, to accept intuition and metaphor as legitimate and indeed indispensable ways of knowing in a scientific sense.

We noted earlier that "operationism," or what was later termed logical positivism, became the dominant view of the philosophy of science for psychology in the late 1920s. By the 1960s this was seen by many psychologists as a rigid and sterile approach to research that ignored important issues, while providing sophisticated answers to trivial questions. For these people, humanistic psychology provided both a home and a rallying cry.

In 1984, a study of the views and values of psychologists (Kimble, 1984) suggested the presence of two distinct cultures or worldviews within the ranks of organized psychology. These two cultures were seen to differ in terms of the following dimensions.

1. The importance of scientific vs. humanistic values;
2. The lawfulness of behavior: determinism vs. indeterminism;
3. The basic sources of knowledge: observation vs. intuition;
4. The appropriate setting for research: the laboratory vs. field or case studies;
5. The generality of laws: nomethic vs. ideographic; and
6. The appropriate level of analysis: elementism vs. holism.

The differences described above of course strike at the very heart of a science. If indeed contemporary psychologists disagree on such fundamental issues, then perhaps, as Koch (1981) has long suggested, there is no one psychology, but rather a cluster of "psychological studies." Perhaps, more succinctly, the question was whether psychology is a science of human behavior, or the study of inner experience.

## Humanistic Therapies

The "Humanistic Therapies," as they are sometimes called, have provided much less embarrassment to professional psychology than have the humanistic views of the limits of science and nature of human beings. Humanistic therapies are usually defined as including Client-Centered Therapy, Gestalt Therapy, the Logotherapy of Viktor Frankl, and the European approaches, termed *Daseinanalyse*, advanced by Benswanger and Boss. They have influenced many other therapeutic approaches as well as views of education and group work.

It is difficult to define the core beliefs that distinguish humanistic approaches from other therapeutic positions. Rice and Greenberg (1992) cite four basic positions or beliefs systems that are distinctive and crucial in all humanistic therapies. These are:

1. A commitment to a phenomenological approach;

2. The belief in some kind of inner actualizing or growth force within all human beings;
3. A belief in the human capacity for self-determination; and
4. A deep-seated concern for and respect for each person. This includes respect for each person's unique subjective experiencing. Being allowed to share in another person's world is viewed as a special privilege requiring a special kind of relationship.

If we accept the above positions as the core beliefs of humanistic therapies, the continuing impact of the humanistic tradition on counseling psychology seems unmistakable.

## THE HUMANISTIC LEGACY

Clearly, the concepts outlined above as the central principles of humanistic therapies have to a considerable extent influenced nearly all contemporary counseling psychologists. Even though Carl Rogers' rather grandiose notions of the "necessary and sufficient" conditions for therapeutic progress have long since been relegated to the status of historical oddities, the central role Rogers ascribed to the relationship as the foundation of all counseling and psychotherapy is very much alive (Gelso & Carter, 1985; Sexton & Whiston, 1994).

The modern view of "relationship" has been broadened to include the psychoanalytic concepts of working alliance and transference. The original Rogerian conditions and the cluster of concepts added to Rogers' formulation have not been fully operationally defined. At the level of intuition and metaphor on which humanistic psychologists have based their knowledge claims, it is very difficult for any practicing counselor to be against qualities such as warmth, empathy, regard, immediacy, or respect. It seems doubtful that many neurologically intact human beings over the past few thousand years have totally ignored or denied the significance of these qualities for human relationships.

In slightly updated form, the concept of empathy has had a resurgence of interest, both in counseling and psychotherapy and in social and developmental psychology (Duan & Hill, 1996). Empathy is seen by some contemporary researchers as the key ingredient in almost all helping situations and relationships (Batson, 1990).

The basic research tools given us by Carl Rogers and Frank Robinson in the 1930s are still basic to both research and training in counseling and therapy. Without the recording of interviews, our understanding of both counseling process and counselor education would be primitive indeed. Clearly, also, the rules and restrictions that marked a philosophy of science based upon positivistic principles have been loosened. Qualitative research, single case studies, naturalistic studies, and client self-reports have become legitimate approaches to inquiry.

Today, we no longer call those on whom we do research subjects. Rather, we refer to those with whom we do research as participants. We employ elaborate ethical safeguards to protect the dignity and psychological well-being of these indispensable partners in scientific progress. Concepts of informed consent and restrictions upon scientific deceit and deception, too, are part of the humanistic legacy.

Watson (1977) gave an even more succinct view of humanistic therapies than we cited above. He said:

> What can be termed a "humanistic creed" is adhered to by, and influences all humanistic therapies. The creed rests on two basic beliefs. First, the therapist must have a fundamental *respect* for the patients with whom he or she works, and must see them as *active agents capable of change*. Second, the therapist must perceive each patient as an *individual* with whom one must have an interpersonal relationship for the therapy to be effective. (pp. 162–163) (italics added)

To some extent humanistic therapy, as a term, has gradually become less of a distinctive and potent force in the field in recent years (Rice & Greenberg, 1992). Perhaps this is because so much of what the humanistic approach advocated for 20 or 30 years ago has been quietly accepted as an essential part of mainstream counseling and psychotherapy.

If the two basic tenets of humanistic therapy cited in the quote above are central to its creed, all of us, as counseling psychologists, should hope that we share fully in the humanistic legacy.

## REFERENCES

Batson, C. D. (1990). How social an animal? *American Psychologist, 45*, 336–346.

Duan, C., & Hill, C. E. (1996). The current state of empathy research. *The Counseling Psychologist, 43,* 261–274.

Gelso, C. J., & Carter, J. A. (1985). The relationship in counseling and psychotherapy: Its components, consequences and theoretical antecedents. *The Counseling Psychologist, 13,* 155–243.

Gendlin, E. T. (1988). Carl Rogers (1902–1987). *American Psychologist, 43,* 127–128.

Gross, M. L. (1978). *The psychological society.* New York: Random House.

Halleck, S. L. (1971). *Politics of therapy.* New York: Science House.

Hilgard, E. R. (1987). *Psychology in America: A historical survey.* Orlando, FL: Harcourt Brace, Johanovich.

Jourard, S. M. (1964). *The transparent self.* Princeton, NJ: Van Nostrand.

Kimble, G. A. (1984). Psychology's two cultures. *American Psychologist, 39,* 833–839.

Kirschenbaum, H., & Henderson, V. L. (Eds.). (1989). *The Carl Rogers reader.* Boston: Houghton Mifflin.

Koch, S. (1981). The nature and limits of psychological knowledge: Lessons of a century of qua "science." *American Psychologist, 36,* 257–269.

Lambert, M. J., DeJulio, S. D., & Stein, D. M. (1978). Therapists' interpersonal skills: Process, outcome, methodological considerations and recommendations for further research. *Psychological Bulletin, 85,* 407–489.

Lecky, P. (1945). *Self-consistency: A theory of personality.* New York: Island Press.

May, R. (1950). *The meaning of anxiety.* New York: Ronald Press.

Rice, L. N., & Greenberg, L. S. (1992). Humanistic approaches to psychotherapy. In D. K. Freedheim (Ed.), *History of psychotherapy: A century of change* (pp. 197–224). Washington, DC: American Psychological Association.

Rogers, C. R. (1939). *The clinical treatment of the problem child.* Boston: Houghton Mifflin.

Rogers, C. R. (1942). *Counseling and psychotherapy.* Boston: Houghton Mifflin.

Rogers, C. R. (1951). *Client-centered therapy: Its current practice, implications and theory.* Boston: Houghton Mifflin.

Rogers, C. R. (1956). Some issues concerning the control of human behavior (Symposium with B. F. Skinner). *Science, 124,* 1057–1066.

Rogers, C. R. (1957). The necessary and sufficient conditions for personality change. *Journal of Consulting Psychology, 21,* 95–103.

Rogers, C. R. (1958). The characteristics of a helping relationship. *Personnel and Guidance Journal, 37,* 6–16.

Rogers, C. R. (1961). *On becoming a person.* Boston: Houghton Mifflin.

Rogers, C. R. (1968). Some thoughts regarding the current pre-suppositions of the behavioral sciences. In W. Coulson & C. R. Rogers (Eds.), *Man and the science of man* (pp. 55–72). Columbus, OH: Charles E. Merrill.

Rogers, C. R., & Dymond, R. F. (1954). (Eds.). *Psychotherapy and personality change.* Chicago: University of Chicago Press.

Rogers, C. R., Gendlin, E. T., Kiesler, D. J., & Truax, C. B. (Eds.) (1967). *The therapeutic relationship and its impact: A study of psychotherapy with schizophrenics.* Westport, CN: Greenwood Press.

Royce, J. R. (1967). Metaphoric knowledge and humanistic psychology. In J. Bugental (Ed.), *Challenges of humanistic psychology* (pp. 21–28). New York: McGraw-Hill.

Sexton, T. L., & Whiston, S. C. (1994). The status of the counseling relationship: An empirical review, theoretical implications, and research directions. *The Counseling Psychologist, 22,* 6–78.

Super, D. (1988). Comment on Carl Rogers's obituary. *American Psychologist, 44,* 1161–1162.

Truax, C. B., & Carkhuff, R. R. (1967). *Toward effective counseling and psychotherapy: Training and practice.* Chicago: Aldine.

Watson, R. I. (1977). An introduction to humanistic psychotherapy. In S. J. Morse & R. I. Watson (Eds.), *Psychotherapies* (pp. 162–181). New York: Holt, Rinehart and Winston.

Wertheimer, M. (1978). Humanistic psychology and the humane but tough-minded psychologist. *American Psychologist, 33,* 739–745.

Zax, M. (1980). History and background of the community mental health movement. In M. S. Gibbs, J. R. Lachenmier, & J. Sigel (Eds.), *Community psychology* (pp. 1–28). New York: Gardner Press.

# 9

# The Behavioral Tradition

A scientific analysis of behavior must, I believe, assume that a person's behavior is controlled by his genetic and environmental histories rather than by the person himself as an initiating, creative agent . . .

—B. F. Skinner, 1974

In the spring of 1917, the Russian city of Petrograd, or St. Petersburg, as it was called in the West, was convulsed in the end of imperial rule, the collapse of its armies on the Eastern Front, and the beginning of the Bolshevik Revolution. On March 15, Czar Nicholas abdicated, and after some 6 months of riots, street-fighting, interim governments, and bloody mutinies came the October Revolution. The Second All-Russian Congress of Soviets convened, and the future of the Union of Soviet Socialist Republics was in the hands of Vladimir Ilyich Ulyanov, alias Nikolai Lenin (Smith, 1985).

In the midst of that turmoil and chaos, a lone worker who had apparently not yet heard of the dictatorship of the proletariat dodged stray bullets, street riots, and angry demonstrators to arrive late but whole at one of the few places in that tortured city that seemed to be operating on a business-as-usual basis. It was a forbidding, fortresslike building with walls some 3 feet thick, surrounded by a moat.

Inside, safe but shaken, the tardy worker received a stern reprimand from the master of the establishment, one Ivan Petrovich Pavlov. The thick walls and moat surrounding the laboratory were not there to protect Pavlov and his assistants from the turmoil of war and revolution, but rather to shut out all noise and smell from the sensitive ears and wet noses of the building's most important residents, Pavlov's dogs.

## THE FIRST BEHAVIORIST

Ivan Pavlov was born in 1849 in the Russian farming village of Ryazan. He was descended from a family of serfs who had been emancipated some generations earlier because they were employed in the Orthodox Church. Ivan's father was an ordained priest and his mother was the daughter of a priest. Both parents, however, had to earn their living in the fields as peasants, working the estates of wealthy landowners.

Young Ivan did well at the village school, and in line with the tradition in his family, was entered in a nearby seminary to prepare for the priesthood. He began to read widely, particularly in the area of the natural sciences, and was fascinated by the blossoming ideas of Darwin and evolutionary biology. The appeal of science clearly outweighed whatever interest he had held for the priesthood.

As a poor, but outstanding, student, young Pavlov won a government-sponsored scholarship to the University of Petrograd. He chose the natural sciences as a major field and a career was born (Fancher, 1990). Pavlov received a degree in physiology in 1875 and continued his education at the Military Medical Academy in Petrograd. He had no intention of pursuing a career in medical practice, but was already actively involved in physiological research.

After receiving an M.D. degree in 1883, Pavlov spent some time working as a researcher in German laboratories. In 1890, Pavlov's great opportunity arrived as he became a professor at the Military Medical Academy. A year later he organized a department of physiology in the newly formed Imperial Institute of Experimental Medicine. He soon became a world-renowned researcher on the physiology of the digestive system. In 1904, Pavlov received the Nobel Prize in Physiology.

As a personality, Ivan Pavlov was a study in extremes and contrasts. Outside of the laboratory he was sentimental, impractical and financially irresponsible, almost a stereotypical example of the legendary absent-minded professor. He became engaged to be married while still a student, and lavished much of his meager income on flowers, candy, and theater tickets for his fiancee—all of the necessities of a young man hopelessly in love.

Once, when he did buy his future wife a practical gift—a new pair of shoes to take on a trip—she found only one shoe in her bag, along

**Figure 9.1    Ivan Petrovich Pavlov**

with a note from Pavlov telling her not to look for the other shoe, since he had taken it as a remembrance and placed it on his desk.

After marriage, he often forgot to pick up his salary, and once, when he did remember, promptly loaned it to an irresponsible acquaintance who was unable to repay the debt. On a trip to New York in 1929 to attend an International Congress of Psychology, Pavlov carried all of his money in a conspicuous wad protruding from his pocket as he entered the subway at rush hour. The predictable occurred, and his American hosts had to take up a collection to replace his funds (Fancher, 1990).

While in the laboratory, however, a complete metamorphosis in Pavlov's personality occurred. There he was a punctual, persistent, and perfectionistic organizer and supervisor. He fought ferociously for funds to ensure that his laboratory was well-equipped and that his precious animals were well-fed. He was a meticulous supervisor who attended to all the details. Pavlov supervised a large staff of experimenters who produced literally dozens of scientific papers and reports each year. When others did not observe his high professional and scientific standards, he was known for his explosive emotional tirades (Windholz, 1997).

From 1890 to his death in 1936, I. P. Pavlov managed a highly organized and superbly productive factory of physiological and eventually psychological research. The First World War and the Russian Revolution were only minor interruptions to either his career or his work. While Pavlov spoke against the Communist Regime on occasion, he was clearly the pampered darling of the Soviet Establishment. Remarks that would have sent a lesser public figure on an unplanned sojourn to Siberia, or worse, were simply ignored. Indeed, Pavlov's canine castle laboratory, which was begun with a grant from a wealthy businessman, was completed and equipped with funds from the Bolshevik government in the newly named city of Leningrad.

Pavlov probably basked in this unusual official favor and ideological indulgence for several reasons. His own peasant background and humble beginnings made his life a virtual testament to the slogans of the Revolution. He was also one of the very few world-renowned scientists in the new Soviet Union as it strove for international recognition. Finally, Pavlov's mechanistic concept of the human being as a walking bundle of semiautomatic reflexes waiting to be conditioned fit nicely with the philosophy of a regime and movement committed not only to re-engineering Russian society, but also with producing a new breed of person: the compliant, cooperative, and above all, hardworking Soviet citizen.

Pavlov's reputation as a physiologist had been built around perfecting a series of surgical procedures that allowed him to observe directly the digestive processes of his laboratory animals. He was able to create surgically a pouch or fistula that brought to the surface portions of the dog's esophagus and stomach. When this was stimulated with food, Pavlov could observe the workings of the digestive system. He performed similar surgeries to expose the workings of the salivary glands in the dog's mouth.

Using these surgical techniques, Pavlov made fundamental discoveries on the nature of gastric glands, the functions of the pancreas, and the motility of the gastrointestinal tract (Dewsbury, 1997). These discoveries brought him the Nobel Prize.

## From Physiology to Psychology

The traditionally accepted version of Pavlov's reluctant transition from physiology to psychology credits the process to his desire to study a puzzling reaction in the salivary secretions of his dogs that seemed to interfere with certain of his experiments. At times, the salivary response was already underway well prior to the presentation of any food. This phenomenon was called a "psychic response" and was given a "mentalistic" explanation by the laboratory staff in terms of the dog's supposed anticipation or "thinking about" the imminent arrival of food.

Supposedly, Pavlov was fiercely opposed to such explanations, and his efforts at soundproofing his laboratory were intended to insulate against extraneous stimuli that might trigger unwanted responses in the dogs. Pavlov's own discussion of the events many years later seemed to support such a set of serendipitous circumstances.

Recently, more careful study of the circumstances and early research on the "psychic secretions" problem suggests that Pavlov, himself, initially credited mentalistic explanations of the phenomenon, recognized its significance, and consciously began the line of research that eventually led to the recognition and understanding of the "conditioned reflex" and the whole process of what we now call classical conditioning (Todes, 1997).

Regardless of how the research began Pavlov's contribution to psychology is immense. His 1927 book that was mentioned earlier is clearly one of the most influential and durable pieces of work ever produced. Very early in the research, clinically trained people were brought in and the human significance and applications of the results were recognized and were explored (Todes, 1997).

Conceptions of classical conditioning processes have been greatly broadened in recent years, and it remains an active and productive area of research (Rescorta, 1988). Current approaches to psychotherapy, particularly in the area of treatments for anxiety and phobias, still owe much to Ivan Pavlov and his dogs (Wolpe & Plaud, 1997).

## THE ANTECEDENTS OF BEHAVIORISM

Ivan Pavlov never referred to himself as a behaviorist. As we saw earlier, that term appears to have been coined by J. B. Watson in

1913. The roots of behaviorism, however, go back far beyond either Pavlov or Watson. For centuries, thinkers have pondered the problems posed by human learning and memory. The whole topic has been described by the term "learning theory"; modern behaviorism is in a sense simply one approach to that age-old problem.

The roots of modern learning theory can be traced to two groups of British philosophers whose approach has been called associationism. The labels "British Associationists" and "British Empiricists" have been given to these philosopher-psychologists who were active in the eighteenth and nineteenth centuries. We should note that the term "empiricism" does not have the modern meaning of being rooted in research. These scholars were "armchair psychologists" who built their points of view around rational analysis of everyday, informal observations of human behavior. For them, the term "empirical" meant a view rooted in experience. One of the positions that came out of the work of this group was phenomenology, the philosophical orientation that is, ironically, central to the humanistic tradition discussed earlier.

One of the crucial concepts in this approach to human learning is that of the *tabula rasa*, or blank tablet, with which all human beings are seen to come into the world. All learning, all associations, all thinking and all behavior, then, are products of experience, not of prenatal or genetic tendencies. The term "empiricism" came from "experience," as opposed to "nativism," the belief that there are already concepts, tendencies, or instincts present in the mind at birth. This 300-year-old argument is by no means an extinct issue. It is still at the heart of the controversy over the process of language acquisition between Skinnerian psychologists and psycholinguists such as Noam Chomsky (Chomsky, 1980).

More than 2,000 years ago, Aristotle had thought about many of the same questions and had concluded that we tend to associate events or ideas that occur close together in space or time, or are seen as similar or opposite to each other. Today these are two of the oldest "laws of association," namely; contiguity and similarity. During the seventeenth, eighteenth and even much of the nineteenth centuries, the associationists simply concluded that human learning and thought were primarily products of contiguity, similarity, and frequency; in other words, that our ideas are learned or formed out of what is frequent, familiar, and pervasive in our experience. This is a strong environmentalist position that occupies the extreme nurture end of the nature-nurture continuum.

Lest we think that the associationists were simplistic or naive in their understanding of human behavior, a quote from John Locke, who was one of the first and foremost of the group, may show how really "modern" was his understanding of human behavior.

John Locke (1693), in giving advice to the parents of a fearful child wrote the following prescription:

> [I]f your child shrieks and runs away at the sight of a frog let another catch it and lay it down at a good distance from him; at first accustom him to look upon it; when he can do that, to come nearer to it, and see it leap without emotion, then to touch it slightly, when it is held fast in another's hand; and so on until he can come to handle it as confidently as a butterfly or a sparrow. (p. 24)

The process that John Locke described more than 300 years ago is today termed "in vivo graduated desensitization" and is considered to be at the core of most successful treatments for phobias (Emmelkamp, 1986). Other things being equal, John Locke could probably participate intelligently in a symposium on behavior therapy alongside Joseph Wolpe and his colleagues.

The first really experimental work on human learning was accomplished by Herman Ebbinghaus (1850–1909). Ebbinghaus was a contemporary of Wundt, but utilized experimental methods that were much more like those in use in experimental psychology today. He is often remembered for inventing the "nonsense syllable," a device for measuring memorization that is not contaminated by prior learning or association.

Ebbinghaus demonstrated the permanent nature of learning by showing that lists of nonsense syllables once learned could be recalled with fewer relearning trials or repetitions than were required to master new material. His results are still cited in general psychology texts today.

Around the beginning of the twentieth century, learning theory split along two divergent paths. German Gestalt psychology began to approach human learning in terms of the way human beings organize their perceptions of the world. The Gestaltists, influenced by the phenomenological notions of the associationists and empiricists, sought to understand learning in terms of sudden "insights" or problem-solving strategies. A half century later many of these ideas were, as we saw, incorporated into Client-Centered Therapy, and became part of the humanistic tradition of counseling psychology.

The second path was that taken by Ivan Pavlov. He was particularly opposed to, and even incensed by, the claims of the Gestaltists who attributed higher level problem-solving behaviors to animals. Pavlov went so far as to try to replicate Kohler's famous study of problem-solving in apes to show that it was merely the result of trial and error. Predictably, Pavlov's ape turned out to be a less efficient problem-solver than Kohler's.

Pavlov's own work, of course, followed the other path out of associationism, as he showed that "neutral stimuli," when presented in close contiguity with eliciting stimuli, could produce a new *conditioned reflex*.

## BEHAVIORISM IN AMERICA

The second facet of modern behaviorism really began in America in the work of William James and his students. James in his famous *Principles of Psychology* (1890) argued that much of human behavior can be explained simply as a function of habits, that is, behavior learned through repetition or frequency.

James had what we consider today to be two careers, one as a psychologist and one as a philosopher. In his latter role, James had been one of the founders of the philosophical approach called pragmatism. The central concepts of pragmatism are that the truth of any proposition is measured by its correspondence with actual observable results, and that the value of any action is determined by its practical consequences or effects.

James's notions about the worth or value of habits were based on their practical consequences for the behaving individual. Bad habits were self-defeating, leading to negative consequences, while good habits furthered the individual's goals and satisfactions. The process of positive learning, or growth, simply consisted of making useful actions automatic and habitual. Good habits are acquired through frequent and consistent repetition or exercise, while bad habits are eliminated by equally careful avoidance. This view is pretty much the essence of behaviorism.

## The Dissertation that Reshaped Psychology

Edward Lee Thorndike (1874–1949) was an undergraduate student at Weslyan College in Connecticut when he read and reviewed James's *Principles* for a prize competition. He began graduate work at Harvard and took courses with James.

Thorndike wanted to do research on children and pedagogy, but shortly before he began his research, a major scandal erupted in Boston. Franz Boas, the anthropologist/psychologist, who was in G. Stanley Hall's little stable of luminaries at Clark University, attempted to do anthropometric research on children in the Boston Schools. The physical measurements involved an unfortunate loosening of some of the children's clothing, and a scandal ensued in prudish and puritanical Boston (O'Donnell, 1985). Although Harvard was not directly involved, its administrators banned all research with children.

Since children were put off limits for research, Thorndike began his research with animals, at first using chickens. James even gave Thorndike space in his own basement after Harvard refused him official research space. Before completing his doctoral research, Thorndike was offered a fellowship by Cattell at Columbia. There he continued his research on animal learning.

In 1898 Thorndike published the report of his doctoral research under the title *Animal Intelligence: An Experimental Study of the Associative Processes in Animals*. It was accepted as his doctoral dissertation.

Thorndike argued that the only way to study animal learning or intelligence was to design experiments that completely controlled the animal's situation. To this end, he designed a set of ingenious "puzzle boxes," each of which could be opened by the animal in a different way. When the animal escaped, it was fed. Thorndike used a number of animal subjects including cats, dogs, and chickens.

What Thorndike found, of course, was that the animal made a variety of responses to the situation. When one of these was rewarded with escape and food, the response was learned. If the response was not rewarded, it gradually disappeared. Thorndike's experimental results led him to reject the view that animals "reasoned." They learned, he said, purely by trial and error, reward and punishment.

Interestingly, although Thorndike's research was accepted as his doctoral thesis, he did not quite dare to set forth its full implications until later, when his own career as an educational psychologist was well established.

In 1911, Thorndike republished his findings in a volume called simply *Animal Intelligence.* Thorndike stated that the process of learning is the establishment of connections between situation and response. He contended that objective or experimental methods could be applied to human beings and predicted that psychology would become a science of behavior. He made the stimulus-response connection or S-R bond the fundamental focus of psychological research.

Thorndike proposed two basic laws of behavior that applied to both human and animal behavior. The first he called "the law of effect." Basically, Thorndike stated that when several responses are made to the same situation, those which are accompanied or closely followed by satisfaction to the organism, will, other things being equal, be more firmly connected with the situation and so will be more likely to recur when the situation is repeated. Thorndike's second law was the "law of exercise," which asserted that the strength of the connection was related to the frequency of repetition of the response-situation pairing. He later modified this proposition, and it was never really accepted by other behaviorists, although it would have been pleasing to Thorndike's old professor, William James, who had died a year earlier in 1910.

With some minor modifications, Thorndike's "law of effect" became the defining and crucial concept of American behaviorism and what we call today operant learning. When we combine the law of effect with Pavlov's concept of the conditioned reflex, much of the rest of behavioral psychology is reduced to the level of a set of tiresome reiterations of the obvious.

Thorndike's seminal contribution, the notion of the stimulus response bond or connection, did not really define his career. He went on to become the outstanding figure in American educational psychology, and is sometimes not even described as a behaviorist. His doctoral research, however, became "the dissertation heard round the world."

# JOHN BROADUS WATSON: AMBASSADOR OF BEHAVIORISM AND BEYOND

Although it was clearly the research of Edward Lee Thorndike that provided the scientific impetus for American behaviorism, it was the flamboyant personality and unbridled rhetoric of John Broadus Watson that moved it into public prominence. As we saw earlier, it was the sudden downfall of James Mark Baldwin that catapulted Watson from relative obscurity to a position of eminence and influence in American psychology. Beginning in 1910, Watson controlled the *Psychological Review* and later the *Journal of Experimental Psychology*, two of the most prestigious psychological journals in America.

In 1912 Watson delivered a series of lectures at Columbia University in which he expounded his views on the nature of psychology. In 1913 he published these ideas in the *Psychological Review* in an article entitled "Psychology as The Behaviorist Views It." In the article Watson declared his independence from traditional psychology, asserted that the field must be an objective science, and, perhaps most importantly, claimed that there was no essential dividing line between animal and human learning or behavior. In 1914 Watson published a textbook entitled *Behavior: An Introduction to Comparative Psychology* and his brief but meteoric career took off. In 1915 Watson was elected to the Presidency of the American Psychological Association, and behaviorism was a recognized and respected part of American psychology.

## The Misbehavior of a Behaviorist

Clearly, J. B. Watson was a rebel throughout his academic career. He railed against introspectionism, dismissed "functionalism" as a vestige of outworn philosophical speculation, and almost singlehandedly turned the world of American experimental psychology upside down.

Unfortunately, Watson's personal life was as turbulent as his academic career was belligerent. John Broadus Watson was born in 1878 in a poor rural area near Greenville, South Carolina. In the aftermath of the Civil War the rural South was a region plagued with poverty, torn by racial strife and bigotry, and haunted by a heritage of faded grandeur. Watson's father had a reputation as a brawling drunk whose main contribution to both the community and his family were his long and frequent absences (O'Donnell, 1985).

John Watson's mother was almost obsessively religious, deeply imbued with Southern Baptist convictions about both sin and salvation. Young John was baptized in a millpond, but it was, as he remarked in later years, a "vaccination that didn't take" (O'Donnell, 1985).

When John was 12 years old, the family moved to Greenville, where opportunities for both education and delinquency were somewhat greater. Watson apparently had few positive memories of those years. He described himself later as lazy, insubordinate, and academically inferior. He was often teased and ridiculed. He was arrested twice, once for firing a revolver in the city limits and once for interracial fighting.

Since South Carolina had no public high schools at the time, Watson entered Furman University at age 16. Apparently, the college experience broadened his intellectual horizons, without converting him to sound Baptist beliefs and behaviors. He graduated in 1899, requiring an extra year because he accepted the challenge of a professor who had declared that he would fail any student who handed in a term paper with the pages backward (Brewer, 1991). It was a tragically prophetic gesture.

Watson spent a year as principal of a country school before applying to enter the University of Chicago. He arrived at Chicago full of burning ambitions, but with nearly empty pockets. John Watson worked as a janitor, a waiter, and as a caretaker for laboratory rats to put himself through graduate school. His studies were concentrated in philosophy, neurology, physiology, and experimental psychology.

In 1903, at the age of 25, John Broadus Watson received his Ph.D. in experimental psychology. He graduated with great distinction and was invited to remain, first as an assistant to his advisor, James Angell, and later as a regular faculty member. At this time, the University of Chicago was one of the most intellectually stimulating and exciting universities in the country. John D. Rockefeller's bounty had been put to good use.

In 1904, Watson publicly married Mary Amelia Ickes, the daughter of a prominent and politically connected family. Mary Ickes had been a student in one of Watson's classes. According to family legend, the 19-year-old Mary had developed a crush on Watson and had included a love poem to him in a paper she handed in.

Mary Ickes' brother, Harold, both detested and distrusted Watson, reportedly to the point of having him investigated by a private detective. Harold Ickes was prominent in the Democratic Party and was later Secretary of the Interior in Franklin Roosevelt's New Deal Cabinet.

Harold Ickes apparently forced his sister to leave the University of Chicago and to join an aunt in the East. Before her departure, however, Mary Ickes and John Watson were secretly married in 1903 (Brewer, 1991). The 1904 ceremony was a concession to propriety. The marriage was never a happy one, and Harold Ickes was apparently a good judge of prospective brothers-in-law, if not of psychologists. The couple had two children, a son, John Junior, and a daughter, Mary, nicknamed Polly.

J. B. Watson spent 6 undistinguished years on the Chicago faculty, engaging in animal research and remaining at the lowly rank of instructor. In 1909 Baldwin's invitation to join the Johns Hopkins faculty, and the events we have already recounted, propelled Watson to academic stardom.

Watson served as a major in the Signal Corp during World War I. He narrowly escaped being court-martialed for insubordination. Upon Watson's return to Hopkins, the scandal that forever ended his academic career erupted.

Watson had begun his research on the emotions of children. One of his research assistants was a 20-year-old Vassar graduate. Their collaboration produced two widely publicized "cases." One was an almost sadistically unethical effort to condition an experimental neurosis in a helpless human infant, "Little Albert." Today, Watson and his research assistant, Rosalie Rayner, would have lost both their jobs and their APA memberships for unethical research.

The second case was "Watson vs. Watson," a sensational divorce case, complete with torrid love letters and lurid testimony. It seems that the Watson-Rayner collaboration had focused more on adult emotions than those of children. Their affair resulted in a divorce trial on grounds of adultery, and in the ensuing scandal, Watson was forced to resign from the Hopkins faculty. At age 42, at the pinnacle of prestige and influence, his academic career ended forever.

An ironic blend of tragedy and success followed J. B. Watson for the rest of his days. Shortly after being forced out of Hopkins, Watson entered the world of advertising, an environment well-suited for his talents for hyperbole. He joined the J. Walter Thompson agency, and became an acknowledged expert on the motivation of consumers.

Watson outdid the testimonials of mere movie stars by getting the Queens of both Spain and Rumania to endorse Pond's Cold Cream. He personally made one of the first radio commercials for toothpaste, and convinced mothers that babies should be powdered after each diaper change. Watson convinced the American public that the mother who used talcum powder was responsible and loving and that the mother who didn't was uncaring. Within 3 years, he was vice president of the agency.

Watson also wrote numerous books and articles for popular audiences, including a number of prescriptions for childrearing. His views of parenting and caregiving were almost antithetical to everything that we know today. He urged parents not to show children the slightest affection, or do any unnecessary touching, in order to avoid "fixations." He also urged that children be held to rigid behavioral performance standards.

Despite great financial success, Watson remained a bitter man, convinced of the injustice of his exile from academia and angry that his former colleagues in psychology had not come to his defense.

Rosalie Rayner Watson, the woman for whom J. B. Watson had sacrificed a career, died at the age of 35, leaving two sons, Billy and Jim.

John B. Watson's granddaughter is Mariette Hartley, the film actress and television personality, perhaps best known for a series of television commercials with James Garner. In 1990, Ms. Hartley authored a Hollywood style tell-all autobiography, *Breaking the Silence*, that detailed her own emotional problems as well as those of three generations of her troubled and dysfunctional family. She described the fate of John B. Watson's four offspring as follows:

> Billy became a highly respected psychiatrist in New York, fulfilling his father's dream. Ironically, that same Billy, brought up with "minimal fixations," took an overdose of sleeping pills in his office in Manhattan but was stopped by Jimmy. His second suicide attempt while in his thirties was successful.
>
> . . . John, brought up with "minimal fixations," became a deeply religious man but continued to have a queasy stomach and intolerable headaches . . . he died in his early fifties of bleeding ulcers.

Uncle Jimmy . . . after intensive analysis is alive and doing well. My mother, brought up with "minimal fixations" attempted suicide over and over and over and over. (p. 48)

John B. Watson was an enormously talented and charismatic personality who profoundly changed American psychology and popularized behaviorism. He also apparently blighted the lives of all whom he touched, including his own. He died in New York in 1958 at the age of 80.

# THE DECLINE AND RENEWAL OF BEHAVIORISM

The years following the fall from grace of J. B. Watson were difficult ones for experimental psychology. It was a period of what would later be termed "paradigm shifts" (Kuhn, 1970). Introspectionism collapsed under the weight of its own mindless efforts to analyze the structure and parameters of the mind. Functionalism, with its broad interest in the whole range of human problems, was more or less absorbed into the mainstream of psychological pursuits, and ceased to exist as a separate school of psychology (Hergenhahn, 1992).

The new positivistic approaches to the philosophy of science increasingly pushed experimental psychology into the area of animal research. The broad claims of the early behaviorists like Thorndike, Yerkes, and Watson that behaviorism would soon re-energize and even revolutionize child-rearing practices, education, and even social relationships were largely forgotten.

Animal learning was the chief preoccupation of psychology laboratories, and researchers such as Guthrie, Tolman, and Hull developed more or less elaborate theoretical models to account for the maze-running proclivities of albino rats. Clark Hull's monumentally complex theory of learning had a brief moment in the sun, yet is today considered merely a quaint relic of the past. By mid-century, the experimental psychology that was built around the marriage of stimulus-response reductionism and logical positivism had seemed to run out of intellectual energy (Leahey, 1980).

One respected historian of the field (Roback, 1952) went so far as to proclaim the death of behaviorism in American psychology. Like the premature announcements of Mark Twain's demise, this report proved to greatly exaggerated.

## B. F. Skinner and Radical Behaviorism

As we noted earlier, B. F. Skinner entered psychology greatly impressed by the work of Pavlov and Watson. It was Skinner who breathed new life into behaviorism almost singlehandedly. In doing so, he became one of the paramount figures in the history of psychology.

For Skinner, behaviorism was far more than a body of animal research with possible implications for limited aspects of human behavior. Behaviorism was instead an approach to the philosophy of science and a key to a new way of knowing about the natural world. Above all, it was a way of understanding the nature of the human organism and the human condition.

Learning theory had bogged down in its efforts to create grandiose and complex theories to explain even simple animal behavior. Clark Hull's hypothetical-deductive megatheory was more complex than the mazes run by his rats, while Tolman's metaphor of rodents with "cognitive maps" left, as one critic put it, his rats deep in thought.

Skinner solved the dilemma of learning theory and rescued the field from the brink of intellectual bankruptcy by simply rejecting the need for theories at all. Skinner's "radical behaviorism" was based upon empiricism, pure and simple. Skinner (1950) contended that simple, direct observation of organisms under carefully controlled conditions would reveal the regularities and order that existed and would generate "laws of behavior" without the need to develop and test armchair hypotheses or build comprehensive or coherent theoretical frameworks.

Following Thorndike's approach, Skinner invented a tightly controlled experimental environment, the "Skinner Box," within which an organism's responses could be manipulated, observed, and recorded. Skinner further devised a simple "data language" with which to describe fully observable behavior without conjecturing about internal or intervening processes or events. For Skinner, it was dealing with an "empty organism." He chose, as had Thorndike, to study "operant" behavior, that is, behavior that produced reactions from the environment.

**Figure 9.2   B. F. Skinner**

Skinner's overall system was called simply the "experimental analysis of behavior." It was perhaps the most far-reaching and influential set of ideas ever formulated in American psychology.

For some 50 years prior to his death in 1990, B. F. Skinner was the most prolific and most widely quoted and cited American psychologist. His contributions are far too extensive to be recounted here. A special issue of the *American Psychologist* (1992) was required simply to describe his impact on the field.

Skinner's impact on society was even more profound than was his laboratory work. Clearly, from the very beginning, B. F. Skinner sought to change the ways in which human beings perceived themselves, and the ways in which they organized their society. Skinner, the frustrated wouldbe novelist, managed to influence his culture far more than most best-selling authors.

At least four of B. F. Skinner's many books were aimed at influencing the public to accept his views regarding human nature and the optimal ways to organize society. In 1948, he wrote a utopian novel, *Walden Two*, in the tradition of Edward Bellamy's *Looking Back-*

*ward*. Skinner outlined in novel form his ideas of a society operated and regulated by the shaping and maintaining of behavior through reinforcement. A few years later, he published *Science and Human Behavior* (1953) that again sought to spell out the implications of behaviorism for human conduct. His *Beyond Freedom and Dignity* (1971) and *About Behaviorism* (1974) followed and continued to seek popular acceptance of Skinner's ideas and social philosophy. Ironically, the aspiring young writer who abandoned the field of literature believing he had nothing to say sold more than a million copies each of *Walden Two* and *Beyond Freedom and Dignity*.

The essence of B. F. Skinner's view of the human condition was that all human behavior, including consciousness itself, is shaped and controlled by the environment, specifically by contingencies for reinforcement operating in the environment. Freedom, autonomy, creativity, and human agency were all illusions. Skinner revised and revitalized controversies that had divided philosophers for centuries. His ideas are certain to be debated, denounced, and defended for many years to come.

## BEHAVIOR THERAPY: RADICAL BEHAVIORISM IN ACTION

It is neither surprising nor coincidental that radical behaviorism, and its technology, the experimental analysis of behavior, was quickly applied to altering human behavior. Clearly, as we have seen, from the very beginning Skinner saw the paradigm as fully applicable to human beings. The use of laboratory animals such as rats and pigeons was for experimental control and convenience in the laboratory, not because the model was considered inappropriate for human behavior.

The essence of the experimental analysis of behavior is that the behavior of organisms, including humans, is repeated, shaped, and maintained or extinguished out of interaction with the reinforcement contingencies operating in the environment. Behavior that differs across situations does so because the organism discriminates among stimuli, while behavior that persists across situations does so because the organism generalizes to similar stimuli.

Some accounts credit Ogden Lindsley and others of Skinner's doctoral students at Harvard with initiating the first efforts at practical applications with humans (Glass & Arnkoff, 1992). These early efforts gradually became known as behavior modification.

Actually, the application of learning theory to counseling and therapy had begun well before the work originating in the Harvard laboratory. E. J. Shoben wrote a prophetic article in 1949 describing psychotherapy as a problem in learning theory (Shoben, 1949). In 1950, Dollard and Miller published their classic effort to reconcile psychoanalysis and learning theory. Their book was, interestingly, dedicated jointly to Sigmund Freud and Ivan Pavlov.

At about the same time that operant conditioning principles were applied to human behavior, classical conditioning approaches were also being adapted by clinicians such as Joseph Wolpe, Arnold Lazarus, and Hans Eysenck. The term "behavior therapy" was probably coined by Lazarus around 1958, while Eysenck was the first to use the term in the title of a book (Glass & Arnkoff, 1992).

In the earlier years, the term "behavior modification" was used broadly to describe operant approaches, while the term "behavior therapy" was reserved for strictly clinical applications, usually those based on classical conditioning models. Behavior modification was used widely in education, parent consultations, family therapy, and in correctional settings, as well as in mental health applications. Eventually, all of the clinical approaches stemming from operant or classical models, or even from social learning, have been lumped together as behavioral therapies.

By the 1960s, radical behaviorism and behavioral therapies had become powerful and pervasive forces in psychological science and professional practice. Differences between behaviorists and other psychologists divided academic departments and polarized the field of psychotherapy.

Eysenck's 1952 critical review of psychotherapeutic effectiveness was followed by a war of words disputing Eysenck's conclusion that traditional psychotherapy, especially psychoanalytic approaches, were largely ineffective. As the number of studies of the efficacy of psychotherapy increased, it became clear that behavioral approaches focusing on changing specific symptoms or reducing or increasing the frequency of clearly targeted behaviors had a much easier time demonstrating positive results than did the traditional therapies that purported to produce global, but ambiguous, "personality change."

Even as the behavioral therapies began to compile impressive bodies of data supporting their efficacy, however, a storm of controversy continued to grow around their use on ethical and philosophical grounds. Much of this "viewing with alarm" today seems slightly naive. Most of the controversy was and is centered around discomfort with the concept of control. Although Watson and the other early behaviorists had loudly proclaimed their view that the basic purpose of psychological science was the prediction and control of behavior, including human behavior, they were seldom taken seriously. As the "new behaviorism" began to develop a technology for actually controlling some aspects of behavior, its possible ethical and philosophical implications were both apparent and, to some, appalling.

Much of the reaction to behavior modification or behavior therapy seemed to assume that some new and diabolical technology had just been invented to put power in the hands of a white-coated class of unfeeling and uncaring scientists, intent upon bending helpless individuals to their own will or whim.

Actually, behavioral therapies were based upon principles that had been well documented for more than a half-century. Both Pavlov's and Thorndike's research, as we have seen, had really defined the basic parameters of behavioral learning theory at the turn of the twentieth century. It is also doubtful that many neurologically intact human beings over the last 10,000 years or so of human history had not intuitively understood the "law of effect." The manipulation of human behavior through reward and punishment is obviously age-old.

Similarly, as we saw, the associationists saw learning as a product of contiguity, similarity, contrast, vividness, frequency, and recency. They understood principles of desensitization, and saw the psychological life of adults as primarily an unfolding of the individual's earlier learning history. They would probably have viewed Pavlov's salivating dogs with a "what else is new" attitude.

What really was and is disturbing to both psychologists and nonpsychologists is the fact that in this, the second century of their existence, the psychological sciences have at least two almost totally incompatible and irreconcilable concepts of human nature and of the human condition.

As we saw earlier, humanistic psychology holds the image of existential man and woman as creatures who define their own reality, are active and creative agents on behalf of their own destinies, and who make choices and take responsibility for their own lives. This branch of the science has defined its own philosophy of science, methods of inquiry, and rules of acceptable scientific evidence.

Behavioral psychology, on the other hand, has an equally vivid and persuasive image of the human organism as inextricably tied to cycles of reward and punishment in the environment, whose very consciousness is externally determined, but who clings stubbornly to the illusions of freedom and dignity (Park, 1999). It views attempts to tease out the meanings and nuances of inner or mental experiencing as largely unnecessary and unscientific. Efforts to reconcile these two visions of reality either scientifically or philosophically have made slow progress.

## COUNSELING PSYCHOLOGY AND BEHAVIORAL COUNSELING

In 1962 Leonard Krasner wrote a provocatively titled chapter called "The Therapist as a Social Reinforcement Machine." Many counselors and therapists began to think of themselves and their methods in a new and different way. Meyerson and Michael (1962) in the same year pointed up the implications of behavioral technologies for counseling and guidance. John Krumboltz (1964) expanded on this view in a seminal article in the *Personnel and Guidance Journal*. Behavioral counseling became a major approach to professional practice in a remarkably short period of time. In 1969, Krumboltz and Thoreson published an edited book that was a virtual catalog of behavioral counseling cases and techniques. Charles B. Truax (1966) published case material to suggest that even Carl Rogers practiced selective reinforcement of clients' utterances.

Like Client-Centered Therapy and psychoanalysis before it, Behavioral Therapy tended to emerge as a separate and distinct "school." Separate journals and professional associations published behavioral research and promoted the field as something new and revolutionary. Dozens of "innovative" behavioral interventions were designed, and consultation and training programs were employed, to teach the wonders of behavior modification techniques to parents, teachers, corrections officers, and others working with problem populations (Dustin & Blocher, 1984).

In point of fact, for many of these behavioral "innovations," all that was actually new was the behavioral terminology with which the program was clothed. "Token economies," for example, were introduced to promote various kinds of desirable behaviors. These programs may have seemed like old wine in new bottles for elementary school teachers, who had been awarding gold stars for perfect spelling papers and redeeming them for pencils and crayons for many years.

Behavioral contracting was often little more than a system of bonuses for specific achievements. Concepts of "time out from positive reinforcement" and "prompting and fading" of cues were familiar to a great many teachers or parents under different names. To many children, it probably made little difference whether being "kept in" from a playground recess was called "time out from positive reinforcement" or something else.

The use of a behavioral data language designed for use in the laboratory, and intended to reflect a radical behavioral point of view in the philosophy of science, initially may have had some utility in differentiating behavioral counseling and consulting techniques from more traditional approaches. Functional analyses of behavior as compared with trait-and-factor-oriented assessment techniques gave some new insights into the nature and source of psychological dysfunctions. Above all, the behavioral language forced counselors and therapists to define their treatment goals and objectives with greater clarity and specificity than ever before.

Predictably, however, a strict behavioral orthodoxy was much more difficult to maintain in the counseling office or consulting room than in an animal laboratory. It was much easier to think of pigeons as "empty organisms" than to conceptualize clients as such. By the end of the 1960s, both learning theorists and counselors were beginning to broaden the behavioral data language to include "covert responses," "vicarious reinforcement," and other cognitively mediated events (Bandura, 1965; Breger & McGaugh, 1965; Mahoney, 1974).

## Cognitive-Behavioral Counseling: A Contradiction in Terms, A Contribution to Practice

Behavioral therapies really existed in a "pure" form for only about a decade. Clearly, clinicians found the language and conceptual framework of radical behaviorism too confining and simplistic for the practice of counseling and psychotherapy. The result was the advent of a dozen or more new approaches that were given the label of "cognitive-behavioral" therapies. From the standpoint of the philosophy of science, of course, the term cognitive-behavioral is a complete contradiction in terms. To a radical behaviorist such as B. F. Skinner, dealing in covert responses, vicarious reinforcements and "things people say to themselves" is a little like dining on apple pie in the Garden of Eden. These are all forbidden fruits in a pure behaviorism.

The cognitive-behavioral approach had a number of sources. One of these was what has been called the "cognitive revolution" (Gardner, 1985). The resurgence of behaviorism that was energized in the 1950s and 1960s by Skinner and his associates had already began to wane in the 1970s.

The final push in counseling and therapy came from the growing trend toward eclecticism. Practicing counselors and therapists were much more interested in finding anything that worked, rather than something that was theoretically pure and unadulterated. The 1960s and '70s had seen the demise of global personality theories and grandiose worldviews. The so-called cognitive-behavioral theories were really the first steps in a growing eclecticism. Much of the awkward and contorted attempts to retain vestiges of the behavioral data language stemmed more from the fact that many of the innovators had been trained in the behavior modification approach than from a conceptual fit with the new techniques.

The actual conceptual foundations for the cognitive-behavioral therapies stemmed more from the work of Albert Ellis than from any other source. Strangely, he is seldom given the credit deserved for his pioneering work. Ellis had drawn upon the philosophical stance of the Stoic and Epicurean philosophers of the ancient world to develop his Rational Emotive Therapy (Ellis, 1962). Basically, Ellis simply asserted that negative emotional reactions are triggered not by unfortunate events, but by the irrational ways in which people construe those events. Effective therapy should be aimed at replacing irrational thinking with reasoned interpretations. Ellis's approach was really the foundation for cognitive-behavioral therapies.

Aaron Beck's "Cognitive Therapy" (1970) was also influential in the development of a variety of cognitive-behavioral therapies. Beck also places his approach in the realm of eclectic therapies.

Cognitive-behavioral interventions have been developed around a number of specific problems and techniques. These include "Anxiety-Management Training" (Suinn & Richardson, 1971); "Problem-Solving Therapy" (D'Zurilla & Goldfried, 1971); "Stress-Inoculation Training" (Meichenbaum, 1977); and "Rational-Behavior Therapy" (Maultsby, 1984), as well as numerous others.

So-called cognitive-behavioral therapies were based upon a set of assumptions that struck at the heart of all that was dear to radical behaviorism (Kendall & Bemis, 1983). These include:

1.   That human beings respond primarily to cognitive representations of the environment, rather than to the actual physical features of that environment;

2.   Most human learning is cognitively mediated;

3.   Thoughts, feelings and behavior are closely and causally interrelated;

4.   Cognitive activities, such as attitudes, expectations, and attributions, are essential to understanding, predicting, or intervening in human behavior;

5.   It is possible and desirable to combine cognitive treatment strategies with behavioral strategies; and

6.   The task of the cognitive-behavioral therapist includes working with the client to change *both* dysfunctional cognitions and related behavior patterns.

These assumptions may form the bases for behavior therapies in the sense that treatment goals and subsequent evaluations are based upon specific observable behaviors. Such therapies are clearly not behavioristic in the tradition of Thorndike, Watson, and Skinner. They are much more products of the cognitive revolution than of radical behaviorism.

Behavior modification began with an almost ideological fervor, promising great things to all people. Its opening rhetoric would have done credit to J. B. Watson himself. To a considerable extent, "theoretically pure" behavior modification ended not with a bang, but with a whimper. Less than two decades after its inception, advocates were calling for "an end of ideology in behavior modification" (London, 1972, p. 913). Nineteen years after coining the term, the man who had first written of behavior therapy was asking whether it had outlived its usefulness (Lazarus, 1977). Lazarus went on to deplore the connection between behavior therapy and behaviorism and redefined his own position as one of "technical eclecticism" (Lazarus, 1976).

# THE BEHAVIORAL LEGACY

Over the past 30 years, both the rhetoric and the substance of behavior therapy has mellowed and moved closer to the mainstream of counseling and psychotherapeutic theory and practice. Even in orthodox behavior therapy, the importance of the relationship has long been recognized (Ford, 1978). The effective behavior therapist is no longer regarded even by critics as a cold, remote, or subtle manipulator of "positive reinforcements." Clearly, qualities such as warmth, empathy, and positive regard, or trustworthiness, attractiveness, and competence form the very basis for positive reinforcement in the counseling situation.

Many of the essentially semantic differences that separated behavioral approaches from other positions in counseling and psychotherapy have gradually disappeared. What remains constitutes a very significant contribution to the profession of counseling psychology.

This contribution can be summarized in several major emphases:

1. Behavioral counseling has influenced the field to define the client's problem or presenting situation in terms that involve overt behaviors as well as internal states.

2. Behavioral counseling has influenced the field to establish objective, operational and measurable goals and objectives, and to focus interventions primarily around attaining those client-specific goals.

3. Behavioral counseling has influenced the field to make continuous monitoring and measurement of client goal attainment a central and essential part of the counseling process.

4. Behavioral counseling has influenced counselors to focus their attention and their language on empirical and definable aspects of counseling and to question the relevance of impressive, but totally ambiguous or undefinable, rhetoric.

Nearly 20 years ago Brown and Hosford (1981) summarized a process of reconciliation and integration of behavioral counseling with other approaches:

It appears that the counseling process historically identified with a behavioral model has evolved over the years to represent not a model for the practice of one form of counseling, but rather as a generic model outlining the process that all counselors should follow. (p. 11)

The behavioral tradition began in an atmosphere of rebellion against the status quo in psychology and was clothed with outrageous rhetoric and radical philosophies. For counseling psychology, at least, it has become one important thread in the fabric of a profession slowly moving toward philosophical unity and theoretical integration.

## REFERENCES

American Psychological Association. (1992). Reflections on B. F. Skinner and psychology. *American Psychologist, 47* (whole issue).

Bandura, A. (1965). A case of no-trial learning. In L. Berkowitz (Ed.), *Advances in experimental social psychology* (Vol. 2). New York: Academic Press.

Beck, A. T. (1970). Cognitive therapy: Nature and relation to behavior therapy. *Behavior Therapy, 2,* 184–200.

Breger, L., & McGaugh, J. L. (1965). Critique and reformulation of "learning theory" approaches to psychotherapy and neuroses. *Psychological Bulletin, 63,* 338–358.

Brewer, C. L. (1991). Perspectives on John B. Watson. In G. A. Kimble, M. Wertheimer, & C. L. White (Eds.), *Portraits of pioneers in psychology* (pp. 171–188). Hillsdale, NJ: Erlbaum.

Brown, S. D., & Hosford, R. E. (1981). The future of behavioral counseling: Recommendations for a continuing empiricism. *Behavioral Counseling Quarterly, 1,* 9–28

Chomsky, N. (1980). *Rules and representations.* New York: Columbia University Press.

Dewsbury, D. A. (1997). In celebration of the centennial of Ivan P. Pavlov's (1897–1902). *The work of the digestive glands. American Psychologist, 52,* 933–935.

Dollard, J., & Miller, N. E. (1950). *Personality and psychotherapy.* New York: McGraw-Hill.

Dustin, R., & Blocher, D. H. (1984). Theories and models of consultation. In S. Brown & R. Lent (Eds.), *Handbook of counseling psychology* (pp. 751–781). New York: Wiley.

D'Zurilla, T. J., & Goldfried, M. R. (1971). Problem-solving and behavior modification. *Journal of Abnormal Psychology, 78,* 107–126.

Ellis, A. (1962). *Reason and emotion in psychotherapy.* New York: Stuart.

Emmelkamp, P. M. (1986). Behavior therapy with adults. In S. Garfield & A. Bergin (Eds.), *Handbook of psychotherapy and behavior change* (pp. 385–442). New York: Wiley.

Fancher, R. E. (1990). *Pioneers of psychology* (2nd ed.). New York: Norton.

Ford, J. D. (1978). Therapeutic relationship in behavior therapy: An empirical analysis. *Journal of Consulting and Clinical Psychology, 46,* 1302–1314.

Gardner, H. (1985). *The mind's new science: A history of the cognitive revolution.* New York: Basic Books.

Glass, C. R., & Arnkoff, D. B. (1992). Behavior therapy. In D. C. Freedheim (Ed.), *History of psychotherapy: A century of change* (pp. 587–628). Washington, DC: American Psychological Association.

Hartley, M., & Commire, A. (1990). *Breaking the silence.* New York: Signet.

Hergenhahn, B. R. (1992). *An introduction to the history of psychology* (2nd ed.). Belmont, CA: Wadsworth.

James, W. (1890). *Principles of psychology.* New York: Holt.

Kendall, P. C., & Bemis, K. M. (1983). Thought and action in psychotherapy: The cognitive behavioral approaches. In M. Hersen, A. E. Kazdin, & A. S. Bellak (Eds.), *The clinical psychology handbook* (pp. 565–592). Elmsford, NY: Pergamon.

Krasner, L. (1962). The therapist as a social reinforcement machine. In H. H. Strupp & L. Luborsky (Eds.), *Research in psychotherapy* (Vol. 2, pp. 67–74). Washington, DC: American Psychological Association.

Krumboltz, J. D. (1964). Parable of the good counselor. *Personnel and Guidance Journal, 43,* 118–124.

Krumboltz, J. D., & Thoreson, C. E. (Eds.) (1969). *Behavioral counseling: Cases and techniques.* New York: Holt, Rinehart Winston.

Kuhn, T. S. (1970). *The structure of scientific revolutions* (2nd ed.). Chicago: University of Chicago Press.

Lazarus, A. A. (1976). *The practice of multimodal therapy.* New York: McGraw-Hill.

Lazarus, A. A. (1977). Has behavior therapy outlived its usefulness? *American Psychologist, 32,* 550–557.

Leahey, T. H. (1980). *A history of psychology.* Englewood Cliffs, NJ: Prentice-Hall.

Locke, J. (1693). *Some thoughts concerning education.* London: Ward, Lock.

London, P. (1972). The end of ideology in behavior modification. *American Psychologist, 27,* 913–920.

Mahoney, M. J. (1974). *Cognition and behavior modification.* Cambridge, MA: Ballinger.

Maultsby, M. C. (1984). *Rational behavior therapy*. Englewood Cliffs, NJ: Prentice-Hall.

Meichenbaum, D. H. (1977). *Cognitive behavior modification*. New York: Plenum.

Meyerson, L., & Michael, J. (1962). A behavioral approach to counseling and guidance. *Harvard Educational Review, 32*, 382–402.

O'Donnell, J. M. (1985). *The origins of behaviorism: American psychology, 1870–1920*. New York: University Press.

Park, D. C. (1999). Acts of will. *American Psychologist, 54*, 461.

Rescorta, R. A. (1988). Pavlovian conditioning: It's not what you think it is. *American Psychologist, 43*, 151–160.

Roback, A. A. (1952). *A history of American psychology*. New York: Literary Publishers.

Shoben, E. J. (1949). Psychotherapy as a problem in learning theory. *Psychological Bulletin, 46*, 366–392.

Skinner, B. F. (1948). *Walden two*. New York: Macmillan.

Skinner, B. F. (1950). Are theories of learning necessary? *Psychological Review, 57*, 193–216.

Skinner, B. F. (1953). *Science and human behavior*. New York: Macmillan.

Skinner, B. F. (1971). *Beyond freedom and dignity*. New York: Bantam Books.

Skinner, B. F. (1974). *About behaviorism*. New York: Knopf.

Smith, P. (1985). *America enters the world: A people's history of the progressive era and World War I*. New York: Penguin.

Suinn, R. M., & Richardson, F. (1971). Anxiety management training: A nonspecific behavior therapy program for anxiety control. *Behavior Therapy, 2*, 498–510.

Todes, D. P. (1997). From the machine to the ghost within: Pavlov's transition from digestive physiology to conditional reflexes. *American Psychologist, 52*, 947–955.

Truax, C. B. (1966). Reinforcement and non-reinforcement in Rogerian psychotherapy. *Journal of Abnormal Psychology, 71*, 1–9.

Windholz, G. (1997). Ivan Pavlov: An overview of his life and psychological work. *American Psychologist, 52*, 941–946.

Wolpe, J., & Plaud, J. J. (1997). Pavlov's contributions to behavior therapy. *American Psychologist, 52*, 966–972.

# PART III

# From Here to Uncertainty

## INTRODUCTION

In Part II, we traced the influence of four basic traditions that have shaped the evolution of counseling psychology. Each tradition has contributed seminal ideas, values, and frames of reference to the field. Yet, to some extent, these disparate and often contentious approaches have also divided and fragmented both counseling psychology and the larger science and profession of psychology itself.

Over the last two decades, counselors and therapists have labored mightily to weave these separate threads together to provide a comprehensive, yet reasonably well-integrated approach to professional practice. In Part III, we will trace the progress of that effort.

At the same time, counseling psychology has struggled to define, assert, and maintain a unique professional identity within the helping professions generally and more particularly within applied psychology.

One of the reasons that counseling psychology is difficult to define is that it really has two interrelated but distinct aspects. It is a subdiscipline of the science of psychology. As such, it is concerned with generating, interpreting, and testing knowledge within several specific content domains.

Counseling psychology is also a specialty in the practice of professional psychology, offering services to clientele around several different kinds of needs and problems. As a professional specialty, counseling psychology affiliates with and seeks recognition from other professional specialties.

In Chapter 10 we will look at the efforts of the science to move toward greater theoretical integration, generate evidence of effectiveness, and create models for future research. In Chapter 11, we will trace the recent development of the profession and some of its current problems and probable futures.

# 10

# From Theoretical Divisiveness to Eclectic-Integrative Therapies

> There is no one "right way" to treat a client, no one "right theory" to explain a client's problems, and no one "right therapist" for a particular client.
>
> —Okun, 1990 (p. 1)

By 1986 more than 400 distinct, if not distinguished, approaches to counseling and psychotherapy had been identified (Karasu, 1986). This represents more than a sixfold increase in 25 years (Kazdin, 1986). The field seemed to spawn new therapies at a rate that makes a warren of rabbits seem like a testimonial for population control.

This proliferation of therapeutic approaches was not, unfortunately, accompanied by a wealth of evidence about their effectiveness. Most were brought into the world without much convincing evidence supporting their claims to either scientific or clinical respectability (Garfield & Bergin, 1986).

Perhaps equally distressing was the fact that a great number of these approaches were endowed with the title of "theories of counseling or psychotherapy." The very fact that we have so many so-called "theories" is eloquent testimony to the fact that few are really scientific theories in any legitimate sense of the term.

A scientific theory is a way of organizing what is known about some phenomenon in order to generate interesting, plausible, and, above all, refutable propositions or hypotheses about what is unknown. Scientific theories exist to advance knowledge through research.

**263**

Most of our multitude of clinical approaches are simply prescriptions or, as one graduate student put it, "recipes," that describe one clinician's way of dealing with clients. The history of counseling and psychotherapy is, as we have seen, predominantly the story of one charismatic figure after another articulating opinions generated from personal clinical experience, while attracting an admiring set of disciples who somehow transform a loosely organized collection of impressions and opinions into a so-called "theory." Most of these recipes are theories only in the popular sense that they are unverified.

As Goldfried (1980) noted, the popularity of a given therapy school is often a function of a set of variables having nothing to do with its efficacy. That popularity often depends upon the charisma, energy level, and longevity of the leader, or guru, as well as the "spirit of the times."

There are literally more brands of counseling and psychotherapy than there are remedies for the common cold. One after another, most of these promising panaceas have first dazzled, then disappointed, practitioners as the new approaches were exposed to the rigors of evaluation or the realities of full-scale professional practice.

It is not surprising that over the past 40 years the percentage of clinicians who classify themselves as adherents to specific "theoretical" models has steadily shrunk. More than 20 years ago, a survey of clinical psychologists indicated that a clear majority classified themselves as "eclectic" (Garfield & Kurtz, 1977). A similar study of counseling psychologists (Watkins, Lopez, Campbell, & Himmell, 1986) produced similar results. A more recent study (Norcross, Prochaska, & Farber, 1993) suggested that the trend has continued unabated.

To a considerable extent, in the midst of this profusion of untested and untestable "brand names," to represent oneself as "eclectic" may seem the only alternative to appearing gullible. Unfortunately, claiming to be eclectic often means little more than refusing to be a "true believer."

The fact that a majority of counseling psychologists classify themselves as eclectic does not tell us much about what else they have in common. The term "eclectic" simply means drawn from more than one source. In one sense, the approach of any individual counselor is always drawn from both some body of knowledge or theory, and from his or her own interpretation and translation of that approach in terms of the counselor's general beliefs and personality.

Pioneering counseling psychologists such as Shoben (1962) and Williamson (1962) recognized early on that the personality of the counselor was a very important variable in the counseling process, and that this process could never be represented solely in terms of some set of abstract ideas or theories. Over the years since then, many critiques of research methodology have pointed out the fallacy of treating counselors as "fixed effects" in evaluating counseling treatments (Martindale, 1978).

Similarly, early counseling psychologists saw counseling and personality theories more as heuristics that helped the counselor to recognize important aspects of a client's situation or personality than as a prescription to be followed or a blueprint to be read. Leona Tyler (1958) characterized personality theories as spotlights playing upon a many-faceted surface, lighting up some facets while allowing others to remain in darkness. Hobbs (1962) wrote of theories as containing multiple "sources of gain" to be recognized and employed as they became relevant to the needs and situations represented by particular cases and clients. Berdie (1959) defended even an unsystematic eclecticism in employing theoretical constructs for practical purposes.

These views are the core of the eclectic position. They leave, however, to the practitioner both the burden and the opportunity to organize and systematize the various elements of an eclectic approach. This has the advantage of allowing the counselor to tailor the conceptual components of an approach to the personal factors represented in the counselor's own belief system and personality characteristics. It also, unfortunately, offers the opportunity for some counselors to mask a totally mindless and shallowly opportunistic approach under the cloak of eclecticism.

Early eclectic approaches called upon the counselor to build a "personal theory of counseling" that was systematic, yet carefully fitted to the individual practitioner (Blocher, 1966; Lister, 1964).

This approach still represents one of the paths taken by eclecticism. Brammer, Abrego, and Shostrum (1993), in the 6th edition of a book that has been a classic counseling text since 1960, endorsed such an approach to eclecticism in this way:

> Each counselor and psychotherapist ultimately must develop a point of view that is uniquely his or her own. Freud was not a Freudian, Jung not a Jungian, and Rogers not a Rogerian. Each of them was himself

most fully and completely, while building upon the wisdom of the past. (p. 19)

Despite support from a growing number of leaders in the field and the quiet shifting of allegiances among practitioners that was mentioned above, eclectic approaches were viewed with considerable suspicion for many years. To some extent, being eclectic was considered being unsystematic, tenderminded, or simply intellectually undisciplined. Much of this came from the distrust and disdain for practitioners that was evident in some members of the "theory class," that is, those with a vested interest in maintaining the status quo. Support for the development of systematic eclectic or integrative approaches has always been strong in counseling psychology. The field had come into existence without being wedded to particular theoretical models or forced to work in professional settings where strong theoretical biases were embedded in the power hierarchy.

## THE QUEST FOR A SYSTEMATIC ECLECTICISM

The search for systematic eclectic approaches is as old as counseling psychology, itself. E. G. Williamson (1950) defined four basic intellectual tasks that must be accomplished in the search for a unifying and integrative approach to counseling. Such a search should, in his view, attempt to reconcile various conflicts and contradictions among existing theories. It should bring into the open and examine critically the often unrecognized and unspoken assumptions that underlay various theories. The search should also seek out the commonalities and points of agreement among various theoretical positions. Finally, the search should identify and define areas and problems across theories that need to be explored through research.

Obviously, after half a century, counseling psychology and related fields have not yet fully completed Williamson's proposed agenda. The need for a systematic eclectic or integrative approach was echoed by a number of writers in the years following Williamson's prophetic article. Harper (1959), Callis (1960), and Carkhuff (1966) all called for eclectic-integrative approaches.

Perhaps the greatest impetus for eclecticism during this period came from a research paper published by Fred Fiedler (1950). Fiedler's study has been cited, interpreted, and misinterpreted for half a century (Poznanski & McLennan, 1995). Fiedler conducted a rather simple study in which therapists from different theoretical orientations and varying levels of training and experience were asked to describe an "ideal therapeutic relationship." Fiedler found that the better trained and more experienced therapists tended to agree with each other more closely across theoretical orientations than they agreed with less well-trained or inexperienced clinicians within the same orientation. In a second study, Fiedler found that psychologically naive raters generally agreed with the clinicians in regard to the nature of an ideal therapeutic relationship. Fiedler's sample was limited to only eight clinicians: six psychologists and two psychiatrists. On the basis of these results, Fiedler drew the conclusions that well-trained, experienced therapists generally agree on the nature of effective therapeutic relationships; that their concepts of such relationships are very similar to those of psychologically naive raters, and that theoretical differences are the result of poor communication or semantic differences among schools. This study has been used for half a century to minimize practical differences among different theoretical orientations. Seldom has so little data been used to such great effect (Peterson & Bradley, 1980).

## THE SEARCH FOR COMMON ELEMENTS

The most obvious and logical way to begin building an eclectic-integrative approach is by examining the commonalties that exist across theories of counseling and psychotherapy. One of the first attempts to examine such common factors was undertaken by Shaffer and Shoben (1956). They pointed up the common effects of support, acceptance, reassurance, and encouragement. They also urged counselors to avoid commitment to a rigid "religion of psychotherapy" and to maintain an open mind. They noted that an eclectic position is frequently treated with disdain by fanatics of all persuasions.

Schofield (1964), in a book provocatively entitled *Psychotherapy: The Purchase of Friendship*, declared that regardless of theoretical allegiances, the therapist is an expert conversationalist who is sensitive to the nuances of the client's communication, uses suggestion and influence tactfully and skillfully, and provides acceptance and respect.

These skills and attitudes were, according to Schofield, simply extensions of those qualities found in close and positive social relationships or friendships.

The most thorough and influential contributor to the "common factors" approach was Jerome Frank (1961). Frank viewed all clients coming into therapy as suffering from stress that they were unable to manage satisfactorily in their lives. This inability was, according to Frank, due largely to faulty learning that arises from their interpersonal experience. This faulty learning leads to persistent difficulties, both in the client's interpersonal relationships and his or her inner, emotional life.

In order to function more effectively, the client must develop a way of imposing order and consistency upon the welter of events and experiences that impinge upon his or her life. This order and consistency is supplied by developing a set of assumptions about the nature of the world and the people in it, including one's self. These assumptions enable people to predict the behavior of others and the outcomes of their own actions.

When clients are severely stressed, it is usually because their assumptions are faulty and maladaptive. The principal function of all psychotherapy is to teach the client new or more adaptive assumptions and thus to modify what Frank termed the client's "assumptive world."

All therapies in essence teach sets of assumptions which, while they may differ from each other, all help clients to experience greater consistency, structure, and effectiveness in their lives than they had prior to therapy. According to Frank, all psychotherapy, then, tries to relieve a person's distress and to improve functioning by helping to reduce errors and resolve conflicts in basic assumptions about self and others. Differences in detail or semantics among theories are of little importance so long as the therapeutic intervention results in an improved set of assumptions on the part of the client.

Frank took a very broad view of therapy and then conceptualized theoretical models merely as special applications of a more general set of tasks, techniques, and purposes.

The search for common factors and the construction of systematic eclectic models based upon them has continued for the past 40 years. As new theoretical models have been developed and researched, a longer and longer list of common factors has been compiled. Garfield (1995) identified an impressive list. These include:

Relationship Factors including the Working Alliance

Cognitive Factors including Insight, Cognitive Restructuring and Self-understanding

Catharsis, Emotional Expression and Release

Reinforcement

Desensitization

Information-giving

Reassurance and Support

Positive Expectations including Hope and Optimism

Any or all of these "sources of gain" can and probably do operate at some point in virtually all counseling situations. None is the exclusive property of any one narrow theoretical model. None is philosophically repugnant or ethically inimical to the value systems of practicing counselor or therapists.

The common factors approach to systematic-eclectic counseling and therapy has great practical credibility and utility to practitioners. It is probably largely responsible for the steady increase in the percentage of eclectic therapists that we noted above. Using all of these factors in a consistent and intentional way as they become relevant is probably simply the mark of an effective practitioner of any theoretical persuasion.

Over the years, the number of eclectic-integrative approaches has steadily mounted. The cognitive-behavioral approach, described earlier, was an effort to meld theoretical approaches at the level of basic theory to combine major emphases from both cognitive and behavioral therapies into a new theoretical formulation. The pragmatic emphasis in this approach clearly overcame major contradictions in terms of underlying philosophies of science. As we saw, even Arnold Lazarus, who coined the term "behavior therapy," joined the movement as he defined what he termed technical eclecticism (Lazarus, 1976).

The movement toward eclectic-integrative therapies has finally achieved full respectability with its own journals, handbooks, and advocates. It has even been referred to as a "revolution in mental health" (Norcross & Arkowitz, 1992).

The success and acceptance of eclectic-integrative approaches has been driven by more than the enthusiasm of its principal advocates or even by their research findings. As new therapies have come and gone, psychotherapy has looked for more durable foundations.

## Back to Basic Psychology

Most of the earlier psychotherapeutic models came out of the clinic and searched for some sort of psychological infrastructure well after the fact. The Client-Centered approach was, as we saw, a prime example. With the exception of behavior modification, that kind of evolution has tended to be the rule. Many of the psychodynamic spinoffs from psychoanalysis never really made an effort to tie into mainstream psychological foundations at all.

More recent attempts to build theoretical frameworks for counseling and therapy have addressed basic bodies of psychological knowledge, particularly in social psychology, that seem to address situations and problems that are also fundamental to counseling.

One of the first to urge this kind of approach was Frank Robinson (1955). Robinson had pioneered in the study of audio-recording of counseling interviews at Ohio State University even prior to Carl Rogers' arrival there. Robinson saw the counseling situation as a special kind of social interaction, and urged the further study of what he called "the social psychology of the interview."

One of Robinson's colleagues at Ohio State, Harold Pepinsky (1974), attempted to analyze counselor-client interaction as a form of social exchange with its own kind of rules and structure. This kind of research marked a decided shift from the earlier efforts at theory-building and research in counseling and therapy. Most of the earlier efforts were directed toward inventing specific, self-contained, and supposedly original models of counseling or therapy. These "recipes," if we pursue that rather inelegant analogy, represented one theorist or another's way of "baking a cake." The newer, more fundamental research programs were more concerned with establishing the specific properties of the basic ingredients that went into all cakes.

## The Social Influence Approach

The most influential and far-reaching effort of this kind was launched by Stanley R. Strong in a seminal paper titled "Counseling: An Interpersonal Influence Process" (Strong, 1968). Strong drew on basic social psychological research on opinion/change, reasoning that this was relevant to counseling since it involved both interpersonal communication processes and changes in client cognitions and behavior.

The study of social influence and opinion change had a long and distinguished history in American social psychology. As early as World War II, a series of studies in communication and persuasion had been undertaken at Yale University under the general direction of Carl Hovland (Hovland, Janis, & Kelly, 1953). This research and the work that was built on it studied the effects of persuasive communications, small group interactions, and mass media on judgments and opinions.

The aspect of this research that Strong and his later colleagues focused upon most directly concerned the characteristics of communicators who are successful in making influence attempts in interpersonal situations. The persuasion research indicated that such attempts tended to be successful when the persuader was seen by the target audience as expert, trustworthy, and attractive.

From this beginning has come nearly three decades of research exploring almost every conceivable aspect of the social influence process in counseling and psychotherapy. Major reviews of this line of research have been done by Corrigan, Dell, Lewis, and Schmidt (1980) and Heppner and Claiborn (1989). A full-scale rationale for the implications of social influence dynamics on counseling and therapy was presented in Strong and Claiborn (1982).

The social influence model has been perhaps the most active and certainly the most controversial line of research in counseling psychology over the last 20 years. It has ironically brought the old, unproductive, and largely forgotten "directive-nondirective" debate around full circle. The author was privileged to be a participant in Strong's first presentation of his model at an APA convention. The reaction of an audience of diehard nondirective counselors to being told that they had spent their careers in exerting social influence over clients was both profound and explosive.

Regardless of one's reaction to the utility of the social influence approach to counseling practice, it has clearly had both a stimulating and liberating effect on research and theory in counseling psychology. Attention to what is called the "interface" between counseling and social psychology has energized and broadened the scope of vision in the field. The view of the counseling psychologist as an applied social psychologist is an exciting one (Forsyth & Leary, 1997; Heesacker, Connor, & Prichard, 1995; Strong, Welsh, Corcoran, & Hoyt, 1992).

## Counseling and the Cognitive Revolution

The return to grace of cognitive psychology and what has been termed the "Cognitive Revolution" (Dember, 1974) provided opportunities for counseling theorists and researchers to turn increasingly to studies about cognition and the relationship between and among thoughts, feelings, and actions. Slowly, the almost phobic reactions of psychologists to self-report that accompanied the decline and fall of introspectionism faded, and psychology recovered its "lost mind" (Mahoney, 1977; Pribram, 1986).

Theorists like George Kelly (1955) developed a "psychology of personal constructs" that was unabashedly "cognitive" and which formed the basis for a new therapy. The return of cognition to legitimacy created a resurgence of interest in psychodynamic concepts and even the "unconscious" once again became fair game for research, as well as speculation (Epstein, 1994).

Edward Bordin (1955), in a classic book, had helped to define psychological counseling and so counseling psychology. Bordin (1980) 25 years later helped to revive interest in psychodynamic concepts as they relate to counseling psychology. Bordin connected psychodynamic theories of personality structure to counseling processes and areas such as brief therapy and career development.

More recently (Bordin, 1994) helped to reintroduce the psychodynamic concept of the "therapeutic working alliance." The working alliance is currently a major focus in counseling process and relationship research (Hill & Corbett, 1993).

Another psychoanalytic concept to return to visibility in counseling research is "object relations" theory, a concept developed by Melanie Klein more than 60 years ago (Klein, 1932). Basically, this spinoff from psychoanalysis asserts that interpersonal behavior patterns at both conscious and unconscious levels are determined by very early experiences with parents and other caregivers. Traumatic experiences in infancy are held responsible for irrational and neurotic behavior in interpersonal relationships in later life.

In somewhat updated form, concepts drawn from ethnological research by Ainsworth and Bowlby (1991) have been combined with

Klein's views in what is called "attachment theory," an important way of looking at the effects of early relationships on personality development (Lopez, 1995).

Psychoanalytic concepts have probably been more widely used in counseling psychology in the past two decades than ever before (Robbins, 1989). Through time, even psychoanalysis has mellowed and compromised with the spirit of the times. In reporting on a long-term follow-up study comparing orthodox psychoanalysis with psycho-dynamic therapy at Menninger Foundation (Wallerstein, 1989, p. 195) reported that "supportive mechanisms *infiltrated* all of the therapies." Apparently, the pull of eclecticism has been felt even in the inner sanctum of psychoanalysis.

## PROCESS RESEARCH IN COUNSELING

Perhaps the most frustrating and disappointing situation in the history of counseling and psychotherapy has been the inability of counseling research to contribute a body of data upon which to base actual practice. More than 20 years ago, Leo Goldman, one of the most respected statesmen in the field, opened an article urging a "revolution in counseling research" with this sentence: "Published research in counseling, has, on the whole, been of little value as a base or guide for professional practice" (Goldman, 1976, p. 543).

In a subsequent article, Goldman put his discontent with research findings this way:

> What has research told us? Research has told us that most theories seem to have some validity, but the variation in findings among different studies that test any one theory usually leaves us with no conclusive answers. Research tells us that some counselors make some contributions to some clients, but rarely does a study tell us what the crucial factors are that lead to success in one case and failure in another. (Goldman, 1977, p. 363)

Goldman's criticisms and call for drastic change have been echoed repeatedly over the past quarter-century (Barlow, 1981; Beutler, Williams, Wakefield, & Entwistle, 1995; Hoshmond, 1989; Stricker, 1997). Apparently they have sounded to little avail.

In 1986 Orlinsky and Howard reported the results of what must have been one of the most exhaustive and exhausting reviews of research ever accomplished in the field of psychotherapy. They reviewed some 1,100 studies of psychotherapy process and outcome, all done on real patients and therapists, in real treatment situations. The treatments were provided in outpatient clinics, university counseling centers, psychiatric hospitals, social agencies, and private practice. The patients were people receiving psychological help for personal or interpersonal problems and for disturbances in emotional, cognitive, or behavioral functioning. All of the studies attempted to analyze process variables, that is, anything that can be observed to occur between the patient and therapist during their work together. The basic question that was asked in this review was "What is effectively therapeutic in psychotherapy?" Some 1,100 studies later, the authors answered the question in this way:

> [O]ur provisional answer to the question is as follows: (1) the patient's and therapist's therapeutic bond—that is their reciprocal role investment, empathic resonance and mutual affirmation—is effectively therapeutic. (2) Certain therapeutic interventions, when done skillfully with suitable patients, are effectively therapeutic. (3) Patients and therapists focusing their interventions on the patient's feelings is effectively therapeutic. (4) Preparing the patient adequately for participation in therapy and collaborative sharing of responsibility for problem solving are effectively therapeutic. (5) Within certain limits more rather than less therapy is effectively therapeutic. (p. 371)

Essentially, 1,100 studies yielded a set of conclusions that are likely to be known intuitively by any graduate student who has successfully completed one semester of counseling practicum: The relationship is important; Some things work with some clients better than others; Try to stay with the client's feelings; Structure with the client what counseling is all about, and be sure the client knows his or her responsibility for what happens; Counseling works better if you can keep the client going past the third interview.

Lest we think that the results reviewed in the 1986 report are obsolete, a slightly updated review by Orlinsky, Graive, and Parks was not greatly different (1994).

# The Beginning of Process Research

Counseling process research is usually considered to have begun with the work of Robinson and Rogers in audiorecording interviews that we have mentioned earlier. This work began in the late 1930s, although abortive attempts to make such recordings occurred as early as 1929 with psychoanalytic sessions (Hill & Corbett, 1993). As we noted earlier, Rogers used the results of early interview analyses both to advance his own ideas, and to discredit those of his critics.

Process and outcome research has been undertaken in a wide variety of settings and in the context of a wide range of theoretical models, including behavioral and cognitive approaches, psychoanalytic theory, family systems approaches, interpersonal theory, and the social influence model discussed above (Hill & Corbett, 1993).

The problem of devising units within which to analyze interviews has been a daunting one. Much of the early analyses simply counted various kinds of responses and dealt with frequencies and ratios of talk under a few simple categories.

After a half century of process and outcome research, as we saw, little useful evidence has been assembled to either guide counseling practice or answer questions about the relative efficacy of various theoretical models.

# Problems With Process and Outcome Research

One basic problem with almost all approaches to process and outcome research involves the assumptions made in aggregating data across cases, that is, across individual clients and counselors. These assumptions include the notion that process variables and effects must be essentially similar across counselor/client pairings and across types of presenting problems. Kiesler (1966) pointed out the fallacies in what he termed the "uniformity myth."

Similarly Krumboltz (1966), Blocher (1966), and Paul (1967) pointed out that outcome research must be directed not to the question of whether counseling works, in a global sense, but to a whole set of much more specific questions, such as: what treatment, delivered by whom, is most effective for this client with that specific problem under these particular circumstances.

There has been almost no opposition to the basic positions asserted by Kiesler, Krumboltz, Blocher, and a host of others over more than 30 years. They have simply been ignored in terms of the vast preponderance of studies done. Gradually, client variables, such as gender, age, race and ethnicity have been recognized as crucial variables, although the actual number of process and outcome studies to employ them in research designs is still minuscule. Actually, one review (Hill, Nutt, & Jackson, 1994) suggests that the number of process-outcome studies in major journals has actually decreased.

Over the past 30 years, a large number of suggestions have been made to improve both the quality and relevance of process-outcome research. Single case experiments that demonstrate control of dependent variables during the course of treatment, or which compare changes on "target" vs. "nontarget" variables, have been proposed and used in limited ways (Barlow, Hayes, & Nelson, 1984; Thoresen & Anton, 1974). Such designs compare initial or baseline frequencies of target or control behaviors before, during, and after intervention. Various kinds of sequential analyses have been proposed to allow the researcher to study the timing of specific interventions and their immediate within-session effects (Lichtenberg & Hummel, 1976).

Another approach (Greenberg, 1986) is to study clinically "significant" events that lead to client "movement" or positive changes. These events may be recognized by a "marker," or noteworthy incident. The sequences of therapist-client interactions following the marker can be studied to create an analysis of a clinically meaningful episode within the ongoing session or sessions.

## RESEARCH AND PRACTICE: NARROWING THE GAP

Some 50 years ago at the Boulder Conference, as we saw in Chapter 4, professional psychology consigned its fortunes and entrusted its future to the scientist practitioner model of doctoral preparation. The hope was that this model of training could both prepare competent practitioners, and produce researchers who could nourish and inform the field. Counseling psychology in particular has remained wedded to that ideal for half a century. In terms of fulfilling the hopes and aspirations on which it was founded, the "Boulder Model" has obviously enjoyed only limited success.

As we saw, the gap between science and practice in counseling and clinical psychology has been profound. Practitioners have addressed researchers with growing skepticism (Stricker, 1997), and researchers have tried to defend their contributions to practice (Strupp, 1989). Some researchers (Beutler et al., 1995; Forsyth & Strong, 1986) have questioned whether research findings with direct relevance to practice are possible.

One somewhat encouraging development in helping to narrow the research-practice gap has been in what is called exploratory or discovery-oriented process-outcome research. Elliott (1983) wrote of fitting process research to the needs of practicing therapists, and predicted that over the ensuing decade great progress in that direction would be made. Elliott's predictions have only partially been fulfilled.

Clara Hill (1990) reviewed a number of these "exploratory" studies in areas such as counselor techniques, client behavior, covert processes, process models, and interactions between therapists and clients.

Hill defined exploratory research as essentially atheoretical studies that describe what goes on in therapy sessions, develop ways of analyzing that interaction, and describe the experiences of the participants. Ideally, in this approach, researchers maintain an attitude of openness to learning about the process through observation. The approach is somewhat analogous to ethnological research in child development, or the participant observer model of anthropological research. Exploratory research sometimes involves debriefing counselors and clients, or asking them to react to the videotapes of just-completed sessions. The goal of exploratory research is eventually to build theoretical formulations that are both relevant to practice and testable through research.

Hill (1990) described the exploratory approach in these terms:

> Exploratory research thus follows the spirit of the scientific method, in which the observation of clinical phenomena leads to hypothesis formulation and testing, which leads to refinement of the hypotheses, replication of the results, and finally development of the theory. . . . Because of the few replicated results in process research I believe that our research is presently in the observation and hypothesis-building stages, rather than at the theory-building stage. (p. 288)

Mahrer (1988) pointed up the difficulties for psychotherapy research in pursuing a traditional hypothesis-testing approach. As we pointed out earlier, most of our "theories" of counseling or therapy simply do not generate refutable propositions or hypotheses that are actually crucial to the integrity or credibility of the would-be theory. As Mahrer put it:

> I know of no established theory of psychotherapy that has declared bankruptcy because of research that failed to confirm, disconfirmed, or falsified its theoretical propositions and network of theoretical assumptions. (p. 694)

The rise and fall of theories in counseling and psychotherapy is more often tied to the spirit of the times than to the number of times that its crucial tenets have been supported by research findings.

Meehl (1978) in a scathing critique of theory-building and research in the field put it this way:

> It is simply a sad fact that in soft psychology theories rise and fall, come and go, more often as a function of baffled boredom than anything else. (p. 807)

Philosophers of science have long recognized that there are two distinct aspects of the scientific enterprise. These are sometime termed the context of discovery and the context of justification (Reichenbach, 1938). The context of discovery is every bit as "scientific" as is the process of testing null hypotheses.

Somehow over the past 50 years, in psychology generally and certainly in counseling psychology, the process of discovery has been neglected and trivialized. As this has happened, the gap between science and practice has only widened.

The development of exploratory research models is a lone bright spot in the otherwise dismal picture of theory and research on process and outcome. Researchers such as Clara Hill, Myrna Friedlander, Robert Elliott, Leslie Greenberg, and Norman Kagan, among many others have all made notable contributions to increasing the relevance of counseling research.

The relatively small number of exploratory studies appearing in major journals, compared to the usual diet of statistically sophisticated and practically sterile studies, shows how far we have to go to realize the aspirations of those who formulated the scientist-practitioner model a half century ago.

Hoshmond (1989, 1991) has shown how teaching research can be integrated into clinical training in ways that can breathe life back into the scientist-practitioner model. The context of discovery, discussed above is the bedrock of both scientific research and science-based counseling practice.

## THE NEW PHILOSOPHY OF SCIENCE

Counseling psychology was conceived in the era of dustbowl empiricism. Many of its founders were convinced that the answer to almost all of the field's scientific problems would be solved by the use of regression equations and ANOVA formulae. Scientific rigor was considered to lie in rigid specification of variables and strict adherence to operational definitions. Herbert Feigl, the distinguished philosopher of science, was fond of saying that every conversation among scientists was reducible to two questions: "What do you mean?" and "How do you know?"

For many of the counseling psychologists of the 1940s and '50s, those questions were considered to be answerable only with operational definitions of variables and sophisticated statistical manipulations of data.

In point of fact, relatively few of the actual terms that filled the conversations of psychologists in those or any other times were operationally defined or definable. Constructs like anxiety, intelligence, motivation, defensiveness, insight, paranoia, and a multitude of others all carried surplus meaning that went far beyond any acceptable operational definitions. The modest level of intercorrelations among psychometric instruments purporting to measure "intelligence," for example, was eloquent testimony to that fact.

Personality theories and theorists bandied about terms like "self-concept," "ego," "self-actualization," "achievement motivation" and so on. If, indeed, psychologists had conversed only in terms that were operationally defined and spoke only of well-replicated experimental results, they would have had very little to say.

Radical behaviorists like Skinner, as we have seen, tried to avoid the confusing morass of hypothetical constructs and intervening variables by claiming that they had no need for theories at all. More than anything else, "logical positivism," as the approach was called gradually changed from a set of maxims to guide research to become a convenient club with which to assault one's opponents in a scientific debate when all else had failed.

Even in the early years of counseling psychology, cautions were sounded about the stultifying effects of rigid or extreme efforts to adhere to positivistic doctrines. Henry Borow (1956), writing in the third volume of the *Journal of Counseling Psychology*, gave such a warning. In the 20 years following Borow's prophetic warning, discontent with rigid approaches to operationism was voiced from several quarters. Rychlak (1968), Bergin, Garfield, and Thompson (1967), and Tyler (1978) all noted that the very subject matter of psychology dictated a need for flexible and comprehensive models of inquiry.

By 1984, a special issue of the *Journal of Counseling Psychology* had organized a veritable chorus of critics advocating a loosening of the bonds of epistemology, and a new liberating and pluralistic approach to the philosophy of science.

Donald Polkinghorne, the special editor of that issue put it this way:

> The practical work of counseling psychologists brings them into relationships with people as integrated, whole beings who are able to reflect on and struggle over decisions, who sometimes make courageous choices . . . and who develop . . . imaginative responses to the stresses in their environments. Yet the research designs that are acceptable emphasize the passive and overt aspects of people—the empirically observable aspects. The designs seem incapable of explaining the everyday social behavior of human beings that is actually experienced by counseling psychologists . . . (p. 422)

The campaign to loosen the bonds of traditional scientific inquiry has been waged courageously and valiantly virtually throughout the entire history of counseling psychology. For Carl Rogers, his own concepts of the sources of knowledge were the guiding conviction of his career. Humanistic psychology, as we saw, came into existence around a profound discontent with traditional canons of scientific inquiry.

Outside of counseling psychology, the chorus of criticism has been just as loud. Koch (1981) and Rychlak (1977) have called for major revisions in the philosophy of science. Kenneth Gergen (1985) went beyond Thomas Kuhn's (1962) position to declare that not only is science itself a social invention, but its findings are inevitably rooted in the perceptions, beliefs, and biases of the society that has created and maintained it.

At the level of discourse at least the windows of change have opened. Hermeneutics (Packer, 1985) has been accepted as a way of teasing out deeper meanings in patterns of human actions and communications. Laboratory models of research design have been acknowledged to have only limited applicability (Manicus & Secord, 1983).

Within counseling psychology, Borow, Tyler, and Goldman all sounded the same call for change many years ago. Contemporary leaders such as Donald Polkinghorne, George Howard, Fred Borgen, Clara Hill, and Lisa Hoshmond, among others, have waged an eloquent and courageous campaign to create a more flexible and open-ended vision of the role and nature of scientific inquiry.

As Howard (1986) pointed out, even relatively modest changes in the approach to research in counseling psychology would help to close the gap between research and practice and help to revive the scientist-practitioner model. Hill, Thompson, and Williams (1997) have shown how consensual qualitative methods can be used to begin the discovery process.

A perusal of recent research published in major journals shows that some limited progress has been made in creating an interface between research and practice. The viability of the science-practitioner model and the scientific foundations of counseling psychology are still very much in the balance.

## THE EFFICACY OF COUNSELING
## AND PSYCHOTHERAPY

The history of counseling and psychotherapy is largely one of the perseveration of efforts to provide sophisticated answers to fundamentally flawed questions. Although the field has seemingly acknowledged for more than 30 years the necessity to specify all sorts of counselor, client, and situational variables in any evaluation study, the search for sweeping answers to vague questions has gone on unabated.

Efforts to evaluate the efficacy of counseling began early in its history. John Rothney (1957) conducted a series of evaluation studies of high school counseling and concluded that counseling helps. One well-controlled study (Merenda & Rothney, 1958) showed that counseled students entered and succeeded in college more frequently than the non-counseled. Williamson and Bordin conducted a series of studies of counseling results in the 1930s and 1940s (Williamson & Bordin, 1941), also with positive results, even on a 25-year follow-up (Campbell, 1963). The Rogers and Dymond studies of client-centered therapy were done in the 1950s. The famous Eysenck critique of therapy results rocked the field in the 1950s and stimulated both more research and more sophisticated methods and critiques.

Most of the careful reviews of counseling and psychotherapy done in the early 1960s were devastatingly critical. Barry and Wolf (1962) sounded an "epitaph" for vocational guidance, and Astin (1961) wrote of the "functional autonomy" of psychotherapy, characterizing it as an activity that continued in the absence of any real evidence of its effectiveness. Cross (1964) critiqued the methodologies of psychotherapy studies and concluded that the better the research design, the more negative the results.

Bergin (1963) reviewed data from therapy studies, noting that the variance among treated groups often increased even when means between treatment groups and controls were not significantly different. Bergin concluded that these changes might be due to negative effects of therapy on some clients that counterbalanced positive changes in others. The specter of therapy as a two-edged scalpel, capable of harming as often as helping, was a haunting one. Truax and Carkhuff (1967) speculated that these effects might be due to the failure of many therapists to provide "facilitative" relationship conditions.

Throughout the 1960s and 1970s, assessments of the effectiveness of psychotherapy tended to be cautious, if not downright pessimistic (Bergin, 1971; Bergin & Strupp, 1971; Strupp, 1978).

Ford and Urban (1963), in a book optimistically titled *Systems of Psychotherapy*, concluded, after reviewing and comparing 10 of the major theories, that verification of any of the theories was impossible until more careful studies of process and outcome could be accomplished.

Ironically, it was not an innovation in research design or a sudden clarification of outcome criteria or process variables that suddenly changed the atmosphere of doom and gloom that had pervaded psychotherapy research since Eysenck's bombshell of 1952. In 1976 Gene Glass, an educational researcher at the University of Colorado, published an article describing a new way of reviewing or summarizing the results of experimental studies (Glass, 1976). The new approach that Glass christened meta analysis consisted simply of entering the effect sizes or differences between the means of treated and control groups into a frequency distribution and analyzing them statistically as one might the scores of single subjects in a regular experimental analysis. One of the first areas that Glass chose to review with this new methodology was psychotherapy outcome. Basically, Glass entered the results of a large number of outcome studies of psychodynamic, client-centered, behavior-modification, and rational-emotive therapies into his equation. What Glass found was that the average treated subject was placed at about the 75th percentile of a distribution of *untreated* subjects. He found only very slight differences among the four types of psychotherapy.

Glass's little 5-page illustration of a statistical exercise in comparing research findings became one of the most widely cited and frequently copied concepts in the history of psychological and educational research. Although the method left untouched many issues of the equivalence of research designs, client populations, and outcome criteria for inclusion in the statistical hopper, meta-analysis was clearly an idea whose time had come.

Within a few years, literally hundreds of meta-analyses had been accomplished on a very wide range of experimental studies. By 1983 the *Journal of Consulting and Clinical Psychology* had devoted a special section to meta-analyses of psychotherapy research (Garfield, 1983). Some ten years later (Lipsey & Wilson, 1993), the *American Psychologist* carried a lengthy paper titled "The Efficacy of Psychological, Educational and Behavioral Treatment: *Confirmation* from Meta-analysis" (italics added). How wonderful is the aura of scientific respectability conferred by the crunching of numbers, as opposed to attempts to draw rational conclusions around complex issues. Interestingly, at about the same time, psychotherapy received a sort of Good Housekeeping Seal of Approval from *Consumer Reports* magazine, attesting to its efficacy (Seligman, 1995).

It appears that all that is left to the psychotherapy researcher is to find out why therapy works when it does work, how therapists should be selected and trained, and what variations in treatment should be provided for the many kinds of clients and presenting problems that lurk outside the door of every consulting room. Perhaps the next 20 years will provide answers to those questions.

Lest the reader interpret the foregoing statements as pessimistic: it is clear that the subdiscipline of counseling psychology and its associated fields have made substantial, if not spectacular, progress over the past 20 years. The era of simple-minded parochialism and divisiveness in counseling theory has faded into the past. Steady progress is being made in terms of psychotherapy integration. A promising beginning has been made in closing the gap between research and practice and in resuscitating the ideal of the scientist-practitioner. Slow progress is being made in focusing evaluation efforts toward specific groups of clients and presenting problems.

In terms of research methodology, counseling research is as sophisticated as any other area of research in psychology. Valiant efforts have been made in loosening the epistemological bonds of a rigidly positivistic philosophy of science. The long-awaited "revolution" in counseling research is upon us. As in all revolutions we must, ourselves, not merely get rid of our old masters, but also shake off the theoretical chains and conceptual blindfolds that we still wear.

# REFERENCES

Ainsworth, M., & Bowlby, J. (1991). An ethnological approach to personality development. *American Psychologist, 46*, 341–353.

Astin, A. W. (1961). The functional autonomy of psychotherapy. *American Psychologist, 16*, 75–78.

Barlow, D. H. (1981). On the relation of clinical research to clinical practice: Current issues, new directions. *Journal of Consulting and Clinical Psychology, 49*, 147–155.

Barlow, D. H., Hayes, S. C., & Nelson, R. O. (1984). *The scientist-practitioner: Research and accountability in clinical and educational settings.* New York: Pergamon.

Barry, R., & Wolf, B. (1962). *Epitaph for vocational guidance.* New York: Teachers College, Columbia University.

Berdie, R. F. (1959). Counseling principles and presumptions. *Journal of Counseling Psychology, 6*, 175–182.

Bergin, A. E. (1963). The effects of psychotherapy: Negative results revisited. *Journal of Counseling Psychology, 10*, 244–249.

Bergin, A. E. (1971). The evaluation of therapeutic outcomes. In A. E. Bergin & S. L. Garfield (Eds.), *Handbook of psychotherapy and behavior change* (pp. 217–270). New York: Wiley.

Bergin, A. E., Garfield, S. L., & Thompson, A. S. (1967). The Chicago conference on clinical training and clinical psychology. *American Psychologist, 22,* 307–316.

Bergin, A. E., & Strupp, H. H. (1971). *Changing frontiers in the science of psychotherapy.* Chicago: Aldine-Atherton.

Beutler, L. E., Williams, R. E., Wakefield, P. J., & Entwistle, S. R. (1995). Bridging scientist and practitioner perspectives in clinical psychology. *American Psychologist, 50,* 984–994.

Blocher, D. H. (1966). *Developmental counseling.* New York: Ronald Press.

Bordin, E. S. (1955). *Psychological counseling.* New York: Appleton-Century-Crofts.

Bordin, E. S. (1980). A psychodynamic view of counseling psychology. *The Counseling Psychologist, 9,* 62–70.

Bordin, E. S. (1994). Theory and research on the therapeutic working alliance. In A. O. Horvath & L. S. Greenberg (Eds.), *The working alliance: Theory, research and practice* (pp. 13–37). New York: Wiley.

Borow, H. (1956). Research notes from here and there. *Journal of Counseling Psychology, 3,* 292–294.

Brammer, L. M., Abrego, P. J., & Shostrum, E. (1993). *Therapeutic counseling* (6th ed.). Englewood Cliffs, NJ: Prentice-Hall.

Callis, R. (1960). Toward an integrative theory of counseling. *Journal of College Student Personnel, 1,* 2–9.

Campbell, D. A. (1963). A counseling evaluation study with a better control group. *Journal of Counseling Psychology, 10,* 334–339.

Carkhuff, R. (1966). Counseling research, theory and practice. *Journal of Counseling Psychology, 13,* 467–480.

Corrigan, J. D., Dell, D. M., Lewis, K. N., & Schmidt, L. D. (1980). Counseling as a social influence process: A review. *Journal of Counseling Psychology, 27,* 395–417.

Cross, H. J. (1964). The outcomes of psychotherapy: A selected analysis of research findings. *Journal of Consulting Psychology, 28,* 413–417.

Dember, W. N. (1974). Motivation and the cognitive revolution. *American Psychologist, 29,* 161–168.

Elliott, R. (1983). Fitting process research to the practicing psychotherapist. *Psychotherapy, Theory and Research, 20,* 47–55.

Epstein, S. (1994). Integration of the cognitive and the psychodynamic unconscious. *American Psychologist, 8,* 709–724.

Fiedler, F. E. (1950). The concept of an ideal therapeutic relationship. *Journal of Consulting Psychology, 14,* 239–245.

Ford, D. H., & Urban, H. B. (1963). *Systems of psychotherapy: A comparative study*. New York: Wiley.

Forsyth, D. R., & Leary, M. R. (1997). Achieving the goals of the scientist-practitioner model: The seven interfaces of social and counseling psychology. *The Counseling Psychologist, 25*, 180–200.

Forsyth, D. R., & Strong, S. R. (1986). The scientific study of counseling and psychotherapy: A unificationist view. *American Psychologist, 41*, 113–119.

Frank, J. (1961). *Persuasion and healing*. Baltimore: Johns Hopkins University Press.

Garfield, S. L. (Special Editor). (1983). Meta-analyses and psychotherapy [Special Section]. *Journal of Clinical and Consulting Psychology, 51*, 3–75.

Garfield, S. L. (1995). *Psychotherapy: An eclectic-integrative approach* (2nd ed.). New York: Wiley.

Garfield, S. L., & Bergin, A. E. (1986). Introduction and historical overview. In S. L. Garfield & A. E. Bergin (Eds.), *Handbook of psychotherapy and behavior change* (3rd ed., pp. 3–22). New York: Wiley.

Garfield, S. L., & Kurtz, R. (1977). A study of eclectic views. *Journal of Consulting and Clinical Psychology, 45*, 78–83.

Gergen, K. J. (1985). The social constructionist movement in modern psychology. *American Psychologist, 40*, 266–275.

Glass, G. (1976). Primary secondary and meta-analysis of research. *Educational Researcher, 5*, 3–8.

Goldfried, M. R. (1980). Toward the delineation of therapeutic change principles. *American Psychologist, 35*, 991–999.

Goldman, L. (1976). A revolution in counseling research. *Journal of Counseling Psychology, 23*, 543–552.

Goldman, L. (1977). Toward more meaningful research. *Personnel and Guidance Journal, 56*, 363–368.

Greenberg, L. S. (1986). Change process research. *Journal of Consulting and Clinical Psychology, 54*, 4–9.

Harper, R. A. (1959). *Psychoanalysis and psychotherapy*. Englewood Cliffs, NJ: Prentice-Hall.

Heesacker, M., Connor, K., & Prichard, S. (1995). Individual counseling and psychotherapy: Applications from the social psychology of attitude change. *The Counseling Psychologist, 23*, 611–632.

Heppner, P. P., & Claiborn, C. D. (1989). Social influence research in counseling: A review and critique. *Journal of Counseling Psychology, 36*, 365–387.

Hill, C. E. (1990). Exploratory in-session process research in individual psychotherapy: A review. *Journal of Consulting and Clinical Psychology, 58*, 288–294.

Hill, C. E., & Corbett, M. M. (1993). A perspective on the history of process and outcome research in counseling psychology. *Journal of Counseling Psychology, 40*, 3–24.

Hill, C. E., Nutt, E. A., & Jackson, S. (1994). Trends in psychotherapy research: Samples, measures, researchers and classic publications. *Journal of Counseling Psychology, 41*, 364–377.

Hill, C. E., Thompson, B. J., & Williams, E. N. (1997). A guide to conducting consensual quantitative research. *The Counseling Psychologist, 25*, 517–572.

Hobbs, N. (1962). Sources of gain in psychotherapy. *American Psychologist, 17*, 741–717.

Hoshmond, L. L. (1991). Clinical inquiry as scientific training. *The Counseling Psychologist, 19*, 431,433.

Hoshmond, L. L. S. (1989). Alternate research paradigms: A review and a teaching proposal. *The Counseling Psychologist, 17*, 3–79.

Hovland, C. I., Janis, I. L., & Kelly, H. H. (1953). *Communication and persuasion*. New Haven, CT: Yale University Press.

Howard, G. S. (1986). The scientist-practitioner in counseling psychology: Toward a deeper integration of theory research and practice. *The Counseling Psychologist, 14*, 61–105.

Karasu, T. B. (1986). The specificity vs. non-specificity dilemma: Toward identifying therapeutic change agents. *American Journal of Psychiatry, 143*, 687–695.

Kazdin, A. E. (1986). The evaluation of psychotherapy: Research design and methodology. In S. L. Garfield & A. E. Bergen (Eds.), *Handbook of psychotherapy and behavior change* (3rd ed., pp. 23–68). New York: Wiley.

Kelly, G. A. (1995). *A theory of personality: The psychology of personal constructs*. New York: Norton.

Kiesler, D. J (1966). Basic methodological issues implicit in psychotherapy research. *American Journal of Psychotherapy, 20*, 135–155.

Klein, M. (1932). *The psychoanalysis of children*. London: Hogarth Press.

Koch, S. (1981). The nature and limits of psychological knowledge: Lessons of a century of science qua "science." *American Psychologist, 36*, 257–269.

Krumboltz, J. D. (1966). *Revolution in counseling: Implications of behavioral science*. Boston: Houghton-Mifflin.

Kuhn, T. (1962). *The structure of scientific revolutions*. Chicago: University of Chicago.

Lazarus, A. (1976). *Multimodal behavior therapy*. New York: Springer Publishing Co.

Lichtenberg, J. W., & Hummel, T. J. (1976). Counseling as a stochastic process: Fitting a Markov chain model to initial counseling interviews. *Journal of Counseling Psychology, 23*, 310–315.

Lipsey, M. W., & Wilson, D. B. (1993). The efficacy of psychological, educational and behavioral treatment: Confirmation from meta-analysis. *American Psychologist, 48,* 1181–1209.

Lister, J. L. (1964). The counselor's personal theory. *Counselor Education and Supervision, 3,* 207–213.

Lopez, F. (1995). Contemporary attachment theory: An introduction with implications for counseling psychology. *The Counseling Psychologist, 23,* 395–415.

Mahoney, M. J. (1977). Reflections on the cognitive-learning trend in psychotherapy. *American Psychologist, 32,* 5–13.

Mahrer, A. R. (1988). Discovery-oriented psychotherapy research: Rationale, aims and methods. *American Psychologist, 43,* 694–702.

Manicus, P. T., & Secord, P. F. (1983). Implications for psychology of the new philosophy of science. *American Psychologist, 38,* 399–413.

Martindale, C. (1978). The therapist-as-fixed-effect fallacy in psychotherapy research. *Journal of Consulting and Clinical Psychology, 46,* 1526–1530.

Meehl, P. C. (1978). Theoretical risks and tabular asterisks: Sir Karl, Sir Ronald, and the slow process of soft psychology. *Journal of Consulting and Clinical Psychology, 46,* 806–834.

Merenda, P., & Rothney, J. W. (1958). Evaluating the effects of counseling eight years after. *Journal of Counseling Psychology, 5,* 163–168.

Norcross, J. C., & Arkowitz, H. (1992). The evolution and current status of psychotherapy integration. In W. Dryden (Ed.), *Integrative and eclectic therapy: A handbook* (pp. 1–40). Buckingham, UK: Free University Press.

Norcross, J. C., Prochaska, J. O., & Farber, J. A. (1993). Psychologists conducting therapy: New findings and historical comparisons on the Psychotherapy Division membership. *Psychotherapy, 30,* 692–697.

Okun, B. F. (1990). *Seeking connections in psychotherapy.* San Francisco: Jossey-Bass.

Orlinsky, D. E., Graive, K., & Parks, B. K. (1994). Process and outcome in psychotherapy. In A. E. Bergin & S. L. Garfield (Eds.), *Handbook of psychotherapy and behavior change* (4th ed., pp. 270–376). New York: Wiley.

Orlinsky, D. E., & Howard, K. I. (1986). Process and outcome in psychotherapy. In S. L. Garfield & A. E. Bergin (Eds.), *Handbook of psychotherapy and behavior change* (3rd ed., pp. 311–384). New York: Wiley.

Packer, M. J. (1985). Hermeneutic inquiry in the study of human conduct. *American Psychologist, 40,* 1081–1093.

Paul, G. (1967). Strategy in outcome research in psychotherapy. *Journal of Consulting Psychology, 31,* 109–118.

Pepinsky, H. B. (1974). A metalanguage for systematic research on human communication. *Journal of the American Society for Information Science, 25,* 483–498.

Peterson, G., & Bradley, R. W. (1980). Counselor orientation and theoretical attitudes toward counseling: Historical perspective and new data. *Journal of Counseling Psychology, 27,* 554–560.

Polkinghorne, D. E. (1984). Further extensions of methodological diversity for counseling psychology. *Journal of Counseling Psychology, 31,* 416–429.

Poznanski, J. J., & McLennan, J. (1995). Conceptualizing and measuring counselor's theoretical orientation. *Journal of Counseling Psychology, 42,* 411–422.

Pribram, K. H. (1986). The cognitive revolution and mind/brain issues. *American Psychologist, 41,* 507–520.

Reichenbach, H. (1938). *Experience and prediction.* Chicago: University of Chicago Press.

Robbins, S. B. (1989). Role of contemporary psychoanalysis in counseling psychology. *Journal of Counseling Psychology, 36,* 267–278.

Robinson, F. P. (1955). The dynamics of communication in counseling. *Journal of Counseling Psychology, 2,* 163–169.

Rothney, J. W. (1957). Counseling does help. *Vocational Guidance Quarterly, 6,* 15–19.

Rychlak, J. F. (1968). *A philosophy of science for personality theory.* Boston: Houghton-Mifflin.

Rychlak, J. F. (1977). *The psychology of rigorous humanism.* New York: New York University Press.

Schofield, W. (1964). *Psychotherapy: The purchase of friendship.* Englewood Cliffs, NJ: Prentice-Hall.

Seligman, M. E. P. (1995). The effectiveness of psychotherapy. *American Psychologist, 50,* 965–974.

Shaffer, L. F., & Shoben, E. J. Jr. (1956). *The psychology of adjustment.* Boston: Houghton-Mifflin.

Shoben, E. J., Jr. (1962). The counselor's theory as personal trait. *Personnel and Guidance Journal, 40,* 617–621.

Stricker, G. (1997). Are science and practice commensurable? *American Psychologist, 52,* 442–448.

Strong, S. R. (1968). Counseling: An interpersonal influence process. *Journal of Counseling Psychology, 15,* 215–223.

Strong, S. R., & Claiborn, C. (1982). *Change through interaction: Social psychological processes of counseling and psychotherapy.* New York: Wiley.

Strong, S. R., Welsh, J. A., Corcoran, J. L., & Hoyt, W. T. (1992). Social psychology and counseling psychology: The history, products and promise of an interface. *The Journal of Counseling Psychology, 39,* 139–157.

Strupp, H. H. (1978). Psychotherapy research and practice: An overview. In L. S. Garfield & A. E. Bergin (Eds.), *Handbook of psychotherapy and behavior change* (2nd ed., pp. 3–32). New York: Wiley.

Strupp, H. H. (1989). Psychotherapy: Can the practitioner learn from the researcher? *American Psychologist, 44,* 717–724.

Thoresen, C. E., & Anton, J. L. (1974). Intensive experimental research in counseling. *Journal of Counseling Psychology, 21,* 553–559.

Truax, C. B., & Carkhuff, R. R. (1967). *Toward effective counseling and psychotherapy: Training and practice.* Chicago: Aldine.

Tyler, L. E. (1958). Theoretical principles underlying the counseling process. *Journal of Counseling Psychology, 5,* 3–11.

Tyler, L. E. (1978). *Individuality: Human possibilities and personal choice in the psychological development of men and women.* San Francisco: Jossey-Bass.

Wallerstein, R. S. (1989). The psychotherapy research project of the Menninger Foundation: An overview. *The American Psychologist, 57,* 195–205.

Watkins, C. E., Lopez, F. G., Campbell, V. L., & Himmell, C. D. (1986). Contemporary counseling psychology: Results of a national survey. *Journal of Counseling Psychology, 33,* 301–309.

Williamson, E. G. (1950). A concept of counseling. *Occupations, 29,* 182–189.

Williamson, E. G. (1962). The counselor as technique. *Personnel and Guidance Journal, 41,* 108–111.

Williamson, E. G., & Bordin, E. S. (1941). A statistical evaluation of clinical counseling. *Educational and Psychological Measurement, 1,* 117–132.

# 11

# Coming of Age As a Profession

In recent years . . . counseling psychologists have increased their participation in a variety of settings. Through the increased diversity of settings, counseling psychologists have carried with them certain beliefs and values in common, including (a) the importance of the scientist-practitioner model, (b) an emphasis on prevention, developmental enhancement, and remediation and (c) the necessity of understanding development across the life span, with special emphasis on the importance of career development and the role of work. (Kagan et al., 1988)

A study of the history of psychology might lead a cynic to believe that there are only two kinds of psychologists, those who envy physicists and those who envy physicians. When one looks at the history of counseling psychology, however, it is apparent that there is a third type: those who envy both as well as most other psychologists.

In 1980, John Whiteley and Bruce Fretz produced an edited book, *The Present and Future of Counseling Psychology*. Whiteley was the founding and longtime editor of *The Counseling Psychologist*, the Division 17 house journal. He was also the chief chronicler of the early years of counseling psychology (Whiteley, 1984). Without his efforts we would know much less about the founding and formation of the Division and its early directions.

Whiteley and Fretz assembled a series of papers from a dazzling array of luminaries in the field, including many who had been responsible for the directions taken by the field since its inception.

The editors asked one group of authors to address the lingering question of the professional identity of counseling psychologists, an issue that had supposedly been resolved some 15 years earlier at the Greyston Conference. A second group was invited to write about their vision of the future of the field, specifically, what counseling psychology would be like in the year 2000.

As we mentioned in Chapter 5, a number of these papers displayed a profound discontent with the present status of the field. Titles like "Counseling Psychology: Tyranny of a Title" (Hurst & Parker, 1980), "We Have Met the Enemy and They is Us—and Everybody Else" (Weigel, 1980), and the "Identity Crises of Counseling Psychologists" (Super, 1980) all deplored the lack of either clear identity or full recognition of the field. One paper (Foreman, 1980) even blamed the problems of the field on its affiliation with those plebeian schools of education.

Not all of the papers were negative. Gilbert Wrenn (1980) saw strength in the field's diversity and cautioned against expecting certainty in an uncertain world. Lyle Schmidt (1980) pointed out that counseling psychology only reflected the needs and values represented in the larger society.

There were critical commentaries on the field from outsiders, including counselor educators and a clinical psychologist. The clinical psychologist (Nathan, 1980) urged counseling psychologist to stay away from psychotherapy, where they would be seen as second-class citizens.

A rejoinder to the papers from active leaders of the Division had been invited, and Norman Kagan (1980) provided a temperate and even lighthearted rebuttal to the tone of doom and gloom, and the assertions that the field had no legitimate identity, in these words:

> Are we then a group of professionals with no known parentage? It would appear that by magic we 2300 bastards found each other. From that point of view can you imagine the early meetings that stimulated the formation of Division 17? I can see one counselor saying to the other "You know your professional parentage?" "Nope." "Me neither, let's write some by-laws and apply for divisional status in APA. We'll call ourselves counseling psychologists, whenever we're with counselors we'll talk psychology, whenever we're with psychologists we'll talk counseling. If we're ever with a group of counselors and psychologists we'll talk about the weather." (pp. 80–81)

Kagan went on, in more serious tones, to point out that counseling psychology does have a legitimate lineage and purpose in helping as many people as possible to "live well, work well, and love well" (p.

81). For Kagan, the identity of counseling psychology clearly issued from its heritage as a social service and social reform movement, motivated more by the need to provide help than by the need to achieve status.

The second group of papers focused upon visions of the future: where we would be in the year 2000. Many of the writers drew upon the faddish writings of those "experts" who dignify their speculations and guesswork with the title futurists. Almost all of the predictions vastly overestimated the rates of both technological and social change. Whiteley (1980) quoted a pair of futurists who blithely predicted that within 20 years, among other things, effective appetite and weight control methods would be available, and there would be practical use of direct electronic communication with the brain. Unfortunately, Americans are fatter than ever and, fortunately, mental telepathy has not replaced the telephone. Some saw a virtual end to one-to-one counseling services. Some doubted the continued existence of the field at all. Perhaps the most honest and forthright response came from Harold Pepinsky (1980) who titled his paper "You Tell Me What's Going to Happen." As we look at the predictions made by the leaders of counseling psychology 20 years ago, it is clear that neither they nor the futurists they consulted were able to predict our present world.

Fretz (1980) wrote hopefully of the existence of 50 APA approved counseling psychology programs. Today, there are, in fact, around 70. Membership in the Division has grown from around 2,300 to around 3,000. A great many of the members are actively involved in APA governance activities (Yee & Bingham, 1999). In the past 20 years, the life of counseling psychology has gone on, not spectacularly, but steadily, and not at all badly.

The diversity which many of the pessimistic pundits so deplored has been, as Gilbert Wrenn predicted, a source of strength. The society has changed and counseling psychology has changed with it.

Some of the self-deprecating tone and pessimistic outlook of the papers could be attributed to the fact that the 1970s were not good years for psychologists, especially those in academia. The flow of federal money that had helped to sustain the operation of various training, research, and service programs since the heady days of NDEA had pretty well dried up. Academic jobs for new doctoral graduates were scarce indeed. Universities were in a belt-tightening mode. In

1972, there were only 19 APA-approved counseling psychology programs in operation. Some state licensing boards were sniffing suspiciously at the credentials of counseling psychology graduates, especially those prepared in schools of education. These were not good times.

It is interesting to note the composition of the group of contributors to the Whiteley and Fretz volume. All but one listed affiliations with universities. That lone non-academic psychologist was from the Veterans Administration. All but one—Leona Tyler—were White males.

Perhaps more even than the content of the papers, the composition of the group of contributors reflected the state of the field in 1980. For the first 30 years of its existence, Division 17 had been predominantly comprised of university professors and college counselors. At the time of the Greyston Conference in 1964, nearly two thirds of a random sample of Division 17 members listed educational settings as their places of employment (Samler, 1964). A similar study in 1973 (Krauskopf, Thoresson, & McAleer) found that fully 70% listed their main job locations in universities and colleges. It is not surprising, then, that a group of leaders would be drawn almost solely out of those settings.

To a considerable extent, prior to 1980, the Division of Counseling Psychology was an organization of people who taught counseling psychology or who practiced it in a very narrow range of settings, primarily in colleges and to a lesser extent in the Veterans Administration Hospitals. The male Caucasian makeup of this group of senior leaders was also largely a reflection of the times.

This is not to say that this group failed to supply skillful direction and much-needed leadership to the field. It was largely a group of scholars from academia who kept counseling psychology alive and growing in the 15 years after the Greyston Conference. To a considerable extent, they were the colleagues and former students of the little group of people who had founded the field in the first place.

It is also not surprising that this group was preoccupied with questions of identity and status for counseling psychology. At the level of institutional identity, counseling psychology is a frail vessel, indeed. Its continued existence rests on its status as a Division of the APA, on the operation of two journals, and the survival of a group of APA-approved doctoral programs.

The governance of the Division, and so really the continued existence of the field, tended to be in the hands of a small, rather closely knit group of very dedicated and fiercely protective people. Most of this group shared close personal and professional ties and were as we saw, very homogeneous in terms of their professional roles. The governance of the Division tended to be informal and the result of consensus judgments among likeminded friends and colleagues.

## THE 1980S: A DECADE OF CHANGE

The 1980s was a decade of beginnings and endings for counseling psychology, and for professional psychology generally. At the beginning of the decade, it was apparent that the Division 17 governance structure no longer fully represented the increasing range of settings in which counseling psychologists were working, and that the new generation of members needed to be represented and involved in the governance of the Division. It was also clear that much greater attention needed to be given to issues of diversity, both within counseling psychology itself, and in terms of the client populations the field sought to serve.

Throughout the 1970s and 1980s a series of surveys of counseling psychologists reported very rapid changes in both the settings in which they worked and the nature of the activities in which they were engaged. Most of the surveys had very low return rates, many under 60%. While that might well have disqualified them from serving as master's theses, it did not prevent them from raising considerable anxiety within the profession.

Whether these surveys were highly accurate in reflecting the settings, views, and activities of counseling psychologists as a total group, they were remarkably consistent in portraying a changing profession.

Clearly, while the core (50 to 60%) of the profession, at least of those who returned questionnaires, remained in colleges and universities, the remaining group, particularly the younger, more recent graduates, were occupied in much more varied settings than ever before. They were also engaged much more frequently in the practice of psychotherapy.

Fretz and Simon (1992) summarized the results of several of these studies and extrapolated the results to give a picture of what these trends might mean in the future.

Extrapolation of these trends suggests that for the first time in the history of counseling psychology, *less* than 50% of all counseling psychologists will soon be in academic settings, *and* private practice will be the most frequent first placement of new doctorates in counseling psychology. . . .

In all of these surveys there is consistent evidence that far more time is being spent on remedial therapeutic activities than on the preventive and developmental/educative activities that have long been identified as major themes in the profession. (pp. 4–5)

It seems less than shocking that for the first time a majority of counseling psychologists might actually be doing counseling rather than teaching, talking, or writing about it. Neither is the fact shocking that many contemporary counseling psychologists refer to their work as "psychotherapy." Many of the semantic problems around the counseling vs. therapy distinction were, as we saw largely the result of the failure of an earlier generation of leaders to make clear that psychological counseling is a form of psychotherapy. The tremendous expansions of brief, behavioral, and cognitive-behavioral therapies has made the ancient counseling vs. therapy distinction even less relevant than before.

As we saw earlier, 40 years ago Leona Tyler (1960) described counseling as "minimum change therapy" in terms that could apply very well to today's brief therapies. To decide whether a given therapist is "remedial" or "developmental" in approach, or both, requires more than a questionnaire. It is quite possible to both define and practice psychotherapy in ways that are fully compatible with a preventive, developmental, and educative orientation.

Practicing psychotherapy is neither the mark nor the monopoly of any single profession. Therapy is done by psychiatrists and several denominations of psychologists, as well as by social workers, nurses, and a variety of so-called paraprofessionals.

Most of the changes noted in these surveys were actually healthy signs of the acceptance given to counseling psychologists both by the public and by employers. Counseling psychologists were and are now demonstrating their competence and worth in community mental health settings, medical centers, business and industry, government, and a host of other settings. The only challenge that this presents to the field is for the professional organizations and the training programs to keep up with a changing reality. Over the past generations, the leaders of counseling psychology had tended to lock themselves into the paradoxical stance of both deploring the status quo and viewing changes with alarm.

Fortunately, the Division of Counseling Psychology began the process of both adapting to change and endeavoring to be proactive some 20 years ago. In the early 1980s, under Presidents Blocher and Borow, new administrative structures and procedures were put into place and efforts were began to reach out to the "grass roots" of the organization. A special committee composed of Tom Magoon, Naomi Meara, and Lyle Schmidt helped to create a new and more effective governance framework for the Division.

In 1982, a major project looking at counseling psychology in the next decade was completed. The project led by Norman Kagan, Bruce Fretz, Roger Myers, Lenore Harmon, and Faith Tanney involved many counseling psychologists in discussions held over a period of more than two years. The final papers (Kagan, 1982) looked at the future of the Division from a number of perspectives, including those of changing work settings and professional opportunities.

Some 3 years later, an even more comprehensive study of the organization was began under the leadership of George Gazda. This project culminated in "The Third National Conference for Counseling Psychology: Planning the Future," or what has become more familiarly known as the Georgia Conference, held in Atlanta in the Spring of 1987 (*The Counseling Psychologist,* 1988).

This conference was called the third such project, following the Northwestern Conference of 1951, that gave the field its name, and the Greyston Conference of 1964. The Georgia Conference dealt with a wide range of problems and perspectives. A large number of counseling psychologists were involved in planning and participating in the Conference, although, predictably, the majority were from university counseling psychology programs.

The Georgia Conference, while still heavily preoccupied with issues of identity and status, managed to take a relatively broad look at both the problems and opportunities confronting the field. The conference planners (Rude, Weissberg, & Gazda, 1988) summarized the achievements of the meeting as follows:

> A number of common themes emerged. Discussions of identity affirmed the value of the scientist-practitioner model and of traditional strengths

such as prevention, life-span development and skill-building as well as innovative and nontraditional functions. Among the ideas . . . were strategies to enhance counseling psychology's visibility and political strength and to build proactive planning into governance. Ways to improve the training of counseling psychologists by enhancing rigor, scientific thinking, professional identity and ability to work in diverse and emerging settings also received substantial attention. (p. 423)

On the whole, the conference demonstrated an increasing ability of the leadership of the field to raise their gaze above the level of their navels and to reach out and recognize both problems and possibilities in the world outside of academia. The obsessive concern over who we are and how others see us was still present, but was considerably tempered as compared to the past. Overall, organized counseling psychology has shown considerable maturity and vision in adapting to rapidly changing times and in facing difficult challenges over the past 20 years.

## ACHIEVEMENTS AND CHALLENGES IN THE 1990S

In 1992, the American Psychological Association officially celebrated its 100th birthday. Counseling as a professional activity was rapidly approaching the century mark—depending upon how one calculated its date of birth. The 1990s were a time of looking back as well as forward, and of savoring accomplishments, rather than agonizing over failures or anticipated failures.

A whole series of historical essays tracing the history of various aspects of the field appeared in the *Journal of Counseling Psychology* in 1992 and 1993. Most of them have been cited in this book. For the first time, counseling began to see its diversity as a source of strength rather than as a symptom of disintegration.

Watkins (1994), in an optimistic paper on "Hope, Promise and Possibilities" examined the accomplishments and possible future of the field. He described the present status of counseling psychology in these terms:

For all of the struggle, counseling psychology has come a long way. . . . We as a group are scientists, practitioners, and scientist-practitioners. We are eclectic, behavioristic, cognitive and so forth. . . . We are academics, private practitioners, and counseling center psychologists among others. We spend time in varied activities, ranging from teaching to counseling to supervision to assessment. We do not lack for diversity in activities performed, in theoretical orientations endorsed, in settings where employment is found, in views about ourselves and our specialty. (pp. 315–316)

Watkins went on to cite ten unifying trends or themes that he saw as representative of the strength and progress of the field. These included many of the achievements that we have already traced earlier in this and the previous chapter. At least four such themes deserve further attention, however.

## Leadership in the Counseling and Career Development of Women

One area in which counseling psychologists have taken notable leadership and produced an outstanding body of research is in the counseling and career development of women. As far back as 1978, a Division 17 Committee on Women produced a set of principles concerning the counseling and psychotherapy of women (Fitzgerald & Nutt, 1983). This document was approved as policy by Division 17 and contributed to important guidelines for practice throughout professional psychology. Distinguished leadership for the development of policies regarding the counseling of women came from people such as Ursula Delworth, Lenore Harmon, and Naomi Meard among many others.

Counseling psychologists have also produced an impressive body of knowledge and theory in the long-neglected area of the career development and vocational behavior of women. Major contributions have been made by people such as Helen Astin, Nancy Betz, Helen Farmer, Ruth Fassinger, Louise Fizgerald, Gail Hackett, Lenore Harmon, and many others. These joint efforts have placed counseling psychology in a position of real leadership in the field of the psychology of women.

## Multicultural Counseling and Therapy

Counseling psychology has also made a notable contribution to the study of the effects of ethnic and cultural differences on counseling and psychotherapy. Important theoretical frameworks regarding the influences of acculturation and racial identity have again put counseling psychology in a position of leadership in this area. Major contributions have been made by Donald Atkinson, Janet Helms, and Charles Ridley, among others.

## Supervision of Counseling and Therapy

Again, counseling psychologists have produced a body of theory and research on the supervision and training of counselors that leads the field. Counseling psychologists have pioneered the use of audio- and videotaped interviews and supervisory techniques to prepare counselors and therapists. Contributors include Elizabeth Holloway, Everett Worthington, Norman Kagan, Cal Stoltenberg, and Michael Ellis, among many others.

## Social Skills Training

Counseling psychologists have pioneered the use of various kinds of skill training programs to treat a wide range of problems. Training in interpersonal relationship skills, assertiveness, and basic parenting, teaching, and managerial skills have also been developed and evaluated by counseling psychologists. Contributors include George Gazda, Norman Kagan, Robert Carkhuff, and Allen Ivey among others. Training has indeed become a preferred method of treatment in many situations.

## OPPORTUNITIES MISSED

While, as we saw, counseling psychology has had its share of success stories, it has also had notable failures and missed opportunities. The most notable of these has been the failure to lead or even to be involved in the area of prevention. Even though the counseling literature has always given lip service to the importance of prevention-oriented intervention, counseling psychologists have largely failed to give leadership, or even to participate effectively in preventive efforts.

## Prevention

Over the past decade, there have been major efforts to develop what is called a "science of prevention" (Coie et al., 1993). Conceptual frameworks have been developed and calls made for a national research program on prevention of psychopathology. These efforts have been coordinated by a Basic Behavioral Science Task Force of the National Advisory Mental Health Council (1996). Prevention has been described as a major aspect of health psychology (Taylor, 1990; Winett, 1995). Social action theories that stress the cultivation of personal responsibility for health through educative and other environmental structures have been proposed in what has been called a "public health psychology" (Ewart, 1991). For 20 years Albee (1982) has stressed the relationship between primary prevention, social change, and the effort to promote human potential.

In the midst of a major effort by psychology, supported by public policy initiatives, one glaring question remains: Where are counseling psychologists?

## The Renewed Emphasis on Positive Psychology

One of the most important and dramatic developments in psychology in the 1990s has been the resurgence of interest in what is called "positive psychology." Martin Seligman (1999), in his 1998 presidential address to the American Psychological Association, called for a new "science of human strengths." As he noted:

> At this juncture psychology can play an enormously important role. We can articulate a vision of the good life that is empirically sound and, at the same time, understandable and attractive. . . . I look not toward the lessons of remedial psychology with its emphasis on repairing damage. Instead, I look to a new social and behavioral science that seeks to understand and nurture those human strengths that can prevent the tragedy of mental illness. (pp. 560–561)

Seligman announced a series of initiatives by the APA to promote positive psychology. Major books by psychologists such as Csikszentmihalyi (1990), Goleman (1995, 1998), Gardner (1983), Sternberg (1996), Salovey and Sluyter (1997), and Spencer and Spencer (1993) have broadened concepts of intelligent behavior, focused upon practical competence in work settings rather than schools, and have placed an emphasis upon healthy personality development, including interpersonal sensitivity and emotional control, as requisites for effective personal and vocational functioning. This movement and its literature have virtually exploded over the past few years.

Again, the question remains, Where are counseling psychologists?

## Occupational Health and Safety

For the past 20 years, as survey after survey reported a lessening of interest and involvement of counseling psychologists in vocational assessment or counseling, complaints are heard that we are getting away from our roots. One area that clearly ties the roots of counseling psychology to problems of health and with some of the most immediate concerns of our society is the field of occupational health. A reading of any metropolitan newspaper, a viewing of the 6 o'clock news, or simply a drive in the evening rush hour will convince any observer that Americans are working more and enjoying it less.

Stress in the workplace has become one of the most immediate and severe problems facing society. Work has moved from providing the spice of life to inflicting the kiss of death (Levi, 1990). Some estimates suggest that as many as one half of all workers are actively unhappy in their jobs, and up to 90% feel that their work is not moving them toward life goals. As many as three fourths of referrals for mental health problems may be traceable, at least in part, to a lack of job satisfaction or the inability to deal with work-related stress (Levi, 1990). Violence in the workplace makes headlines. Stress-related morbidity is buried, like its victims, in the obituary section. Major initiatives in the prevention of work-related psychological disorders have been proposed by the National Institute of Occupational Safety and Health (Sauter, Murphy, & Hurrell, 1990).

Occupational health promotion programs have been reviewed in terms of reducing risk of cardiovascular disease (Glasgow & Terborg, 1988). Counseling psychologists have become involved in research around problems of workplace stress in limited ways (Bowman & Stern, 1995; Decker & Borgen, 1993; Kagan, Kagan, & Watson, 1995; Long, 1998; Osipow & Spokane, 1987; Ross & Altmaier,

1994), and a special section of the *Journal of Counseling Psychology* has been devoted to the topic.

However, a 1992 review of health-related applications of counseling psychology (Altmaier & Johnson) did not mention work-related stress. In the same volume, the topic was treated very briefly in a chapter on counseling and career adjustment (Myers & Cairo, 1992). Gerstein and Shullman (1992), in a review of counseling psychology and the workplace, stated that "Counseling psychologists have generally not been affiliated with workplace wellness, medical and safety programs" (p. 592).

Again, except for a few pioneering spirits we can ask the question, Where are the counseling psychologists?

## Developmental Human Ecology

A final area of missed opportunities is in the study of those environmental conditions that nurture, rather than negate, human developmental processes. This study is sometimes called developmental human ecology (Bronfenbrenner, 1979). As we have seen, both the concept of human development and a focus on person-environment fit have been central to counseling psychology since its very beginning.

As early as 1939, E. G. Williamson, in a book titled *How To Counsel Students*, recognized the importance of what we now call an ecological approach. He noted:

> [T]he counselor must also have acquired some understanding and appreciation of the possible effects upon the student of social, educational and occupational situations. The counselor will need to predict the effect which these situations will have on the student. Will they help him grow intellectually socially and emotionally, or will they lead to maladjustments, wasted efforts and emotional conflicts? . . . The effect of the occupation on the student, for example, is as important as are the student's chances for success in the job. (p. 176)

This view was repeated frequently throughout the early years of counseling psychology. Wrenn (1962), Mok (1960), and Shoben (1962) all pointed to the roles counselors could play in helping to shape educational institutions to the needs of developing students. Danskin, Kennedy, and Friesen (1965) described the central focus of guidance as the "ecology of students." Stewart and Warnath (1965) described the role of the counselor as one of "social engineering." Blocher (1974) pointed to an integration of theoretical models to provide foundation for an ecology of human development. Banning and Kaiser (1974) and Conyne and Clack (1981) applied ecological formulations to the design and function of college environments.

The ecological view was apparently short-lived in counseling psychology, but it has provided a durable basis for research in developmental psychology, and it is widely applied in community psychology. A quote from developmental psychologists Sundberg, Snowden, and Reynolds (1978) illustrates the promise that an ecological focus could have had for counseling psychology:

> We define competence as personal characteristics (knowledge, skills and attitudes) which lead to adaptive pay-offs in significant environments. The notion of adaptation points to the need to assess the demands and resources of the environment. Competence suggests an ecological situation: individuals are actively moving through settings which provide "nutrients" or support for certain kinds of coping, but hinder others. . . . Considerations of competence raises such questions as "In which situations can a person best function?" It moves from the "how much" question of traditional trait psychology to "where" and "which" questions concerning the surroundings people will encounter and their coping resources and active interests. (p. 196)

The above quotation captures the very essence of counseling psychology as it was conceived by its founders and elaborated upon by its pioneers.

Apparently, an ecological approach in counseling psychology died along with the spirit of idealism and social reform of the 1960s and early 1970s. Twenty years ago, Zimmer (1978) reviewed research published in counseling psychology and was able to identify only a handful of studies with an ecological focus or emphasis. Little seems to have changed since.

In 1998, a special issue of the American Psychologist (Hetherington, 1998), reporting the applications of developmental science, reviewed almost every problem area involving children and adolescents. Virtually all of those reviews took an ecological approach. One could again ask the question, Where was counseling psychology?

# PROBLEMS OF PROFESSIONAL PSYCHOLOGY

Many of the problems confronting contemporary counseling psychology are problems of professional psychology, generally. For the past 20 years, professional psychology has labored mightily to reinvent itself as "health psychology." Some of this effort has stemmed from a genuine appreciation of both a broader view of what is encompassed by the notion of good health, and by a more realistic view of human functioning. The inevitable intertwining of what had traditionally been separated into "physical" and "mental" processes by the ancient mind-body dualism of philosophy has given way to a much more holistic vision of an integrated thinking, feeling, and acting human being.

To a considerable extent, however, the urgency with which this new version of professional psychology was pursued was based upon political and economic realities as much as by a sudden scientific enlightenment. It had as much to do with how psychological services would be paid for, as with how they should be conceptualized.

As America moved through the 1980s and 1990s, it was clear that political winds were shifting. Massive cuts in human services programs seemed imminent. The one area that seemed to be partially insulated from "Reagonomics" was health care.

Throughout the period, the possibility of a broad-based National Health Insurance Program that would include mental health care delivered by psychologists was like a carrot on a stick, luring organized psychology further and further along the path to "medicalization." Unfortunately, counseling psychology's response to this siren song was an enthusiastic "Me too!"

What organized psychology sought throughout this period was inclusion in a national health insurance program. What it got was managed care.

The pipe dream of a new, private practice-based, professional psychology operating on the same level of status and financial reward as medicine has, to an extent, turned into a nightmare of escalating insurance costs, micromanagement of clinical decisions, external reviews of privileged, confidential records, and 9:00 to 5:00 salaried positions in clinical "factories" run for profit by third-party payers (Zimet, 1989).

The ebullient tones with which professional psychology greeted the 1980s has given way to frustration, if not despair, as the century ends. Wiggins (1994) titled his Presidential Address to the American Psychological Association "Would You Want Your Child To Be A Psychologist?" A front-page headline in the *APA Monitor* (1999) reads "Angered by Managed Care, Practitioners Look to Unions."

Some of the response to threats to the status, autonomy, and financial prosperity of psychologists has been to call for postdoctoral training of psychologists similar to medical residencies (Wiens, 1993) and tightening and narrowing of professional preparation and licensing requirements to fit a PsyD. rather than the Ph.D. model of professional training (Shapiro & Wiggins, 1994). Numerous calls have been made for psychologists to demand hospital admission and drug prescription privileges to help them compete with psychiatrists. Unfortunately, since many of the problems afflicting psychologists are also besetting physicians, getting on the medical bandwagon seems less and less attractive.

Perhaps the most lucid approach to the crisis in managed care, and the one most relevant to counseling psychologists, comes from a disillusioned clinical psychologist (Fox, 1994). Ronald Fox called for radical changes in preparing psychologists for the twenty-first century in these words:

> It is critically important that we do not slip into confusing our profession with specific techniques (such as psychotherapy) or with sub-domains of practice . . . or with limited problem areas (such as mental health). Professional psychology is much broader . . . and includes applications to human problems far afield from mental illness. . . . Professional psychology is that profession which is concerned with enhancing the effectiveness of human behavior. (pp. 200–202)

The definitions that Fox provided for "professional psychology" fit almost exactly the basic purposes, competencies, and goals articulated in counseling psychology over the past half-century. The best strategy for the survival of counseling psychology is to remain true to its basic purposes and orientation. Counseling psychology does not need a life raft, but simply a compass to steer by, and a steady hand on the wheel. An understanding and appreciation of its own history may go a long way towards providing both.

# REFERENCES

Albee, G. W. (1982). Preventing psychopathology and promoting human potential. *American Psychologist, 37,* 1043–1050.

Altmaier, N. M., & Johnson, B. D. (1992). Health-related applications of counseling psychology: Toward health promotion and disease prevention across the life-span. In S. Brown & R. Lent (Eds.), *Handbook of counseling psychology* (2nd ed., 315–348). New York: Wiley.

*APA Monitor.* Angered by managed care, practitioners look to unions (1999, September). *30*(8), p. 1

Banning, J. H., & Kaiser, L. (1974). An ecological perspective and model for campus design. *Personnel and Guidance Journal, 52,* 370–375.

Basic Behavioral Science Task Force of the National Advisory Mental Health Council (1996). Basic behavioral science research for mental health: Vulnerability and resilience. *American Psychologist, 51,* 22–28.

Blocher, D. H. (1974). *Developmental counseling* (2nd ed.). New York: Ronald Press.

Bowman, G. D., & Stern, M. M. (1995). Adjustment to occupational stress: The relationship of perceived control to effectiveness of coping strategies. *Journal of Counseling Psychology, 42,* 294–303.

Bronfenbrenner, U. (1979). *The ecology of human development.* Cambridge, MA: Harvard University Press.

Coie, J. D., Watt, N. F., West, S. G., Hawkins, D., Asarow, J. R., Markman, H. J., Ramey, S. L., Shure, M. B., & Long, B. (1993). The science of prevention: A conceptual framework and some directions for a national research program. *American Psychologist, 48,* 1013–1022.

Conyne, R. K., & Clack, R. J. (1981). *Environmental assessment and design.* New York: Praeger.

*The Counseling Psychologist. Third National Conference for Counseling Psychology: Planning the Future. (1988). 16* (special issue).

Csikszentmihalyi, M. (1990). *Flow: The psychology of optimal experience.* New York: Harper.

Danskin, D., Kennedy, C. E., & Friesen, W. S. (1965). Guidance: The ecology of students. *Personnel and Guidance Journal, 45,* 130–135.

Decker, P. J., & Borgen, F. H. (1993). Dimensions of work appraisal: Stress, strain, coping, job satisfaction, and negative affectivity. *Journal of Counseling Psychology, 40,* 470–478.

Ewart, C. K. (1991). Social action theory for a public health psychology. *American Psychologist, 46,* 931–946.

Fitzgerald, L. F., & Nutt, R. (1986). The Division 17 principles concerning the counseling/psychotherapy of women: Rationale and implementation. *The Counseling Psychologist, 14,* 180–216.

Foreman, M. E. (1980). The changing scene in higher education and the identity of counseling psychology. In J. Whiteley & B. Fretz (Eds.), *The present and future of counseling psychology* (pp. 50–55). Monterey, CA: Brooks/Cole.

Fox, R. E. (1994). Training professional psychologists for the twenty-first century. *American Psychologist, 49*, 220–206.

Fretz, B. (1980). Counseling psychology: 2001. In J. Whiteley & B. Fretz (Eds.), *The present and future of counseling psychology* (pp. 105–112.). Monterey, CA: Brooks/Cole.

Fretz, B., & Simon, M. (1992). Professional issues in counseling psychology: Continuity, change, and challenge. In S. Brown & R. Lent (Eds.), *Handbook of counseling psychology* (2nd ed., pp. 3–36). New York: Wiley.

Gardner, H. (1983). *Frames of mind*. New York: Basic Books.

Gerstein, L. H., & Shullman, S. L. (1992). Counseling psychology and the workplace: The emergence of organizational counseling psychology. In S. Brown & R. Lent (Eds.), *Handbook of counseling psychology* (pp. 581–626). New York: Wiley.

Glasgow, R. E., & Terborg, J. R. (1988). Occupational health promotion programs to reduce cardiovascular risk. *Journal of Counseling Psychology, 56*, 365–373.

Goleman, D. (1995). *Emotional intelligence*. New York: Bantam Books.

Goleman, D. (1998). *Working with emotional intelligence*. New York: Bantam Books.

Hetherington, M. (Guest Editor). (1998). Applications of Development Science. *American Psychologist, 53* (special issue).

Hurst, J. C., & Parker, C. A. (1980). Counseling psychology: Tyranny of a title. In J. Whiteley & B. Fretz (Eds.), *The present and future of counseling psychology* (pp. 21–28). Monterey, CA: Brooks/Cole.

Kagan, N. (1980). Perspectives on counseling psychology: Where are we, who are we. In J. Whiteley & B. Fretz (Eds.), *The present and future of counseling psychology* (pp. 80–89). Monterey, CA: Brooks/Cole.

Kagan, N. (Guest Ed.). (1982). Counseling psychology: The next decade. *The Counseling Psychologist, 10* (special issue).

Kagan, N., Armsworth, M., Altmaier, E., Dowd, E. T., Hansen, J., Mills, D., Schlossberg, N., Sprinthall, N., Tanney, M. F., & Vasquez, M. (1988). Professional practice of counseling psychology in various settings. *The Counseling Psychologist 16*, 347–365.

Kagan, N. I., Kagan, H., & Watson, M. G. (1995). Stress reduction in the workplace. *Journal of Counseling Psychology, 42*, 71–78.

Krauskopf, C. J., Thoreson, R. W., & McAleer, C. A. (1973). Counseling psychology: The who, what, and where of our profession. *Journal of Counseling Psychology, 20*, 370–374.

Levi, L. (1990). Occupational stress: Spice of life or kiss of death. *American Psychologist, 45*, 1142–1145.

Long, B. C. (1998). Coping with workplace stress: A multiple group comparison of female managers and clerical workers. *Journal of Counseling Psychology, 45*, 65–78.

Mok, P. (1960). *A view from within.* New York: Garden Press.

Myers, R. A., & Cairo, P. C. (1992). Counseling and career adjustment. In S. Brown & R. Lent (Eds.), *Handbook of counseling psychology* (pp. 549–580). New York: Wiley.

Nathan, P. E. (1980). A clinical psychologist views counseling psychology. In J. Whiteley & B. Fretz (Eds.), *The present and future of counseling psychology* (pp. 69–73). Monterey, CA: Brooks/Cole.

Osipow, S. H., & Spokane, A. R. (1987). *Occupational stress inventory.* Odessa, FL: Psychological Assessment Resources.

Pepinsky, H. B. (1980). You tell me what's going to happen. In J. Whiteley & B. Fretz (Eds.), *The present and future of counseling psychology* (pp. 188–194). Monterey, CA: Brooks/Cole.

Ross, R. R., & Altmaier, E. M. (1994). *Intervention in occupational stress: A handbook for stress at work.* London: Sage.

Rude, S. S., Weissberg, M., & Gazda, G. M. (1988). Looking to the future: Themes from the Third National Conference for Counseling Psychology. *The Counseling Psychologist, 16*, 423–430.

Salovey, P., & Sluyter, D. J. (Eds.) (1997). *Emotional development and emotional intelligence.* New York: Basic Books.

Samler, J. (1964). Where do counseling psychologists work? What do they do? What should they do? In A. Thompson & D. Super (Eds.), *The professional preparation of counseling psychologists* (pp. 43–68). New York: Columbia Teaches College.

Sauter, S. L., Murphy, L. M., & Hurrell, J. J., Jr. (1990). Prevention of work-related psychological disorders: A national strategy proposed by the National Institute for Occupational Safety and Health (NIOSH). *American Psychologist, 45*, 1146–1158.

Schmidt, L. D. (1980). Why has the professional practice of psychological counseling developed in the United States. In J. Whiteley & B. Fretz (Eds.), *The present and future of counseling psychology* (pp. 29–33). Monterey, CA: Brooks/Cole.

Seligman, M. (1999). The President's address. *American Psychologist, 54*, 559–562.

Shapiro, A. E., & Wiggins, J. G. (1994). A PsyD degree for every practitioner: Truth in labeling. *American Psychologist, 49*, 207–210.

Shoben, E. J., Jr. (1962). Guidance: Remedial function or social reconstruction? *Harvard Educational Review, 32*, 430–443.

Spencer, L. M., & Spencer, S. M. (1993). *Competence at work.* New York: Wiley.

Sternberg, R. (1996). *Successful intelligence.* New York: Simon and Schuster.

Stewart, L., & Warnath, C. (1965). *The counselor and society.* Boston: Houghton-Mifflin.

Sundberg, N. A., Snowden, L. R., & Reynolds, W. M. (1978). Toward assessment of personal competence and incompetence in life situations. *Annual Review of Psychology, 29,* 179–221.

Super, D. E. (1980). The identity crises of counseling psychologists. In J. Whiteley & B. Fretz (Eds.), *The present and future of counseling psychology* (pp. 15–20). Monterey, CA: Brooks/Cole.

Taylor, S. (1990). Health psychology: The science and the field. *American Psychologist, 45,* 40–50.

Tyler, L. (1960). Minimum change therapy. *Personnel and Guidance Journal, 38,* 475–479.

Watkins, C. E. (1994). On hope, promise and possibility in counseling psychology or some simple, but meaningful observations about our specialty. *The Counseling Psychologist, 22,* 315–334.

Weigel, R. G. (1980). I have seen the enemy and they is us: and everyone else. In J. Whiteley & B. Fretz (Eds.), *The present and future of counseling psychology* (pp. 56–61). Monterey, CA: Brooks/Cole.

Whiteley, J. (1980). Counseling psychology in the year 2000 AD. In J. Whiteley & B. Fretz (Eds.), *The present and future of counseling psychology* (pp. 91–104). Monterey, CA: Brooks/Cole.

Whiteley, J., & Fritz, B. (Eds.) (1980). *The present and future of counseling psychology.* Monterey, CA: Brooks/Cole.

Whiteley, J. M. (1984). A historical perspective on the development of counseling psychology as a profession. In S. D. Brown & R. W. Lent (Eds.), *Handbook of counseling psychology* (pp. 3–55) (1st ed.). New York: Wiley.

Wiens, A. W. (1993). Post-doctoral education: Training for specialty practice. *American Psychologist, 48,* 415–422.

Wiggins, J. G., Jr. (1994). Would you want your child to be a psychologist? *American Psychologist, 49,* 485–492.

Williamson, E. W. (1939). *How to counsel students.* New York: McGraw-Hill.

Winett, R. A. (1995). A framework for health promotion and disease prevention. *American Psychologist, 50,* 341–350.

Wrenn, C. G. (1962). *The counselor in a changing world.* Washington, DC: American Personnel and Guidance Association.

Wrenn, C. G. (1980). Landmarks and the growing edge. In J. Whiteley & B. Fretz (Eds.), *The present and future of counseling psychology* (pp. 7–14). Monterey, CA: Brooks/Cole.

Yee, C. S., & Bingham, R. P. (1999). American Psychological Association Division 17 governance members. *The Counseling Psychologist, 27,* 616–619.

Zimet, C. N. (1989). The mental health care revolution: Will psychology survive? *American Psychologist, 44,* 703–708.

Zimmer, J. (1978). Concerning ecology in counseling. *Journal of Counseling Psychology, 25,* 225–230.

# Epilogue

We have traced the course of psychology for more than a century, and the course of counseling for nearly a century. We have seen a half century of pain and progress in what we now call counseling psychology. We have examined four powerful streams of influence and tradition that have shaped, and sometimes splintered, the field.

We have seen an evolution from a social reform movement imbued with social concern, but woefully short of scientific substance, to a highly organized profession, still beset with doubts about its own identity and status within the family of psychology. We have seen the field expand from a focus on the transition from school to work, to a concern with the myriad problems, challenges, and traumas of lifespan development. We have seen the impact of two world wars, the Great Depression, the return of millions of veterans, and the tension of the Cold War. We have seen a second wave of social reform in a massive Civil Rights movement and a second Women's Movement. All have shaped our present, and will continue to influence our future.

In the course of this journey, we have looked at the contributions of a host of gifted and productive people who have helped to build a profession that all counseling psychologists can join with pride. More than anything else, the history of counseling psychology is their story.

In 1956, a Committee on Definition (American Psychological Association, 1956), consisting of Edward Bordin, Milton Hahn, Donald Super, C. Gilbert Wrenn, and Harold Pepinsky, tried to enunciate and elaborate on the nature of a new profession called counseling psychology. They described it thus:

At the present time, the specialty of counseling psychology is approaching a state of balance among emphases upon contributions to (a) the development of an individual's inner life through concern with his or her motivations and emotions, (b) the individual's achievement of harmony with his or her environment through helping him or her to develop the resources that he or she must bring to this task . . . and (c) the influencing of society to recognize individual differences and to encourage the fullest development of all persons within it. (p. 283)

This statement or definition contained the essence of psychological counseling, the overriding emphases on development, the concern with person-environment fit and the heritage of social reform.

In 1998, counseling psychology received approval of a new charter, or "Archival Description of Counseling Psychology," from the APA (APA, 1999). This definition was prepared after broad consultation among members and the Division 17 Governance bodies. The new description was prepared under the leadership of James Lichtenberg, chair of a special task group including Louise Douce, Rodney Good-year, Sharon Bowman, Michael Duffy, and Roberta Nutt.

The brief definition of counseling psychology, 1998, follows:

Counseling psychology is a general practice and health-service provider specialty in professional psychology. It focuses upon personal and inter-personal functioning across the life span and on emotional, social, vocational, educational, health-related, developmental and organiza-tional concerns. Counseling psychology centers on typical or normal developmental issues as well as atypical or disordered development as it applies to human experience. . . . Counseling psychologists help people with physical, emotional and mental disorders improve well-being, alleviate distress and maladjustment, and resolve crises. In addi-tion, practitioners . . . provide assessment, diagnosis and treatment of psychopathology . . .

Within the context of lifespan development counseling psychologists focus on healthy aspects and strengths of the client, . . . environmen-tal/situation influences, . . . and the role of career and vocation on individual development and functioning. (p. 589)

After more than 40 years, the 1998 definition clearly contains the emphases on development, person-environment fit, and psychological dynamics. The last vestiges of the social reform antecedents of counsel-ing psychology are apparently gone forever. The 1998 definition is also clearly a turf-defining statement, laying claim to almost every conceivable area of professional practice. After 40 years, counseling psychologists, like nature, obviously still abhor a vacuum.

# REFERENCES

American Psychological Association, Division of Counseling Psychology, Committee on Definition. (1956). Counseling psychology as a specialty. *American Psychologist, 11,* 282–285.

American Psychological Association (Division 17). (1999). Archival description of counseling psychology. *The Counseling Psychologist, 27,* 589–592.

# Appendix A

**TABLE 1   The Expansion of Counseling and Counseling Psychology: Settings, Clientele, and Goals by 20-Year Intervals**

| 1900s | 1920s | 1940s |
|---|---|---|
| *Settings* | | |
| Settlement houses | High schools | Junior high schools |
| Vocational schools | Colleges | High schools |
| | Child guidance clinics | Colleges |
| | Employment and youth programs | Veterans Hospitals |
| | | Veterans benefits offices |
| | | Employment services |
| *Clientele* | | |
| Youth leaving school | High school students | Children |
| Vocational training students | College students | Adolescents |
| | Troubled children and adolescents | Young adults |
| | Job seekers | Veterans |
| | | Job seekers |
| | | Disabled |
| *Goals* | | |
| Vocational | Vocational | Vocational |
| Social reform | Educational | Educational |
| | Developmental | Rehabilitative |
| | | Developmental |

*(continued)*

**TABLE 1.** *(continued)*

| 1960s | 1980s | 2000s |
|---|---|---|
| *Settings* | | |
| Elementary schools | Elementary schools | Elementary schools |
| Junior high schools | Junior high schools | Junior high schools |
| High schools | High schools | High schools |
| Colleges | Community Colleges | Community colleges |
| Hospitals | Colleges | Rehabilitation services |
| Corrections | Rehabilitation agencies | Hospitals |
| Alcohol and drug | Hospitals | Community Mental |
|   programs | Community Mental |   Health Agencies |
| Employee Services |   Health Agencies | Employee Services |
| | Corrections | Health Agencies |
| | Employee assistance | Family services |
| |   programs | Alcohol and drug |
| | Private practice |   programs |
| | | Corrections |
| | | Employee assistance |
| | |   programs |
| | | HMOs |
| | | Private practice |
| *Clientele* | | |
| Full range, including women, minorities, emotionally disturbed, disabled, job seekers | Full age range, women, minorities, couples, parents, disabled | Full age range, women, minorities, emotionally disturbed, disabled |
| *Goals* | | |
| Developmental | Developmental | Developmental |
| Therapeutic | Therapeutic | Therapeutic |
| | Preventive | Preventive |

# Appendix B

## MARKERS AND MILESTONES IN THE EVOLUTION OF COUNSELING PSYCHOLOGY

**1879**     Wilhelm Wundt's Psychological Laboratory at Leipzig opens.

**1882**     Galton's Laboratory begins testing and measuring human characteristics and capacities.

**1883**     G. Stanley Hall establishes a psychological laboratory at Johns Hopkins University.

**1890**     James McKeen Cattell coins the term "mental tests."

**1892**     The American Psychological Association is formed.

**1896**     Lightner Witmer founds a psychological clinic.

**1898**     Jesse B. Davis begins a career as a high school counselor.

**1899**     William Rainey Harper, President of the University of Chicago, calls for "the scientific study of the college student."

**1908**     The Vocation Bureau of Boston opens its doors directed by Frank Parsons.

**1909**     Parson's book *Choosing a Vocation* is published posthumously.

**1913**     The National Vocational Guidance Association is founded.

**1915**     The Division of Applied Psychology is founded as an academic department at Carnegie Institute of Technology.

**1917**     American psychologists devise and administer the Alpha and Beta tests to millions of soldiers.

**1920** College Personnel Programs and Testing Bureaus are opened in several universities, including Northwestern and the University of Minnesota.

**1931** The Minnesota Employment Stabilization Research Institute, under the direction of Donald G. Paterson, begins counseling the unemployed of the Great Depression.

**1933–** The New Deal Depression Era programs begin, including
**1935** the Civilian Conservation Corps (CCC), the National Youth Administration, and the United States Employment Service. Counselors work to stem the tide of the Great Depression.

**1941** The Second World War begins. Counseling psychologists work in selecting air crewmen and other specialists.

**1944** The G.I. Bill is passed. Returning veterans get educational benefits, including counseling.

**1945** APA reorganizes. Division 17 becomes the Division of Counseling and Guidance.

**1949** The Boulder Conference adopts the scientist-practitioner model of preparation for doctoral preparation in professional psychology.

**1951** The Northwestern Conference coins the name "counseling psychology" and tries to define itself. The Veterans Administration creates the position after the same name. The American Personnel and Guidance Association is formed organizing the "other counselors."

**1957** The National Defense Education Act is passed and thousands of school counselors are trained.

**1960** Reform movements in the areas of civil rights, rights for women and antiwar protests begin to sweep the country. Political activism becomes part of campus life. The profession is caught up in a second wave of social reform.

**1964** The Greyston Conference attempts to deal with issues of identity, status, and confidence in the profession.

**1965** A rash of new therapies brings an end to the dominance of psychodynamic theories. Psychologists become involved in psychotherapy and enter private practice in great numbers.

**1969** Behavior Modification becomes a major force as one of the new therapies.

**1970** Cognitive and Cognitive-Behavioral Therapies begin to replace behavior modification.

**1977** Humanistic psychology becomes a "Third Force" in American Psychology.

**1986** More than 400 different therapies can be identified. Practitioners and researchers move toward eclectic-integrative approaches.

**1988** The Georgia Conference meets to plan the future of Counseling Psychology.

**1992** The American Psychological Association reaches the century mark. The field, including counseling psychology, looks at itself.

**1998** Counseling psychology receives a new charter, or archival definition. The process of redefinition continues.

**2000** A new millennium begins.

# Name Index

Abrego, P. J., 265, 285
Acord, J., 79, 94
Addams, Jane, 11, 17, 23, 29
Adler, Alfred, 124, 126–127
Ainsworth, M., 272, 284
Albee, G. W., 301, 307
Albertson, Ralph, 17
Alexander, F., 189, 202
Alexik, M., 172, 174
Allen, F. L., 7, 29
Allen, Frederick, 126
Allport, Gordon, 154–155, 173–174, 195, 202, 226
Altmaier, N. M., 302–303, 307, 309
American Psychological Association, 165, 174
Anderson, John E., 99
Anderson, S., 172, 174
Angell, James, 55
Anton, J. L., 276, 290
Arkowitz, H., 269, 288
Arnkoff, D. B., 251, 259
Astin, A. W., 282, 284
Astin, Helen, 299
Atkinson, Donald, 300
Aubrey, R. F., 3, 29, 153, 174

Baldwin, James Mark, 182–184, 243
Bandura, A., 254, 2
Banning, J. H., 304, 307
Barlow, D. H., 273, 276, 284

Barone, M., 164, 174
Barry, R., 282, 284
Baruch, R. W., 197, 205
Batson, C. D., 229–230
Baumgardner, S. R., 172, 174
Beck, Aaron, 255, 258
Beers, Clarence, 88, 129–130, 132
Bell, Hugh, 101
Bellamy, Edward, 9, 249
Bemis, M. K., 256, 259
Benjamin, L., 42, 53, 56, 72, 79, 82, 92, 94, 98, 118
Berdie, R. F., 265, 284
Berg, I., 113–114, 117–118
Bergin, A. E., 263, 280, 282, 284–286
Bernreuter, Robert, 158
Bersoff, D. M., 165–166, 174
Betz, Nancy, 299
Beutler, L. E., 273, 277, 285
Binet, Alfred, 43–47, 49, 120, 169, 177–178, 181
Bingham, R. P., 293, 311
Bingham, Walter V., 52–55, 67, 72, 90–91
Binswanger, 226, 228
Blocher, D. H., 201–202, 253, 258, 265, 275–276, 285, 297, 304, 307
Block, N. J., 160, 174
Bloomfield, Meyer, 16–17
Blumenthal, A. L., 76, 94

Boas, Franz, 120
Bordin, Edward, 71, 107–108, 118, 135, 144, 272, 282, 285, 290
Borgen, Fred, 281
Borgen, J. H., 302, 307
Boring, E. G., 34, 38, 40, 72
Boring, Edwin, 94
Borow, Henry, 172, 174, 196–198, 202, 280–281, 285, 297
Boss, 226, 228
Bowen, M., 140, 144
Bowlby, J., 272, 284
Bowman, G. D., 302, 307
Bowman Sharon, 314
Bradley, R. W., 267, 289
Brammer, L. M., 137, 144, 265, 285
Brandenberg, Broughton, 62
Breger, L., 254, 258
Breuer, Josef, 122
Brewer, C. L., 244–245, 258
Brewer, John, 8, 13, 15, 21, 25–26, 30, 67, 72, 217
Bridgeman, P. W., 59–60, 72
Brigham, Carl C., 63, 65, 93
Brill, A. A., 120
Brim, O., 194, 202
Bringmann, M. W., 77, 95
Bringmann, W. G., 77, 95
Brodin, Edward, 313
Bronfenbrenner, U., 303, 307
Broughton, J. M., 182, 202
Brown, S. D., 257–258
Bryan, Alice, 94
Buber, Martin, 226
Bugental, James, 226
Buhler, Charlotte, 197, 203
Bulatao, E. Q., 92, 95
Burt, Cyril, 179

Cahan, E. D., 182, 203
Cairo, P. C., 303, 309
Calia, V. F., 172, 174
Calkins, Mary Whiton, 218
Callis, R., 266, 285
Campbell, D. A., 264, 282, 285
Campbell, V. L., 264, 290

Cantril, Hadley, 226
Carkhuff, Robert, 172, 174, 224, 232, 266, 282, 285, 300
Carroll, J. B., 168, 174
Carter, J. A., 229, 231
Cattell, James McKeen, 40–42, 46, 52–54, 80, 121, 149–150, 166, 241
Cattell, James, Sr., 149–150
Cattell, R. B., 158
Catton, W. B., 8, 12, 22, 30, 61, 73, 86, 95
Charcot, Jean Martin, 122
Childs, H. G., 49–50
Chiriboga, D., 193, 204
Chock, S., 142, 145
Chomsky, Noam, 238, 258
Clack, R. J., 304, 307
Claiborn, C. D., 271, 286, 289
Clark, Jonas, 79
Cohen, L. D., 123, 144
Coie, J. D., 301, 307
Connor, K., 272, 286
Conyne, R. K., 304, 307
Cooley, Charles H., 218
Coolidge, Calvin, 54, 164
Coon, D. J., 79, 95
Corbett, M. M., 272, 275, 287
Corcoran, J. L., 272, 289
Corrigan, J. D., 271, 285
Corsini, R., 139, 144
Costa, P. T., Jr., 170, 175
Cronbach, Lee, 34, 72, 166, 174
Cross, H. J., 282, 285
Csikszentmihalyi, M., 301, 307
Cummings, N., 125, 146
Cushman, P., 122, 124, 144

Danish, S. J., 201, 203
Danskin, D., 303, 307
Darley, John G., 71, 90, 96, 98–101, 109, 115, 117, 133
Darrow, C., 193, 204
Darwin, Charles, 36, 39–40, 152, 162–163
D'Augellli, 201, 203

Davis, Jessie B., 17–19
Dawis, R., 153, 156–158, 173–174
Dean, Arthur, 18
Dearborn, W. F., 57
Deary, I. J., 40, 72
Decker, P. J., 302, 307
DeJulio, S. D., 224, 231
DeLeon, P. H., 125, 146
Dell, D. M., 271, 285
Delworth, Ursala, 299
Dember, W. B., 272, 285
Dewey, John, 20–22, 80, 160, 163,
    186–187, 200, 203, 217–218
Dewsbury, D. A., 236, 258
Dix, Dorothea, 130–131
Dixon, D., 56, 72
Doll, Edgar, 94
Dollard, J., 251, 258
Douce, Louise, 314
Dreese, Mitchell, 101
Duan, C., 229, 231
Duffy, Michael, 314
Dugan, Willis E., 207
Durkin, M., 79, 94
Dustin, R., 253, 258
Dvorak, B., 157, 174
Dworkin, G., 160, 174
Dymond, 282
Dymond, R. F., 219, 232
D'Zurilla, T. J., 255, 258

Early, C. E., 77, 95
Ebbinghaus, Clark, 120
Ebbinghaus, Herman, 239
Edgerton, Harold A., 101
Eliot, Charles, 10–11, 17, 30
Elliot, G. L., 90, 95
Elliot, H. S., 90, 95
Elliott, Richard, 94, 99
Elliott, Robert, 277–278, 285
Ellis, Albert, 141–142, 144, 255
Ellis, Michael, 300
Entwistle, S. R., 273, 285
Epstein, S., 272, 285
Erickson, C., 188, 203
Erickson, C. E., 69, 72

Erikson, Erik, 128, 191, 203
Eurich, Alvin C., 101
Evans, R. B., 92, 95, 106, 118, 120–
    122, 144
Ewart, C. K., 301, 307
Eysenck, Hans, 140, 142, 144, 251,
    283

Fancher, R. E., 179, 203, 234–235,
    259
Farber, J. A., 264, 288
Farmer, Helen, 299
Fass, P., 68, 72
Fassinger, Ruth, 195, 201–203, 299
Ferenczi, Sandor, 120
Fiedler, Fred, 266–267, 285
Fitzgerald, Louise, 299, 307
Flanagan, John, 109
Ford, D. H., 282, 286
Ford, J. D., 257, 259
Foreman, M. E., 292, 308
Form, W. H., 197, 204
Forrest, D. W., 36–37, 72
Forsyth, D. R., 272, 277, 286
Fox, Ronald, 306, 308
Frank, Jerome, 268, 286
Frankl, Victor, 226, 228
Frederiksen, N., 168, 174
French, J. L., 42, 50, 72
Fretz, Bruce, 291, 293, 295, 297,
    308
Freud, Sigmund, 43, 119–124, 126,
    128–129, 141, 189–190, 251
Friedlander, Myrna, 278
Friedman, H., 56, 72
Friesen, W. S., 303, 307
Fromm, Erich, 126, 190, 203
Fromm-Reichmann, Frieda, 126
Fryer, Douglas, 91
Fulcher, R., 92, 95
Fuller, Florence, 56

Galton, Francis, 36–40, 44, 65–66,
    150, 152, 156, 159, 169
Gardner, Howard., 59, 72, 169, 174,
    255, 259, 301, 308

Garfield, S. L., 133–134, 140–141, 144, 263–264, 268, 280, 283, 285–286
Garmezy, N., 195, 203
Garraty, J. A., 5–6, 30
Gazda, George, 297, 300, 309
Gelso, C. J., 195, 201, 203, 229, 231
Gendlin, Eugene T., 212, 222–223, 231–232
Gergen, Kenneth, 280, 286
Gerstein, L. H., 303, 308
Gesell, Arnold, 57
Gilbert, W., 135, 144
Ginsberg, M. R., 201, 203
Glaser, R., 168, 174
Glasgow, R. E., 302, 308
Glass, C. R., 251, 259
Glass, Gene, 283, 286
Glasser, William, 141, 144
Goddard, Henry, 49, 51, 62–63, 65, 163
Goldfried, M. R., 255, 258, 264, 286
Goldman, Leo, 159, 174, 273, 281, 286
Goleman, D., 169, 174, 301, 308
Goodenough, Florence, 56, 161
Goodyear, Rodney, 314
Gordon, E. W., 167, 174
Graive, K., 274, 288
Graue, M. E., 165, 175
Greenberg, L. S., 126, 145, 226, 228, 230–231
Greenberg, Leslie, 276, 278, 286
Grinder, R. E., 163, 175
Grinker, R. R., 130, 144
Grob, G. N., 131, 144–145
Gross, M. L., 227, 231
Gruenberg, Benjamin, 18
Grundlach, R. H., 92, 95
Guilford, J. P., 168, 175
Guthrie, 247

Hackett, Gail, 299
Haeckel, Ernst, 185, 203
Hahn, Milton, 71, 106, 137, 145, 313

Hall, G. Stanley, 17, 48–49, 57, 77–80, 119–120, 122, 163, 183–186, 190, 203, 241
Halleck, S. L., 213, 231
Hamrin, S., 69, 72, 188, 203
Harding, Warren, 22, 163
Harlow, Harry, 61
Harmon, Lenore, 297, 299
Harper, R. A., 266, 286
Harper, William Rainey, 28, 80
Hartley, Mariette, 246, 259
Hartmann, H., 128, 145, 190, 203
Harvey, O. J., 199, 203
Hathaway, Starke, 158
Havighurst, Robert, 192, 203
Hayes, S. C., 276, 284
Heesacker, M., 272, 286
Helms, Janet, 300
Heppner, P. P., 271, 286
Hergenhahn, B. R., 34, 38, 43, 47, 73, 184, 203, 247, 259
Herrnstein, R. J., 63, 73, 169, 175
Hetherington, M., 304, 309
Hilgard, Earnest. R., 83, 94–95, 99, 102–103, 118, 123–124, 129, 141, 145, 186, 203, 218, 231
Hill, Clara, 229, 231, 272, 275–278, 281, 286–287
Himmell, C. D., 264, 290
Hobbs, Nicholas, 109, 265, 287
Holland, J., 173, 175
Hollingsworth, Leta, 59, 73, 83, 210
Holloway, Elizabeth, 300
Holtzman, W. H., 167, 175
Hoover, Herbert, 50, 54, 86
Hopkins, L. B., 89
Horn, J. L., 168, 174
Horney, Karen, 126, 128
Horvath, J. A., 169, 175
Hosford, R. E., 257–258
Hoshmond, Lisa, 273, 279, 281, 287
Hovland, C. I., 271, 287
Howard, George, 274, 281, 287
Howard, K. I., 274, 288
Hoyt, W. T., 272, 289
Hull, Clark, 59, 247

Hummel, T. J., 276, 287
Humphreys, K., 132, 134, 145
Hunt, D. E., 199, 203
Hurrell, J. J., Jr., 302, 309
Hurst, J. C., 292, 308

Ickes, Harold, 245
Ickes, Mary Amelia, 244–245
Israel, Harry, 61
Ivey, Allen, 300

Jackson, S., 276, 287
Jahoda, Marie, 194, 203
James, William, 48, 78–80, 121–122, 129, 218, 240–242, 259
Janis, I. L., 271, 287
Jaspers, 226
Jastrow, Joseph, 76, 79–80, 121
Johnson, B. D., 303, 307
Johnson, R. C., 37, 73
Jones, Ernest, 120
Jourard, S. M., 227, 231
Jung, Carl Gustav, 120, 124–125, 180, 191, 204

Kagan, H., 302, 308
Kagan, J., 194, 202
Kagan, Norman, 278, 291–293, 297, 300, 302, 308
Kaiser, L., 304, 307
Kallikak family, 49
Kamin, L. J., 65, 73
Kaplan, D. M., 124, 145
Karasu, T. B., 263, 287
Kazdin, A. E., 263, 287
Kegan, R., 201, 204
Kelly, George, 200, 204, 272, 287
Kelly, H. H., 271, 287
Kendall, P. C., 256, 258
Kennedy, C. E., 303, 307
Kierkegaard, Soren, 224–226
Kiesler, Donald, 223, 232, 275–276, 287
Kimble, G. A., 228, 231
Klein, D. B., 33, 73
Klein, E., 193, 204

Klein, Melanie, 272–273, 287
Kobasa, S. C., 195, 204
Koch, S., 228, 231, 280, 287
Koelsch, W. A., 120–122, 144
Kohlberg, Lawrence, 200, 204
Kohler, 240
Krasner, Leonard, 253, 259
Krauskopf, C. J., 294, 308
Krumboltz, J. D., 253, 259, 275–276
Kuder, G. Frederick, 101, 157–158
Kuhlman, Frederick, 50, 163
Kuhn, Thomas, 247, 259, 281
Kurtz, R., 264, 286

Lambert, M. J., 224, 231
Lazarus, Arnold, 251, 256, 259, 269, 287
Leahey, T. A., 62, 73
Leahey, T. H., 247, 259
Leary, M. R., 272, 286
Lecky, Prescott, 218, 231
Lens, Sidney, 4, 30, 57, 73
Levi, L., 302, 308
Levinson, D., 193, 204
Levinson, M., 193, 204
Lewis, K. N., 271, 285
Lichtenberg, James, 276, 287, 314
Lincoln, Abraham, 5
Lindsley, Ogden, 250
Link, A. S., 8, 12, 22, 30, 61, 73, 86, 95
Link, M., 79, 94
Lippmann, Walter, 159–160
Lipsey, M. W., 283, 288
Lister, J. L., 264, 288
Lloyd-Jones, E., 89–90, 95
Locke, John 239, 259
Lodge, Henry Cabot, 17
Loevinger, Jane, 200, 204
Lofquist, 173
London, P., 256, 259
Long, B. C., 302, 309
Lopez, F., 264, 273, 288, 290
Lowenthal, M., 193, 204
Lykken, D., 170, 175

Magoon, Tom, 297
Mahoney, M. J., 254, 259, 272, 288
Mahrer, A. R., 277–278, 288
Manicus, P. T., 281, 288
Mann, A., 13, 30
Marshall, Helen, 56
Martindale, C., 265, 288
Maslow, Abraham, 195, 204, 226
Maultsby, M. C., 256, 260
May, Rollo, 133–134, 145, 225–226,
   231
May, T. M., 159, 175
McAleer, C. A., 294, 308
McCall, W. A., 65, 73
McClelland, David, 166, 175
McCrae, R. R., 170, 175
McGaugh, J. L., 254, 258
McKee, B., 193, 204
McKinley, J. C., 158
McLennan, J., 267, 289
McNemar, Quinn, 161
Mead, George Herbert, 20, 218
Meara, Naomi, 64, 73, 153, 175,
   297, 299
Meehl, P. C., 278, 288
Meichenbaum, D. H., 256, 260
Merenda, P., 282, 288
Merrill, George Arthur, 9
Meyer, Adolf, 129, 131
Meyerson, L., 253, 260
Michael, J., 253, 260
Miller, C. H., 3, 25–26, 30, 66, 68,
   73, 88, 95
Miller, D. C., 197, 204
Miller, N. E., 251, 258
Miller-Jones, D., 165, 175
Mitchell, David, 83
Mok, P., 303, 309
Moore, Bruce, 67, 90, 94
Mosher, Ralph, 200, 204
Muers, 303
Munsterberg, Hugo, 24, 27, 46–47,
   52, 80, 82, 122, 159
Murphy, L. M., 302, 309
Murray, C., 63, 73, 169, 175
Muuss, R. E., 185, 204

Myers, Roger, 297, 309

Naisbitt, John, 97
Napoli, D. S., 151, 175
Nathan, P. E., 292, 309
National Society for the Promotion of
   Industrial Education (NSPIE), 10,
   16
Neimeyer, G. J., 201, 204
Neisser, A., 45, 73
Nelson, R. O., 276, 284
Neugarten, B., 193, 204
Norcross, J. C., 264, 269, 288
Norris, W., 23–24, 30
Norton, M. B., 6, 30
Nutt, E. A., 276, 287
Nutt, Roberta, 299, 307, 314

O'Donnell, J. M., 42, 73, 149, 175,
   183, 204, 241, 244, 260
O'Hara, R. P., 197, 205
Okun, B. F., 201, 204, 263, 288
Orlinsky, D. E., 274, 288
Osipow, S. H., 302, 309
Otis, Arthur, 52–53

Pace, Edward, 80
Packer, M. J., 281, 288
Park, D. C., 253, 260
Parker, C. A., 292, 308
Parks, B. K., 274, 288
Parsons, Frank, 13–15, 23–24, 29,
   30, 171, 217
Paterson, Donald G., 28, 30, 66–67,
   69, 73, 87, 90–91, 93, 99, 157,
   159
Patterson, Cecil, 226
Paul, G., 275, 288
Pavlov, Ivan Petrovich, 59–60, 233–
   238, 240, 242, 248, 251–252
Pearson, Karl, 35, 39, 73, 156
Pepinsky, Harold, 101–102, 104,
   106, 111, 113, 117–118, 270,
   289, 293, 309, 313
Pepinsky, Pauline, 106, 118
Perls, Fritz, 141–142, 145, 226

Perls, Laura, 226
Perry, W., 200, 204
Pershing, John J., General, 53
Peterson, D. R., 143, 145
Peterson, G., 267, 289
Piaget, Jean, 179–182, 199, 204
Pinel, Philippe, 131
Plaud, J. J., 237, 260
Polkinghome, Donald, 280–281, 289
Pope, K. S., 109, 118
Poznanski, J. J., 267, 289
Pribram, K. H., 272, 289
Prichard, S., 272, 286
Prince, Morton, 122–123
Pritchard, D. H., 136, 145, 172, 175
Prochaska, J. O., 264, 288

Raimy, Victor, 119
Rank, Otto, 124, 126
Reed, Anna, 16–17, 23, 26, 30
Reich, Wilhelm, 124
Reichenbach, H., 278, 289
Reisman, J. M., 82, 95
Reschly, D. J., 165, 175
Rescorta, R. A., 237, 260
Resnick, R. J., 82–83, 95, 133–134, 145
Reynolds, W. M., 304, 310
Rice, L. N., 126, 145, 226, 228, 230–231
Richardson, F., 255, 260
Ridley, Charles, 300
Roback, A. A., 46–47, 73, 247, 260
Robbins, S. B., 273, 289
Robinson, Francis, 142
Robinson, Frank, 230, 270, 275, 289
Rockefeller, John D., 77, 244
Rockwell, P., 23, 30
Rodgers, D. T., 5, 11, 30
Roe, Ann, 197, 204
Rogers, Carl, 71, 89, 91, 94–95, 99–100, 108, 118, 126, 135, 141–142, 145, 188, 195, 204, 207–212, 214–224, 227, 229–232, 253, 274, 280, 282
Roosevelt, Franklin Delano, 86

Rosenzweig, S., 120, 145
Ross, D., 78, 95
Ross, R. R., 302, 309
Rothman, S., 169, 175
Rothney, John, 23, 30, 282, 289
Rousseau, Jean-Jacques, 181, 205
Routh, D. K., 83, 85, 95
Royce, Josiah, 80, 227, 232
Rude, S. S., 297, 309
Rush, Benjamin, 130
Rychlak, J. F., 280, 289

Salovey, P., 301, 309
Samelson, F., 84, 92, 95
Samler, J., 136, 145, 172, 175, 294, 309
Samson, G. E., 165, 175
Sartre, 226
Sauter, S. L., 302, 309
Schlossberg, N., 201–202, 203, 205
Schmidt, Lyle, 142, 145, 271, 285, 292, 297, 309
Schneidler, G. G., 66, 69, 73
Schofield, W., 267–268, 289
Schroder, H. M., 199, 203
Scott, C. Winfield, 100–101, 112, 115, 118
Scott, K. J., 159, 175
Scott, Walter Dill, 52–54, 89–90, 96
Seashore, Harold, 106
Secord, P. F., 281, 288
Seligman, Martin, 283, 289, 301, 309
Sexton, T. L., 224, 229, 232
Shaffer, L. F., 267, 289
Shapiro, A. E., 306, 309
Sharma, S., 131, 145
Shartle, Carrol L., 101
Shear, B. E., 26, 30
Shoben, E. J., Jr., 112–113, 117–118, 194, 205, 251, 260, 265, 267, 289, 303, 309
Shostrum, E., 137, 144, 265, 285
Shullman, S. L., 303, 308
Shurkin, J. N., 48, 50, 63, 68, 74, 160–162, 175
Simon, M., 295, 308

Simon, Theodore, 42, 45, 47, 49, 179–180
Skinner, Burrhus Frederick, 60, 141, 221, 233, 248–250, 255–256, 260
Sluyter, D. J., 301, 309
Smith, P., 8, 11, 30, 233, 260
Snowden, L. R., 304, 310
Snyderman, M., 169, 175
Sokal, M. M., 53–55, 61, 74, 78–79, 80, 82, 96
Spearman, Charles, 39, 156–157
Spencer, Herbert, 12, 152
Spencer, L. M., 301, 309
Spencer, S. M., 301, 309
Spokane, A. R., 302, 309
Sprinthall, Norman, 200, 204
Stefflre, B., 137–138, 145
Stein, D. M., 224, 231
Stekel, Wilhelm, 124
Stephens, W. R., 11, 13, 18, 20, 27, 30
Stern, M. M., 302, 307
Stern, William, 120
Sternberg, R., 301, 310
Sternberg, R. J., 169, 175
Stewart, L., 304, 310
Stoddard, George G., 161
Stoltenberg, Cal, 300
Stone, Calvin, 94
Stough, C., 40, 72
Strang, R., 90, 96
Stricker, G., 273, 277, 289
Strickland, B. R., 84–85, 96
Strickland, C. E., 163, 175
Strong, E. K., 57, 157, 175
Strong, Stanley R., 270–272, 277, 286, 289
Strupp, H. H., 277, 282, 285, 290
Suinn, R. M., 255, 260
Sullivan, Harry Stack, 126, 128, 191, 205
Sundberg, N. A., 304, 310
Super, Donald, 52, 66, 69, 74, 88, 91, 96, 104, 106, 112, 116–118, 172–173, 176, 195, 197, 201, 205, 212, 232, 292, 310, 313
Swenson, 201
Szasz, Thomas, 226

Taft, Jesse, 126
Taft, William Howard, 19
Tanney, Faith, 297
Taylor, S., 301, 310
Tellegen, A., 170, 175
Terborg, J. R., 302, 308
Terman, Lewis, 47–51, 53, 56–57, 62, 68, 74, 159–163, 166–167, 176
Terrell, M. D., 167, 174
Thelen, D. B., 8, 31
Thompson, A. L., 280–281, 285
Thompson, Albert S., 116–118, 136, 145, 172, 176
Thompson, B. J., 281, 287
Thoresen, C. E., 276, 290
Thoreson, R. W., 294, 308
Thorndike, Edward Lee, 55, 185, 205, 241–242, 247–248, 256
Thurnher, M., 193, 204
Thurstone, L. L., 156–157, 168, 176
Thurstone, Thelma, 168
Tichener, E. B., 80
Tiedeman, David, 114, 197, 205
Tildsley, John, 69
Tillich, Paul, 226
Titchener, Edward Bradford, 46, 58–59, 66, 74, 120, 122
Todes, D. P., 237, 260
Tolman, Edward, 109, 247–248
Traxler, A., 70, 74
Truax, Charles B., 223, 224, 232, 253, 282, 290
Tyler, Leona, 106–107, 114–116, 118, 136, 146, 188, 201, 205, 265, 280–281, 290, 294, 296, 310

Urban, H. B., 282, 286

Vaillant, G., 193, 205
Van de Kamp, H. V., 78, 96

VandenBos, G. R., 125, 127, 132, 143, 146
Vasquez, J. F., 109, 118
Vernon, 38
Vestal, M., 79, 94
Von Mayrhauser, R. T., 51, 74

Wagner, R. K., 169, 175
Wakefield, P. J., 273, 285
Walberg, H. J., 165, 175
Wallen, J. L., 99
Wallerstein, R. S., 273, 290
Wallin, Wallace, 83
Warnath, C. F., 172, 176, 304, 310
Watkins, C. E., 264, 290, 298–299, 310
Watson, John Broadus, 55–56, 60, 74, 184, 221, 237–238, 243–248, 252, 256
Watson, M. G., 302, 308
Watson, R. I., 40, 57, 74, 230, 232
Watson, Rosalie Rayner, 246
Weaver, Eli, 17, 23
Wechsler, David, 168, 176
Wedding, D., 139, 144
Weigel, R. G., 139, 146, 292, 310
Weinstein, T., 165, 175
Weissberg, M., 297, 309
Wellman, 162
Wells, H. G., 60
Welsh, J. A., 272, 289
Wertheimer, M., 227, 232
Wesman, A. G., 168, 176
Whiston, S. C., 224, 229, 232
White, Robert, 191, 199, 205
Whiteley, J. M., 189, 201, 205
Whiteley, John, 114, 291, 293–294, 310
Wiebe, F., 86, 96
Wiebe, Robert, 5, 8, 31
Wiens, A. W., 306, 310

Wiggins, J. G., Jr., 306, 309, 310
Williams, E. N., 281, 287
Williams, R. E., 273, 281, 285
Williams, W. M., 169, 175
Williamson, E. G., 27–28, 31, 66–67, 69–71, 74, 89–90, 96, 98–101, 115, 133, 154, 176, 188, 205, 207–209, 265–266, 282, 290, 303
Wilson, D. B., 283, 288
Wilson, Woodrow, 3, 19
Windholz, G., 236, 260
Winett, R. A., 301,3 10
Witmer, Lightner, 42–43, 53, 81–83, 86, 96, 98, 183
Wolf, B., 282, 284
Wolf, T. H., 43–45, 74, 178, 205
Wolfle, D., 93, 96
Wolpe, Joseph, 141, 146, 237, 251, 260
Wood, Ben D., 28
Woodworth, Robert, 154
Worthington, Everett, 300
Wrenn, C. Gilbert, 90, 96, 104., 106, 110, 114, 116, 118, 135, 144, 146, 292–293, 303, 310, 313
Wundt, Wilhelm, 34, 40, 42, 46, 58, 76, 79, 120, 149, 159, 183, 239

Yalom, Irving, 226
Yates, Dorothy, 56
Yees, C. S., 293, 311
Yerkes, Robert, 51, 55, 65, 62–64, 74, 93–94, 99, 159, 247
Yoakum, C. S., 28, 31

Zax, M., 226, 232
Zimet, C. N., 305, 311
Zimmer, J., 304, 311
Zytowski, D. G., 3, 31

# Subject Index

About Behaviorism (Skinner), 250

Accreditation, 110, 124

Acculturation, 300

Adjustment Service, 88

Adlerian theory, 126

*Adolescence: Its Psychology and Its Relations to Physiology, Anthropology, Sociology, Sex, Crime, Religion and Education,* 186

Age of Psychotherapy, 143–144

Agricultural Research Station, 187

Alpha tests, 28, 91, 94

American Association for the Advancement of Science, 77

American Association of Applied Psychology (AAAP), 91, 93, 103

American Association of Clinical Psychologists (AACP), 82–83

American Civil War, 4–5

American Council on Education, 29

*American Journal of Psychology, The,* 79

American Personnel and Guidance Association (APGA), 24, 110, 138

American Psychological Association (APA):

Archival Description of Counseling Psychology, 314

Clinical Psychology, Division of, 83–85, 103, 111, 115, 294

Committee on Ethical Standards, 109

Committee on Scientific and Professional Ethics, 108

constitution and by-laws, 97

development of, 77–76, 80–81

Division 17, 98–101, 103–104, 114–116, 294, 299

Education and Training Board, 113–114

Ethical Standards for Psychologists, adoption of, 109

founding members, 80–81, 112

Hall, G. Stanley, role in, 77–80

100 year birthday of, 298

membership in, 82–85, 91–92

professional concerns of, 81–82

reorganization of, 91–94, 108–109

*American Psychologist,* 93, 113, 223, 249, 283, 304

American Youth Commission, 87

Anal fixation, 189–190

*Animal Intelligence* (Thorndike), 241–242

*Annual Review of Psychology,* 135

Antidepressants, 140

Anti-immigration movement, 61–64

Anti-semitism, 61

Anthropometric measurements, 66

Anxiety-management training, 255

Applied psychology:
in America, 40–42

Applied psychology *(continued)*
  clinical method, development of,
      42–43
  counselors, need for, 66–68
  development of, 27, 33–36
  Galton, Francis, role in, 36–40
  immigration debate, 62–64
  interview guidelines, 68
  IQ tests, 43–46
  mental testers, 64–65, 164
  professional organization in, 83–84
  during the Roaring Twenties, 53–57
  Stanford-Binet test, 47–51
  testing, value of, 47, 62–63, 164
  women, psychology of, 59–60
  World War I, psychological impact,
      51–53, 62
Appraisal, in guidance, 69
Aptitude testing, 88, 168–170
*Aptitude Testing* (Hull), 59
Armchair psychologists, 238
Army General Classification Test, 91
Association for Humanistic Psychology,
      227
Attachment theory, 273
Austen Riggs Center, 126
Automatism, 122
Aviation Psychology Program, 91

Bag of virtues approach, 195
Behavioral contracting, 254
Behavioral counseling, 253–258
Behavioral tradition:
  in America, 240–242
  antecedents to, 237–240
  counseling, counseling psychology
      and, 253–256
  decline and renewal of, 247–250
  historical development, 234–237
  legacy of, 257–258
  overview, 233
  Pavlov, Ivan, role in, 234–238
  radical behaviorism, 248–250, 256
  therapy, 250–253
  Watson, John Broadus, role in,
      243–247

*Behavior: An Introduction to Compar-
    ative Psychology* (Watson),
      243
Behaviorism, 154
Behavior modification, 251–252, 256,
      283
Behavior therapy, 269
Belief system, in humanistic psychol-
      ogy, 228–229
*Bell Curve, The* (Murray), 63, 169
Beta tests, 28, 94
*Beyond Freedom and Dignity* (Skin-
      ner), 250
Biological psychiatry, 140
Bolshevik Revolution, 61
Boulder Conference, 103–104, 106,
      276
Boulder Model, 103, 276
Brief therapy, 296
British Associationists/British Empiri-
      cists, 238

Career development:
  overview, 172–173
  stages of, 197
  of women, 299
Certification issues:
  consulting psychology, 82–84
  psychologists/psychotherapists, 134
Chestnut Lodge Sanitarium, 126
Child guidance clinics, 88–89, 132,
      187
Child Guidance Movement, mental
      health issues, 132
Child labor, 6, 9
Children, generally:
  developmental psychology, *see* Devel-
      opmental tradition
  psychosexual development of, 190
Child Study Department of the Society
      for the Prevention of Cruelty to
      Children, 214–215
*Choosing A Vocation* (Parsons),
      14–17
Civic Service House, 14
Civilian Conservation Corps (CCC), 87

Civil Rights Movement, 165, 214
Clark University Vicennial Conference on Psychology and Pedagogy, 119–120
Classical conditioning, 237, 251
Client-centered therapy:
  components of, 141–142, 283
  1951 model, 219–220
  relationship conditions, 220–222
  with schizophrenics, 222–224
  therapeutic change, conditions for, 221
*Client-Centered Therapy* (Rogers), 108, 135, 219–220
Clinical counseling model, 71
Clinical interviews, 159
Clinical psychologists:
  counseling psychology distinguished from, 114–115
  psychotherapy and, 132–133
  VA standards for, 102–103, 105
Clinical Psychology, in American Psychological Association (APA), 83–85
*Clinical Treatment of the Problem Child, The,* (Rogers), 215
Cognitive-behavioral therapies, 254–256
Cognitive development theories, 199–201
Cognitive functioning, 157
Cognitive growth, 198–199
Cognitive maps, 248
Cognitive revolution, 272–273
College aptitude tests, 166
Colleges and universities, counseling programs in, 89–91
Common factors approach, 267–269
Community psychology, 129
Complexes, in psychoanalytic theory, 122
Concept of competence, 191
Conditioned reflex, 237, 240
*Conditioned Reflexes* (Pavlov), 59
Conflicts, in psychoanalytic theory, 122

Confrontation, 227
Constructivists, 178 182
Cooperative Test Service, 28
Correlational analysis, 156
Counseling, generally:
  cognitive revolution, 272–273
  expansion of, 317–318
  personal theory of, 265
  procedures, historical perspective, 70–71
  psychology, *see* Counseling psychology
  versus counseling psychology, 109–113
*Counseling and Psychotherapy* (Rogers), 90, 99, 215–217
Counseling psychologists:
  counselors distinguished from, 110
  identity problems of, 136
  pioneers of, 265
Counseling psychology:
  clinical psychology and, 114–115
  development of, 71, 319–320
  expansion of, 317–318
  future directions of, 292, 301–304
  identity of, 293
  in the 1980s, 295–298
  in the 1990s, 298–300
  psychological counseling, 137–139
  research-practice gap, 276–279, 281
Counseling Psychology, Division of, 135, 138, 189
*Counseling with Returned Servicemen* (Wallen/Rogers), 99
*Counseling and Psychotherapy* (Rogers), 71–72
*Counseling Theory and Practice* (Pepinsky), 106–107
Counter Conditioning Therapy, 141
Cult of adjustment, 70, 213
Cultural bias, in testing, 65
Curriculums, historical perspective, 26

Dark Year (Skinner), 60
Darwinian biology, 152–153

*Daseinanalyse,* 228
Deliberate psychological education, 200
*Democracy and Education* (Dewey), 187
Desensitization, 239, 252
Determinism, 221
*Developmental Counseling* (Blocher), 201
Developmental human ecology, 303–305
Developmental psychology, social impetus for, 186–189. *See also* Developmental tradition
Developmental tasks, 192
Developmental tradition:
  in America:
    Baldwin, John Mark, 183–184
    Hall, G. Stanley, 184–186
    social impetus of, 186–189
  developing mind, 178–182
  education, developmental, 198–201
  impact of, 201–202
  lifespan development:
    optimal development concepts, 194–196
    overview, 189–192
    research, 193–194
  overview, 177–178
  vocational development, 196–198
Differential diagnosis, 219
Differential psychology, 166–170
Directive counseling, 108, 188, 214–219
Directive-nondirective controversy, 215–218, 271
Director of Attendance and Vocational Guidance, 26
Directors of Guidance, 26
Disabled Veterans Rehabilitation Act, 102
Division 16, 98
Division 17, of the APA, 98–101, 103–104, 114–116, 294, 299
Division of Clinical Psychology, 83–85, 103, 111, 115, 294

Eclecticism:
  common elements, search for, 267–273
  eclectic, defined, 264–265
  systematic, 266–267
Eclectic psychologists, 264–265
Economic depression, impact of, 8. *See also* Great Depression
Education:
  colleges and universities, counseling programs in, 89–91
  during Guidance Movement:
    Progressive, 20–22
    vocational, 9–11
  Great Depression, impact on, 86
Education and Training Board, APA, 113–114
*Education as Guidance* (Brewer), 25–26
Efficacy, of counseling and psychotherapy, 281–284
Ego, 128
Ego-psychologists, 190
Eight Stages of Man, 191
Electric shock treatment, 131
Ellis Island, 63
Emotional intelligence, 169
Empathy, 229
Ethical principles, development of:
  overview, 108–109
  political issues, 113–116
Ethical Standards for Psychologists, adoption of, 109
Eugenics movement, 65
Existentialism, 224–227
Experimental psychology, 60, 239. *See also* Behavioral tradition
Exploratory research, 277–278

Factor analysis, 156
Finger and Tweezer Dexterity test, 171
Fixation, in psychoanalytic theory, 189
Free will, 221
Freudian theory, 121–122, 128. *See also* Psychoanalysis
Functionalism, 154

General Aptitude Test Battery, 157, 171
Genetic epistemology, 182, 199
Georgia Conference, 297
Gestalt psychology, 239–240
Gestalt Therapy, 141, 226–228
G. I. Bill, impact of, 102
Gilded Age, 4, 6, 76
Grand Rapids Conference, 19–20, 22
Great American Desert, 5
Great Awakening, 131
Great Depression, psychological impact of:
  child guidance clinics, 88–89
  colleges and universities, 89–91
  overview, 85–87
  unemployed population, 87–88
Greyston Conference, 112, 116–117, 139, 291, 294, 297
Group guidance, 26
Guidance, generally:
  clinical method, 70–71
  historical background, 3–7
  ideals/identity, search for, 24–27
  moral philosophies, 11–13
  National Vocational Guidance Association (NVGA), 16–18, 22–24
  Parsons' legend, 13–16
  professionalism, 22–24
  Progressive Education, 20–22, 133
  Progressive Movement, 19–20
  social conscience, 7–9
  testing technology, 27–29
  vocational education, 9–11
Guidance counselors, identity of, 138
*Guidance in the Secondary School* (Hamrin/Erickson), 69–70
Guidance Movement, 6, 133, 153

*Handbook of Counseling Psychology* (Fassinger/Schlossberg), article, 202
*Handbook of Psychology* (Baldwin), 183
Harvard Studies in Career Development, 197

Heuristic realism, 155
*How to Counsel Students* (Williamson), 90, 303
*How to Interview* (Moore), 67–68
Humanistic psychologists, 195
Humanistic psychology, 141. *See also* Humanistic tradition
Humanistic tradition:
  development of, 226–228
  historical perspective:
    client-centered therapy, 219–224
    directive-nondirective controversy, 215–218
    existentialism, 224–226
    overview, 207–215
  humanistic psychology, 226–228
  legacy of, 229–230
  therapies, 228–229
Hygiology, 195
Hypothetical-deductive megatheory, 248

Id, 128
Ideals, in guidance, 24–27
Identity, *see* Professional identity
Idol-smashing, 226
Immigration:
  demographic impact of, 68
  perceptions of, 61–64
Immigration Act, 62, 64
Individual differences tradition:
  Darwinian biology and, 152–153
  differential psychology, 166–170
  intelligence, 156–157
  interest measurement, 157–158
  nature-nurture controversy, 159–162
  overview, 150–152
  personality, measurement of, 157–158
  trait-and-factor psychology, 153–156, 158–159
Individual Psychology, 24, 126
Industrial Revolution, 4, 6
Informed consent, 230
Insight therapies, 128, 240
Insulin shock, 131

Intellectual functioning, Piaget's theory of, 181–182, 198
Intelligence, individual differences tradition, 156–157
*Intelligence Tests and School Reorganization* (Terman), 68
Interest inventories, 157–158, 171
Interviews:
  in applied psychology, 68
  clinical, 159
Interview therapy, 215
Introspectionism, 58, 247
Intuition, 229
Iowa Child Welfare Research Station, 187
IQ testing:
  cognitive growth and, 198–199
  historical development:
    overview, 43–46, 177–178
    in schools, 68–69
  nature-nurture controversy, 159–162

Jewish Occupational Council, 88
Job descriptions, 138
Job placement programs, 88
*Journal of Consulting and Clinical Psychology*, 283
*Journal of Consulting Psychology*, 91, 140, 158
*Journal of Counseling Psychology*, 106, 280
*Journal of Experimental Psychology, The*, 243
Journals:
  *American Journal of Psychology, The*, 79
  *American Psychologist*, 93
  *Journal of Consulting and Clinical Psychology*, 283
  *Journal of Consulting Psychology*, 91
  *Journal of Counseling Psychology*, 106, 280, 298, 303
  *Psychological Review*, 184

Kuder Preference Record (Kuder), 157–158
Ku Klux Klan, 61

Labeling, 136
*Laggards in Our Schools* (Ayers), 10
La Societe, 177
Law of effect, 242, 252
Law of exercise, 242
Laws of association, 238
Learning theory, 248, 251
Legislation, impact of:
  Disabled Veterans Rehabilitation Act, 102
  G. I. Bill, 102
  Immigration Act, 62, 64
  National Defense Education Act (NDEA), 110–111
  Smith-Hughes Act, 19
Libido, 189
Lifespan development:
  optimal development concepts, 194–196
  midlife crises, 191
  overview, 189–192
  psychosexual development, 189–190
  research, 193–194
  self-actualization, 191–192, 195
Lobotomies, 131
Logical positivism, 60, 247
Logotherapy, 228
Looking glass self, 218

*Man in a World of Work* (Borow), 197
Marathon nude T-Group, 227
Master-servant economy, 5
*Meaning of Anxiety, The* (May), 225–226
Mechanical test, 171
Menninger Clinic, 126
Menninger Foundation, 273
*Mental Development in the Child and in the Race* (Baldwin), 183
Mental health:
  etiology of, 140
  psychotherapy and, 129–132
Mental hospitals, 131–132
Mental hygiene movement, 129, 187
Mental Hygiene Society, 131
Mental retardation, perceptions of, 48–49

Mental testers, 64–65, 160, 164
Mental testing:
  decline and fall of, 165–166
  psychology of, 164
  traditional, 150, 164
Meta analysis, 283
Metaphor, 229
Midlife crises, 191
*Mind That Found Itself, The* (Beers), 129
Minimum change therapy, 136–137
Minnesota Clerical test, 171
Minnesota Multiphasic Personality Inventory (MMPI), 158
Minnesota Paper Form Board test, 171
Minnesota Point of View, 71
Moral development, 200
Moral philosophies, Guidance Movement, 11–13
Moral therapy, for mentally ill, 131
Multicultural counseling and therapy, 299–300
Mutualism, 14

National Advisory Mental Health Council, 301
National Association for the Study of Childhood, 186
National Defense Education Act (NDEA), 110–111
National Education Association (NEA):
  Commission on the Reorganization of Secondary Education, 25
  development of, 18
  IQ testing, 69
  psychological testing and, 66–67
National Health Insurance Program, 305
National Institute of Mental Health, 115, 129, 222
National Institute of Occupational Safety and Health, 302
National Research Council, 29, 92–94
National Society for the Promotion of Industrial Education (NSPIE), 10–11, 16, 18–20

National Vocational Guidance Association (NVGA), 16–18, 20, 22–24, 197
Nativism, 61–62
Nature of Man, 226
Nature-nurture:
  continuum, 239
  controversy, 159–162
Necessary and sufficient theorem, 221–223, 229
Neoanalytic theorists, 190
Neo-Freudian theory, 128
Neuropsychiatric patients, 102, 133
New Deal Programs, 86–87
New Therapies, 141–142
New York Conference on Vocational Guidance, 18
New York State Association of Consulting Psychologists, 83–84
Non-directive counselors, 25
Nondirective counseling, 99, 108, 188, 215–219
Nonsense syllable, 239
Normal personality, defined, 194
Northwestern Conference, 104–105, 109, 112, 135, 201, 297
Nuclear age, impact of, 225

Occupational health and safety, 302–303
Oedipal conflict, 126
*On Becoming a Person* (Rogers), 224
Operant behavior, 248–251
Operationism, 60, 227
Optimal development, 186, 194–196, 227
Oral fixation, 189–190
Outcome research, 275–276, 283

Paraprofessionals, 296
Pegboard test, 171
Personality, measurement of, 157–158
Personality development, 107. *See also* Developmental tradition
Personality patterns, 170
Personality theories, 279
Person-centered therapy, 227

Personnel bureaus, 28
Personnel psychology, 97–98
Phallic fixation, 189–190
Phenomenological view, 225,
    228–229
Philosophy of science, 279–281
Piaget's theory, development of,
    179–181
Population growth, historical perspec-
    tive, 4–6
Positive functioning, 195
Positive psychology, 301–302
Pragmatism, 240–241
Prejudice, 61
*Present and Future of Counseling
    Psychology, The* (Whiteley/
    Fretz), 139, 291
Primary Mental Abilities Test, 157
*Principles of Psychology* (James),
    240–241
Private practice psychologists,
    133–134
Problem-solving therapy, 255
Process-outcome research, 275–277
Process research:
    beginning of, 275
    problems with, 275–276
Professional identity, development of:
    counseling psychology, establishment
        of, 104–105, 109–113
    ethical principles, 108–109
    Greyston Conference, 112, 116–
        117, 139, 297
    in the 1950's, 105–108
    overview, 24–27, 70, 97–101, 189
    political issues, 113–116
    post-World War II, 101–104
Professionalism, in Guidance, 22–24
Professionalization stage:
    American Psychological Association
        (APA), 76–77, 80–81, 91–94
    certification issues, 82–84
    Great Depression, impact of, 85–91
    Hall, G. Stanley, role in, 77–80
    practitioner organization, 82–85
    science *vs.* practice, 81–82

Professional journals, development of,
    *see* Journals
Professional organizations, 110, 138.
    *See also* American Psychologi-
    cal Association (APA)
Professional psychology, problems of,
    305–306
Progressive education, 20–22, 133,
    187
Progressive Era, 8, 165
Progressive Movement, 8–9, 19–20,
    129, 162
Progressivism, 163
Psychiatrists, role in training programs,
    133–134
Psychic research, 79
Psychoanalysis:
    decline in, 140–141
    historical perspective, 124–128
    orthodox, 123–124
    pioneers in, 122–123
    residential treatment centers,
        126–127
    training in, 127
Psychoanalytic theory, 189
Psychodynamic psychiatry, 140
Psychodynamic therapy:
    decline of, 141
    traditional, 136
Psychological counseling, 133
*Psychological Counseling* (Bordin),
    107–108
Psychological disorders, work-related,
    302–303
*Psychological Review,* 184, 243
Psychological testing, perceptions of,
    151, 155
Psychologists, generally:
    counseling, *see* Counseling
        psychologists
    historical perceptions of, 151
    role of, 132–135
*Psychology of Careers* (Super), 172
Psychometrics, 159, 169–170
Psychopathology, 122
Psychosexual development, 190

Psychotherapist, role of, 190
Psychotherapy, *see* Counseling
    psychotherapy
  Age of, 143–144
  counseling distinguished from,
    135–140
  Freud, Sigmund, 119–124
  mental health and, 129–132
  new therapies, 141–142
  psychoanalysis, 124–128, 140–141
  psychologists, role in, 132–135
  research on, 142–143
  utilization of, 143
*Psychotherapy and Personality
    Change* (Rogers/Dymond,
    eds.), 219
*Psychotherapy: The Purchase of
    Friendship* (Schofield),
    267–268
Public health psychology, 301
Public Law 16, 102
Pupil Personnel Services, 26
Pure intelligence, 160

Qualitative assessment, 159
Q sort, 219

Radical behaviorism, 250–253, 256,
    279–280
Rational-behavior therapy, 256
Rational emotive therapy, 141, 255,
    283
Reality therapy, 141
Recapitulation theory, 185
Reinforcement, 254–255, 257
Relationships, in client-centered ther-
    apy, 220–222
Religious beliefs, Guidance Movement
    and, 11–12
Repression, 122
Research, *see specific types of re-
    search*; Research design
Research design, significance of,
    281–284
Roaring Twenties, 53–57, 86
Rogers Personality Adjustment Inven-
    tory, 215

Schizophrenia, 222–224
*Science and Human Behavior* (Skin-
    ner), 250
Science of prevention, 301
Scientific psychologists, 163
Scientific theory, defined, 263
Scientist-practitioner, 103, 134, 278
Self-actualization, 191–192, 195
Self-concept, 219
*Self-Consistency: A Theory of Person-
    ality* (Lecky), 218
Self-disclosure, 227
Self-report, 272
Self theory, 218
Settings, for psychotherapy, 132–135,
    142, 187, 274
Settlement houses, 11, 14
Shell shock, 179
Skinner Box, 248
16 Personality Factor Questionnaire,
    158
Smith-Hughes Act, 19
Social action theories, 301
Social conscience, development of, 7–9
Social Darwinism:
    defined, 152
    implications of, 12, 64–65, 87
    psychology and, 162–165
Social efficiency, 23
Social engineering, 304
Social gospel, 11–12, 131
Social influence, 270–272
Social policy, 64
Social role theory, 218
Social skills training, 201, 300
Societe Alfred Binet, 177
Somatic causes and cures, 140
Spiritualism, 218
Standing Committee on Certification,
    84
Stanford-Binet test, 159–160
Stimulus-response reductionism, 242,
    247
Stress-inoculation training, 255–256
Strong Vocational Interest Blank
    (Strong), 157

Structuralism, 154, 183
*Student Guidance Techniques* (Paterson/Schneidler/Williamson), 69–70
*Study of American Intelligence, A* (Brigham), 63
Subjective reality, 225
Sunlamp school of psychotherapy, 220
Super-ego, 128, 192
Supervision, in counseling and therapy, 300
Symbolism, 122
*Systems of Psychotherapy* (Ford/Urban), 282

*Tabula rasa,* 238
Testing:
  by clinical psychologists, 134–135
  IQ, *see* IQ testing
  mental, *see* Mental testing
  psychological:
    bias in, 65
    Guidance Movement, 27–29
    IQ testing, 68–69
    purpose of, 65
Thanatos, 179
Theoretical divisiveness, 263–266
Theory-building, 278
Theory class, 266
Theory of multiple intelligences, 169
Therapeutic hospitals, 131
Therapeutic relationship, 267
Therapeutic working alliance, 272
Token economies, 253
Traditional therapy, psychotherapy *vs.,* 136
Training. generally:
  analysis, 125–126
  counseling *vs.* psychotherapy, 137–138
  graduate degrees, 138
  guidance workers, 69–70
  for IQ testing, 69–70
  NDEA legislation and, 111
  programs, *see* Training programs
Training programs:

Boulder Model, 103
  scientist-practitioner model, 103, 134
  Veterans Administration standards, 102–103
Trait, defined, 154–156
Trait-and-factor psychology:
  counseling model, 153–156
  decline of, counseling psychology and, 170–173
  legacy of, 158–159
  vocational development, 196
Tranquilizers, for mentally ill, 132, 140
Transparent self, 227
True reasoning, 136

Unconscious, 272
Uncover and cure approach, 190, 192
Unemployment, dealing with, 87–88
U.S. Office of Education, Occupational Information and Guidance Service, 87
University counseling centers, 132

Veterans Administration:
  Division of Medicine and Neurology, 102
  Division of Vocational Rehabilitation, 102
  training requirements, 102–103, 105
Vienna Psychoanalytic Society, 125
Vocational counseling, Parsonian model of, 170–171
Vocational counselor, 27
Vocational development, rise of, 196–198
Vocational education, development of:
  overview, 9–11
  Parsons, Frank, role in, 13–17
*Vocational Guidance Bulletin,* 23
*Vocational Guidance Quarterly,* 23

*Walden Two* (Skinner), 249–250
White-coat psychology, 201
Women, counseling and career development of, 299

Women's Movement, 165, 214
Worker Trait Requirements, 171
*Work of the Counselor, The* (Tyler),
106
Workplace stress, 302–303

World War I, impact of, 27
World War II veterans, 101–104, 133
World's Fair, 75–76

*Zeitgeist*, 167

**⑤** *Springer Publishing Company*

# Making Collaborative Connections With Medical Providers

## A Guide for Mental Health Professionals

**L. Kevin Hamberger,** PhD, **Christopher Ovide,** EdD, and **Eric L. Weiner,** PhD

*"A helpful primer on collaboration for the wide range of therapists who are considering working closely with primary care physicians. This practical book will help!"*

> **-William Doherty**, PhD
> Dept. of Family and Social Services,
> University of Minnesota

This book provides detailed, concrete, and practical information on successful collaborations between physicians and mental health service providers. The authors draw on their experience working with physicians on referrals in a variety of clinical settings and specialties. Mental health professionals will find important basic skills such as how to present their credentials to medical providers; negotiate through the referral process; follow through after a referral; and report back to physicians on cases. This is a valuable guidebook for clinical psychologists, family therapists, social workers and others who want to establish more effective collaborations with medical colleagues.

**Contents:** Introduction: The Purpose and Scope of this Book • Understanding Culture: Similarities Between Physicians and Mental Health Providers • Cross-Cultural Differences Between Mental Health Professionals and Physicians • Getting Known: Negotiating the Medical Community • First Contacts • Continuing Collaboration • Training Physicians to Collaborate: The Collaborative Family Conference • Summary and Future Directions • References

*1999    160pp.    0-8261-1258-7    softcover  www.springerpub.com*

536 Broadway, New York, NY 10012-3955 • (212) 431-4370 • Fax (212) 941-7842